COMPARISON

COMPARISON

Theories, Approaches, Uses

Edited by
Rita Felski & Susan Stanford Friedman

THE JOHNS HOPKINS UNIVERSITY PRESS
Baltimore

© 2013 The Johns Hopkins University Press
All rights reserved. Published 2013
Printed in the United States of America on acid-free paper
2 4 6 8 9 7 5 3 1

The Johns Hopkins University Press
2715 North Charles Street
Baltimore, Maryland 21218-4363
www.press.jhu.edu

ISBN-13: 978-1-4214-0912-2 (paperback : alk. paper)
ISBN-10: 1-4214-0912-7 (paperback : alk. paper)
ISBN-13: 978-1-4214-0949-8 (electronic)
ISBN-10: 1-4214-0949-6 (electronic)

Library of Congress Control Number: 2012948563

A catalog record for this book is available from the British Library.

Chapter 2 adapted from *PMLA* 126, no. 3 (2011): 753–62.
Chapters 1, 7, 8, 9, 10, 11, 12, 13, 14, and 15 appeared in
New Literary History 40, no. 3 (Summer 2009).

Special discounts are available for bulk purchases of this book. For more information,
please contact Special Sales at 410-516-6936 or specialsales@press.jhu.edu.

The Johns Hopkins University Press uses environmentally friendly book
materials, including recycled text paper that is composed of at least 30
percent post-consumer waste, whenever possible.

CONTENTS

Introduction

Rita Felski and Susan Stanford Friedman

THIS BOOK ADDRESSES THE EPISTEMOLOGY, aesthetics, politics, and disciplinary histories of comparison. To what extent do all modes of thought rely on implicit, if not explicit, forms of comparison? Is comparative analysis compatible with the acknowledgment of singularity or even incommensurability? Can comparison decenter or unsettle our standards of measure rather than reinforce them? How do we rethink the structures of comparison and the history of its uses in order to do justice to past and current postcolonial and global contexts? How do the new spatial modes of analysis based on interrelations, conjunctures, networks, linkages, and modes of circulation draw on or enrich comparative thinking? What are the limitations of comparisons based on similarities and differences, and what other methods of comparative thinking might we envision? What are the contributions of different disciplines and interdisciplinary fields to the archive of comparative scholarship? These questions and more were explored in a special issue of *New Literary History*, to which this volume has added six new essays.[1]

As cultures are forced into ever-greater proximity through the dissemination of new media and escalating patterns of migration, as global flows of texts, ideas, and persons traverse traditional borders and boundaries, acts of comparing seem ubiquitous and inescapable. Yet the idea of comparison is frequently spurned as old-fashioned at best, retrograde at worst. Comparison, it is often said, is never neutral; it develops within a history of hierarchical relations.[2] Scholars of comparative literature, and of anthropology especially, are often eager to disavow their disciplines' entanglement in comparative methodologies, citing the complicity of these disciplines with colonialism and Eurocentrism during their formative years.[3] Comparison, in this light, is seen as a homogenizing process rooted in the encyclopedic ambitions and evolutionary models of nineteenth-century thought—an approach that distorts the uniqueness of the objects being compared, reduces them to variants on a common standard, and relies on a downgrading of certain cultures in relation to others.

The renunciation of comparison, however, seems neither possible nor desirable. Comparison is a mode of thinking, an analogical form of human cognition, that seems fundamental to human understanding and

creativity and that depends upon principles of relation and differentiation. Not just a cornerstone of analytic thought, comparison pervades
everyday life as one of the ways in which we organize and make sense
of the world around us. Forms of comparison are built into the deep
structures of language and constitute the basis for ubiquitous figures
of speech such as metaphor, simile, and analogy. Intertextuality, with
its insistence on the relational and interdependent nature of meaning,
underscores comparison as an inevitable, rather than optional, form
of thought. Moreover, the political stakes of relational thinking call for
more extensive consideration. Comparisons can indeed be insidious,
buttressing complacent attitudes in individuals or cultures while incul-
cating feelings of inadequacy or shame in others. But acts of comparing
are also crucial for registering inequalities and for struggles against the
unjust distribution of resources. Comparison is central to the analysis
of world systems, transcontinental connections, and interculturalism,
not only in the current phase of globalization but throughout human
history. Moreover, comparison does not automatically authorize the
perspective of those doing the comparing, but can also serve as a jolt
to consciousness, initiating a destabilizing, even humbling, awareness of
the limitedness and contingency of one's own perspective.

Here a renewed focus on comparison could re-energize the field
of comparative literature as well as provide a valuable methodological
basis for graduate courses in the field.[4] For much of its recent history,
comparative literature has defined its own distinctiveness in terms of its
affiliation with "theory"—usually understood as a particular tradition
of French and German philosophical argument. Theory, however, as
Haun Saussy remarks, is no longer a badge of special intellectual identity or even a mark of infamy, having become an accepted part of many
curricula in the humanities.[5] In this context, comparative literature,
by reclaiming and reflecting on the adjective in its title, could provide
a rationale for its own distinctive contribution to current scholarship.
Comparative thinking—or, if you prefer, relational thinking—lies at the
very heart of a field that has always sought to make connections across
traditions, boundaries, and identities. Meanwhile, more disciplines across
the humanities are voicing interest in interdisciplinary, transnational, or
other forms of comparative work, while sometimes struggling to reconcile
such interest with their existing commitment to close reading, empirical
studies, or other forms of site-specific analysis. Why not redefine comparative literature as a field that is especially well equipped to explore
the risks and pleasures, the dangers and necessities, the methodologies,
complexities, and pitfalls of comparative thinking?

Whether addressed explicitly or implicitly, whether in the form of a
manifesto or a set of theoretical or philosophical reflections, the issue

of comparison is now being systematically rethought from a range of different perspectives in the humanities and qualitative social sciences. In *Comparing the Incomparable*, for example, Marcel Detienne challenges historians' conventional resistance to comparison by arguing that comparison ought *not* be limited to comparing the comparable, that it is most productive in comparing the incomparable. He defends the "ethical virtue" of comparison, advocates "constructive comparison," and suggests that comparison can help a scholar learn "how to distance oneself from one's basic instincts and to bring a critical eye to bear on one's own traditions so as to see, or at least glimpse, that in all likelihood they represent but one choice among others."[6] Drawing on philosophy, Ming Xie's *Conditions of Comparison: Reflections on Comparative Intercultural Inquiry* focuses on the epistemology of comparison, arguing for a "critical comparativity" that fosters self-reflexivity about comparison and enables comparative interculturalism as a mode of inquiry that is attuned to misrecognition and incommensurability.[7] As contributors to new models of world literature, scholars like David Damrosch in *What Is World Literature?*, Wai Chee Dimock in *Through Other Continents*, Jahan Ramazani in *A Transnational Poetics*, and Franco Moretti in *Graphs Maps Trees* not only greatly extend spatio/temporal literary archives but also suggest new ways of thinking about comparison in the context of global circulation.[8]

From the perspective of area studies, Pheng Cheah observes in *Grounds of Comparison: Around the World of Benedict Anderson* that "in the past, the grounds of comparison were undeniably Eurocentric. Not only was the material starting point of comparison always from Europe or the North Atlantic. Comparison also had a teleological aim . . . One can no longer nonchalantly or dogmatically start a comparative endeavor from Europe or the North Atlantic."[9] But the problem of comparison in area studies goes beyond the critique of Eurocentrism, he contends, for "the claim to begin from any area outside the North Atlantic has also become problematic. In other words, if comparison always presupposed geographical or cultural areas that are a priori distinct and to be compared, how must the grounds of comparison be re-envisioned?" Aram A. Yengoyan's *Modes of Comparison: Theory and Practice* reviews the changing emphases in anthropology's evolution as a discipline based on comparison, from a stress on the similarities among cultures (as in Lévi-Strauss's structuralism) to an insistence on the differences among cultures (as in Geertz's localism). Yengoyan himself considers comparison "a form of discovery [that] can destabilize what we consider natural, raising new and unforeseen implications," and he goes on to suggest provocatively that "all forms of comparison are problems of translation and all problems of translation are ultimately problems of comparison."[10] In this context, Emily Apter's *The Translation Zone: A New Comparative Literature* contributes to the discourse on comparatism with its assertion of "two opposing principles—'Nothing is Translatable' and 'Everything is translatable.'"[11]

Echoing Apter, the field of debate about comparison operates within a similar dynamic contradiction: nothing is comparable, everything is comparable. Whatever the discipline, *how* does the mediation that such a contradiction requires get put into practice? Many of the essays in this volume articulate new methods of comparison that attempt to avoid the problems of older modes based on the familiar delineation of similarities and differences. Shu-mei Shih theorizes what she calls "relational comparison," a mode of analysis that draws on the relational poetics of Édouard Glissant and identifies global networks operating at the level of both integrated world history and the individual text.[12] For historians, Linda Gordon advocates what she calls a method of "light comparison," whereby contexts outside the historian's main area of archival knowledge suggest new questions and approaches that bring the primary archive into fresh focus. Mary N. Layoun develops the concept of "small" comparisons that eschew grand, synthetic schema by juxtaposing texts to emphasize their differences and particularities. Susan Stanford Friedman uses paratactic juxtapositions differently, seeing in them a comparative method that fully contextualizes yet brings to light new generalities not otherwise visible. Borrowing from translation studies theory, Friedman also advocates sustained attention to the gap between the phenomena being compared: the dynamic space of in/commensurability in between. Rebecca L. Walkowitz also draws on translation theory's close relation to comparison by proposing a concept of "comparison literature," texts that are written for near-simultaneous translation and global distribution, thereby inviting a new method for comparative literary studies based on a different kind of attention to language and style.

Gayatri Chakravorty Spivak coins the term *comparison in extremis* to convey a mode of comparative analysis that focuses on situations of extreme violence to reveal underlying structures of power, one that fosters the "close reading" enabled by the deep knowledge of language, culture and history promoted by area studies. Walter Mignolo advocates a decolonial methodology of comparison at direct odds with traditional comparative methodologies in its refusal to accept the notion of value-free comparison and its insistence on the colonial matrix of power that shapes production of knowledge. Like Ming Xie in *Conditions of Comparison*, R. Radhakrishnan asks for attention to misrecognition as a site of illumination produced in much intercultural comparison.

These new methods of comparison add to a growing body of alternatives to the model of "compare and contrast," especially in comparative literary studies. In *Theory in an Uneven World*, Radhakrishnan theorized a method of intercultural comparison based in "reciprocal defamiliarization."[13]

Spivak's persistent advocacy of language-based "close reading" as essential for comparison answers Franco Moretti's sociological comparative method of "distant reading," whereby comparison of such genres as the novel is accomplished through analysis of vast databases.[14] Wai Chee Dimock's method of reading comparatively across "deep time" in *Through Other Continents* emerges out of an archive of radical spatio/temporal juxtapositions. In a *PMLA* forum on comparative literature, Haun Saussy contrasts "tree-shaped comparativism" based on an evolutionary model with an "*and*" method of comparison based on a juxtapositional model of "collision."[15] Taken together, these newer models of comparative methodology offer concrete ways to negotiate the epistemology and politics of comparison.

Part I, The Stakes of Comparison, opens this volume with a cluster of essays that take as their main subject the larger theoretical and political stakes of comparison. "Why Compare?," asks R. Radhakrishnan. He uses the example of his friendly sparring with an autorickshaw driver in Chennai to set the stage for a wide-ranging meditation on comparison. He zeroes in on questions of epistemology as well as politics, elaborating the philosophical complexities of a Self-Other problematic that troubles any notion of comparison as a neutral activity and that inevitably transforms the objects being compared. His subsequent turn to *A Passage to India* underscores the centrality of comparative thinking to the making of literature as well as theory. While aspects of Forster's conception of India seem befuddled or benighted, the novel also allegorizes and reflects on the perils and the promise of cross-cultural recognition. Throughout the essay, Radhakrishnan retains a qualified skepticism in the face of pragmatic defenses of comparison, yet he concludes by acknowledging the crucial utopian dimension of comparative thought.

Susan Stanford Friedman responds in part to Radhakrishnan's essay, pointing out that the various reasons for not comparing are well rehearsed, but the cognitive, cultural, and political imperatives *to compare* need more consideration. What are the consequences (political and otherwise) of refusing to compare? Her essay explores the dangers of insisting on the purely local, particular, and geohistorically contextualized; it also suggests that the production of theory depends on comparative acts of cognition. Turning to methods of comparison, Friedman urges greater attention to the dynamism of comparison in the tension between commensurability and incommensurability, suggesting that modes of comparison/contrast based on identification of similarities and differences are too restricted. The essay concludes by arguing for a juxtapositional method of comparison that can avoid the political and epistemological problems of traditional modes of comparative thinking.

In his essay, Zhang Longxi draws on philosophical and literary texts from both China and Europe to argue that comparison is not something we can refuse to engage in. Rather, it is a condition of our thinking and acting, an inescapable aspect of human communication and self-formation. We are always "facing a crossroads," experiencing the inevitable uncertainties that accompany our experiences of comparing and choosing. The motif of "killing a Chinese mandarin"—once a popular motif among European intellectuals for gauging the limits of empathy toward far-distant foreigners—serves Zhang as a means of illustrating the changing ethics and politics of comparison. As the world becomes increasingly globalized, he argues, so, too, the distance between cultures is shrinking, decreasing the likelihood of moral indifference toward those outside one's own social or racial group. In conclusion, Zhang offers a skeptical assessment of theories of untranslatability, arguing that such theories have the effect of shoring up ethnocentrism and cultural narcissism. Comparison, like translation, is a risky business, but also an ethical and political imperative.

Haun Saussy is equally ready to offer a qualified defense of comparison as a concept that has often been seen as little more than a form of discredited universalism or a "velvet-coated power play" in the recent history of comparative literature. Saussy points to a complex history of comparative thinking across various humanistic and scientific fields, questioning the assumption that such thinking is always a sign of usurpation or misappropriation. Rather, he observes, comparison also serves as a crucial means of challenging injustice and acknowledging the claims of others. Drawing on an account of "structural violence" developed by political scientist Johan Galtung, Saussy argues that any diagnosis of structural inequality depends on comparison—whether across individual nations, cultures, or groups, or between the potential and actual state of being of a particular group at a given historical moment.

Part II, Comparison in the World: Uses and Abuses, contains a wide-ranging array of reflections on the various ways comparison has been deployed and to what effects, particularly in historical, cultural, or literary contexts. Drawing on recent work in world history as well as the writings of Édouard Glissant, Shu-mei Shih develops a model of "comparison as relation" that can reorient comparative literature away from its traditionally Europe-centered perspective. Shih argues that such a method offers a way of theorizing connection and interrelation across national and cultural differences without assuming an implicit Western norm; it also allows us to make connections between poetry and politics without scanting the fundamental differences of scale between global structures and the individual text. Tracing out a "plantation arc" that stretches across Southeast Asia to the southern United States to the Caribbean, Shih examines how literary works by William Faulkner, Chang Kuei-Hsing, and Patricia Powell grapple with histories of indenture and slavery, kinship and culture, land and language as they shape specific contexts of colonialism.

Walter Mignolo proposes that comparison is a triangular business, including at least two objects to be compared plus the subject performing the comparison. The comparative methodologies that developed in nineteenth-century Europe assumed a zero-point epistemology: an objective observer who is detached from the field being observed. Underscoring the epistemic, political, and ethical problems of such assumptions, Mignolo argues that colonial power differentials always saturate acts of comparison. We see such hierarchies especially clearly in Western notions of "literature" that marginalize or radically misunderstand alternative traditions of creative expression. Mignolo's alternative model emphasizes relation, interdependence, and entanglement—concepts better suited, he argues, to the decolonizing of knowledge. Comparative methodology thus gives way to a relational ontology in which the scholar is always implicated in the objects he or she is analyzing.

In their essay, Robert Stam and Ella Shohat undertake to "compare comparisons," analyzing the ways in which the inhabitants of Brazil, France, and the United States deploy transnational and often-triangulated modes of thinking to characterize national and ethnic identities, commonalities, and differences. Drawing on a rich archive of examples, they catalogue the role of comparative thinking in numerous contexts: discourses of national exceptionalism; traditions of ethnic and cultural ranking; comparative histories of France, Brazil, and the United States; popular mythologies of national identity; comparative debates about race and slavery; and a history of encounters between French explorers and intellectuals and Indian and Afro-Brazilian cultures. Their essay underscores both the inescapability and the unpredictability of comparisons serving heterogeneous intellectual and political agendas that can either shore up or subvert the clarity of national, ethnic, or racial differences.

Ania Loomba asks why contemporary discussions of comparison are oriented toward questions of space rather than time. The current wariness of cross-temporal comparison derives, in large part, from the discrediting of evolutionary models of history and other forms of teleological thinking. She shows, however, that transtemporal comparison can be used to destabilize rather than uphold the exceptionalism of Western modernity. Rejecting the often-heard claim that race is a product of modern notions of biological difference, Loomba shows how premodern ideas about race blend elements of religion, culture, and biology in ways that blur lines between the present and the past. Turning to current debates about the status of caste in India, Loomba finds an analogous blurring of biology and culture, a complex overlapping of the ostensibly distinct categories of caste and race. A cautious comparativism, she suggests, can further our understanding of the global histories of race, even as attention to specific racial histories can be used to challenge the ingrained habits of comparative thought.

Pheng Cheah's essay starts with an incisive delineation of differing views of comparison in the work of Rousseau, Kant, and Hegel. This tradition of thought is subsequently revised and turned to new ends; literary works such as José Rizal's *Noli Me Tangere* and Pramoedya Ananta Toer's *Footsteps* recruit comparison to spark revolutionary consciousness, underscoring the painful differences between colonizing and colonized nations. Cheah concludes by proposing that comparison has shifted from a technique of consciousness to an infrastructural relationship in and between nation-states concerned with the maximization of resources and the management of persons. The intimate entanglement of comparison with these new forms of transnational biopower cannot help but qualify its critical or emancipatory potential.

In his contribution, Bruce Robbins zeroes in on the work of a single influential thinker in order to shed broader light on comparison as it informs and sustains cosmopolitan affiliations. Hewing to the Golden Rule, Noam Chomsky embraces a seemingly dispassionate and uncompromising standpoint of comparative critique, claiming to hold the United States to the same moral standard that it applies to other nations. In fact, Chomsky's excoriation of his own country runs the risk of sustaining rather than subverting its centrality (a point also made by Stam and Shohat). Moreover, Chomsky's comparative critiques, like the analogous arguments of Walter Benn Michaels, ignore fundamental inequities and power differentials between the phenomena being compared. This is not to conclude that we should lapse back into a self-defeating and self-contradictory rhetoric of abjuring comparison. Rather, Robbins argues for an imperfect cosmopolitanism informed by partiality and belonging as well as a practice of comparison willing to face up to its own exercise of power and normative claims.

Mary N. Layoun proposes that literary texts not only illuminate the problematic of comparison but can model alternative forms of comparative thinking. Her account of current debates in comparative literature leads her to a close reading of a poem by C. P. Cavafy and a novel by Abd al-Rahman Munif, two texts that share an interest in the calibration of spatial and temporal differences in modernity and in the tensions between a comparison of interest and a comparison of necessity. The "small" literary examples of a novel or a poem, Layoun suggests, may offer a medium for exploring relations among differences that is not grandly authoritative or synthetic in scope, constituting a vital imaginative space for both comparison and for reflection on comparison.

Echoing this idea that literary texts are themselves exercises in comparative thinking, Rebecca L. Walkowitz develops the concept of "comparison literature" to describe a new phenomenon in the history of print culture: texts that are published simultaneously, often in multiple languages, and that circulate transnationally in a global literary market place. J. M. Coetzee's *Diary of a Bad Year* both exemplifies and reflects on this process, exploring the vicissitudes of comparison at a thematic, formal, generic, and even a typographical level, foreshadowing its own future as a work of world literature. The national categories that continue to inform comparative as well as national literature departments and programs lag behind a comparison literature highly attuned to its own international conditions of production and circulation and their ethical and political implications.

Part III, Comparison in the Disciplines, includes essays that probe the standing of comparison within specific disciplines, ranging from comparative literature and anthropology, two disciplines that are rarely examined in the same volume in spite of their shared transnational concerns and comparative methodologies, to history, a discipline typically resistant to sustained comparison. Gayatri Chakravorty Spivak offers an assessment of the field of comparative literature, calling for a "comparativism of equivalence" that works against the field's Eurocentric origins, acknowledging the irreducibility of idiom by questioning the equation of language and nation and by advocating the value of lesser-taught languages. She subsequently introduces the idea of *comparison in extremis* to describe the ways in which postcolonial texts such as Medoruma Shun's short story "Hope" explore the double bind of politics and ethics. *Comparison in extremis* emerges out of a context of unacknowledged suffering, confronting the impossible choice between the anguish of subaltern invisibility on the one hand and ethical prohibitions against killing on the other. Abederrahmane Sissako's film *Bamako*, meanwhile, offers a revealing representation of the discontinuities between African struggles against neocolonialism and the people on whose behalf such struggles ostensibly take place.

Richard Handler distinguishes between a positivist anthropology that aspires toward a taxonomy of cultural similarities and differences in order to advance general hypotheses and causal claims, and an interpretative anthropology where interactions between observer and observed leads to a changed understanding of both cultural worlds. The work of Ruth Benedict offers an illuminating example of an interpretative anthropology that stresses the boundedness and irreducibility of particular cultures, while also engaging in sophisticated practices of translation and comparison. Rejecting the frequent association of incommensurability with untranslatability and the relativist assumptions that other cultures cannot be understood or compared, Handler argues that two-way translation between incommensurable forms of life can allow for a productive estrangement from one's own cultural context, affording, for example, a fresh optic on the ideologies of individualism on display at Colonial Williamsburg.

Caroline B. Brettell parses the divide in anthropology in slightly different terms, as a disagreement between generalizers and particularizers about the merits of comparative methodologies. Rejecting comparison, particularizers emphasize thick description, cultural difference, and the dangers of cross-cultural analogies; embracing comparison, generalizers retain an interest in larger hypotheses and in tracking similarities as well as differences. Drawing on her ethnographic research into Portuguese migrants in the Parisian suburbs as well as in urban areas in Canada and the United States, Brettell uses comparative analysis to clarify the various ways in which host societies incorporate or exclude immigrants. A cross-national comparative consciousness, she argues, is essential for theory-building in migration studies, alerting the researcher to the significance of what is absent as well as present in a given milieu.

In the final essay, Linda Gordon considers the role of comparison in historical scholarship. Historians, she notes, have often been wary of comparative work, pointing to the dangers of oversimplification that adhere in cross-cultural generalization (and that are often evidenced in social scientific forms of comparative analysis that rely on universal categories). Meanwhile, the dominance of the nation as the main unit of analysis in historical scholarship has also hindered the development of comparative thinking. In making a case for the merits of such thinking, Gordon draws on two examples of her recent work: first, an analysis of the position of Mexican American migrant workers in Arizona that draws parallels with the history of European colonialism and, second, a comparative study of the conventions of state-sponsored propagandistic art in the United States, Germany, Russian, and Italy. Comparison here is less a matter of assuming sameness than of drawing attention to differences that would otherwise have escaped notice. Gordon concludes with an advocacy of "light comparison"—less a full-scale project than a partial and often-unsystematic use of comparative thinking to illuminate particular issues.

This collection of essays, then, offers a many-sided consideration of a concept that is often taken for granted or given short shrift in recent theoretical debates. In spite of their diverging frameworks, methods, and subject matter, the contributors to this volume agree that comparison is neither to be rejected out of hand nor unconditionally celebrated as a surefire antidote to parochialism. Rather, they offer sustained reflection on the vicissitudes and complexities of comparison, as a mode of thought central to everyday experience, literary expression, and disciplinary as well as interdisciplinary knowledge.

NOTES

1   Rita Felski and Susan Stanford Friedman, eds., "Special Issue on Comparison," *New Literary History* 40, no. 3 (Summer 2009). The new essays are by Linda Gordon, Walter Mignolo, Haun Saussy, Shu-mei Shih, and Zhang Longxi; Friedman's essay is reprinted from *PMLA* 126, no. 3 (2011): 753–62.

2   For a review of these debates, see Susan Stanford Friedman, "Why Not Compare?," in this volume.

3   See Mignolo in this volume and Natalie Melas's history of comparative literature in the context of colonialism in *All the Difference in the World: Postcoloniality and the Ends of Comparison* (Stanford, CA: Stanford Univ. Press, 2007). Aram A. Yengoyan's "Introduction: On the Issue of Comparison" surveys the advocacy for and resistance to comparison in the development of the social sciences in the twentieth century, especially anthropology, sociology, and history, in his edited book, *Modes of Comparison: Theory and Practice* (Ann Arbor: Univ. of Michigan Press, 2006), 1–27.

4   For earlier discussions of comparative literature as a discipline that have some bearing on comparative methodology, see also Rey Chow, ed., "Forum on Comparison in Literary Studies," *ELH* 71, no. 2 (Summer 2004): 289–344; Djelal Kadir, ed., "Special Issue on Comparative Literature: States of the Art," *World Literature Today* 69, no. 2 (1995); Djelal Kadir, ed., "Special Issue on Globalization and World Literature," *Comparative Literature Studies* 41, no. 1 (2004); "Theories and Methodologies on Comparative Literature," *PMLA* 118, no. 2 (March 2003): 326–41; Haun Saussy, ed., *Comparative Literature in an Age of Globalization* (Baltimore: Johns Hopkins Univ. Press, 2006).

5   Haun Saussy, "Exquisite Cadavers Stitched from Fresh Nightmares: Of Memes, Hives, and Selfish Genes," in Saussy, *Comparative Literature in an Age of Globalization*, 3.

6   Marcel Detienne, *Comparing the Incomparable*, trans. Janet Lloyd (Stanford, CA: Stanford Univ. Press, 2008), 38–39.

7   Ming Xie, *Conditions of Comparison: Reflections on Comparative Intercultural Inquiry* (New York: Continuum, 2011).

8   David Damrosch, *What Is World Literature?* (Princeton, NJ: Princeton Univ. Press, 2003); Wai Chee Dimock, *Through Other Continents: American Literature across Deep Time* (Princeton, NJ: Princeton Univ. Press, 2006); Franco Moretti, *Graphs Maps Trees: Abstract Models for Literary History* (London: Verso, 2005); Jahan Ramazani, *A Transnational Poetics* (Chicago: Univ. of Chicago Press, 2009). See also Rey Chow, "The Old/New Question of Comparison in Literary Studies: A Post-European Perspective," *ELH* 71, no. 2 (Summer 2004): 289–311, and the responses to her in the same issue, 313–44; "Theories and Methodologies on Comparative Literature," *PMLA*.

9   Pheng Cheah, "Grounds of Comparison," in *Grounds of Comparison: Around the Work of Benedict Anderson*, ed. Jonathan Culler and Pheng Cheah (London: Routledge, 2003), 2.

10   Aram A. Yengoyan, "Introduction: On the Issue of Comparison," in *Modes of Comparison*, 26, and his "Comparison and Its Discontents," in *Modes of Comparison*, 151. See also Harry Harootunian and Hyun Ok Park, eds., "Special Issue on Problems of Comparability/Possibilities for Comparative Studies," *boundary 2* 32, no. 2 (Summer 2005).

11   Emily Apter, *The Translation Zone: A New Comparative Literature* (Princeton, NJ: Princeton Univ. Press, 2006), 8.

12   In part, Shih's notion of relational comparison comes out of the network theory of "minor transnationalism" that she has developed with Françoise Lionnet in their edited

volumes *Minor Transnationalism* (Durham, NC: Duke Univ. Press, 2005) and *The Creolization of Theory* (Durham, NC: Duke Univ. Press, 2011). See also Shih's discussion of comparison as a component of racialization in "Comparative Racialization: An Introduction," *PMLA* 123, no. 5 (October 2008): 1347–62.

13   R. Radhakrishnan, *Theory in an Uneven World* (Oxford: Blackwell, 2003), 82.

14   Spivak first responds to Moretti's notion of distant reading in *Death of a Discipline* (New York: Columbia Univ. Press, 2003), 106–7, n. 1. See Franco Moretti, "Conjectures of World Literature," *New Left Review* 1 (January–February 2000): 54–68; "The Novel: History and Theory," *New Left Review* 52 (July–August 2008): 111–24; and *Graphs Maps Trees.*

15   Haun Saussy, "Comparative Literature?" *PMLA* 118, no. 2 (March 2003): 336–41.

Part I **The Stakes of Comparison**

CHAPTER ONE

Why Compare?

R. Radhakrishnan

WE COMPARE, WE COMPARE LIKE MAD: my autorickshaw driver in Chennai, India, and I, each time I visit India—usually, twice a year. We compare life in India and life in the United States; and he always likes to ask where I feel more at home. Do I have a car, what kind of car, and do I have a chauffeur, or do I drive my car myself? Since so much of the conversation happens in motion as he drives me around through the sui generis irrationality of Chennai traffic, it is only natural that we talk about driving and road conditions, the behavior of motorists, the average vehicular speed, and so on. It is around here that I sing the praise of the orderly lane system in the United States. I may as well point out that lanes for the most part do not exist in India; and even where they do, lane logic is observed more in the breach than in the observance. My friend is mystified, even appalled to hear me maintain that lanes make for safe, coherent, and pleasurable driving. He asks me, how then do you overtake (pass) another vehicle creatively, proactively, aggressively? Don't lanes constrict the driver's freedom and creativity? Doesn't everybody reach their destination late? Doesn't driving become boring and mechanical? If lane *dharma* is administered punitively, how can a small and vulnerable vehicle like the autorickshaw maintain its own against the dominance of cars and lorries (trucks)? Even as I try to convince him that his perceptions are wrong and that any sane human being would choose the structure and order of lane-controlled movement over the arbitrary madness of Indian roads, somewhere within me, on another and smaller wavelength, I hear his point of view and the relative autonomy of his rationale within his *Lebenswelt*. Of course, at this juncture I could throw up my hands in despair and abandon the very possibility of a comparatist epistemology. For after all—and this is the ethical dilemma—how can either one of us persuade the other, without perpetrating naked aggression, that somehow one's own "life world" is superior to that of the other? What starts out as a neutral and disinterested comparison of modes inevitably turns into a comparison between life worlds and ways of being. Where and how does one draw a critical line between ways of being and ways of knowing?

The point I want to make here is that comparisons are never neutral: they are inevitably tendentious, didactic, competitive, and prescriptive. Behind the seeming generosity of comparison, there always lurks the aggression of a thesis. Am I guilty here of a hasty, universal condemnation of comparison as such? Clearly, not all projects of comparison are fated to be aggressive. My point is simply this: even when they are not overtly anthropological or colonialist in motivation, comparisons are never disinterested. That in itself is not a major problem. After Karl Marx and after Fredrich Nietzsche, it is almost a truism to claim that all epistemologies are perspectival with reference to their respective subjects: the classed subject, the gendered subject, and so on. But the plot thickens when it comes to comparison for the very simple reason that it is not clear who the perspectival subject of the comparative endeavor is: it is neither A nor B, as each existed prior to its interpellation by comparison. The epistemology of comparison is willed into existence by a certain will to power/knowledge. Such a will is never innocent of history and its burden. Comparisons are discursively implicated in such syntactic imperatives as "as good as," "better than," "the best among": the positive, comparative, and superlative degrees of calibrating value within a single but differentiated world. The cliché "apples and oranges" captures the epistemological impasse that haunts comparison. If comparative studies are to result in the production of new and destabilizing knowledges, then apples and oranges do need to be compared, audaciously and precariously. But this will never happen since it has already been laid down as an a priori that comparing apples and oranges is fallacious. Comparisons work only when the "radical others" have been persuaded or downright coerced into abandoning their "difference," and consent to being parsed within the regime of the sovereign One. When was the last time comparisons were made between "cosmopolitan realism" and "third-world realism?" The answer, of course, is never.

The truth of the matter is that even as I am prepared to grant my friend the rectitude of his thesis, I grant him that value only within his parameters, even as I mutter *sotto voce* that his parameters are all wrong, nay, underdeveloped: oops, did I just even think that? His logic works for him, and mine for me; the comparison remains unproductive, neither of us having learned from the other. The comparison may as well not have taken place. So, why compare at all? What are the epistemological grounds for the initiation of comparative study and understanding? Does there need to be an ideal or at least a developmental model to preside over the relationship between any two empirical/historical instances? If yes, who, then, or which historical subject is responsible, perspectively, for the task of configuring the ideal model? I assume that wanting to learn from "other" experiences that are not one's own is and should be the real motive behind any comparative endeavor and not just the imperative to hector, proselytize, or hierarchize difference in the name of a dominant "superior" identity. Clearly, learning cannot be nontransformative, just as knowledge cannot be the provincialization of reality in the name of one location or the other that we "nativize" as our own. It is only within the restlessness that characterizes the spaces that lie between the way things are and the way they should be (the volatile gap between the actual and the ideal) that learning takes shape—a restlessness, I must add, that is not the progressive or developmental monopoly of any one culture or people. I am aware that the objection could be made that not all learning involves a "should." My point is that, even when not overtly prescriptive or tendentious, all learning (and here I am following the famous Marxian dictum that to know is to change reality) is transformative and interventionary, and if that is the case, then all learning is valuecentric. As in my traffic context, examples of comparison are carriers of value, and it is in the name of this value, that is, efficiency, beauty, orderliness, structure, eloquence, that one example counters another in dialogue and contestation. In other words, it is not possible for me or my driver friend to merely juxtapose descriptively our two respective scenarios and pretend as though we were not interested in winning the debate by way of our examples.

The conversation between my driver and me could be considered an exchange in comparative humanity. But what is comparative humanity, and how did humanity get comparative? Is there something called humanity in the first place that is present to itself in an apodictic mode, and is then, in a supplemental and secondary way, taken away from its self-sufficiency into the zones of comparison where it is pluralized, heterogenized, and rendered radically different from itself? Or, is comparatism constitutive of the human and not just an epiphenomenal gloss or afterthought that can be reduced to the order of a submissive commentary on an already-immaculate and plenary text? Here is the problem as well as the excitement. Once a comparison is initiated, there is no way to retreat safely into a single frame, into the safe haven of a filiative centrism. The epistemology of comparison enjoins on the human subject the simultaneity of the One world with the phenomenology of the many worlds within the One world. The world is one precisely because, and on the basis of, its irreducible plurality and heterogeneity. The identity of the world with itself is predicated on a radically different and disjunctive relationship with itself. It is in the name of difference that the world as One undertakes a conversation with itself. If the world, in its very oneness, were not different, then it would be doomed to a hermetic, solipsistic nonconversation with itself. Emerging realities in different parts of the world are both historically disparate and coeval with one another, and a comparatist epistemology has to come to terms, honestly and accountably, with this chronotopic doubleness. The heart of the world ticks differently in the haiku, in the novel of magical realism, in the street theaters of India, and in a variety of other genres and cultural-literary formations—but not so differently as to necessitate an apartheid policy of "separate but equal."

Comparisons, so goes the platitude, are odious; whether they are odious or not, they are certainly not natural or, should I say, self-evident. Is there anything intrinsic in A that is desperately calling out to be compared with B, or is the comparison intuited gratuitously by an observant scholar who feels that there is something to be gained, by all, through the act of comparison? The point is not just that A is like or not like B, but rather: why is it of epistemological importance that A is like or not like B, and what point of view, informed by a certain worldview and a certain will to knowledge, establishes the cognitive agenda? As we professors of literature always instruct our students: Please, when you are writing a paper that compares two works, make sure that you carefully delineate the grounds of comparison, for these grounds are by no means self-evident. Any act of comparison is predicated on an unavoidable deracination and a yoking together that one hopes will not be violent. The two works to be compared are deterritorialized from their "original" milieu and then reterritorialized so that they may become cospatial, epistemologically speaking. I say "epistemologically" to emphasize the point that the real motivation behind the comparatist project is the desire and the will for a new knowledge. This does not mean that prior to the initiation of the temporality of the comparison the works/objects/identities to be compared were lacking in self-knowledge, each within its own habitat. The project of comparison in a way ups the ante by suggesting perhaps that a knowledge based on comparison could be more sophisticated, progressive, worldly, and cosmopolitan than a form of knowledge that is secure in its own identity and provenance.

The project of comparison finds itself somewhere between the stability of identity and the fluidity of difference. A Venn diagram is a good illustration of what I am talking about. In this diagram, A and B can be seen as both independent and overlapping with each other. Within the new topology, A and B continue their prior existence, that is, their reality outside the frame of comparison, even as they display vividly the common ground where their very difference becomes viable for the comparative project. As I have discussed elsewhere,[1] the questions, postcomparison, are these: What is the relationship, within A and B, between the area that is shaded within the Venn diagram and the area that falls without? And is there a relationship at all between the respective areas in A and B that have not fallen within the shaded area of comparison? Even more significantly, postcomparison, will A and B ever be the same again, that is, having discovered that they have much in common with some one "outside," will they be capable of retaining their internal integrity as well as solidarity? For example, an urban novel based in Mumbai: once it is discovered that the urban reality of Mumbai is eminently comparable to similar realities in Rio de Janeiro, Shanghai, London, Tokyo, and Cairo, will it still be possible to relate, in an accountable mode, the reality of urban Mumbai to its own national hinterland made up of rural, semirural Maharashtra and India? I hope my example points up the problem of unevenness. My point is that the comparative act, in enabling a new form of recognition along one axis, perpetrates dire misrecognition along another. I would argue, for example, that the "global city" is the product of a comparatist coup: a coup that commits the global city to the rationale of transnational flows rather than to the rhythms and needs of the intranation. The point to be made here is that the act of comparison has the capacity and the potential, depending on which powers are backing the project, to supplant a prior epistemological object with a new one.

Comparison foregrounds the following philosophical issues: 1) the politics of representation; 2) the intra- and interidentitarian thresholds of recognition and validation. What happens when a literary critic compares the feminism in Tamil of C. S. Lakshmi, who writes under the pseudonym Ambai, with the feminisms of say, Adrienne Rich, or Virginia Woolf, or Hélène Cixous? This comparison takes place in an ideal as well as a circumstantial and historical world, that is, both within One world and between two worlds whose mutual relationship is structured by dominance. What is indeed amazing is that despite different historical grounding and location, these writers come up with "comparable" articulations of gender, écriture, and possibilities of experiencing the Real beyond the gynocentric versus androcentric divide. But here lies the problem: whereas someone like Cixous achieves this awareness as a function of her interlocution with Sigmund Freud, Jacques Lacan, psychoanalysis, and poststructuralism in general, Ambai's formulations are the result of her interactions with Indian political economy, Indian nationalist and feminist discourses, and aspects of Hindu Advaitic philosophy. Once the commonality is figured out at the level of "knowing," it feels as though the real differences between Ambai and Rich at the level of "being" do not matter; where each of them comes from turns into a mere empirical detail at the service of a more meaningful theoretical enterprise. Even more crucially, what happens to those areas in each work that remain "indigenous" and are not relevant to the common ground area of the comparison? Would these areas be abandoned from critical-theoretical consideration as mere hinterlands whose function is nothing more than prepping and propping up the avant-garde area of comparison?

So, which subject is initiating the comparison and why? What is at stake in the comparison, and who will benefit from the comparative performance? How does comparatism as pedagogy and methodology create its own epistemological object as subject and within what parameters of normativity? To revert to the example of my conversation with my friend the autorickshaw driver: is it possible to have that exchange without having to invoke the temporality of historicism that mandates that the state of traffic in a first-world situation is necessarily superior to the traffic in an underdeveloped third-world context? What I am hinting at is the very point that Chinua Achebe made a few decades ago when he evaluated the comparative humanist gesture made by Joseph Conrad toward his African brethren. Achebe's contention was that in the very act of according equal brotherhood to his fellow African, Conrad had infantilized the African in the role of the younger brother, who, much like the third world, would be destined to play a game of chronic catchup with his older brother who, by fiat, "would already have been" in those very places and historical junctures where the younger brother would follow identically years later. To echo the fraught debates based on Benedict Anderson's groundbreaking work on nationalism and Partha Chatterjee's critique of Anderson, the younger sibling faithfully and derivatively instantiates the impeccable modularity authored originally by the elder sibling. To put it differently, it is as though the Bildungsroman of the worlding of universality is no more than a hand-me-down from the already-developed to the to-be-developed constituencies of humanity.

Comparison, whether intended literally or metaphorically, raises a number of fundamental issues that are philosophical and epistemological in nature. For example, how does a comparative project intervene in the Self-Other problematic? How does a comparison contribute to our understanding of the Identity-Difference theme? How does an epistemology of comparison exacerbate or resolve the tension between the categories of "reciprocity" and "recognition"? To what extent does a comparative endeavor escape the ugly stigma of centrism, of centrism as such? How does a comparative perspective steer its way carefully and rigorously between the Scylla of a dominant universalism and the Charybdis of a solipsistic relativism? How does the perspectivism of comparison negotiate with the uneven reality of the many worlds within the One world? And finally, does the project of comparison succeed in bringing into existence a new object/subject of knowledge, or does it recuperate the semantico-ideological contours of the world as status quo?

I would like to suggest that comparative studies are simultaneously epistemological and political. Insofar as they are epistemological, they are characterized by a certain critical, utopian idealism; and insofar as they are inescapably political, they partake in and are actively symptomatic of the unequal and asymmetrical relationships that have and continue to structure the world in dominance. To state this differently, a comparatist project has to be perennially double conscious: on the one hand, act as though the comparison is being made in an ideal world and at the same time deconstruct such an idealist ethic in the name of lived reality and its constitutive imbalances. A comparatist project has to be rigorously aware that despite its avowed egalitarianism it is incluctably interpellated by a worldview that is captive to dominance and the reproduction of dominance. How then does a scholar of comparative studies, to avail of Saul Bellow's egregious example, compare the complexity of Leo Tolstoy with the richness of Zulu culture?[2] Would such a comparison be irrational, anomalous, unequal, and hopelessly asynchronic? Clearly not everything is or should be comparable; and if that is the case, are we left in a situation where the only legitimate thing to do is to initiate a comparison among "equals" and "compatibles"? But here is the problem: could a comparison among so-called equals and compatibles be anything but an exercise in narcissism? Moreover, who is "unequal" and who is "incompatible"—and says who? Does this mean that the adventure of comparison is nothing but the stale repetition of the rationale of the old boys' network and the chronic parading of one's own tradition and one's own canonicity as the standard bearer of the universal? What happened to that "other" project of rendering the self vulnerable to "other" histories and "other" criteria of the good, the beautiful, and the normative? What about that precarious project of exposing the inequality of equality and of renegotiating compatibility by way of newer and different forms of recognition and reciprocity?

Try as valiantly as one might, the comparatist paradigm flounders in the unquiet of the Self-Other problematic and its politics of recognition. To put it in the context of "our own" departmental academic politics: how does comparative literature transcend the distance between nationalized subjects of literature? Let us say then, that prior to the comparatist endeavor we have the English subject, the French subject, the German subject, the Indian subject, and so on. Each subject conceives of itself within its own interior plenitude, its own sense of an I-We balance and equilibrium. The sense of collectivity, that is, the sense of the "we," is internal or intraidentitarian. What happens to the apparatus of recognition under the aegis of comparison? The truth of the matter is that there is no putative "subject" of comparative literature just as there is no identitarian domain called comparative literature. Comparisons open up a mobile space of the "between" that is nonsovereign—space that cannot be owned and administered as property. The challenge for "comparative literature" is the task of deconstructing the apparatus of recognition; and I use the term "deconstruction" in a precise technical sense to insist that there is no *hors-texte* to the text of recognition. To put it concretely: comparative literature has to coordinate into existence a new subject even as it acknowledges that this new production will remain subject to the binary logic of Self and Other. The problem is simply this: how to produce a new "we," and who will sign in the name of this new "we" to come?

It is only appropriate that Jacques Derrida's *The Politics of Friendship* figures prominently at the very outset of Gayatri Chakravorty Spivak's *Death of a Discipline,* a short work where Spivak evaluates the viability of "comparative literature." Derrida enables Spivak to pose the issue of comparative literature at the highest level of epistemological complexity and to come to terms with what the project really entails, rather than pretend, in the name of an easy and untheoretical pragmatism, that comparison had tinkered its way beyond the Self-Other problematic. Let us hear from Derrida as he appears in Spivak's polemic:

How are we to distinguish between ourselves, between each of us who compose this as yet so determined "we"?

Let us therefore suppose that you hold me responsible for what I say by the mere fact that I am speaking, even if I am not yet assuming responsibility for the sentences that I am quoting.

Then, perhaps, you will grant me this: that as the first result of a practical demonstration, the one that has just taken place—even before the question of responsibility was posed to the question of "speaking in one's name," countersigning such and such an affirmation, etc.—we are caught up, one and another, in a sort of heteronomic and dissymmetrical curving of social space—more precisely a curving of the relation to the other: prior to all organized *socius,* all *politeia,* all determined "government," *before* all "law." Prior to and before all law, in Kafka's sense of being "before the law."[3]

This is a dense passage, replete with multiple possibilities, and my interest in it, for my purposes here, is with the notion of the "as yet to be determined we." Let me explain with a return to my driver friend and myself. Clearly, the two of us constitute a "we" across differences of location, profession, and class. Even as we both are ontologically human, we represent different worldviews, each with its own historicist and developmental calibration. Both of us are marked differently by the regime of nationalism and the nation-state, and each of us lives within a certain bounded space that is capable of forming translocal alliances with other locations. When we begin comparing our respective views on the nature of the traffic, we end up avowing, through our respective narratives, the realities of where each of us is coming from. We recognize our difference from each other and then wonder what to do with, or how to negotiate, this difference. There is an uncomfortable realization that we constitute and at the same time do not constitute a "we." If there is no stable sense of "we" to begin with, then the comparison loses its salience, unless the practice of comparison is able to bring into existence that "other we" that is occluded and precluded by the regnant social and political regimes. It is not at all a coincidence that Derrida invokes "friendship" as that "other" register or wavelength with the potential to reconfigure and reassemble the apparatus of recognition.

In whose name will the comparison be valorized? Which will be the signature, and which the countersignature? Who will be officially responsible for the comparison: Self or Other or both or neither? There is no easy way, in the name of the piety of the comparison, to escape the dire binary separation between "the ones and the others." Paradoxically, the reciprocity that is enjoined by recognition is anchored in the axiomatics of the Self-Other paradigm. Can "the politics of friendship" somehow adumbrate the "we to come" in a spirit of true coevalness, and in the process deconstruct, from within, the authority of the Self-Other structure of recognition? If the authority of the Self-Other paradigm of recognition is irrefragable, however, then is it at least possible to invoke the "as yet to be determined we" in a noncentrist, nonauthoritative manner? Derrida, as he so often does, reminds us of an inescapable double bind: compare we must, and yet at the same time be scrupulously aware that in the act of comparing we are indeed perpetrating some form of epistemic violence. The difficult questions that Derrida is raising, although ontologically and not historically, are these: How do we decide who is "us" and who is "them"? What do we do with "the heteronomic dissymmetrical curvature of social space"? If all intrahuman interactions are ordained to take place within such a social space, what constitutes recognition, and what constitutes misrecognition?

Can the project of comparison escape the arrogance of centrism? What, for example, is the normative assumption behind "our" desire to compare traffic conditions "here" and "there"? As I enter the world of comparison, am I capable of decentering myself from my Euro- or Indocentric or first-world- or third-world-centric frame of reference? Am I capable of the hermeneutic task of thinking through and beyond the circularity of my own frame of reference? The double bind of comparison works thus: on the one hand, comparative methodology has to persuade each of the entities implicated in the comparison to reidentify itself with respect to the other; and on the other hand, it has the obligation to "let each entity be" (the Heideggerian principle of *Gelassenheit*), rather than violate each in the name of the comparison. It all depends on where the interpellation is issuing from. As I have discussed elaborately in chapter two of *Theory in an Uneven World*, the Self-Other problematic needs to be understood simultaneously as philosophical as well as political, theoretical as well as historical. Philosophically and theoretically speaking, the Self requires the position as well as the gaze of the Other for its own self-recognition. Recognition by definition demands the analytic breakup of the solipsistic plenitude of the Self. All selves, dominant, subaltern, hegemonic, and others, are caught up in the rationale of what after Lacan and Slavoj Žižek we could term the big O. But the question that Derrida and Lacan often fail to ask is this: How is this symbolic or categorical (a priori) law of the big O exemplified and instantiated in history? How is the historical dynamic of uneven and unequal relationships between Master and Slave, Colonizer and Colonized, related to the philosophical thesis of the big O? Or to put it somewhat reductively, how can "equal comparisons" be undertaken in an unequal world?

Commenting astutely on Derrida's rhetoric, Spivak says:

> Given the irreducible curvature of social space—the heteronomic curvature of the relationship with the other—the political must act in view of such a "perhaps." Because we cannot decide it, it remains decisive, the unrestricted gamble of all claims to collectivity, agonistic or otherwise. Derrida knows the interminable indeterminacy of epistemic change in the agent, not only through his theoretical elaborations but also, as his specific invocation of the classroom at the beginning of *Politics of Friendship* indicates, as a teacher in the humanities. It is in that class that the question "How many are we?" is asked.
>
> The law of curvature—that one cannot access another directly and with a guarantee (by "appresentational analogy" only, Husserl will write)—is not a deterrent to politics. By suggesting that the philosophical position of being called by the other be accessed by its inscription into political responsibility, Derrida demands a more risky political activity.[4]

The pressing question here is that of the "we"—a "we" that is yet to come—in whose heralding and delineation the "we" as we are needs to take a crucial role. The critical utopian hope is that somehow the "we" of the present that is hopelessly mired in the binary logic of Us-Them and Self-Other will find a way to launch into history the "other we" that will not be complicit with the wretched binary rationale. As both Derrida and Spivak emphasize, with comparison comes responsibility: but responsibility in whose name—in the name of whose location or subject position?

So, in the comparative enterprise, who is calling and who is responding—and in the name of which "we"? Within the "heteronymic and dissymmetrical curvature of social space" what can comparisons realize, philosophically and theoretically as well as politically? What is manifest, for example, in the radical move from national literary formations to departments of comparative literature is a fundamental dissatisfaction with a certain form of collectivity and a corresponding yearning after a differently axial collectivity that will have deployed the apparatus of recognition and reciprocity "otherwise." The two assumptions that should not underwrite the comparative project are that the other be accessible, with guarantee, to the self, and that the performance of comparing as a pragmatic political activity can somehow neutralize, transcend, or short-circuit the deep philosophic structure of the Self-Other problematic. To put it differently, the task of expanding perennially the domain of the "we" has to acknowledge the theoretical-conceptual incorrigibility of "the heteronymic and dissymmetrical curvature of social space" and observe rigorously the double predicament of the Self-Other structure: 1) the relationship of reciprocal recognition between any historical Self and Other, and 2) the binding normative relationship of all historical selves to the ontological Other that by definition has or knows "no other."

Is it possible to start provisionally from one's given position and yet not consecrate that position as a center? Is it possible—and here I am thinking of Judith Butler in theory and Amitav Ghosh in fiction—to think from elsewhere, or cultivate one's assigned location ek-statically, eccentrically, a-centrically, pluri-centrically? Is the center where one thinks or lives or both? Or, is there something about the modality of thinking that cannot but make a center of its provenance, however fortuitous? Even if an extraordinary injection of empathy makes possible an other-oriented thinking, isn't such a thought, as Maurice Merleau-Ponty has pointed out, undertaken as a performance by the Self as though it were the Other? Even if these questions cannot be answered in theory, what is possible is to make a clear distinction between centrism as descriptively unavoidable and a critical or deconstructive deployment of centrism in the name of the other. Awareness of centrism, whether Euro-, logo-, Afro-, Sino-, Indo-, gyno-, or andro-, can initiate perennial critique as the only valid mode of knowing. How far does a critique go and what is its mode of validating recognition? When two centrist worldviews or knowledges meet in conversation, are they capable of divesting from their respective anchorages substantively or strategically; or to put it in hermeneutic terms, can each centrism do no more than lay bare its prejudices and forestructures of understanding in the presence of the "other"? In other words, to revert to Derrida and Spivak, no direct access to the other is possible; but what is indeed eminently possible is rigorous autocritique and autodefamiliarization in coeval response to the presence of the other. The assumption, of course, is that the "other self" is performing something similar from its own location.

But the question still remains: how many worlds are there? Whether one invokes the myth of the Tower of Babel or any other allegory, the crucial problem is: in what sense are "we" one and of the same world, and in what sense are we different and of different worlds? If the One world worlds differently in Christianity, Hinduism, Judaism, Islam, Sikhism, Buddhism, Zorastrianism, and secularism, which is to say, if the world is

one in its reality but irreducibly plural in its knowability, where and how
should the project of comparison be situated: in the one, the many, or
in an ecstatic mode that constantly reorganizes the apparatus of recognition? The charm, as well as the challenge, is that even if the world is one
in its objective givenness, it will have to be recognized historically as one
by the many constituencies and perspectives that constitute the world;
and unfortunately, with recognition comes duality and the possibilities of
dire misrecognition, as in the recognition structure between Master and
Slave, between the Colonizer and the Colonized, and between dominant
and subaltern. Alas! Recognition of all the historical selves and others
by the big O cannot be secured transhistorically; that recognition has
to be worked out historically through fierce contestations, violence, and
war, by way of actual, on-the-ground recognitions that are structured in
dominance and asymmetry. It is not that recognition does not happen
under Jim Crow or colonialism or apartheid or heteronormative patriarchy; but these recognitions are extreme misrecognitions that need to
be set right, not immaculately or miraculously, but in the name of other
and different historical possibilities.

   With these thoughts in mind, it is time now to turn to literature. It is
not coincidental that "friendship," just as it is in Derrida, is the driving
theme in E. M. Forster's *A Passage To India*. Is humanistic friendship viable
in the ugly context of colonial modernity and its brutal Manichaeism? Is it
possible to invoke an equal and reciprocal politics of human recognition
during times when the human has been betrayed by the binary machinery
of colonialism? Is it really the case that the East is East and the West is
West, and if so, under what conditions? Is it conceivable that once England
and India are both emancipated from the savagery of colonialism, they
can be friends under the same sky? How will "recognition" change both
as apparatus and as vision postcolonially? Throughout the book comparisons are made between Christianity and Hinduism, Hinduism and
Christianity, tradition and modernity, between being English in England
and being English in colonial India, between secularism and spirituality,
between Italy and India, and so on. Will the comparative experiment
lead to civilizational monadism, syncretism, symbiosis, fusion, mystery,
or muddle? Here is a famous passage that dramatizes the predicament
of recognition between two forces that are trying to understand each
other both naturally and historically:

They are dark caves. Even when they open towards the sun, very little light pen-
etrates down the entrance tunnel into the circular chamber. There is little to
see, and no eye to see it, until the visitor arrives for his five minutes, and strikes
a match. Immediately another flame rises in the depths of the rock and moves
towards the surface like an imprisoned spirit: the walls of the circular chamber

have been most marvelously polished. The two flames approach and strive to unite, but cannot, because one of them breathes air, the other stone. A mirror inlaid with lovely colours divides the lovers, delicate stars of pink and grey interpose, exquisite nebulae, shadings fainter than the tail of a comet or the midday moon, all the evanescent life of the granite, only here visible. Fists and fingers thrust above the advancing soil—here at last is their skin, finer than any covering acquired by the animals, smoother than windless water, more voluptuous than love. The radiance increases, the flames touch one another, kiss, expire. The cave is dark again, like all the caves.[5]

The allegory of the passage is obvious; but what can we learn from the allegory? Are the lessons to be learned from allegory historical or timeless? And what about the allegory itself, its coming into being at a certain moment in history? If all humanity is one big indivisible collectivity, and if every human being partakes of the spirit of that collectivity and is therefore coextensive and consubstantial with every other human being, why and how then does recognition go wrong? If an inclusive and nondenominational humanism mandates love and friendship and solidarity, it should surely be able to transcend and triumph over the perversions and distortions of the Colonizer-Colonized as well as the East-West divide. Why can't the Eastern self and the Western self, the Colonized self and the Colonizer self, disinvest from their present history of binary recognition and invest together in their common accountability to the big O? Within the comparative format of recognition, why can't each flame perform both as mirror and as window to the other so that transcendence into the utopian Real may be effected in radical transgression of the colonialist mode of recognition?

Forster takes care to begin with the tenebrous and, shall we say, monistic primordiality of the caves that is in fact not available to human perception or illumination at all. Against the backdrop of the impenetrable alterity of the caves, a dualist drama of recognition takes place. The flame is lit by the visitor's, and not the native's, striking the match. If the caves are conceptualized as Hindu or Jainist or Buddhist, then clearly the visitor can be identified as British-colonial. But if the caves are understood as Nature or Being, then the visitor's intrusion stands for the anthropocentric invasion by the *cogito* of the mystery of Nature/Being. Can the allegory be made to work on both levels? Recognition is a dyadic structure, but latent in this structure is the authority of a third term; and it is in the name of the symbolic authority of the third term that the dyadic structure can be instrumentalized. Forster's problem as a narrator is not all that different from that of Frantz Fanon's "new humanism" or Derrida's "we to come." The temporality of recognition flutters between the here-and-now historicity of colonialism, which mandates a certain kind of reciprocity between India and England, and that "other" utopian temporality that is postcolonial and therefore "yet to come" and "as yet undefined." And here is the catch: there is no way to get to that "other" utopian recognition except by way of colonialist misrecognition. Are the two flames antagonists or collaborators working by way of a pregiven solidarity? Whatever transpires between the two flames, as they reflect and converse with each other, would also result in an effective illumination of the mystery of the caves. Forster compares the phenomenology of the two flames, one breathing air and the other stone, and attributes the failure in coming together to their elemental difference. But what is interesting is that procedurally or modally speaking, the lighting of the one flame produces instant and spontaneous reciprocity. What is more, in having been hailed by the first flame and thus having been cast as the "object" of recognition, the answering flame moves from a state of imprisonment toward subjecthood. Subtended by the categorical a priori of recognition, how should the two flames behave? Should they continue to play the Self-Other game interchangeably and maintain duality, or should they meld and fuse into each other erotically in the name of oceanic love and transcendent friendship? In Forster's heightened rhetoric, there is a fleeting instant of coming together that has no duration at all. The flames die, and the darkness prevails and thwarts recognition. In this allegory, recognition is the *pharmakon*: the poisoned present that is both the poison and the remedy. In the time of colonialism, recognition can go this far and no further.

The ontopological questions that Forster raises are the following: Whence does a comparison emerge, and to where does it return? And correspondingly, where does recognition begin and where does it find a home? In the very literal-semantic spacing of recognition, how does repetition reach the original—or does it? Why should the two flames merge at all? Why can they not maintain their discrete luminosity? Would this result unfortunately in "a separate but equal situation"? It is interesting that Forster chooses to distinguish the two flames elementally: air and stone. Is Forster suggesting, in anticipation of Samuel P. Huntington, that there are essential-civilizational differences that cannot be bridged or overcome by historical, secular practices? So, which is the truth and which the illusion; which one is real and which mere appearance? Is an irreconcilable and incommensurable duality the result of colonial violence and its programmatic strategies of "othering" the Colonized; or is duality inscribed in the very ontology of the human condition? In the postcolonial period, would the two flames unite forever, and Aziz and Fielding ratify their friendship in the name of the human liberated from the alienating regime of colonialism? Hovering over this entire discussion is the problem of the One: its epistemological as well as historico-temporal status. Are "we" part of one indivisible humanity, or are we part of several different, contradictory, incompatible, and perhaps even incommensurable communal groupings brought about by the circumstantiality of history? Are comparisons made on the tacit understanding that A and B, to avail of Walter Benjamin's rhetoric, are "fragments" of the same totality, shattered and betrayed by the circumstances of history? Or, should comparisons be wary of the ploy of the One: the One disingenuously anchored in some dominant centrism? Here then is Benjamin. "Fragments of a vessel which are to be glued together must match one another in the smallest details, although they need not be like one another. In the same way, a translation, instead of resembling the meaning of the original, must lovingly and in detail incorporate the original's mode of signification, thus making both the original and the translation recognizable as fragments of a greater language, just as fragments are part of a vessel."[6] I am not for a moment suggesting that the task of comparison and the task of translation are synonymous. I invoke Benjamin in a very limited context. Both translation and comparison foreground the problem of "identity" and "difference."

Whether we are translating or comparing, we come up with the theme of recognition and misrecognition, and the deeper problematic of Self and Other. It is customary in the fields of philology and translation studies to talk about families of languages, such as the Indo-European, Semitic, Slavic, and Dravidian, by way of calibrating the proximity and distance between languages. By this rationale, two Slavic languages, in spite of their differences, could be understood as partaking in a common familial self or identity; and ergo, the differences between them could be parsed and understood as intrafamilial variations. In contrast, the difference between Tamil and English would be of a different order. In the field of comparison, centrism functions—much like the concept of a family—to measure and adjudicate the distance between two literatures or cultures. The degree of incommensurability or reciprocal intelligibility between any two flames, to go back to the Forster scene, would vary depending on whether the flames were both Occidental or Oriental, or Occidental and Oriental. But whether the differences are intra- or inter- in nature, the question remains: are differences that are parsed into meaning through comparison or translation part of the same cultural world or not? Are they fragments of the same vessel called Being or Humanity or the human condition? When I compare, say, the musical concept of improvisation in jazz with the practice of improvisation in the use of *kalpana swaras* in Carnatic music, am I assuming that jazz and Carnatic music belong to the same aural world? Or am I demonstrating the thesis, precisely because "improvisation" inheres and performs differently in each of the two systems, that these are two differently structured musical worlds that need to be understood separately?

A propos of the "two flame" mutual recognition predicament, there is another passage in *A Passage to India*, where Forster attempts, with partial success, the Benjaminian allegorical task of destabilizing and defamiliarizing all "fragment meanings" in the name of a primordial negative ontology. I refer here to the much quoted and discussed semantics of the "echo"—the echo that through its very reiterative structure frustrates all stable recognition and traumatizes any and every attempt at a centrist shoring of human meaning. The echo as nonlanguage unleashes in Forster's fiction the terrifying thesis of undecidability and the obligatory horizon of nothingness that "nihilates" every endeavor of meaning making. The echo returns, in an atavistic mode, linguistic sense back to the arbitrariness of sound. In the beginning is not the Word, Christian, Islamic, Hindu, or Buddhist, but the primordiality of sound and its absolute anteriority relative to each and every language. The universalist thesis here is that when linguistic sense is desemanticized in the name of aurality, all languages are rendered vulnerable: they become gibberish.

Here, then, is the famous passage from Forster:

The echo in a Marabar cave . . . is entirely devoid of distinction. Whatever is said, the same monotonous noise replies, and quivers up and down the walls until it is absorbed into the roof. "Boum" is the sound as far as the human alphabet can express it, or "bou-oum," "ou-boum,"—utterly dull. Hope, politeness, the blowing of a nose, the squeak of a boot, all produce "boum." Even the striking of a match starts a little worm coiling, which is too small to to complete a circle but is eternally watchful. And if several people talk at once, an overlapping howling noise begins, echoes generate echoes, and the cave is stuffed with a snake composed of small snakes, which writhe independently.[7]

This allegorical elucidation of the One-Many nexus has a critical bearing on the cultural politics of comparison that I have been discussing in this essay. The overriding problematic is that of recognition, inter- as well as intra-, under the aegis of what I have been calling the big O, the big Other. My contention is that comparison initiates echoes of recognition that need to be read back into language—but in the name of which language? Should it be in the name of any language at all, or in the name of a primordial aural, but prelinguistic "nothingness" that deconstructs the semantic integrity of each and every language? Once the economy of the echo is galvanized, every language is obligated to try and recognize "its self" in its determinate echo. In other words, the sovereignty of meaning has to be understood as a mode of vulnerability to the echo rather than as a masterful self-evidence that preempts the "dangerous" alterity of the echo. In the colonial-modern historical context of Forster's novel, can one echo be compared with another: English with Urdu, Judaeo-Christian with the Hindu or the Islamic? Unable on the one hand to cut himself

loose from the seductions of Orientalist thinking, and on the other, from
the exhortations of a humanism desperately trying to authenticate itself
in the very heart of colonialism, Forster offers the reader a befuddled
allegory—allegory as muddle. The "nothingness" in this passage is a vicious manifestation of nescience rather than an affirmative celebration
of a relational universality that demonstrates the finitude of each and
every perspective. Despite Forster's best narrative intentions, India and
the caves have to be demonized in the service of the devastating negative
ontology: its meaning-hating nihilism. It is precisely by not recognizing
the Hindu "Oum" in the "boum" that the narrative is able to promote
the allegorical recognition that all meaning comes to naught in the caves.

Forster's narrative fails to create an accountable articulation between
colonialist historiography and the "new humanism" that lies beyond.
The classic problem with the allegory of the caves in Forster's novel is
the tension between "who is saying" and "what is being said." When the
primordial Hindu-Vedantic sound "Oum" (a sound that in the Hindu
metaphysical imagination embodies the spiritual self-presence of meaning before meaning is fractured into the semantic and the phonetic) is
haunted by its own echo and is misrecognized into the meaninglessness
of "Boum." Which ears register that loss: Hindu ears, Christian ears, or
human ears in general? Why is it that the allegory of linguistic meaninglessness as such has to be shored up in the name of the meaninglessness
of "Oum" rather than that of the Christian logocentric word or the Alpha
and the Omega of Greek thought? Could the same failure of meaning
and linguistic cognition have taken place in Stonehenge, the Acropolis,
or the Parthenon? Why is the onus on the Marabar Caves to bear the
burden of the universal loss of sense? My point is that Forster's allegorical
construction of the Marabar Caves remains complicit with anthropological exoticism. First, the caves and the landscape of Chandrapore have
to be exoticized, the river Ganges (Ganga in local languages) denied
coevalness with the Thames, and all of India essentialized as unknow-
able mystique; only then, can the "Boum" work its devastating allegorical
effect. Forster's allegory remains trapped within the colonial imaginary
and its mode of recognition and reciprocity: a mode that requires that
the language of the Colonized bear the burden, in a symptomatic and
pathological mode, of the futility of all languages. The cognitive failure
is coterminous with the body of the Colonized, but it requires the *cogito*
of the Colonizer to redeem failure as an allegorically oriented negative
ontology.

As I conclude my essay, I wish to speculate briefly about the possibilities
of postcolonial comparatism. Why indeed compare, if all that comparison
does is to reiterate the economy of a world structured in dominance?
Why compare, unless the performance of comparison transforms the

world and the many actors who have volunteered to participate in the project? Why compare, if, after the comparison, each actor goes back to her corner to pursue business as usual? I think there is a way to play out the allegory of the Marabar Caves, multidirectionally. There is a way to simultaneously celebrate the world as one, and honor the world as the ongoing effect of heterogeneous and relational worldings. Despite my overall critical take on the possibilities of comparison in this piece, I would like to return to one of my earlier essays where I had envisioned an affirmative potential for projects of fusion and hybridity.[8] And it is interesting that my context then also had to do with the "semanticization" of sound, and I was talking then about fusion and hybridity in music. The question is, how does any system of music remain anchored in its own structure and at the same time recognize the valences of a different system? Let us assume that comparisons persuade each system to acknowledge and thematize its own musical finitude, not in the privacy of its own provincial chamber, but in an open world-historical site where every musical system is in the process of defamiliarizing itself along with other systems. What you hear in such a polymelodic, polyharmonic echo chamber is the simultaneous staging of multiple alienations. The alienation is intra-, inter-, and presystemic. My *raga* sounds both meaningful and random to me in the context of a harmonic musical progression that is alien to my system. I find myself wondering what my *raga* would sound like in alien ears if it were stripped of its taxonomic recognition known as the "*raga* structure." Likewise, the Western musical enthusiast wonders what "counterpoint" would sound like if it were derecognized and heard merely as "sound." What takes place in such a transverse echo chamber is an initial relativization of every system that is eventually parsed and rerecognized, not in its own name, but in the name of a radical nothingness or namelessness that has been misrecognized historically as Hindustani, Carnatic, jazz, rap, blues, Western classical, and so on.

In this postcolonial context that is mindful not only of each history and where it comes from, but also of the interimbrication of every history with every other history, the echo chamber performs differently. For starters, there is the simultaneous staging of multiple misrecognitions and not the singling out of the Oum-Boum fiasco. The caves are simultaneously Platonic, Marabar, British, Algerian, French, Western, Eastern, and whatever else. I began by suggesting that comparisons should lead to fundamental epistemological transformations, that comparisons should be weaned away from the hegemony of centrism. Comparisons, to be educative, need to happen in a site that belongs to no one. Comparisons should not be the vehicles of a latent calculus that has predetermined who, within the comparative continuum, is more developed than whom. Rather, they should function as precarious and exciting experiments where every normative "Self" is willing to be rendered vulnerable by the gaze of the "Other" within the coordinates of a level playing field. So, to revert to my initial example, perhaps traffic in the United States is "better" than my friend's traffic in Chennai, India, along some developmental scale; but that should not come in the way of my learning from my friend, on another wavelength not fully accounted for by the theme of the comparison.

NOTES

1   R. Radhakrishnan, *Theory in an Uneven World* (Malden, MA: Blackwell, 2003), 31–87.

2   Saul Bellow, quoted in Charles Taylor, "The Politics of Recognition," in *Multiculturalism: A Critical Reader* (Malden, MA: Blackwell, 1994), 84.

3   Jacques Derrida, *Politics of Friendship*, trans. George Collins (New York: Verso, 1997), 231.

4   Gayatri Chakravorty Spivak, *Death of a Discipline* (New York: Columbia Univ. Press, 2003), 29–30.

5   E. M. Forster, *A Passage to India* (New York: Harcourt Brace, 1924), 137–38.

6   Walter Benjamin, "The Task of the Translator," in *Illuminations: Essays and Reflections*, ed. Hannah Arendt, trans. Harry Zohn (New York: Schocken Books, 1968), 78.

7   Forster, *A Passage to India*, 163.

8   Radhakrishnan, *Theory in an Uneven World*, 31–87.

CHAPTER TWO

Why Not Compare?

Susan Stanford Friedman

WHY NOT COMPARE? It's a Janus-faced question, a double enten-
dre, its dual meanings depending on emphasis.[1] On the one
hand, what are all the reasons why we should *not* compare? But
on the other hand, why *shouldn't* we compare, and what are the costs if
we do not? Embedded in these questions are even more fundamental
ones ranging from the epistemological to the methodological. What do
we mean by comparison, what effects do our comparisons have, and how
do we actually do comparison? By "we," I address those involved in intellectual work who face choices about whether to engage in comparison;
I do not, in this essay, address those who study how and why individuals
or human societies compare and with what consequences.[2]

Those who compare, even in disciplines like comparative literature
and anthropology, which are founded on the principle of comparison
and are often engaged in self-reflexive assessments, seldom address
these questions of the what, why, and how of comparison.[3] The nature
and methods of comparison are typically assumed as givens, left largely
uninterrogated as comparison is simply performed (or not) across
the disciplines and interdisciplines. Discussions of comparison, when
they occur at all, typically focus on its politics, most often to attack
comparison, but occasionally to defend it. There are some significant
exceptions, including essays in this volume.[4] And yet, comparison is an
ever-expanding necessity in many fields, including literary studies, where
the intensification of globalization has encouraged more comparative
analysis of literature and culture on a transnational, planetary scale.

Epistemology and Politics

The reasons *not* to compare are legion, centering in ways in which
comparison presumes a normative standard of measure by which the
other is known and often judged. In describing one thing in terms of
another, comparison assumes knowledge of the one to which the other
is compared. The known then operates as measure of the unknown,
standing in an unequal relationship to it. As Gayatri Chakravorty Spivak

writes, "comparison assumes a level playing field and the field is never level . . . It is, in other words, never a question of compare and contrast, but rather a matter of judging and choosing."[5] Similarly, R. Radhakrishnan recalls "a comparative evaluation I was used to hearing as a boy growing up in India":

Telugu, a rich and euphonious language spoken in the South Indian state of Andhra Pradesh, was often referred to, in an honorific vein, as "the Italian of the East." Both Italian and Telegu were obviously considered "sweet and musical" languages, and it is on the basis of that linguistic sweetness (which is the tenor of the comparison) that the languages were being identified in terms of each other. And yet this comparison is not without its own hierarchical assumptions. Why not call Italian "the Telugu of the West?" In whose image is the comparison being initiated and who indeed is being honored by the comparison? Why is Telugu being named and regionalized as Eastern/Oriental while Italian remains unlocated and universal as the standard bearer of linguistic euphony or sweetness?[6]

In making Italian the basis for knowing Telugu, the comparison replicates a system of dominance on a global scale. "The point," Radhakrishnan continues, "is that in a world structured in dominance, comparisons are initiated in the name of those values, standards, and criteria that are dominant. Once the comparison is articulated and validated, the values that underwrote the comparison receive instant axiomatization as universal values . . . Let me reiterate that behind the will to comparison lies the will to judge and evaluate" (74). The "grounds of comparison," argues Pheng Cheah, have been "undeniably Eurocentric" and "teleological."[7] In political terms, comparison on a global landscape runs the risk of ethnocentrism, the presumption of one culture's frame of reference as universal and known; the other's as different, unknown, and thus inferior.[8]

As yet another reason *not* to compare, the inequity written into global comparisons reproduces an epistemological instrumentalism built into metaphoric thought as a form of analogy. In the terms I. A. Richards established, a metaphor uses an image or figure (the "vehicle") to explain something else (the "tenor").[9] "Petals on a wet, black bough" are the vehicle through which Ezra Pound describes the "apparition of these faces in the crowd" in "In a Station of the Metro."[10] What drives the comparison—the metaphoric equivalency—is the need to understand the tenor (apparition of these faces in the crowd), not the vehicle (petals on a wet, black bough). The image exists to serve the concept, which remains primary. Of course many poets work deeply against this privileging of the tenor to entangle the two parts of the comparison in a reverberating echo chamber, as H. D. does in "Oread": "Whirl up, sea—Whirl your pointed pines, / . . . / Cover us with your pools of fir."[11] Even Pound's tenor contains its own metaphor: the "apparition" is a ghostly vehicle that describes "these faces." In much poetic language, the vehicle steals the show, however much it appears to serve the tenor. Nonetheless, the fundamental instrumentalism of metaphor raises questions about the ethics of comparison. In a world structured in dominance, why should one thing exist to explain another, instead of being seen as a thing in itself?

Although metaphor always embeds comparison, not all comparison is metaphoric. In analytic as opposed to analogic terms, comparison identifies similarities and differences, commensurability and incommensurability, areas of overlap and of discontinuity. In so doing, comparison decontextualizes; that is, it dehistoricizes and deterritorializes. It removes what are being compared from their local and geohistorical specificity. Consequently, one reason *not* to compare is the potential violence such removals can accomplish, the damage they can do to the requirements of a richly textured understanding of any phenomenon in its particularity. For example, Mary Daly's comparison in *Gyn/Ecology* of foot-binding in China and genital cutting in Africa as instances of universal patriarchy left her open to charges of such decontextualization.[12] With her emphasis on similarity, Daly wrenched each so far out of its context that the meanings of both appeared inadequate; the nature, history, function, and even politics of foot-binding and genital cutting were distorted or at least inadequately understood in comparison. Given her position outside the cultures she described, Daly could hardly avoid the "Self-Other" dilemma of comparison that Radhakrishnan articulates in "Why Compare?," in this volume. Comparative analysis of similarities and differences goes against the grain of the "thick description" required for the kind of "local knowledge" Clifford Geertz advocates in *Local Knowledge*.[13]

And now to reverse the question: shift the emphasis in "why not compare?" and the question embeds an insistence on comparison.[14] "Why *not* compare?" implies that there is an imperative to compare. We compare because we must. We compare because if we do not, there are worse consequences than the political, decontextualizing problems of comparison. What are the ethics of not comparing? To refuse comparison is also a political act, one that can potentially reinstate the existing hierarchies by not challenging them.

There is, in the first place, the cognitive imperative to compare. Comparison is one of the ways in which the brain thinks and knows, essential to analogic and analytic thought processes.[15] This is not to say that comparison is a fixed cognitive universal; as a complex and flexible organ, the brain shapes and is shaped by all kinds of environments. But some form of comparison, however culturally specific, is a central mode of cognition. Comparison is at the heart of all analogy (x is like y), which means that all forms of figural thought—from metaphor to metonym, symbol, and allegory—embed implicit or explicit comparisons. And figural thought—as distinct from other modes of thought like narrative—is a vital component not only of literature but also of everyday life and language itself. Additionally, comparison as the capacity to see first sameness in difference, then difference in sameness, is one of the key modes of analytic or conceptual thought. You can't compare apples and oranges, the adage goes. But in fact you can: apples and oranges share the properties of fruit. As fruit, they are the same; as types of fruit, they differ. The concept of fruitness depends upon a comparison of what apples and oranges have and do not have in common. As Radhakrishnan argues in *Theory in an Uneven World*, comparison performs the conceptual operation of the Venn diagram, visualizing similarities and differences in terms of circles that partially overlap (75).

Second, there is the social or cultural imperative to compare. Whether individual or collective, identity requires comparison, an interplay of sameness and difference. Social comparison, according to psychologists, is a major building block of human behavior and experience.[16] The Self-Other relationship that constitutes individual and collective identities enfolds comparison at its core. At the level of the individual, I am myself because I am not the same as the other, even though we are both human; at the level of the collective, we are different from others, even though our groups are both human. The identity of a group also depends upon its members being seen as the same as the others in it and different from those outside it—a fundamentally comparative perception. As Pheng Cheah writes in "Grounds of Comparison," "imagining the nation is essentially a comparative process in which the nation is always haunted by something that is at one and the same time both spatially other or exterior to it but also similar to it" (10). The colonized, conversely, are haunted by engagements with the colonizer, Rey Chow argues in her discussion of comparative literary studies. Outside the national frame, comparison is also essential to notions like the *umma*, the worldwide community of Muslims. Whether regarded from inside or outside the group, members of the *umma* are the "same" in their identification with their religion, but "different" in their races, genders, ethnicities, classes, national origins, sects, degrees of observance, and so forth. Identity requires sameness in difference, difference in sameness—in a word, comparison.[17]

A final imperative to compare lies in the myriad epistemological and political consequences of not comparing. For all the problems of comparison, in the end, it is worse not to compare than to compare. Cognitively speaking, the possibility of conceptual thought that comparison fosters moves knowledge beyond pure particularity and thereby enables theory. By "theory," I mean the cognitive capacity to conceptualize, generalize, and see patterns of similarity as part of a broadly systematic form of thinking.[18] Theory in this sense requires comparison. Without the concept of fruit, we would be limited to an infinite regress of items, of things; knowledge would be confined to the purely particular and individual. Fruitness includes similarities and differences in an arbitrarily constructed category that is part of a larger theory of biological classification based on identification of patterns. An example closer to literary studies is Vladimir Propp's narrative theory, based on his empirical collection of Russian folktales.[19] Comparing hundreds of tales, he established a typology of thirty-one functions, patterns (similarities) that took particular forms (differences) in actual tales but that were striking enough to allow for the development of a narrative theory. If the danger of comparing is the potential erasure of the particular and nonnormative, the danger of not comparing involves the suppression of the general and the theoretical. Comparison's attention to the particular and the theoretical negotiates between the potential parochialism of the purely local and false universalism of the purely global.[20]

Politically speaking, the refusal to compare can potentially turn into a romance of the local, a retreat into the particular and identity based, a resistance to the cosmopolitan. The political problem, that comparison can reaffirm the universalism of the dominant as the implied standard of measure, is real. But there are also political consequences of restricting the inquiry to one cultural group, one nation, or one region of the world. As Radhakrishnan writes in *Theory in an Uneven World*, "there can be no serious multicultural experience or multicultural perception of value without a responsible theory of comparison" (75). Comparison across cultures defamiliarizes what one takes as "natural" in any given culture. This is, of course, a familiar experience of travel: to learn about one's own society, go to another—a double learning that involves comparison. To learn through comparison that others see things differently is to recognize the constructedness of one's own frame of reference. Such defamiliarization of "home" through engagement with the "other" is often the cornerstone of transcultural political analysis. In other words, one effect of comparing cultures is to call into question the standards of the dominant precisely because it is unveiled as *not* universal. Scholars who develop narrative theory out of a purely Western literary archive—without global comparisons of different narrative traditions—are caught, politically speaking, in a hermeneutic circle that confirms Western narrative forms as dominant, universal.[21] A more inclusive comparison of narratives from different sites on the globe can dismantle the false universalism of Western forms.

The decontextualization upon which comparison relies as it moves beyond the particular and local also involves a recontextualization that is potentially illuminating. A literary text, for example, has many potential contexts, not just linguistic, national, temporal, or generic.

The refusal to compare texts from different places, times, or cultures privileges one temporal-spatial context and renders other contexts invisible. Anthropologist Aram A. Yengoyan describes comparison as a form of carrying over from one context to another: "The rise of comparative histories—of gender relations and colonialism, slavery, migration and immigration, and more recently transnationalism—all emerge from a single case or context from which issues are carried into other contexts. Through comparison, the initial assumptions from the original case can be questioned and rethought."[22]

The comparative study of women writers from different historical periods, national cultures, and world regions is a form of carrying over from one context to another. This recontextualization opens up insight into how gender functions across time and space—in/commensurably, as both similar and different. Take, for example, how a comparison of Virginia Woolf's *Three Guineas* and Marjane Satrapi's *Persepolis* reframes current debates about "old" versus "new" cosmopolitanism—the old as elite, as cosmopolitanism "from above"; the new as subaltern, "from below."[23] The cosmopolitanism of both texts, I have argued, posits a link between war, the nation-state's violence against its own citizens, and the circumscription of women's lives in the name of protection.[24] Similar in what I have called their gender-based "cosmopolitanism-from-the-side," *Three Guineas* and *Persepolis* also differ as products of incommensurable locations: imperial London and the once-semicolonial, now defiantly anti-Western Iran. The comparison I made has been challenged as illegitimate because it "left out important contexts," particularly "Woolf's cosmopolitanism as the product of a certain European or English moment."[25] Here in spades is the argument against comparison based on decontextualization. I suggest instead that this comparative recontextualization of Woolf and Satrapi renders visible ways in which women's writing about the nation-state and their second-class citizenship within it leads to less-polarized theories of cosmopolitanism. Transhistorical, transcultural comparison enables the production of a cosmopolitan feminist theory based on an expanded archive of women's writing.

Methodology: Comparative Practice

Comparison is rudimentary for human cognition, identity, and culture. But *how* is comparison done? How should it be done? How can it be done to minimize its negative aspects? There is, as Yengoyan writes in *Modes of Comparison*, no "single all encompassing method" (8), and I would encourage more reflection on the plurality of methods and the pros and cons of each. The ABCs of comparative method taught in school are a standard pedagogical exercise of "comparison and contrast" based on similarities and differences, stressing that the similarities must be significant enough to warrant comparison in the first place. This kind of comparison can produce mind-numbingly dull college papers. The method is essentially static, not sufficiently dialogic. It obscures the contradictory core of all comparison, the tension between commensurability and incommensurability.[26] In yoking together things that are simultaneously alike and unalike, comparison sets in motion a dynamic, irresolvable paradox. On the one hand, comparison compels recognition of commensurability—likeness—but on the other hand, comparison acknowledges incommensurability—difference. Oranges cannot be reduced to apples no matter how much we consider their fruitness. Conversely, the fruitness of apples and oranges depends on a cognitive abstraction wherein similarity resides. Aligned with particularity, local knowledge assumes the incommensurability of apples and oranges. Aligned with abstraction, comparative knowledge identifies what is commensurate in apples and oranges. Comparison contains a contradictory pull between the particular and the abstract, between identification of parallels and insistence on contrasts. Comparison puts incommensurability and commensurability into dynamic interplay reflected in the slash that separates and connects: *in/commensurability*.

Methodologically speaking, the dynamism of in/commensurability can itself be the focus of comparison just as much as the specifics of what is being compared. Comparative methodology in this sense performs a kind of translation of one thing into another through the act of comparison. Translation—from the purely linguistic to the broadly cultural—incorporates a comparative logic of in/commensurability: the languages or cultures undergoing translation are both similar and different.[27] The gap between original and translation is increasingly the subject of analysis, one that brings into visibility what the languages or cultures share and don't share. Moreover, the comparison doubles back to highlight aspects of each that might have gone undetected without the attempt at translation.

The dialogic pull of in/commensurability invites a comparative methodology that is juxtapositional, contrapuntal, and reciprocal, thus opening the possibility for a progressive politics of comparison. A juxtapositional model of comparison sets things being compared side by side, not overlapping them (as in a Venn diagram), not setting up one as the standard of measure for the other, not using one as an instrument to serve the other. Juxtaposition can potentially avoid the categorical violence of comparison within the framework of dominance. The distinctiveness of each is maintained, while the dialogue of voices that ensues brings commonalities into focus.

A rhetoric of juxtapositional comparison has appeared sporadically in some discussions of comparison. Haun Saussy rejects what he calls an outmoded "tree-shaped comparatism" based on an evolutionary model (literature as trunk with branches) in favor of one based on "reading as collision," what he calls the "and" model of linked texts.[28] The "new comparativism," Spivak writes, is "comparativism as equivalence."[29] Djelal Kadir reads for sites of "contrapuntal juxtaposition," especially for loci of the peripheralized and displaced, "where comparison is an implacable necessity."[30] Kenneth Reinhard advocates a comparative "reading in which texts are not so much grouped into 'families' defined by similarity and difference, as into 'neighborhoods' determined by accidental contiguity, genealogical isolation, and ethical encounter."[31]

To move beyond the rhetoric of juxtapositional comparison, I propose three modes of juxtapositional comparison, each with its own, distinctive focus on dynamic in/commensurability: collision, defamiliarization, and collage. I do so aware that all methods of comparison can fail. The danger of juxtapositional comparison is the license it might provide to juxtapose willy-nilly, for the sake of conjunction without assurance of productive comparison. (Sometimes juxtaposition is just juxtaposition, not comparison.) Collision is the juxtapositional methodology that Mary N. Layoun envisions in "Endings and Beginnings" when she calls for comparison based on "relational literacy" and "recognition of difference."[32] Returning to the Greek concept of comparison as *synkrisis* (from *krino*, "to distinguish, discern"; *syn*, "with, among"), Layoun posits comparison as a "listening to, speaking with, and inhabiting diverse communities and a diverse world." Comparison is the "great jostling of differences," anchored in the "massive movements and dislocations of peoples in the modern period, the radical juxtaposition—in metropolitan cities or in colonial centers, for example—of different peoples and ideas and things that were hitherto not colliding with one another in quite the same close fashion" (584–85). Her collisional comparative methodology then sets in play different voices coming out of distinctive geohistorical and asymmetrical contexts. Comparison's utopian potential emerges out of a commitment "to the effort to cohabit with, listen to, and consider alternate stories of those who are different" (602).

"Reciprocal defamiliarization" is a juxtapositional methodology that Radhakrishnan advocates in *Theory in an Uneven World*, a Derridean mode that displaces the Self-Other binary and emphasizes unknowability (82). Radhakrishnan suggests that each element in a comparison be taken out of its own larger system of meaning, that it open itself to other influences and frameworks in a hybridizing comparative process in which each transforms the other reciprocally. In comparing the sitar of Ravi Shankar and the violin of Yehudi Menuhin, he asks that "the sitar and violin" become "audible to each other as they problematize themselves both in relationship to each other and in acknowledgement of the transcendent authority of aurality as such. The dialogue between the two musical horizons is not an egocentric palaver, but a mode of surrender to the radical unknowability of aurality as such" (87). This reciprocal defamiliarization unravels the Self-Other opposition that reproduces systems of epistemological dominance. Politically speaking, a defamiliarizing comparison can enhance reciprocal understanding and coexistence.

Collage as a juxtapositional comparative methodology borrows from early twentieth-century modernist poetics, especially dadaism but also paratactic modernist poetics. It maintains the particularity of each, refuses hierarchy and instrumentalism, and fosters identification of new generalities based on what texts share. I have called this comparative method "cultural parataxis" or "cultural collage," by which I mean the radical juxtaposition of texts from different geohistorical and cultural locations.[33] Put side by side, each in its own distinctive context but read together for their in/commensurability, texts-in-collage produce new insights about each, as well as new theoretical frameworks. Collaging Aimé Césaire's *Notebook for a Return to the Native Land* and Theresa Hak Kyung Cha's *Dictée*, for example, radically disrupts the contexts in which their experimental long poems are typically read—francophone/Caribbean/Pan-African negritude/surrealist; Korean/Asian American/postmodernist.[34] Juxtaposition allows for some of the particularities of these conventional contexts, but it also brings into focus a form of diasporic modernism that seeks not to wipe out the past ("make it new") but to revisit it, reclaim it, re-vision it as the basis of new beginnings based in painful psychologies of decolonization. Comparison through cultural collage enables the production of new theories.

In suggesting modes of juxtaposition as strategies for comparison that potentially avoid the problems of epistemological hierarchy, instrumentalism, and stasis, I do not want to foreclose other forms of comparative practice. The identification of similarities and differences will no doubt always have a place in comparative studies, although I would urge greater focus on the dynamic relation between them. Some comparative methods are likely to emphasize commonalities; some, differences.[35] Tracing the intertextual evolutions and revolutions of ideas, themes, and motifs continues to be a comparative methodology in literary studies. Newer concepts of "traveling theory" (Said), "traveling cultures" (Clifford), "friction" (Tsing), and "teleopoiesis" (Spivak) fundamentally involve comparison, as one idea or practice transplants to or indigenizes into another location, as one text is written anew or cut and pasted into another text.[36] They have served as comparative frameworks for literary and cultural studies on a globalized landscape of encounter.

Conclusion

Radhakrishnan asks, "why indeed compare, if all that comparison does is to reiterate the economy of a world structured in dominance? Why compare, unless the performance of comparison transforms the world and the many actors who have volunteered to participate in the project? Why compare, if, after the comparison, each actor goes back to her corner to pursue business as usual?" ("Why Compare?," in this volume). These are, of course, rhetorical questions that set in opposition dystopian and utopian forms of comparison. Somewhat differently, I ask: why *not* compare? Comparison is an inevitable mode of human cognition. We need, for certain, strategies of comparison that resist the politics of domination and otherness. We need, as well, greater reflexivity about the epistemology and practice of comparison. We should aim, in my view, for modes of comparison that work with the contradictions inherent in comparison, that expand the voices put in play, that creatively open up dialogue and new frameworks for reading and acting in the world. I have suggested that various juxtapositional methods of comparison in literary and cultural studies work with comparison's in/commensurability in powerfully suggestive ways consistent with efforts to move past centrisms and instrumentalisms of all kinds.

To refuse comparison *in toto* is to stick your head in the sand.

NOTES

1. My title riffs on R. Radhakrishnan's "Why Compare?," *New Literary History* 40, no. 3 (2009): 453–675. That essay and his discussion of the politics of comparison in *Theory in an Uneven World* (Oxford: Blackwell, 2003), 72–81, represent, in my view, the most cogent examinations of comparison as a mode, politics, and practice of knowing.

2 For discussions of comparison as a significant historical phenomenon, see in this volume the essays by Richard Handler, Ania Loomba, Walter Mignolo, Bruce Robbins, Robert Stam and Ella Shohat, and Rebecca L. Walkowitz. See also Harry Harootunian, "Some Thoughts on Comparability and the Space-Time Problem," *boundary 2* 32, no. 2 (Summer 2005): 23–52; Natalie Melas, *All the Difference in the World: Postcoloniality and the Ends of Comparison* (Stanford, CA: Stanford Univ. Press, 2007) and "Versions of Incommensurability," *World Literature Today* 69, no. 2 (1995): 2275–80; and Shu-mei Shih, "Comparative Racialization: An Introduction," *PMLA* 123, no. 5 (2005): 1347–62.

3 For comparative literature's self-reflexivity, see Emily Apter, *The Translation Zone: A New Comparative Literature* (Princeton, NJ: Princeton Univ. Press, 2006); Anna Balakian, "Theorizing Comparison: The Pyramid of Similitude and Difference," *World Literature Today* 69, no. 2 (1995): 263–67; Charles Bernheimer, *Comparative Literature in the Age of Multiculturalism* (Baltimore: Johns Hopkins Univ. Press, 1995); Jonathan Culler, "Comparability," *World Literature Today* 69, no. 2 (1995): 268–70; David Damrosch, "Comparative Literature?," *PMLA* 118, no. 2 (2003): 326–30; Abdul Nabi Isstaif, "Beyond the Notion of Influence: Notes toward an Alternative," *World Literature Today* 69, no. 2 (1995): 281–87; Djelal Kadir, "Comparative Literature Hinternational," *Comparative Literature Studies* 41, no. 1 (2004): 245–48; Clayton Koelb and Susan Noakes, eds., *Comparative Practice on Literature: Approaches to Theory and Practice*

(Ithaca, NY: Cornell Univ. Press, 1988); Chandra Mohan, ed., *Aspects of Comparative Literature: Current Approaches* (New Delhi: India Publishers and Distributors, 1989); Haun Saussy, "Comparative Literature?," *PMLA* 118, no. 2 (2003): 336–41 and *Comparative Literature in an Age of Globalization* (Baltimore: Johns Hopkins Univ. Press, 2006); Gayatri Chakravorty Spivak, *Death of a Discipline* (New York: Columbia Univ. Press, 2003); "Theories and Methodologies: Comparative Literature," *PMLA* 118, no. 2 (2003): 326–41.

4   Other significant exceptions include Robert Borofsky, ed., *Assessing Cultural Anthropology* (New York: McGraw, 1994); Rey Chow, "The Old/New Question of Comparison in Literary Studies: A Post-European Perspective," *ELH* 71, no. 2 (2004): 289–311; Culler "Comparability," 268–70; Jonathan Culler and Pheng Cheah, eds., *Grounds of Comparison: Around the Work of Benedict Anderson* (London: Routledge, 2003); Dedre Gentner, Keith J. Holyoak, and Boicho N. Kokinov, eds., *The Analogical Mind: Perspectives from Cognitive Psychology* (Cambridge, MA: MIT Press, 2001); Harry Harootunian and Hyun Ok Park, eds., "Special Issue on Problems of Comparability/Possibilities for Comparative Studies," *boundary 2* 32, no. 2 (Summer 2005): 1–251; Isstaif, "Beyond the Notion of Influence"; Djelal Kadir, ed. "Special Issue on Comparative Literature and Globalization," *Comparative Literature Studies* 41, no. 1 (2004): 1–184; Melas, *All the Difference in the World* and "Versions of Incommensurability"; Laura Nader, "Comparative Consciousness," in Borofsky, *Assessing Cultural Anthropology*, 84–96; Saussy, "Comparative Literature?," and *Comparative Literature in the Age of Globalization*; Ann Laura Stoler, "Tense and Tender Ties: The Politics of Comparison in North American History and (Post)Colonial Studies," *Journal of American History* 88, no. 3 (2001): 829–65; Jerry Suls and Ladd Wheeler, eds., *Handbook of Social Comparison: Theory and Research* (New York: Plenum, 2000); "Theories and Methodologies: Comparative Literature," *PMLA*; Aram A. Yengoyan, ed., *Modes of Comparison: Theory and Practice* (Ann Arbor: Univ. of Michigan Press, 2006).

5   Gayatri Chakravorty Spivak, "Rethinking Comparison," in this volume.

6   Radhakrishnan, *Theory in an Uneven World*, 74.

7   Pheah Cheng, "Grounds of Comparison," in Jonathan Culler and Pheah Cheng, *Grounds of Comparison*, 2.

8   For attacks on comparison as an imperial project allied with European modernity, see Harootunian, "Some Thoughts on Comparability"; Peter Osborne, "On Comparability: Kant and the Possibility of Comparative Studies," *boundary 2* 32, no. 2 (Summer 2005): 3–22; Chow, "The Old/New Question of Comparison," 289–311; Shih, "Comparative Racialization"; Melas, *All the Difference in the World*. Shih and Melas see comparison as an agent of both colonization and decolonization. For defenses of comparison in anthropology, see Borofsky, *Assessing Cultural Anthropology*; Caroline B. Brettell, "Anthropology, Migration, and Comparative Consciousness," in this volume; Nader, "Comparative Consciousness," 84–96; Stoler, "Tense and Tender Ties," 829–65; Yengoyan, *Modes of Comparison*.

9   I. A. Richards, *Principles of Literary Criticism* (London: Kegan, 1924).

10   Ezra Pound, "In a Station of the Metro," in *The Selected Poems of Ezra Pound* (New York: New Directions, 1957), 35.

11   H. D., "Oread," in *Collected Poems of H. D.* (New York: New Directions, 1983), 55.

12   Mary Daly, *Gyn/Ecology: The Meta-ethics of Radical Feminism* (Boston: Beacon, 1978), 134–78.

13   Clifford Geertz, *Local Knowledge: Further Essays in Interpretative Anthropology* (New York: Basic, 1985).

14   In spoken American English, the meaning-bearing difference of emphasis in the two forms of "why not compare?" are tonal: the "not" in the first is flat; the "not" in the second has a rising tone.

15   For comparison in cognitive psychology, see Gentner, Holyoak, and Kokinov, eds., *The Analogical Mind*. For Kant's views on comparison in human cognition, see Cheah, "The Material World of Comparison," in this volume; Osborne, "On Comparability."

16   See Jerry Suls and Ladd Wheeler, eds., *Handbook of Social Comparison*.

17 Arguments that regard comparison as the product of a post-1500 Western modernity ignore how the mobility and intercultural contact that characterizes millennia of human history has always engendered comparison.

18 See Susan Stanford Friedman, "Theory," in *Modernism and Theory: A Critical Debate*, ed. Stephen Ross (London: Routledge, 2009), 237–46.

19 V. Propp, *Morphology of the Folktale*, 1928, trans. Laurence Scott (Bloomington: Indiana Research Center, 1958). •

20 Mary Louise Pratt suggests that comparison should be "vertical" (global to local), not just "horizontal" (A to B), in "Comparative Literature and Global Citizenship," in Bernheimer, *Comparative Literature in the Age of Multiculturalism*, 63–64.

21 For extended discussion, see Susan Stanford Friedman, "Towards a Transnational Turn in Narrative Theory: Literary Narratives, Traveling Tropes, and the Case of Virginia Woolf and the Tagores," *Narrative* 19, no. 1 (2011): 1–32.

22 Yenhoyan, *Modes of Comparison*, 11.

23 Virginia Woolf, *Three Guineas*, 1938 (New York: Harcourt, 2006); Marjane Satrapi, *Persepolis: The Story of a Childhood*, 2000, trans. Mattias Ripa and Blake Ferris (New York: Pantheon, 2003).

24 Susan Stanford Friedman, "Wartime Cosmopolitanism: Cosmofeminism and Virginia Woolf's *Three Guineas* and Marjanne Satrapi's *Persepolis*," *Tulsa Studies in Women's Literature* 31, no. 1 (Spring 2012).

25 Letter to author from editorial board of a prominent journal in rejecting the essay, May 15, 2009. Versions of the essay have been delivered as lectures, keynotes, or conference panels nine times from 2007 to 2012.

26 See Culler, "Comparability," 245–303; Melas, *All the Difference in the World*, 32–43, and "Versions of Incommensurability"; Handler, "Uses of Incommensurability in Anthropology."

27 In *The Translation Zone*, Apter sees translation ("everything is translatable"; "nothing is translatable") as the basis for a new comparatism (esp. xi–xii, 3–11). Mohan argues that India's multilingualism compels Indian literary studies to be comparative (viii).

28 Saussy, "Comparative Literature?," 336–39.

29 Spivak, "Rethinking Comparison," in this volume.

30 Djelal Kadir, "Comparative Literature Hinternational," 246.

31 Kenneth Reinhard, "Kant with Sade, Lacan with Levinas," *MLN* 110, no. 4 (1995): 785.

32 Mary N. Layoun, "Endings and Beginnings: Reimagining the Tasks and Spaces of Comparison," in this volume.

33 Susan Stanford Friedman, "Paranoia, Pollution, and Sexuality: Affiliations between E. M. Forster's *A Passage to India* and Arundhati Roy's *The God of Small Things*," in *Geomodernisms: "Race," Modernism, Modernity*, ed. Laura Doyle and Laura Winkiel (Bloomington: Indiana Univ. Press, 2005), 245–61; "Modernism in a Transnational Landscape: Spatial Poetics, Postcolonialism, and Gender in Césaire's *Cahier/Notebook* and Cha's *Dictée*, *Paideuma* 32, nos. 1–3 (2003): 39–74.

34 Aimé Césaire, *Cahier d'un retour au pays natal* (Notebook of a Return to the Native Land), 1939, *The Collected Poetry*, trans. Clayton Eshleman and Annette Smith (Berkeley: Univ. of California Press, 1982), 34–85; Theresa Hak Kyung Cha, *Dictée*, 1982 (Berkeley, CA: Third World Women, 1995).

35 Comparative literature's original emphasis on commonality and its increasing stress on difference are discussed in Balakian, "Theorizing Comparison"; Bernheimer, *Comparative Literature*.

36 Edward W. Said, "Traveling Theory," in *The World, the Text, and the Critic* (Cambridge, MA: Harvard Univ. Press, 1983), 226–47; James Clifford, "Traveling Cultures," in *Routes: Travel and Translation in the Late Twentieth Century* (Cambridge, MA: Harvard Univ. Press, 1997), 17–46; Anna L. Tsing, *Friction: An Ethnography of Global Connection* (Princeton, NJ: Princeton Univ. Press 2005); and Spivak, *Death of a Discipline*, 31.

CHAPTER THREE

Crossroads, Distant Killing, and Translation: On the Ethics and Politics of Comparison

Zhang Longxi

> The way (*tao*) of Heaven, isn't it comparable to
> pulling a bow?
> That which is too high is lowered down; that
> which is too low is lifted up.
> That which is too much is reduced; that which
> is not enough is compensated.
> The way of Heaven is to reduce what is too
> much and compensate what is not enough.
> The way of man is not like this:
> It takes from those who have not enough and
> gives it to those who already have too much.
> Who can take the too much and give it to all
> under heaven?
> Only the one who is in possession of the *tao*.
>
> *Laozi*, chapter 77

T O COMPARE OR NOT TO COMPARE, unlike to be or not to be: that is *not* the question. On a most basic level, ontologically speaking, we cannot but compare, and we compare all the time in order to differentiate, recognize, understand, make judgments or decisions, and act upon our decisions. All our actions in cognitive and physical terms depend on making comparisons, and we have no other alternative but to compare, because as human beings we all rush into existence *in medias res*, with our living conditions and social environment, including language and culture, already in place, and our life is always caught in between what is given and what is yet possible, external reality and our dreams, desires, and choices. High or low, superfluity or destitution, all these are impossible to conceive without comparison, and it is impossible to achieve the appropriate equilibrium between having too much and having not enough without making the right choice in comparison. It is one of life's little ironies that we have no choice but to choose, and when we choose, we must compare. The contrast between the self-plenitude of identity and the multiple dependence of difference is an illusion, because the very concept of identity is established through comparison and differentiation, as Sigmund Freud has argued in psychoanalysis and Ferdinand de Saussure in linguistics.

Freud describes the ego as developing according to the "reality principle" by constantly comparing and interacting between the desires and impulses of the id on the one hand and what is available in the external world on the other. For my purposes here, I cite a short piece by Freud that deals with the problem of identity and difference with direct reference to language in a way that reminds us of Saussure's linguistic understanding. "Our conceptions arise through comparison," says Freud in a review of Karl Abel's *Über den Gegensinn der Urworte*. "Were it always light we should not distinguish between light and dark, and accordingly could not have either the conception of, nor the word for, light," Freud reminds us with Abel. "'It is clear that everything on this planet is relative and has independent existence only in so far as it is distinguished in its relations to and from other things ... Man has not been able to acquire even his oldest and simplest conceptions otherwise than in contrast with their opposites; he only gradually learnt to separate the two sides of the antithesis and think of the one without conscious comparison with the other.' "[1] In psychoanalytic understanding, nothing exists without comparison with, and in contradistinction to, its opposite. The naive belief in one's own plenitude is mere "narcissism," typical of children and "primitive man," which Freud sees as gradually dismantled by the progress of science: "the self-love of humanity suffered its first blow, the *cosmological* one," when the Copernican heliocentric theory was generally accepted; Darwinian evolution dealt "the second, *biological* blow to human narcissism"; and Freud's own psychoanalysis constitutes the third blow, "the *psychological* one."[2] The human self is fundamentally and dynamically constructed in comparison and differentiation, and its development a process of *Bildung* that proceeds through a constant cycle of alienation and return, an endless process of learning from what is different and alien.

We find an eminently comparable formulation of identity and difference in Saussure's structural linguistics. "The linguistic mechanism is geared to differences and identities," says Saussure, "the former being only the counterpart of the latter." He considers language as a system of mutually defining terms, in which the value of each sign is determined in comparison with those of other signs, and what is seen as identical is actually equivalent, that is, of equal values in comparison. He illustrates this characteristic of linguistic signs by drawing comparisons with non-linguistic examples. "For instance, we speak of the identity of two '8:25 p.m. Geneva-to-Paris' trains that leave at twenty-four hour intervals. We feel that it is the same train each day, yet everything—the locomotive, coaches, personnel—is probably different. Or if a street is demolished, then rebuilt, we say that it is the same street even though in a material sense, perhaps nothing of the old one remains."[3] The examples bring out the point that what we consider to be the same or the identical may in fact be quite different, and what counts as same or different is determined by an entire network of signs in mutual differentiation. "In language there are only differences," says Saussure. "Even more important: a difference generally implies positive terms between which the difference is set up; but in language there are only differences *without positive terms*."[4] The point is that identity is not self-sufficient but is defined by what it is not more than what it is. In other words, identity is established in and through comparisons. Human existence is one of relations, and the necessity of comparison is a given in life, which presents both a good opportunity and a serious challenge.

Crossroads and Parallelism

The difficulty of comparing and making choices is well illustrated by the story about an ancient Chinese philosopher Yang Zhu, who "wept at a crossroads, for it could lead to the south or to the north."[5] This may sound odd, but it takes a philosopher to weep at the juncture of uncertain possibilities, where philosophical Angst is as much about making comparison as it is literally about choosing the right road. Facing a crossroads is of course a conceptual metaphor for facing the dilemma of uncertain possibilities and difficult choices. As George Lakoff and Mark Turner argue, "metaphor resides in thought, not just in words."[6] Conceptual metaphors reveal the deep-seated metaphoricity of the mind that constantly puts things in comparison and maps them over one another. It would be sheer stupidity to take a road that may lead to the south or to the north without considering what may lie ahead, but it is the figurative or metaphorical meaning of a crossroads that enables us to understand Yang Zhu's anxiety—not that he was perplexed by roads going in different directions, but that he feared the consequences of making a wrong move.

In facing roads that diverged in a wood, Robert Frost may have shown, in comparison with the Chinese philosopher, a more robust sense of determination in simply saying that "I—/ I took the one less traveled by, / And that has made all the difference."[7] The last line seems to make a factual statement about the consequences of the road taken or the choice made, but what about the road not taken (which is, after all, the title of this famous poem)? Isn't the statement made "with a sigh"? Isn't there the suggestion of a sense of loss or regret, a tinge of sadness perhaps in those words? As another American poet, John Whittier, puts it, "for all sad words of tongue or pen, / The saddest are these: 'it might have been!'"[8] It is in comparison with what "might have been," the lost opportunity of an imagined better condition, that sadness sets in. Happiness or sadness is of course a matter of perception in comparison. "All happy families resemble one another, each unhappy family is unhappy in its own way," so begins Leo Tolstoy's great novel *Anna Karenina* in a neat parallelism.[9] The Chinese novel *Romance of the Three Kingdoms* starts likewise with a comparison, a cyclical notion of history, which presents unity and division as the two choices alternately made in the unfolding of dynastic history: "Speaking of the overall condition of all under heaven, it tends toward unity after prolonged division, and division after prolonged unity."[10]

It could be instructive to see how many memorable beginnings of great novels tell us about the world, real or fictional, by way of comparison. Here is one of the most well known, the beginning of Charles Dickens's *A Tale of Two Cities*:

It was the best of times, it was the worst of times, it was the age of wisdom, it was the age of foolishness, it was the epoch of belief, it was the epoch of incredulity, it was the season of Light, it was the season of Darkness, it was the spring of hope, it was the winter of despair, we had everything before us, we had nothing before us, we were all going direct to Heaven, we were all going direct the other way—in short, the period was so far like the present period, that some of its noisiest authorities insisted on its being received, for good or for evil, in the superlative degree of comparison only.[11]

The parallel structure of this passage is fundamentally comparative, and comparison is, as noted above, not just a structural given in language, but in the mind itself. "In giving shapes to human beings, nature always makes their bodies in symmetry with limbs in pairs. Through the use of divine principles, nothing is left in isolation," says Liu Xie (465?–522), a fifth-century Chinese critic, as he traces parallelism in language and thinking to a natural, even divine, origin. "The mind creates literary expressions, and puts a hundred thoughts in the right design. The high and the low are mutually dependent, thus one-to-one parallels are naturally formed."[12] Liu Xie's words seem perfectly suited to what we experience in reading the passage from Dickens. The rhetorical juxtaposition, antithesis, and parallelism are all predicated on the mental work of thinking in comparisons, and in reading Dickens's depiction of an age full of contradictions, we seem to detect a strong rhythmic impulse that reveals a natural tendency toward comparison.

For Roman Jakobson, parallelism embodies Saussure's legacy, his "radical distinction between the 'syntagmatic' and 'associative' planes of language," a "fundamental dichotomy."[13] Jakobson further develops that dichotomy into the two axes of "positional (namely, syntactic) contiguity" represented by metonymy and "semantic similarity" represented by metaphor, the interaction of which can be seen everywhere in language, but is particularly pronounced in literary parallelism. "Rich material for the study of this relationship is to be found in verse patterns which require a compulsory parallelism between adjacent lines," says Jakobson, and he mentions examples "in Biblical poetry or in the West Finnic and, to some extent, the Russian oral traditions."[14] If he knew Chinese, he would probably have added Chinese poetry as the most exemplary, for the second and third couplets in a Chinese *lü shi* or regulated verse, also known as "recent-style poetry," require the parallel structure of an antithesis far more strict than most other prosodies. A famous poem by the great Tang poet Du Fu (712–70) is unusual in having parallelism in every couplet, which may give us some idea of the strict prosodic rules for making a regulated verse in classical Chinese poetry:

The wind is strong, the sky high, sadly the gibbons are crying,
The islets are clear, the sands white, in circles the birds are flying.
Boundless forests shed their leaves swirling and rustling down,
The endless river flows with waves rolling and running near.
Ten thousand miles, in sorrowful autumn, often as a wanderer I sigh,
A hundred years, old and sick, alone up the high terrace I climb.
In misery and hardships, I hate to see my hair turning all white,
Out of ill fortune and poor health, I have lately abstained from wine.[15]

    In my translation above, I try to keep the word order as close to the original as possible so that the parallelism of each couplet can be seen clearly. Each word in the adjacent lines of a couplet is put in comparison with its counterpart—thus "the wind is strong" and "the islets are clear," "the sky high" and "the sands white," "the gibbons are crying" and "the birds are flying," "boundless forests" and "the endless river," "ten thousand miles" and "a hundred years"—all these are strictly parallel and must contrast to one another in meaning, grammatical category, and particularly tone, as Chinese has four tones and the tonal pattern forms the basis of the musical quality of the language. As Yu-kung Kao and Tsu-lin Mei note, "Jakobson's theory can account for the facts of [Chinese] Recent Style poetry with greater ease than for those of Western poetry—for which the theory was originally intended."[16] In discussing the formation of Chinese phrases and the required antithetical structure of regulated verse, James J. Y. Liu claims that "there is a natural tendency in Chinese towards antithesis." He makes a distinction between antithesis in Chinese poetry and parallelism in other literatures and argues that "antithesis, known as *tuei* in Chinese, differs from 'parallelism,' such as in Hebrew poetry. Antithesis consists of strict antonyms, allowing no repetition of the same words, as parallelism does."[17] It is true that Chinese poetry requires a more strictly antithetical structure than biblical parallelism, but the principle of its structure is comparative, and in that sense, antithesis can be seen as a subspecies of parallelism, not something entirely different in kind. Indeed, whether it is identity through differentiation in a psychological or a linguistic sense, crossroads as a conceptual metaphor or contradictions juxtaposed at the beginning of a novel, the antithesis in a Chinese regulated verse or parallelism in biblical poetry, all these are fundamentally related to comparison, which proves to be the *modus operandi* of thinking and language.

In the postmodern critique of fundamentals, we are told not to essentialize anything and not to hold things in a metaphysical hierarchy, as though any kind of comparison or differentiation, any value judgment, or any order of things would result in a repressive regime that privileges one and, of necessity, excludes all other alternatives. That may explain why some feel uneasy about comparison and question its validity, but if we do not compare and prioritize at all among a number of possibilities, we cannot move, and there would be no action, no narrative, no literature, and no history. Weeping at a crossroads may be in itself a temporary choice, but eventually you need to choose a road and move on. Otherwise, you may shed a lot of tears, but your life remains an empty possibility, not a lived experience. The point is, again, not that we can choose to compare or not to compare, but that we need to make reasonable comparisons and good choices rather than bad ones. Good and bad, in a profoundly ethical and political sense as the comparison and the choice we make, have consequences affecting our own lives as well as the lives of others. Since comparison is something we always do anyway, all the talk about whether to compare is but idle talk. The question is not whether, but how; it is a matter of the relevance or reasonableness of the comparison we make, and of its consequences and implications.

Killing a Chinese Mandarin

Kwame Anthony Appiah presents cosmopolitanism as a moral choice, the idea that "no local loyalty can ever justify forgetting that each human being has responsibilities to every other."[18] Here local closeness is compared with, or contrasted to, the distance of the "other," whose fate and condition may seem far from one's immediate concerns. Distance in time and space is a matter of comparison: How far does one's obligation or responsibility extend to a stranger as compared to one's relatives or close friends? How does one treat someone unseen or even unknown in comparison with one's own group or community? In this context, Appiah recalls a scene in Balzac's novel *Le Père Goriot*, where Eugène Rastignac talks to a friend and poses a question he attributes, erroneously, to Jacques Rousseau. "Have you read Rousseau?," asks Rastignac. "Do you recall the passage where he asks the reader what he'd do if he could make himself rich by killing an old mandarin in China merely by willing it, without budging from Paris?"[19] The killing of a Chinese mandarin far from France by mere volition, without ever getting close and dirtying one's hands, and therefore without the danger of being found out and punished, is presumably something a Frenchman might fancy in view of getting the mandarin's wealth in return. Like Yang Zhu weeping at a crossroads, wondering whether to kill a mandarin in China may serve as another conceptual metaphor with philosophical implications. "Rastignac's question is splendidly philosophical," Appiah notes. "Who but a philosopher would place magical murder in one pan of the scales and a million gold louis in the other?"[20] Weighing a stranger's life on a balance against a million gold louis vividly evokes the point of moral choice and challenges one to consider the ethical and political implications of comparison, and also the core idea of cosmopolitanism as extending one's moral responsibilities to distant outsiders and strangers.

Rastignac's question, however, does not come from Rousseau, but more likely from Adam Smith in a passage in *The Theory of Moral Sentiments* (1760), where Smith speculates how a European might react to the news of an imagined earthquake that suddenly wiped out "the great empire of China." Though a decent European might feel sorry for "the misfortune of that unhappy people" and reflect on "the precariousness of human life," the death of millions of Chinese would seem insignificant in comparison with the smallest pain that might happen to his own person. "If he is to lose his little finger to-morrow," writes Smith, "he would not sleep to-night; but, provided he never saw them, he will snore with the most profound security over the ruin of a hundred millions of his brethren, and the destruction of that immense multitude seems plainly an object less interesting to him, than this paltry misfortune of his own."[21]

Appiah sees both Smith and Balzac posing a question about the moral implications of physical and psychological distance, responsibility, and emotional involvement, all based on the comparison of gain and loss: "If we were to apportion our efforts to the strength of our feelings, we would sacrifice a hundred millions to save our little finger (Smith's inference); and if we would do that (this is Rastignac's corollary), we would surely sacrifice a single faraway life to gain a great fortune."[22] Ethics is all about making the right moral choice, and what constitutes the right choice is based on the comparison of the good and the bad, and sometimes the bad and the less bad. For Appiah, cosmopolitanism implies giving up killing a mandarin in China, even if it also means giving up the opportunity to get rich without much effort or risk. It is a moral choice made not because of a simple sense of sympathy, but because "we are responsive to what Adam Smith called 'reason, principle, conscience, the inhabitant of the breast.'"[23] Cosmopolitanism, therefore, is not something natural or intuitive, but it requires a lot of sound thinking and reasonable comparison, a choice consciously made after careful deliberations.

In a learned essay on the theme of killing a Chinese mandarin, Carlo Ginzburg traces the idea of the moral implications of distance to the works of Diderot and Chateaubriand, thus establishing a French lineage for Rastignac's question in *Le Père Goriot.* "Distance in space or time weakened all feelings and all sorts of guilty conscience, even of crime," says Diderot. "The assassin, removed to the shores of China, can no longer see the corpse which he left bleeding on the banks of the Seine. Remorse springs perhaps less from horror of oneself than from fear of others; less from shame at what one has done than from the blame and punishment it would bring if it were found out."[24] It is interesting that both Adam Smith and Diderot used China to suggest huge distance. In the eighteenth century, because of the Jesuit missionaries' letters and reports, China was very much on the minds of European thinkers, though for the average person, it was still a faraway place, probably on the margins of some imaginary *mappa mundi,* and thus suitable as a symbol of the greatest distance possible.

Ginzburg points out that the assassin who left Paris for China in Diderot's work re-emerged in François-René de Chateaubriand's popular work *The Genius of Christianity,* where the author writes, "I put to myself this question: 'If thou couldst by a mere wish kill a fellow-creature in China, and inherit his fortune in Europe, with the supernatural conviction that the fact would never be known, wouldst thou consent to form such a wish?'"[25] The question obviously responds to Diderot's hypothetical situation and is almost identical to Rastignac's in Balzac's novel. Chateaubriand, as Ginzburg notes, "created a new story: the victim is a Chinese; the murderer, a European; a reason for the murder—financial gain."[26] Chateaubriand, however, used that hypothetical murder of a Chinese to prove the ubiquitous presence of conscience, particularly from a Christian point of view. However he tried to rationalize the distant killing of a Chinese, eventually, says Chateaubriand, "in spite of all my useless subterfuges, I hear a voice in the recesses of my soul, protesting so loudly against the mere idea of such a supposition, that I cannot for one moment doubt the reality of conscience."[27] In Balzac's novel, Rastignac's friend likewise eventually rejects the temptation and chooses to extend his moral responsibility to a stranger despite the enormous distance.

In *The Hypothetical Mandarin*, Eric Hayot considers "killing a Chinese mandarin" to be "a generic philosopheme for the question of how best to be, or to become, a modern, sympathetic human being."[28] In the "civilizing" process of European life and sentiments during the eighteenth and the nineteenth centuries, China was both on the margin as a sign of the distant "Other" *and* an "empire of cruelties," a barbaric foil to contrast with civilized Europe, "a horizon of horizons."[29] In an article on the same subject, Iddo Landau discusses killing a mandarin as a thought experiment, a philosophical hypothesis that reveals the deep-seated self-deception of all human beings, that people are often worse than they think they are, that most people "are ready to, or have significant difficulty in refusing to, murder a human being, if it is clear that we would never be caught," thus highlighting "the importance, or centrality, of society's supervision over us."[30] From a European or American point of view, a Chinese mandarin signifies an unknown person from a distant place, but the philosophical import of this thought experiment needs not be limited to just European or American. In fact, the fantasy of killing a person at great distance without the risk of dire consequences is not at all an alien idea in Chinese imagination. In a satirical essay on "Chinese Fantasies," the influential modern writer Lu Xun observes: "There is another small fantasy. That is, with a gentle hum a man can send out a ray of white light from his nostrils and kill his hated enemy or opponent, no matter how far away it is. The white light will return and no one will know who's done the killing. How nice and carefree it is to be able to kill someone and have no troubles for it!"[31] In his study of classical Chinese fiction, Lu Xun notes that such fantasies, stories of "riding on clouds and flying daggers," were already popular in the literature of the Song dynasty from the twelfth to the mid-thirteenth centuries.[32] Such fantasies of distant killing seem to anticipate the Western fantasy of killing a Chinese mandarin, but the significant difference is that the Chinese fantasy does not have a Frenchman or Englishman as the target. This lack of particularity reveals something specific about modern and European coloniality that we cannot relate to those classical stories of Chinese fantasies.

Hayot refers to a version of killing a Chinese mandarin in Gertrude Stein's *Everybody's Autobiography*, in which she remarks that "many people had thought it was funny when, in her opera *Four Saints in Three Acts*, 'they asked Saint Therese what would she do if by touching a button she could kill three thousand Chinamen and the chorus said Saint Therese not interested.'"[33] Saint Therese here shows her saintly quality and moral conscience, but thanks to the progress of science and technology, particularly in the manufacturing of increasingly more sophisticated and powerful modern weaponry, the distant killing of thousands of people by pushing a button in a bomber or a missile base is no longer an abstract philosophical hypothesis or literary fantasy, but a real choice available for the politicians and military commanders to make (and have made) in the world today. On the one hand, the development of science has made it possible to kill from a distance, but on the other, because the fantasy of distant killing has become a real and lethal possibility, and more importantly a possibility no longer exclusively European and American, killing a Chinese mandarin has lost its guarantee of safety in its original imaginary form. In comparison with the time of Diderot and Balzac, then, science and moral sensibility in our time have almost eliminated the distance—physical and psychological—between China and the West, and has given the metaphor of killing a Chinese mandarin a definite feel of datedness, an unsavory flavor of Western racism and imperialism, which the original metaphor purports to question and challenge in the works of Adam Smith, Diderot, Chateaubriand, Balzac, and others.

When Adam Smith imagined an earthquake that destroyed "the great empire of China," he probably had in mind the real, devastating earthquake that had destroyed the city of Lisbon in 1755, which inspired Voltaire to write his *Poème sur le désastre de Lisbonne* and *Candide,* in which he satirized Leibniz's optimistic idea of "the best of all possible worlds." That famous earthquake had a profound influence on the Enlightenment philosophers and helped change European thinking and society in many ways. If the Lisbon earthquake was indeed the background for Smith's imaginary earthquake in China, for at the time China seemed so far away from Europe that such natural disasters could only be imagined by the Europeans, then we may compare Smith's imaginary earthquake with the real and hugely destructive Sichuan earthquake that shook China in May 2008, or the horrible earthquake, tsunami, and dangerous radioactive leaks at the Fukushima nuclear power plant in Japan in March 2011. Both these earthquakes in Asia were immediately reported the world over through satellite TV and extensive international news coverage that made them a compelling reality felt far beyond China or Japan, at least in people's consciousness, such that it became rather difficult for an average European or American with any degree of decency to brush it aside as if nothing had happened. Intercontinental travel, Internet, e-mail, Facebook, Twitter, television, and world news reports—all these common features of the digital age—have made the world seem much smaller. What was distant one hundred years ago now seems close to home in the so-called global village.

If distance diminishes the intensity of emotional responses, then, compared with the time of Adam Smith or Balzac, have modern science and technology diminished the distance between different parts of the world, say, between China and Europe? That killing a Chinese mandarin has gone out of currency in the usage of our time may suggest a positive answer. And yet, whether one is to extend one's moral responsibilities to distant strangers as compared to one's relatives and close neighbors is still a choice to be made, still a matter of comparison each time we face a real issue. We find ourselves still facing a crossroads that calls for careful comparisons and reasonable decisions.

A Critique of Untranslatability

Translation is all about comparison, about finding comparable or equivalent expressions in one language for those in another, and in recent theoretical reflections, translation is often taken to be a model for comparative literature. "Global translation is another name for comparative literature," as Emily Apter puts it.[34] So far, I have argued for the necessity of comparison, so translation as inherently comparative is also, I would argue, always necessary and possible. Much of recent Western theorizing, however, has focused on the notion of untranslatability, the idea that translation is impossible. Apter's "Twenty Theses on Translation" begins with "nothing is translatable," though paradoxically or dialectically, it ends at just the opposite position: "everything is translatable."[35] Untranslatability in Apter's argument, however, does not really mean incomparability and therefore does not mean the impossibility of translation. Untranslatability is a misnomer.

There is always this dream of untranslatability, what John Sallis calls "the dream of nontranslation": "What would it mean not to translate?," asks Sallis. "What would it mean to begin thinking beyond all translation?"[36] If thinking is speaking to oneself, as Plato and Kant have argued, it is already thinking in language and therefore, Sallis asserts, "it will never have outstripped such translation . . . in other words, for thinking to begin beyond such translation would mean its collapse into a muteness that could mean nothing at all; incapable of signification, it would have ceased—if thinking is speaking to oneself—even to be thinking. It would have risked a captivation that falls short even of silence, if indeed silence is possible only for one who can speak."[37] But mystics and philosophical mysticism have always dreamed of that silence, and despite his effort to refute it, Sallis has to admit that "attestations to untranslatability abound."[38] They abound particularly in recent theorizing in translation studies, in which the idea of untranslatability denies languages their basic comparability.

In her introduction to a volume of essays on translation, Sandra Bermann reminds us that the semantic "overlap" of words in different languages, on which translation is based, can only be partial, that words seemingly synonymous are in fact untranslatable, "as is attested by Benjamin's famous example of '*Brot*' versus 'pain' or Saussure's equally well-known discussion of '*mouton*' versus the English 'mutton' *and* 'sheep.'"[39] That no two languages or linguistic expressions totally overlap is a basic fact that calls for comparison and translation in the first place, but when Benjamin claims that "the word *Brot* means something different to a German than the word *pain* to a Frenchman, that these words are not interchangeable for them, that, in fact, they strive to exclude each other," he is making a clear distinction, "distinguishing the intended object from the mode of intention." As though to forestall misunderstanding, Benjamin immediately goes on to add: "As to the intended object, however, the two words mean the very same thing."[40] For Benjamin, the mode of intention or the way in which the intended object manifests itself is always couched in a particular language and makes sense only in that language. *Brot* makes sense in German and differs from *pain* in French, but he also argues that different languages with their different modes of intention can intend "the very same thing," or relate to the same referential intentionality. Benjamin does not, in other words, endorse the idea of untranslatability. On the contrary, he emphatically states that "the translatability of linguistic creations ought to be considered even if men should prove unable to translate them."[41] Benjamin argues that beyond their different idioms and modes of intention, all languages want to express a deep intention realized in a "pure language."[42] It is this pure language that one tries to translate, and it is in this pure language that translation finds its ultimate legitimacy.

Benjamin's idea of the task of the translator, as Antoine Berman comments, "would consist of a search, beyond the buzz of empirical languages, for the 'pure language' which each language carries within itself as its messianic echo. Such an aim, which has nothing to do with the ethical aim, is rigorously metaphysical in the sense that it platonically searches a 'truth' beyond natural languages."[43] For Benjamin, translatability is rooted in the very nature of languages and their comparable intentionality; it is confirmation of the possibility of translation on a conceptual level, even though on a technical level, some words or expressions may prove to be untranslatable. "The very aim of translation—to open up in writing a certain relation with the Other, to fertilize what is one's Own through the mediation of what is Foreign," says Berman, "is diametrically opposed to the ethnocentric structure of every culture, that species of narcissism by which every society wants to be a pure and unadulterated Whole."[44] The idea of untranslatability is wrong because it is based, wittingly or unwittingly, on that narcissistic desire of cultural and linguistic purity, the ethnocentric illusion that one's own language and culture are unique, superior to, and incomparable with, any other. Or, in a different way, it is wrong because it keeps the Other as absolutely Other, as totally different from one's self, with no possibility of comparison, understanding, and communication. Translation as comparison of the Other with what is one's Own is thus deeply ethical as the act of communication and the establishment of a human relationship.

But in a discussion of the ethics of translation, Robert Eaglestone deliberately goes against the widely accepted view "that translation is central to the ethical philosophy of Emmanuel Levinas," and puts forward his own counterargument that "Levinas's work offers an understanding of ethics that suggests the impossibility of translation."[45] According to Eaglestone, "Levinas's thought is about translation—but that movement is heading out from the community to the other, precisely where translation is impossible. Levinas argues for an unending (and so infinite) ethical responsibility incumbent on each of us. The counterintuitive conclusion is that we are each responsible for those we do not, cannot, and could not understand."[46] But with such total alienation and lack of understanding, how can one establish an ethical relationship with the Other in an intense engagement, what Levinas calls "the face-to-face with the Other"?[47] What Levinas calls "face" denotes the presence and alterity of the Other, but he speaks of human relationships, not of automatons. "Face to face with the other man that a man can indeed approach as presence," the thinking subject is exposed, says Levinas, "to the defenseless nakedness of the face, the lot or misery of the human . . . to the loneliness of the face and hence to the categorical imperative of assuming responsibility for that misery." For Levinas, it is the "Word of God" that commits us to such a moral responsibility, hence "a responsibility impossible to gainsay."[48] With such an absolute moral command, ethics is injected into hermeneutics, and the dialogic relationship with the Other in understanding is recast as the real and practical questions of human relationships and responsibilities: questions of comparison and moral choice. Denying understanding is thus to deny recognition of the "face" of the Other, its suffering and misery, its basic humanity; it is to put the Other at the fantastic end of exoticism as pure difference, or at the endlessly remote distance where untranslatability turns into total indifference. The ethical implication of translation as communication is the comparison of the Other and one's self, the extension of moral responsibilities to the Other in comparison with one's own relatives and one's own community.

When Emily Apter draws on Alain Badiou to "rethink translation studies from the standpoint of the presumption that 'nothing is translatable,'" she acknowledges that her notion of "the translation zone is established on the basis of the philological relation."[49] To limit comparison to philological relations with common etymons in languages and shared sociohistorical conditions, however, is a very limited view, almost of the old-fashioned *littérature comparée* with its positivistic emphasis on *rapports de fait*. What Badiou does is to discard all those philological and cultural relations in the comfort zone and to compare a classical Arabic poet, Labîd ben Rabi'a, with the French poet Mallarmé across huge chasms and gulfs in culture and language. Badiou does not have much faith in the old-fashioned comparative literature, nor does he consider much translation of great poets adequate, but he is not at all inimical to comparison. On the contrary, he believes "in the universality of great poems, even when they are represented in the almost invariably disastrous approximation that translation represents." "Comparison," says Badiou, "can serve as a sort of experimental verification of this universality."[50] Translation may be miserably inadequate as "disastrous approximation," but it is surely not impossible. Here we may recall Benjamin's remark that "the translatability of linguistic creations ought to be considered even if men should prove unable to translate them." For Badiou, it is comparison that makes understanding possible despite disastrous translations. In his comparative work, as Apter well describes it, "for all the obstacles posed by translation, 'great poems' surmount the difficulty of being worlds apart and manage to achieve universal significance. This poetic singularity against all odds challenges the laws of linguistic territorialization that quarantine language groups in communities 'of their own kind' (as in Romance or East Asian languages) or enforce a condition in which monolingualisms coexist without relation."[51] That is exactly what comparative literature for our time should be—comparison not just within but beyond and across philologically linked language groups, across Romance and East Asian languages. "Badiou's literary universalism, built on affinities of the Idea ('une proximité dans la pensée') rather than on philological connections or shared sociohistorical trajectories," says Apter, "defines a kind of *comparatisme quand même* that complements the militant credo of his political philosophy."[52] For Badiou, the very act of comparison bears witness and serves as "experimental verification" of the universality of radically different literary works brought into comparison. That, in my view, holds out an exciting and promising prospect for comparative literature more effectively than the translatability of everything into everything else by, into, or through digital codes in an age of advanced computer technologies.

Concluding Remarks: The Inevitability of Comparison

The Self and the Other are invariably correlated as identity and difference or, more precisely, as identity through comparison and differentiation. This can find another formulation in Spinoza's famous motto *omni determinatio est negatio* "determination is negation."[53] To determine or ascertain one's Self is necessarily to relate to the Other in an act of comparison and differentiation; thus Spinoza puts forth the following as an *ethical* proposition: "Every individual thing, or everything which is finite and has a conditioned existence, cannot exist or be conditioned to act, unless it be conditioned for existence and action by a cause other than itself."[54] Freud and Saussure made the same argument in psychoanalysis and linguistics, which all confirm that comparison or differentiation is ontologically and epistemologically necessary, inevitable, and always already functioning. That is also the core of this essay's argument.

Parallelism and antithesis are obviously predicated on comparison, while the conceptual metaphors of a crossroads and distant killing help bring out the necessity as well as the challenge of comparison as a risky business with moral and political implications. Cosmopolitanism as a moral choice is seen as deeply comparative in the sense that it measures the distance of the Other against one's loyalty to one's relatives and local community, and argues for extension of one's responsibilities to distant strangers and outsiders. Finally, translation is inherently comparative, as it involves the Self and the Other, what is one's Own and what is Foreign, the close and the distant. It is essential not only because it engages different languages and their comparability, but because understanding and communication are, in a broad sense, necessary for forming any human relationships. Translation, in that sense, is then a fundamental form of communication like dialogue, and thus a form as essential to Mikhail Bakhtin as it is to Levinas. Bakhtin puts it very well: "To be means to communicate dialogically. When dialogue ends, everything ends. Thus dialogue, by its very essence, cannot and must not come to an end."[55] We may say in the same vein that comparison, by its very essence, cannot and will not come to an end. Bakhtin's insistence on dialogue thus becomes as much a moral imperative as Benjamin's insistence on translatability or Badiou's insistence on *comparatisme quand même*. Comparison, we realize, is what we must always do to exist and to act, and therefore what and how we compare—and what follow as consequences of our comparison—truly deserve our critical attention.

NOTES

Epigraph. Wang Bi (226–49), *Laozi zhu* (Laozi with Annotations), vol. 3 of *Zhuzi jicheng* (Collection of Masters Writings), 8 vols. (Beijing: Zhonghua, 1954), 45. All translations from Chinese are mine. The *Laozi* or *Tao te ching* have dozens of English translations, and interested readers may look at *Tao te ching*, trans. D. C. Lau (Harmondsworth: Penguin, 1963) or *The Classic of the Way and Virtue: A New Translation of the* Tao-te ching *of Laozi as Interpreted by Wang Bi*, trans. Richard John Lynn (New York: Columbia Univ. Press, 1999).

1   Sigmund Freud, "The Antithetical Sense of Primal Words," trans. M. N. Searl, in *Collected Papers*, 5 vols. (New York: Basic Books, 1959), 4: 187.

2   Freud, "One of the Difficulties of Psycho-Analysis," trans. Joan Riviere, in *Collected Papers*, 4: 351, 352.

3   Ferdinand de Saussure, *Course in General Linguistics*, trans. Wade Baskin (New York: Philosophical Library, 1959), 108.

4   Saussure, *Course in General Linguistics*, 120.

5   Liu An (?–122 BCE), *Huainanzi* (Master Huainan), vol. 7 of *Zhuzi jicheng* (Collection of Masters Writings), 302. A slightly different version of this story can be found in an even earlier text, *Xunzi*, and we can learn about the life and thoughts of Yang Zhu in several other texts, notably *Liezi*.

6   George Lakoff and Mark Turner, *More Than Cool Reason: A Field Guide to Poetic Metaphor* (Chicago: Univ. of Chicago Press, 1989), 2. The concept of identity is not "autonomous," Lakoff and Turner insist, and they present their argument against the "autonomy claim" of language, that is, the view that conventional language is semantically autonomous and not metaphoric. Instead, they maintain that "conventional language and our conventional conceptual system are fundamentally and ineradicably metaphoric," and that "there are general mappings across both poetic and everyday conventional language." Quoting Robert Frost's lines about roads taken and not taken, they argue that if the metaphor is not fundamentally conceptual, "there would be no way to explain either why we understand this passage to be about life or why we reason about it as we do" (116).

7   Robert Frost, "The Road Not Taken," *Selected Poems* (New York: Gramercy Books, 1992), 163.

8   John Greenleaf Whittier, "Maud Muller," in *American Poetry*, ed. Percy H. Boynton (New York: Scribner, 1918), 254.

9   Leo Tolstoy, *Anna Karenina*, trans. Louise Maude and Aylmer Maude (Oxford: Oxford Univ. Press, 1998), 1.

10   Luo Guanzhong (1330?–1400?), *San guo yanyi* (The Romance of the Three Kingdoms) (Beijing: Renmin wenxue, 1985), 1. For an available English translation, see the work attributed to Luo Guanzhong, *Three Kingdoms: A Historical Novel*, trans. Moss Roberts (Berkeley: Univ. of California Press, 1991).

11   Charles Dickens, *A Tale of Two Cities* (New York: Modern Library, 1996), 3.

12   Liu Xie (465?–522), *Wenxin diaolong zhu* (The Literary Mind and the Carving of Dragons with Annotations), 2 vols., annotated by Fan Wenlan (Beijing: Renmin wenxue, 1958), 2: 588. For an available English translation, see Liu Hsieh, *The Literary Mind and the Carving of Dragons: A Study of Thought and Pattern in Chinese Literature*, trans. Vincent Yu-chung Shih (New York: Columbia Univ. Press, 1959).

13   Roman Jakobson and Morris Halle, *Fundamentals of Language* (The Hague: Mouton, 1956), vi.

14   Jakobson and Halle, *Fundamentals of Language*, 77.

15   Du Fu, "Climbing Up the Terrace," in *Du shi xiangzhu* (Du Fu's Poems with Detailed Annotations), 5 vols., annotated by Qiu Zhao'ao (fl. 1685) (Beijing: Zhonghua, 1979), 4: 1766–67.

16   Yu-kung Kao and Tsu-lin Mei, "Meaning, Metaphor, and Allusion in T'ang Poetry," *Harvard Journal of Asiatic Studies* 38, no. 2 (1978): 287.

17   James J. Y. Liu, *The Art of Chinese Poetry* (Chicago: Univ. of Chicago Press, 1962), 146. For a classic study of parallelism in biblical poetry, see James L. Kugel, *The Idea of Biblical Poetry: Parallelism and Its History* (New Haven, CT: Yale Univ. Press, 1981).

18   Kwame Anthony Appiah, *Cosmopolitanism: Ethics in a World of Strangers* (New York: W. W. Norton, 2006), xvi.

19   Honoré de Balzac, *Le Père Goriot* (Paris: Éditions Garniers Frères, 1961), 154; quoted in Appiah, *Cosmopolitanism*, 155.

20   Appiah, *Cosmopolitanism*, 156.

21 Adam Smith, *The Theory of Moral Sentiments*, ed. Knud Haakonssen (Cambridge: Cambridge Univ. Press, 2002), 157.

22 Appiah, *Cosmopolitanism*, 157.

23 Appiah, *Cosmopolitanism*, 174.

24 Denis Diderot, "Conversation of a Father with His Children," in *This Is Not a Story and Other Stories*, trans. P. N. Furbank (Oxford: Oxford Univ. Press, 1993), 143; quoted in Carlo Ginzburg, "Killing a Chinese Mandarin: The Moral Implications of Distance," *Critical Inquiry* 21 (Autumn 1994): 50.

25 Viscount de Chateaubriand, *The Genius of Christianity: Or the Spirit and Beauty of the Christian Religion*, trans. Charles I. White (Baltimore: John Murphy, 1856), 188; quoted in Ginzburg, "Killing a Chinese Mandarin," 54.

26 *Ginzburg, "Killing a Chinese Mandarin," 54.*

27 Chateaubriand, *The Genius of Christianity*, 188; quoted in Ginzburg, "Killing a Chinese Mandarin," 54.

28 Eric Hayot, *The Hypothetical Mandarin: Sympathy, Modernity, and Chinese Pain* (Oxford: Oxford Univ. Press, 2009), 8.

29 Hayot, *The Hypothetical Mandarin*, 10.

30 Iddo Landau, "To Kill a Mandarin," *Philosophy and Literature* 29 (April 2005): 94.

31 Lu Xun, *Zhongguo de qixiang* (Chinese Fantasies), vol. 5 of *Lu Xun quanji* (Lu Xun's Complete Works), 16 vols. (Beijing: Renmin wenxue, 1981), 239.

32 See Lu Xun, *Zhongguo xiaoshuo shi lue* (A Concise History of Chinese Fiction), vol. 9 of *Lu Xun quanji* (Lu Xun's Complete Works), 100.

33 Gertrude Stein, *Everybody's Autobiography* (New York: Cooper Square, 1971), 89–90; quoted in Hayot, *The Hypothetical Mandarin*, 205.

34 Emily Apter, *The Translation Zone: A New Comparative Literature* (Princeton, NJ: Princeton Univ. Press, 2006), xi.

35 Apter, *The Translation Zone*, xi, xii.

36 John Sallis, *On Translation* (Bloomington: Indiana Univ. Press, 2002), 1.

37 Sallis, *On Translation*, 2.

38 Sallis, *On Translation*, 112.

39 Sandra Bermann, "Introduction," in *Nation, Language, and the Ethics of Translation*, ed. Sandra Bermann and Michael Wood (Princeton, NJ: Princeton Univ. Press, 2005), 5.

40 Walter Benjamin, "The Task of the Translator," in *Illuminations*, trans. Harry Zohn (Glasgow: Fontana, 1973), 74.

41 Benjamin, "The Task of the Translator," 70.

42 Benjamin, "The Task of the Translator," 74.

43 Antoine Berman, *The Experience of the Foreign: Culture and Translation in Romantic Germany*, trans. S. Heyvaert (Albany: State Univ. of New York Press, 1992), 7.

44 Berman, *The Experience of the Foreign*, 4.

45 Robert Eaglestone, "Levinas, Translation, and Ethics," in *Nation, Language, and the Ethics of Translation*, 127.

46 *Eaglestone, "Levinas, Translation, and Ethics," 137.*

47 Emmanuel Levinas, *Time and the Other [and Additional Essays]*, trans. Richard A. Cohen (Pittsburgh, PA: Duquesne Univ. Press, 1987), 79.

48 Emmanuel Levinas, *Outside the Subject*, trans. Michael B. Smith (Stanford, CA: Stanford Univ. Press, 1994), 158.

49 Apter, *The Translation Zone*, 85.

50 Alain Badiou, *Handbook of Inaesthetics*, trans. Alberto Toscano (Stanford, CA: Stanford Univ. Press, 2005), 46.

51 Apter, *The Translation Zone*, 85–86.

52 Apter, *The Translation Zone*, 86.

53   Benedict de Spinoza, "Correspondence," in *The Chief Works of Benedict de Spinoza*, 2 vols., trans. R. H. M. Elwes (New York: Dover, 1951), 2: 370.

54   Spinoza, "Ethics," in *The Chief Works of Benedict de Spinoza*, 2: 67.

55   Mikhail Bakhtin, *Problems of Dostoevsky's Poetics*, ed. and trans. Caryl Emerson (Minneapolis: Univ. of Minnesota Press, 1984), 252. Katerina Clark and Michael Holquist first made the connection between Bakhtin and Levinas. They emphasize Bakhtin's skeptical attitude toward systematizing and put him in a tradition of thinkers "from Heraclitus to Emmanuel Lenivas, who have preferred the powers that inhere in the centrifugal forces." See Clark and Holquist, *Mikhail Bakhtin* (Cambridge, MA: Harvard Univ. Press, 1984), 8.

CHAPTER FOUR

Axes of Comparison

Haun Saussy

R EADERS OF JOSÉ RIZAL'S NOVEL *Noli me Tangere* (1887)—like the readers, perhaps more numerous among comparatist scholars, of Benedict Anderson's *Imagined Communities* (1998)—will remember the visit by the hero of the novel, Ibarra, to the botanical garden of Manila. There, says the narrator, he is beset by the "demon of comparisons." His overly well-traveled eye makes him see this genuinely tropical garden as a faded, diminished replica of the artificially tropical gardens of Madrid, Paris, and London. This is the work of comparison, its violence, one might say.[1] Not in a paradise, but in a parody of Eden where the work of the name-giving Adam is everywhere on display, the returned colonial encounters the devil.[2]

It is hard to elicit many cheers for comparison these days. The editors of this volume admit the good and the bad, saying that comparison may be "a homogenizing process . . . that distorts the uniqueness of the objects being compared, reduces them to variants on a common standard, and relies on a downgrading of certain cultures in relation to others" (that's the bad stuff), but it is also "an analogical form of human cognition . . . indispensable to understanding and creativity" (that's the good stuff). They go on to say that "comparisons can indeed be insidious . . . But acts of comparing are also crucial for the registering of inequalities and for struggles against the unjust distribution of resources."[3] In this essay I attempt to provide more detail on all these counts, and ask if we can successfully separate the goodness of comparison from its bad aspects, or if the bad examples are bad not because they are comparisons but because they misapply, misconstrue, or otherwise abuse a blameless mode of thought.

Several authors in the special issue of *New Literary History* from which this book derives recalled "in broad outline . . . the rise of the modern fields of comparative studies in nineteenth-century Europe."[4] The lexicographical work and to some extent the intellectual history behind these outlines were performed some time ago by René Wellek in a pair of classic essays seeking to trace the origin of comparative literature.[5] Robert Lowth (1710–87), once Professor of Poetry at Oxford University, was one of the first to speak of a comparative method, and it may be typical of our magpie discipline that he did so while trying to illustrate a philological discussion with terms borrowed from astronomy. His *Lectures on the Sacred Poetry of the Hebrews* (1753; translated into English, 1787) demonstrated to the learned of Europe that the psalms, prophets, and many other parts of the Bible were written in verse, but a type of verse that had become unrecognizable: *parallelismus membrorum* he called it, or the articulation of similar or opposite meanings in successive verses, a kind of semantic rhyme.[6] In preparing his readers' minds to receive the inhabitual word-craft of the ancient Hebrews, so far from the standard mid-eighteenth-century English understanding of poetry, Lowth warned them that it is not

enough to be acquainted with the language of this people, their manners, discipline, rites, and ceremonies; we must even investigate their inmost sentiments, the manner and connexion of their thoughts; in one word, we must see all things with their eyes, estimate all things by their opinions; we must endeavor as much as possible to read Hebrew as the Hebrews would have read it. We must act as the astronomers with regard to that branch of their science which is called comparative, who, in order to form a more perfect idea of the general system, and its different parts, conceive themselves as passing through, and surveying the whole universe, migrating from one planet to another, and becoming for a short time inhabitants of each. Thus they clearly contemplate, and accurately estimate what each possesses peculiar to itself with respect to situation, celerity, satellites, and its relation to the rest; thus they distinguish what and how different an appearance of the universe is exhibited according to the different situations from which it is contemplated.[7]

To put oneself into the place of another and survey the universe from that point of view: this is what Lowth knows as the comparative method, and Wellek applauds him for "formulat[ing] the ideal of comparative study well enough."[8] But let us mark what might make his analogy unavailable for the linguistic or cultural pluralism that forms the basis of comparative cultural work today. Lowth's analogy makes sense only if we have agreed that there is a single universe that can be examined from a variety of points of view, points that are mutually intelligible, defined by a common standard, and consistently calculable. But because the disciplines of language and culture deal most of all with questions of value, which put that very mutuality and commensurability always in doubt, our contemporaries would find it impossible to make a claim like Lowth's. Anyone who did so would be considered not well intentioned or empathetic, but presumptuous, oblivious of the other's otherness.

Lowth's usage was not repeated in eighteenth-century literary scholarship. "Comparative" remained a word and a mode for the natural sciences.

Perhaps this has to do with the difference between beauty and truth, or between the particular and the general, for comparison reveals structure by obliterating some of the immediacy and particularity of its objects. So close an observer as George Stubbs, the British animal painter, could use "comparative" as the label for his series of parallel engravings designed to raise observation to theory.[9] They show the dissimilar bodies of a man, a tiger, and a chicken engaged in identical pursuits (standing, running, leaping). Identity of function here draws out the different structures that realize it in each animal. Not a bone-for-bone correspondence, Stubbs's analogies show the tiger's knees and elbows carrying different weight and espousing different shapes from the man's, and the chicken's knee echoing the man's knee, but as if turned back to front. The action of a joint or limb thus separates from its observable anatomical shape and suggests a common body plan, with strong variations, across distinct species.

Wellek credits the French naturalist Georges Cuvier with making the use of the word "comparative" prominent and, through his publications and popular lectures, with extending it into many domains of knowledge. Cuvier's contribution to European intellectual life was not only in classifying the animal kingdom but in a particular idea of organic form. He called it "the law of coexistence," the functional interdependence of the parts of an organism.

In the living state, the organs are not only next to one another, but . . . act on one another and contribute together to a common end. For this reason, should any of the organs undergo a modification, its influence will extend to all the others. Those modifications that cannot coexist rule one another out; other modifications demand their counterparts, so to speak, not only in organs that are in immediate contact with one another but even in those that at first glance appear to be most distant and independent from one another . . .

No bone can vary in its facets, in its curvature, or in its protruberances, without the others undergoing proportionate variations and it is possible to derive from the observation of a single bone conclusions about the whole of the skeleton.[10]

In Cuvier's epistemology, the word "comparative" stood for a double guarantee of systematic character: the idea that an animal was a tightly interdependent system of parts, and the promise that random or mechanical variation would be absent from a synoptic view of the whole animal kingdom. In the inventory of beasts past and present, nature had created prodigious variations limited only by conditions of physical impossibility. Cuvier's zoo is a network of interlocking relationships and the model for such classificatory and genealogical projects as comparative grammar, comparative law, comparative architecture, and comparative literature, all dating from the early nineteenth century and all combining curiosity about difference with a drive toward integration that lets no detail escape into randomness. Ralph Waldo Emerson, visiting the Cabinet of Natural History in Cuvier's Jardin des Plantes in 1833, was overcome: "How much finer things are in composition than alone," he wrote. "The limits of the possible are enlarged, and the real is stranger than the imaginary . . . The Universe is a more amazing puzzle than ever as you glance along this bewildering series of animated forms—the hazy butterflies, the carved shells, the birds, beasts, fishes, snakes—and the upheaving principle of life everywhere incipient in the very rock aping organized forms."[11]

Emerson caught the excitement that once attached to the term "comparative." The method of bringing things "in composition" and letting them reveal their commonalities led to a single "upheaving principle of life" that might even be read in the lifeless rocks, so strong was the impression it made on the human observer. But there precisely is the difference with the situation of the humanities today: no single principle, upheaving, *aufhebend* or otherwise, is easily discernible in the documents we study, and anyone who proposed to discern one would instantly be blamed for bad universalism, heedlessly invading others' fields of research, pursuing an imperial project of reductivism, and the like. I take this to be both a sociological fact about the way we manage our disciplines and an epistemological obstacle: on the one hand, a grand synthesis seems improbable; on the other hand, it seems threatening. Why should this be so? Other disciplines, too, have trouble building their observations into an overarching unity, but the idea that it would be a bad thing to try to do so is not so widespread among historians, philosophers, and linguists, for example, as it is among literary scholars. Aside from our division into national fields and the sense that maintaining the divisions keeps the fields alive (on which more below), the reason we have a bad conscience about such projects is that we, like many anthropologists, are sharply aware of hypocritical universalism. The abhorrence we feel toward it makes us suspicious of the whole comparative enterprise. A vivid example is given in the present collection by R. Radhakrishnan, who observes that "the comparative act, in enabling a new form of recognition along one axis, perpetrates dire misrecognition along another."[12] The two dynamics of recognition and misrecognition—or perhaps, to put it in another critic's idiom, blindness and insight—do not reconcile in a higher synthesis. Radhakrishnan works out the problem through an example:

What happens when a literary critic compares the feminism in Tamil of [Ambai] . . . with the feminisms of say, Adrienne Rich, or Virginia Woolf, or Hélène Cixous? . . . What is indeed amazing is that despite different historical

grounding and location, these writers come up with "comparable" articulations . . . But here lies the problem: whereas someone like Cixous achieves this
awareness as a function of her interlocution with Sigmund Freud, Jacques Lacan,
psychoanalysis, and structuralism in general, Ambai's formulations are the result
of her interactions with Indian political economy, Indian nationalist and feminist
discourses, and aspects of Hindu Advaitic philosophy. Once the commonality
is figured out at the level of "knowing," it feels as though the real differences
between Ambai and Rich at the level of "being" do not matter; where each of
them comes from turns into a mere empirical detail at the service of a more
meaningful theoretical enterprise . . . what happens to those areas in each work
that remain "indigenous" and are not relevant to the common ground area of
the comparison? Would these areas be abandoned . . . as mere hinterlands whose
function is nothing more than prepping and propping up the avant-garde area
of comparison?[13]

More meaningful? To whom? Is this sarcasm? The alliteration in "prepping and propping up" sounds dismissive and telegraphs to the reader
which, of the "indigenous" and the "avant-garde," is to be supported.

Using more general language, Radhakrishnan notes that "the point
to be made here is that the act of comparison has the capacity and the
potential, depending on which powers are backing the project, to supplant a prior epistemological project with a new one." Talk of "powers
backing the project" makes comparison sound instrumental, even mer-
cenary. It sounds as if comparative literature, when it harvests the fruits
of close reading in a particular language and tradition, always does so
in order to package and export them to some alien destination, "sup-
planting a prior epistemological project with a new one." But is "sup-
planting" necessarily the right word? It carries connotations of usurpation, of misappropriation. Is it necessarily true that the "new project" in
the case of the Lakshmi-Rich-Woolf-Cixous comparison will necessarily
obliterate the local flavor and commitments of the writers discussed,
or is the point that this will tend to be the outcome? Is the example a
call to vigilance or an admission of futility? Let us take it as the former.
Rather than assume that the local, empirical, nonmainstream interests
of a writer will always be erased by a new, falsely global but actually
provincial translation into the canon and idiom of the North Atlantic
academy (I assume these to be the "powers" in question), would it not
be better to insist that comparison does its job poorly when it reduces
too effectively, when it discards too much of the prior context that gave
a work its meaning in the first instance? If the trouble with comparison
is that it systematically filters out, as impurities, the elements in a work
of literature that are associated with women, persons of color, speakers
of languages, and users of concepts developed that appear exotic to the
denizens of London, Paris, and Berlin, as Radhakrishnan seems to be

saying, is this a problem that can be corrected by rejecting comparison? Can the postcolonial critic exorcize the "demon of comparisons," or is the haunting definitive?

Seeking a corrective, Radhakrishnan pursues "the unquiet of the Self-Other problematic": "Let us say then, that prior to the comparatist endeavor we have the English subject, the French subject, the German subject, the Indian subject, and so on."[14] Is this a good starting point? It has the advantage of not introducing a falsely universal subject (the human subject in general) as the standard of comparison, but it has the disadvantage of reproducing the structure of our academic departments of "national languages," themselves a diverted reproduction of the structure of the face of the earth as divided into nations, each with its passport, language, customs, laws, ways of being, cuisine, flag, heroines, heroes, and so forth. It has the further disadvantage of potentially legitimating the kind of relativism that political nations like to use to quash debate within their frontiers. Stipulating that what we have prior to the comparatist endeavor is "the English subject, the French subject, the Indian subject, and so on" has the effect of specifying the task of comparison as stating the differences and commonalities of the worldviews of the subjects so constituted—which may be a vain and fruitless task, from the moment we look at conditions that pay no heed to national borders.

The step away from putative universalism is needed. But what is it a step toward? By bringing up national identities, Radhakrishnan wants to point to a condition of inequality among intellectual producers, a condition that guarantees wider distribution and greater remuneration to some people and ideas, while putting formidable obstacles on the path of others. Literary comparison as currently practiced does not often resist this condition. It would be wrong to accept it as the way of the world. The question before comparatists is, does our discipline naturalize this inequality? The discussion about "world literature" has been one of the channels for exploring the issue—or, to put it less blandly, one of the subfields that perpetuate the problem. Analogies with economics and political power are never far from the surface in those discussions—sometimes crude analogies, as when we hear that a rising country deserves a Nobel Prize for one of its admired writers, sometimes more subtle, as with accounts of literary reputation mechanisms that draw from Wallerstein or Bourdieu.[15]

World literature as *comparative* or *competitive*: that is one way of putting the problem. Pheng Cheah summons up Hobbes, Locke, Rousseau, and Kant to trace the emergence of literary comparison from a theme in the history of social thought that sees the act of comparing oneself with others as sometimes generous (putting oneself in another's place) and sometimes invidious (ranking oneself against others), two moves that Cheah calls "a hospitable and a competitive relation to alterity."[16] There is the good comparison that acknowledges the other, and the bad comparison that seeks to outdo and undo him. This is insightful and goes well beyond disciplinary concerns. In the double root of comparison we might see mirrored the modern problem of democratic politics hitched to capitalist economics, an often unstable combination. Within culture, the ambiguity is redoubled. A particularly refined form of dominance today, says Cheah, is the rivalry expressed in an "ethics of comparison . . . as a form of cultural capital that bespeaks the intellectual superiority of national academic institutions capable of cultivating such an ethics."[17] It sounds as if this "ethics of comparison" envelops both the hospitable and the competitive relation, as if the accommodation and toleration we prize as consequences of comparison were just a velvet-coated power play. If this is true, then comparison, even the most well intentioned, is fated to fall on the bad, competitive side, and intellectuals (bent under their "cultural capital") will inevitably fall there with it. Such is precisely the condition that strikes Radhakrishnan as an injustice—a condition of competition among national cultural institutions unequally endowed with the very resources that make for success in the game of comparison. The "demon of comparisons" is alive and well.

Disquiet with comparison might take the form of refusing to compare. Jean-Jacques Rousseau had a model for that. He imagined the "savages" at the dawn of humanity as speaking a language of utter singularities in which both general categories and comparisons would be unthinkable:

Individual things displayed themselves to [the savages'] minds isolated as they are in the image of nature; if one oak tree was named A, another one would be named B; for the first idea one derives from two things is that they are not the same, and it often takes a long time to discover what they have in common. So that the narrower the bounds of their knowledge, the vaster their vocabulary.[18]

A savage could consider his right leg and his left leg separately, or survey them together under the indivisible idea of a "pair," without ever thinking that he had two legs.[19]

Paul de Man sees this second passage as setting a deep baseline of skepticism: "For Rousseau . . . number is par excellence the concept that hides ontic difference under an illusion of identity."[20] The savage will not be taken in; comparison will have no opportunity to mingle or permute difference and identity; one oak tree is not to be spoken of in the same terms as another oak tree. Such a retreat from comparison will not solve the problem of inequality as much as make it inconceivable. Where nothing is equal to anything else, nothing can be unequal either.

In another place, Rousseau imagines the denial of comparison as the healthy or perfect subject refusing to be likened to the broken or incomplete one. "It has always seemed strange to me that anyone should ask a free people why they are free. It's as if someone were to ask a man who has his two arms why he is not an amputee. The right to freedom is self-generated, it is the natural state of man."[21] If freedom is the natural state, then even to raise the theoretical possibility of unfreedom takes us out of that state, disturbs us in the enjoyment of our freedom by the specter of doubt, the specter of comparisons. The topic of amputation appears as the mark or brand of history in its differentiation from nature. The imaginary amputation imputes violence to the current condition that passes for normal, makes this condition the result of a violent act in the past. Man in the state of nature is complete, perfect, in no need of explanation. People who are living in historical conditions of reduced freedom must always be comparing their plight, even if silently, to the lost state of nature, while the contrary is not true.

To say this is, however, to fall for a fiction, because Rousseau explicitly tells us that the state of nature is a theoretical construct and no more. He has invented, for the sake of comparison, a prior "natural state of man" against which all current states are to be judged.[22] The invention of this state has as its purpose to make the current state unnatural, to put it in need of an explanation, to undermine its self-evident character. The state of nature, in Rousseau's political polemics, is a nonexistent baseline generated for the purpose of making difference visible and scandalous: it is pure comparison, comparison for the sake of comparison.

"State of nature" theories have two advantages regarding the paradox of invidious comparison advanced earlier. First, they should operate on a universal basis without juggling the features and merits of particular nations and cultures; and second, they are powerfully aprioristic, they take little for granted and demand much. John Rawls, attempting to construct a just social order (within national frontiers, though these are never named), specifies that "the original position"—his equivalent for the state of nature—"is the appropriate initial status quo which insures that the fundamental agreements reached in it are fair."[23] "The idea of the original position is to set up a fair procedure so that any principles agreed to will be just. The aim is to use the notion of pure procedural justice as a basis for theory."[24] Rawls is not grading on a curve. In comparison with the ideal starting point and the subsequent procedures that aim to preserve its initial fairness, all existing societies are found wanting. One will not find in Rawls the commitments to the local and specific that, for some political thinkers, are the virtues of a humane or communitarian liberalism: "as far as possible the choice of a conception of justice should not be affected by accidental contingencies."[25]

Johan Galtung's scheme for evaluating the degree to which a society can be called "peaceful" addresses these contingencies. His account of "structural violence" is like a negative projection of Rawls's theory of justice. In the attempt to discover a common basis for evaluating all sorts of inequality ranging from nuclear war to malnutrition, Galtung sets the baseline with variables of a temporal and technological nature. As with Rousseau's state of nature, inequality is a result of violence. But violence is not for Galtung an event, an eruption of force or a body count that might be traced to some act and actor in the past, but the result of a comparison that we must make ourselves:

As a point of departure, let us say that *violence is present when human beings are being influenced so that their actual somatic and mental realizations are below their potential realizations* . . . Thus, if a person died of tuberculosis in the eighteenth century it would be hard to conceive of this as violence since it might have been quite unavoidable, but if he dies from it today despite all the medical resources in the world, then violence is present according to our definition. Correspondingly, the case of people dying from earthquakes today would not warrant an analysis in terms of violence, but the day after tomorrow, when earthquakes may become avoidable, such deaths may be seen as the result of violence.[26]

A comparison between potential and actual states, with an assessment of remedies possible at the time, makes possible the diagnosis of violence. Some violence is obvious: people are shot, bombed, sent to camps, deliberately starved, or executed on the basis of falsified testimony. In the less straightforward cases, where no particular person is at fault for the harm, where there is no drama or action, comparison is indispensable as the revealer of violence. "Violence without this relation [of subject and object] is structural, built into structure. Thus, when one husband beats his wife there is a clear case of personal violence, but when one million husbands keep one million wives in ignorance there is structural violence."[27] Structural violence is not an on-off function, but a shaded and multiple thing. Its nature evolves as we do. Not only the failings, but the achievements of humanity, too, redraw its outlines. The discovery of multidrug regimens that turned HIV into a manageable chronic disease changed the relation of potential and actual outcomes, to be sure, but this change merely redrew the boundaries of structural violence in the epidemic, replacing a condition in which all AIDS patients endured pain, stigma, and neglect (compared to other patients) with one in which medication was available only to those with money or insurance.[28]

Galtung's comparative logic is exempt from the state-of-nature claim and its assumptions about essential humanity, from historical triumphalism, and from national boasting. It instead asks: What was the best realization of potential that might have been achieved? Who benefited from it, and who did not? What determined the distribution of pain and comfort? Comparisons are indispensable in framing answers to these questions.

While some forms of inequality happen between nations, or groups roughly specifiable as nations (for example, the corpus of literary traditions framed in particular languages that are spoken in some nations and not in others), and other forms are made visible within nations by the existence of classes or strata of rich and poor, most recently it has been impossible to ignore forms of inequality that wash over national borders as a wave over a shallow dike. For centuries, disease and war have been the prime examples of such conditions (germs ignore borders, armies seek to redraw them), but now we must consider the effects of human energy use: nuclear and fossil fuels and their effects on nature and society. Additionally, in recent times, with the weakening of state prerogatives in economic transactions such as investment and marketing, frontiers are rather filters than walls—no longer outlines determining the contours of national selves, but gates designed to enable or disable particular kinds of exchange among various markets. (As examples, consider the wage and immigration policies of the major industrialized countries, or even of different regions of a country like China, in contrast to the flow of goods among these areas.[29]) It is therefore anachronistic to think of the inhabited globe in terms of nations, flags, and passports, as if those could still serve as the labels and containers of human purpose. These other forms of inequality or violence bypass the nation, and although I am not sure what comparative literature can do to help us understand them, or even to recognize our responses to them, clinging to the nation as our unit of thought will not help in the task.

There is no need to specially castigate scholars of literature for having failed to notice the erosion of the nation as a category. Galtung's own examples often assume a national frame of reference, or a cultural one, in which "societies," taken as units, exhibit greater or lesser degrees of personal and structural violence. But the model is not inherently tied to the nation, as models based on distinctive histories or institutions are. Today, whether under conditions of peace or war, the infliction of pain and the distribution of comfort are global in scope. To cut up this international field into national patches creates distracting mediations.

But when we adopt a wider perspective, do we necessarily adopt the universal human subject as its protagonist? To what new identities do we commit or expose ourselves? Who speaks, after all, in Rousseau, Galtung, or Rawls? Literary scholars ought to be skilled in all questions involving speech, and if they choose to chronicle the history of global inequality, they should first put themselves in the role of universal listeners. The material is ready to hand; people respond to moral imbalance with narrative. Even Rawls, despite his knack for dismissing "accidental contingencies," could admit such evidence: "A rational individual is not subject to envy, at least when the differences between himself and others *are not thought to be the result of injustice* and do not exceed certain limits . . . Those who express resentment must be prepared to show why certain institutions are unjust or how others have injured them."[30]

What does all this mean for comparative literature? It is certainly possible to search out texts that denounce contemporary inequality, even to link several such texts in a traditionally comparative study.[31] What Rousseau, Galtung, and Rawls suggest for the comparatist is not the poetry, but the grammar, of the postnational condition. Grammar must become legible before we can make much of poetry. Moreover, the literary study of transnational conditions does not have to remain on the level of content. Much can be done on the level of structure that might transform our ways of reading. Our organizing principles (the national filing system for authors and works, and the habit of referring to nations interchangeably with languages, to offer two examples) could be rethought. Looking at different constellations of objects might renew the poetics of comparative scholarship (how we research and organize our writing). The politics of comparison today would not concern nations, races, parties, or classes, but conditions—elusively omnipresent—which subtend these, and which all of us help to create. To hold them in our attention might precipitate discoveries.

NOTES

1   On this scene, made archetypal by Benedict Anderson's invocation in *The Spectre of Comparisons: Nationalism, Southeast Asia and the World* (London: Verso, 1998), see Pheng Cheah, "The Material World of Comparison," in this volume.

2   On the delicate question of how to translate Rizal's "el demonio de las comparaciones" ("the spectre of comparisons"? or "the devilry of comparison"? or "the imp of analogy"?), see Cheah, "The Material World of Comparison." Poe's "imp of the perverse," Baudelaire's "Démon," and Mallarmé's "démon de l'analogie" may be significant precursors.

3   Rita Felski and Susan Stanford Friedman, "Introduction," in this volume.

4   Mary N. Layoun, "Endings and Beginnings: Reimagining the Tasks and Spaces of Comparison," in this volume; and see the similar reference to Rey Chow on the hypocrisy of comparison in Bruce Robbins, "Chomsky's Golden Rule: Comparison and Cosmopolitanism," in this volume.

5   René Wellek, "The Term and Concept of Literary Criticism," in *Concepts of Criticism* (New Haven, CT: Yale Univ. Press, 1963), 21–36, and "The Name and Nature of Comparative Literature," in *Discriminations: Further Concepts of Criticism* (New Haven, CT: Yale Univ. Press, 1970), 1–36.

6   Robert Lowth, *Lectures on the Sacred Poetry of the Hebrews*, trans. G. Gregory (Boston: Buckingham, 1815), 258–72.

7   Lowth, *Lectures on the Sacred Poetry of the Hebrews*, 72. The original Latin text reads in part: "Idem . . . nobis faciendum est, quod Astronomi solent in ea suae disciplina parte

quam vocant Comparativam." Lowth, *De sacra poesi Hebraeorum* (Oxford: Clarendon Press, 1753), 47.

8 Wellek, "The Name and Nature of Comparative Literature," 2.

9 George Stubbs, *A Comparative Anatomical Exposition of the Structure of the Human Body with That of a Tiger and a Common Fowl* (1795–1806), reprinted in Terence Doherty, *The Anatomical Works of George Stubbs* (London: Secker and Warburg, 1970).

10 Georges Cuvier, *Leçons d'anatomie comparée* (Paris: Baudouin, 1800), 1: 46, 56–57 (my translation). On Cuvier's epistemology, see Guy Jucquois, *Le comparatisme: Généalogie d'une méthode* (Louvain: Peeters, 1989) and *Le comparatisme: Émergence d'une méthode* (Louvain: Peeters, 1993).

11 Ralph Waldo Emerson, *Journal,* July 13, 1833, cited in Joel Porte, ed., *Emerson in His Journals* (Cambridge, MA: Harvard Univ. Press, 1982), 110–11.

12 R. Radhakrishnan, "Why Compare?," in this volume.

13 Radhakrishnan, "Why Compare?"

14 Radhakrishnan, "Why Compare?"

15 Pascale Casanova, *The World Republic of Letters,* trans. M. B. DeBevoise (Cambridge, MA: Harvard Univ. Press, 2005), draws on Pierre Bourdieu for her sociological framework. Wallerstein is perceptible as a reference in Franco Moretti's "Conjectures on World Literature," *New Left Review* 1 (2000): 54–68, and a recent anthology pursues the methodological point in detail: David Palumbo-Liu, Bruce Robbins, and Nirvana Tanoukhi, eds., *Immanuel Wallerstein and the Problem of the World* (Durham, NC: Duke Univ. Press, 2011).

16 Cheah, "The Material World of Comparison."

17 Cheah, "The Material World of Comparison." Cheah also dissents from the common view that "education is about the enhancement of human capital so that a given country can be comparatively stronger than others." But the countries of North America and Europe seem at this writing to have decided that educating their young and caring for their sick is too expensive; what must be strong, in the postnational framework, is not "a given country" or its citizens but a given economy. Robbins analyzes a similar slippage from nation to economy ("Chomsky's Golden Rule").

18 Jean-Jacques Rousseau, "Discours sur l'origine et les fondements de l'inégalité parmi les hommes" (1755), in *Œuvres complètes,* ed. Bernard Gagnebin and Marcel Raymond (Paris: Gallimard, 1964), 3: 149 (my translation; I have modernized the spelling).

19 Rousseau, "Discours sur l'origine de l'inégalité," Note xiv, in *Œuvres complètes,* 3: 219.

20 Paul de Man, *Allegories of Reading* (New Haven, CT: Yale Univ. Press, 1979), 154.

21 Rousseau, "Histoire du Gouvernement de Genève," in *Œuvres complètes* (Paris: Gallimard, 1995), 5: 519.

22 This point is perennial in discussions of Rousseau. For Victor Goldschmidt, it is a methodological step: "natural right has no need of history, and even repudiates history as it does positive law" in *Anthropologie et politique: Les principes du système de Rousseau* (Paris: Vrin, 1983), 133. Robert Dérathé clarifies the relation of Rousseau's "state of nature" to predecessor political theorists in Jean-Jacques Rousseau et la science politique de son temps (Paris: Vrin, 1970), 125–34.

23 John Rawls, *A Theory of Justice* (Cambridge, MA: Belknap Press, 1971), 17.

24 Rawls, *A Theory of Justice,* 136.

25 Rawls, *A Theory of Justice,* 530.

26 Johan Galtung, "Violence, Peace, and Peace Research," *Journal of Peace Research* 6, no. 3 (1969): 167–91. In a footnote, Galtung clarifies that bad housing for the poor can render earthquakes violent, in the interhuman sense, when such houses collapse and better houses do not. This point was made earlier by Jean-Jacques Rousseau ("Lettre à Voltaire," 18 August 1756, in *Oeuvres complètes* (Paris: Gallimard, 1969) 4: 1061. (I am indebted to

David Damrosch for this reference.) On the philosophical reverberations, see Werner Hamacher, "The Quaking of Presentation," in *Premises: Essays on Philosophy and Literature from Kant to Celan* (Stanford, CT: Stanford Univ. Press, 1999), 261–93.

27 Galtung, "Violence, Peace, and Peace Research," 171.

28 See Paul Farmer, "An Anthropology of Structural Violence," in *Partner to the Poor: A Paul Farmer Reader,* ed. Haun Saussy (Berkeley: Univ. of California Press, 2010), 350–75.

29 For an ingenious play on this difference, see Henry Box Brown, *Narrative of the Life of Henry Box Brown* (Manchester: Lee & Glynn, 1851).

30 Rawls, *A Theory of Justice,* 530, 533 (my emphasis).

31 For a comparative study calling on Galtung's framework among others, see Rob Nixon, *Slow Violence and the Environmentalism of the Poor* (Cambridge, MA: Harvard Univ. Press, 2011).

Part II **Comparison in the World**
Uses and Abuses

CHAPTER FIVE

Comparison as Relation

Shu-mei Shih

COMPARISON, AS THE ACT OF COMPARING SIMILARITIES and differences, has led to two ethical conundrums. First, it led to anxieties toward the grounds of comparison, because when we put two texts or entities side by side, we tend to privilege one over the other. The grounds are never level. A presumed or latent standard operates in any such act of comparison, and it is the more powerful entity that implicitly serves as the standard. Second, the most likely conclusion to these comparisons is further pronouncement of differences and incommensurabilities between the entities, precisely due to an ethical concern over the latent operation of the presumed, usually Eurocentric, standard. Comparing two entities at their intimate juxtaposition therefore paradoxically produces further distances between them.

This essay is a modest proposal for a new theory of comparison that I call relational comparison. It argues for comparison as relation, or doing comparative literature as relational studies. Comparison as relation means setting into motion historical relationalities between entities brought together for comparison, and bringing into relation terms that have traditionally been pushed apart from each other due to certain interests, such as the European exceptionalism that undergirds Eurocentrism. The excavation of these relationalities is what I consider to be the ethical practice of comparison, where the workings of power are not concealed but necessarily revealed. Power, after all, is a form of relation.

To set up the relational framework, I first draw insights from the integrative world history detailed by such scholars as Janet L. Abu-Lughod, John M. Hobson, and André Gunder Frank to consider the potentiality of a world historical study of literature as they do global economy, and to offer a new, and I think more viable, conception of world literature. I synthesize these findings with the theory of Relation developed by Martinican thinker Édouard Glissant as a way to link geocultural and socioeconomic history—the history of worldwide interconnectedness—not only to literature but also to poetics. Literature is part and parcel to the world, and poetics is as much about understanding the text as understanding the world. Glissant's notion of poetics as a certain logic of the world and a theory of literature offers us a creative way to think about the relation between the text and the world in several ways. As a being in the world, the text is not only organic to the world but also enters into relations; its worldliness is its thrownness. Usefully, we can consider the question of scale in literary studies from the world to the text, from the grand geographical scale of the world to the admittedly small physical scale of an individual text. The relational method informed by world history, I contend, allows for the scaling back and forth between the world and the text as well as along the intermediary scales, moving toward a more integrated conception of comparative literature and world literature, where the issue is not inclusiveness or qualification (which text deserves to be studied or designated as "world literature" and which does not) but excavating and activating the historically specific set of relationalities across time and space. These relationalities can be as much about form as content; hence the importance of poetics.

Relational studies of literature in integrated world historical contexts can occur along various axes and pivots, from different perspectives, around different thematics, and in different scales. For example, we can consider the specific decolonial pivot of world history in the global 1960s to analyze literary texts that cross-fertilized each other, or we can consider the axis of women's movements around the world to analyze women's literature in these different places not as discreet entities but in relation. The potential topics are as numerous as the infinite web of world relations within which the text is caught.

In this essay, the specific pivot traces what I call the "plantation arc," stretching from the Caribbean to the American South and to Southeast Asia. From the Caribbean, we follow Glissant's theory of Relation, a theory that is consonant with the widespread tendency to think on a global scale in the late twentieth century (as in chaos theory, which he appropriates, and theories of globalization) and organic to the location from which he theorizes, the Caribbean archipelago or the West Indies. From there, we follow Glissant's reading of the plantation novels of William Faulkner, set in the American South and populated by white and mixed-blood planters harboring dark secrets, a reading which enacts the scaling of the theory of Relation from the worldwide to the textual. From this American South, we move to the British East Indies—the Borneo rain forest of British and Japanese colonizers, Chinese settlers and coolies, Sarawak communists and indigenous Dayaks—in the work of Taiwan-based Sinophone Malaysian author Chang Kuei-hsing. We then loop back to the Caribbean of Patricia Powell, the Jamaica of postabolition blacks, white coolie traders, Chinese coolies, and shopkeepers. The purpose here is twofold: first, to illustrate how doing relational studies with a keen world historical sense demands that world literature take its worldliness more seriously than thought possible; and second, to show

how relational comparison opens up a new arena, perhaps even a new life, for comparative literature.

Integrative World History and World Literature

The two main theses for integrative world historians, simply put, are that the world as we know it has been integrated economically and otherwise for much longer than the modern world system theory proposes, and that the so-called "rise of the West" owed much to the more advanced East. To consider the macrohistory of the world is to learn the interconnectedness of the world since at least around the sixth century, and what this means is that the ideology of "East is East and West is West" is as fictive as it is false.

Historical sociologist J. L. Abu-Lughod identifies in her important book *Before European Hegemony* (1991) the existence of a polycentric world system in the thirteenth century, much before the European-led world system of the sixteenth century, as has been proposed in Immanuel Wallerstein's popular world systems theory. By the eleventh, twelfth, and especially the thirteenth century, the world had become more integrated than ever before. The "increased economic integration and cultural efflorescence" of the thirteenth century can be witnessed in such accomplishments as Sung celadonware, Persian turquoise-glazed bowls, Egyptian furniture with complex inlays of silver and gold, grand cathedrals in Europe, great Hindu temples in south India, as well as developments in technology and social innovations such as navigation and statecraft, all of which happened alongside an international trade system that stretched from northwestern Europe to China.[1] This international trade system was in turn organized around three major circuits of the Far East, the Middle East, and Western Europe, covering most of the world, with the exception of the continental Americas and Australia.

Disputing Abu-Lughod's claim that the thirteenth-century world system then declined when the European-led world system arose, André Gunder Frank's explicitly anti-Eurocentric *ReOrient: Global Economy in the Asian Age* (1998) pays special attention to the structural relations, interconnectedness, and simultaneity in world events and processes during what he calls "the Asian Age," which he dates from 1400 to 1800. Even though he actually locates in his other works the existence of something similar to Wallerstein's world system back by five thousand years, not five hundred years, his main point in this book is to show how Europe "climbed up on the back of Asia, then stood on Asian shoulders," which also asserts the view, contrary to Abu-Lughod's, that Asia did not decline but maintained its economic dominance until 1800.[2] Frank analyzes trade routes, the capillary operation of money, and the interconnectedness of a global economy, making an argument after Joseph Fletcher for a "horizontally integrative history." This is how Fletcher defined integrative history as a method:

> Integrative history is the search for and description and explanation of such interrelated historical phenomenon. Its methodology is conceptually simple, if not easy to put into practice: first one searches for historical parallelisms (roughly contemporaneous similar developments in the world's various societies) and then one determines whether they are causally interrelated.[3]

Here what we have is a proposal to study macrohistory in a horizontal fashion across different geographical regions in terms of structures, simultaneities, and interrelations, as opposed to predominant studies of vertical continuities of national histories. The integrative method is deceptively simple, but it is also the method that historians (not to mention literary scholars) have more than successfully avoided throughout the modern period. This avoidance is telling. To analogize alongside Frank's critique of Eurocentric history, separating the West from the East in literary studies was probably as foundational to the construction of European literary exceptionalism as it was for Eurocentric historical studies. We can now perhaps begin to see the conceit of not only the displacement of horizontal studies (the East is too hard to know), but also the conversion of horizontal to vertical studies (the East is the past of the West) prevalent in literary studies. Fletcher's method begins with finding parallel patterns, and this is but one of the methods one can use to do relational studies, but it can be highly productive for literary studies. When we do modernist studies, for instance, we can no longer turn a blind eye to all those modernisms that occurred in non-Western countries, nor can we see each of these modernisms as autonomous or discreet. Apparent parallelisms are not historical accidents.

Synthesizing many of the views of Abu-Lughod, Frank, and other like-minded world historians, J. M. Hobson's *The Eastern Origins of Western Civilization* (2004) offers specific analyses of the "resource portfolios" (technologies, institutions, and ideas) that the East had to offer to the West to make possible the rise of the "Oriental West," because globalization was first of all Eastern (Far Eastern and Islamic Middle Eastern) or Oriental. What this means is that the world since the sixth century has been a "single global cobweb,"[4] where advancements in the production of iron and steel (not to mention the production of crops, crafts, and arts), the breakthroughs in astronomy and mathematics, and the creation of a whole series of capitalist institutions in the Islamic Middle East—as well as the technological advancements such as printing, gunpowder, navigational sciences (compass and the building of ships)—enlightened ideas of rationality, and agricultural and other technological know-how from the Far East (especially China) made the world a much more interconnected place. It was with the construction of the white racist self-identity, the burgeoning of European social sciences, and the rise of imperial ambitions that the ideas of European exceptionalism and the autonomous "rise of the West" were invented. Methodologically, Hobson does not necessarily offer anything more than Frank does, but substantiates Frank's more theoretical and general claims in greater detail.

Integrative world history, as far as I can see, began as both a reaction against nationalist historiography (where the object of study is one nation and its vertical history of continuity) as well as traditional comparative history (where the two objects of study—two nations—largely run parallel while differences and similarities are calibrated). The new focus is instead, as one historian notes, on "the complex, global network of power-inflected relations that enmesh our world."[5] To be sure, not all parts of the network are equally affecting or evenly affected by the global system, but all parts of the network are constitutive of the system itself, and there is no hiding from an interconnectedness that is thoroughly infiltrated by the operations of power. This means that histories of empire, conquest, slavery, and colonialism cannot in any way be disavowed when one does integrative world history; after all, as noted earlier, power is a form of relation.

Herein lies perhaps the greatest distinction between integrative world history and the theories of world literature offered by literary comparatists in recent years. Franco Moretti's map of world literature, though inclusive of much of the world, is Eurocentric to the extent that he holds up what is essentially an exceptionalist argument about the life story of the novel as rising in the West and traveling to the East.[6] Pascale Casanova's model considers colonial history only to reaffirm Paris as the center of the world republic of letters.[7] David Damrosch's model would grant world literature status only to those texts that have "circulated beyond their culture of origin" through such modes of circulation as translation, publication, and reading.[8] What this implies is that the study of world literature is partly about identifying which texts were translated into and read in which languages. Considering that the United States has the lowest percentage of translated books compared to almost all of the other countries in the world, American scholars should be accordingly least qualified to theorize the system of world literature. More importantly, texts travel over terrain that is by no means even, and the circulation model effectively cuts off from consideration the literatures of many small nations and minor languages that are nonetheless also touched by world historical processes. Wouldn't it make better sense to consider a model of world literature similar to that of integrative world history that sees, instead of discreet national literatures, all literatures as participating in a network of power-inflected relations, with the task of the world literature scholar to excavate and analyze these relations through deep attention to the texts in question in the context of world history? These relations can manifest themselves on formal, generic, and other levels, so the new model will require close readings of the texts (as opposed to Moretti's "distant reading") and will require sensitivity to world history, scaling both the textual and the global without losing sight of either of the scales. To put it differently, form and formation are intimately connected, as are content and history, even in texts that most assiduously flaunt artistic autonomy. The argument for the autonomy of the text is itself a historical formation.

From the West Indies, Relation

While the integrative world historians have given us concrete historical and economic evidence as to the interconnectedness of the world since the sixth century, Martinican thinker Édouard Glissant has theorized Relation as both a way of describing and understanding the globalized world of "infinite interaction of cultures," and as an act (Relation as "an intransitive verb") that changes all the elements that come into relation with each other.[9] Relation is therefore as much a phenomenological description of the world as a movement or a process. As a description, it is akin to the perception of the dynamics of the world in chaos theory; as a movement, it is best exemplified in the worldwide and ceaseless process of creolization. Together, they constitute a poetics. Relation is a network and shaped by history, however chaotic and unpredictable this network may be. It is not "devoid of norms, but these [norms] neither constitute a goal nor govern a method,"[10] just as in the science of chaos, which shows that indeterminacy can be an analyzable fact and accidents can be measurable.[11] Relation therefore allows us to consider the world both in its unity and totality as well as in its infinite diversity. Like the ecological interdependence of all lands on earth, all peoples and cultures are interdependent when seen from the viewpoint of Relation. Cultures cannot be reduced to prime elements, such as prime numbers in mathematics, but are always open and changing through their contacts with other cultures. Hence Relation is movement. In this way, it is not just a description of the past world where Relation did its work, the constantly changing present where Relation is doing its work, but also the unforeseeable future where Relation will continue to do its work in transforming cultures, peoples, and languages.

To do the work of Relation as an exercise in poetics—that is, Relation as a method—is to relate here and elsewhere and to explore the inexhaustible and unpredictable entanglements and confluence among cultures and histories. As the world has been and will always be enmeshed in the unceasing processes of creolization, so should our method be attentive to these processes rather than providing static descriptions of closure and completion. As a method, this also departs dramatically from even the non-Eurocentric methods of comparative literature, where the juxtaposition of different cultural texts has caused some to worry about cultural relativism.[12] Relation work is in fact the opposite of relativism, because relativism is premised on reductive understanding of cultures and assumes essentialism of cultures,[13] as if each culture has a discreet boundary that another culture cannot cross. The West Indies is as exemplary as the place from which to theorize as any other place, as the point is not to elevate the specific to the universal but to deconstruct the universal altogether by way of interrelations among places and cultures. One can start in any place. And it is in this specific sense that Glissant's evocation of Caribbean poet Kamau Brathwaite's famous line "the unity is submarine"—both as an epigraph for his magnum opus, *Poetics of Relation*, and as something unique to the Caribbean in *Caribbean Discourse*—should be understood. It refers to the "subterranean convergence" of the histories of the islands in the Caribbean specifically,[14] but it really also refers to the worldwide confluence of cultures.

In Françoise Lionnet's discussion of the archipelagic dimension of Caribbean thought, she evokes the Southeast Asian nations' declaration of their archipelagoness in the Bandung Conference of 1955, but these two areas are seldom discussed together.[15] The fact is that the West Indies and the East Indies are similar geographic formations, and they also share similar colonial histories. These commonalities alone should prompt comparative archipelago studies.[16] Etymologically, "archipelago" refers to the water between islands, not the islands themselves: "pelagos" is "sea," as in Middle English "arch-sea,"[17] similar to the meaning in Greek and Italian. Viewing from the perspective of the sea, I infer, allows us to see the world as an archipelago, where different land masses (whether the so-called continents or the so-called islands) are all islands; though of varying sizes, they are also all interconnected by the sea. This would be the relational way of looking at the world as a sea of islands, big or small, concretized by integrative world historians' mapping of maritime trade routes that crisscrossed the world. We may say that the archipelago is unique to the West Indies, from where Glissant theorizes, and to the East Indies, where the same European colonizers landed, but it is also a way to comprehend the interconnectedness of the world: the world as an archipelago. After all, "the unity is submarine." Here the geographical scale can be shrunk or expanded in our thinking, but the important point is how one begins specifically (from the West Indies), not to arrive at the universal, but to arrive at interconnections. This is what I mean by doing relational studies, which does not resuscitate old universalisms or construct new universalisms, but works from the specific to arrive at interrelations in history.

How might this theory of Relation (and, related to it, the world as archipelago) be scaled back to the textual level for the literary comparatist? Glissant notes, in one of his many lyrical moments, what the poetics of Relation promises: "The probability: that you come to the bottom of all confluences to mark more strongly your inspirations."[18] It is surely impossible to reach "the bottom of all confluences," and I doubt there is such a place, however abstract that place may be, but it may be the place where we can work toward, from whichever small or large land mass in the arch-sea.

The Plantation Arc

The history about what I call the plantation arc is fairly straightforward; it considers the West Indies, the American South, and the East Indies in the same conjuncture and thereby traces a related but different itinerary from that of a plantation system organized around slavery. Glissant himself notes that the plantation system "spread, following the same structural principles, throughout the southern United States, the Caribbean islands, the Caribbean coast of Latin America, and the northeastern portion of Brazil."[19] In the postslavery context, however, the plantation system also spread throughout the East Indies, where the European colonizers experimented with, mimicked, and transplanted their practices from and to the Americas with varying successes. They experimented, for instance, with tobacco, sugar, and coffee in the East Indies as in the Caribbean, then shifted to rubber and other products such as tapioca and pepper when those crops that had succeeded in the Caribbean could not acclimate to Southeast Asia. Planters across the Americas and Southeast Asia imported indentured laborers—especially coolies from China and India—as labor to the plantation system at the end of slavery. Some of the so-called Chinese coolies brought to the Caribbean were themselves transported across the Indian Ocean and the Atlantic—not from China, but from Southeast Asia, as the European colonizers had brought them there earlier.[20]

This arc from Southeast Asia to the Americas constitutes a portion of the postslavery plantation circuit, a circuit of interconnected histories of European colonialism. One route takes off from Southeast Asia through the Indian Ocean, around Cape Town, and over the Atlantic to the Americas; the other route from Southeast Asia through the Suez Canal to cross the Atlantic from the Mediterranean. These were the routes of the coolie ships in the nineteenth century, along with the route that takes off directly from southeastern China to the Americas over the Pacific.[21] Viewed in terms of integrative world history, this nineteenth-century circuit exceeds the Far Eastern economic circuit that Abu-Lughod identifies for the thirteenth century, as the Far Eastern circuit at the time extended from the Indian Ocean in the west only to the South China Sea in the east, and it did not cross the Pacific to the Americas, nor did it cross the other way through the Atlantic to the Americas. In fact, the coolie ships were often nothing more than repurposed slave ships, and they traversed both the Pacific and the Atlantic to reach the Caribbean islands from China and Southeast Asia. Jamaican writer Patricia Powell aptly and empathetically calls this the "middle passage" of the Chinese coolies.[22]

To trace this arc from the West Indies to the East Indies, a brief loop through the American South helps us actuate the arc in specific literary works, and to consider the possibility of a poetics born of literary relations in the context of world historical relations. We can see this in Glissant's deeply attentive reading of the novels of William Faulkner set in the American South. Not only did Glissant repeatedly refer to Faulkner as an important example for his poetics of Relation in his book *Poetics of Relation* (1991), but he also wrote an entire book devoted to Faulkner, *Faulkner, Mississippi*, five years later. In a sense, we can see *Faulkner, Mississippi* as Glissant's scaling of Relation from the global level to the textual level, from the logic of the world to the logic of the text, and his extension of the theory of Relation from the Caribbean to elsewhere from archipelagic perspectives. Not only are there structural similarities between the two plantation systems in the Caribbean and the American South, Glissant proposes that the American South is actually an "incalculable border" of the Caribbean.[23]

The basis of Glissant's reading of Faulkner's work rests with the question of race and consequences of slavery. In contrast to Faulkner's public position on the question of race where Faulkner was usually racist and at best paternalistic, including in his public conversations with W. E. B. Du Bois,[24] Glissant reads Faulkner's novels as having exposed the torrid undercurrent of sin and perversion among the planters and other southern whites, all tinged with deep racial anxieties; that is, he reads Faulkner's novels as taking the opposite stance from the author's own on the race question. In Faulkner's novels, the southern whites actually live "such bootless daring, such useless majesty, such tragic, miserable, and small-minded lives" with "so much violence, theft, rape, insanity, infirmity, misfortune"[25] that their legitimacy is most fundamentally challenged. A cloud of ambiguity and a mountain of secrets haunt their existence. They all seem to be somehow damned.

This damnation is manifested in the perversion of the descent line, or the irreparable collapse of relationships of filiation. In novel after novel, the descent line between fathers and their children (especially sons) is irrevocably broken, the family members are torn asunder, and some have monstrous births, awkward deaths, and other unexpected misfortunes. And then there are stories that actually include episodes of lynching, as well as those set in the Caribbean. Lucas Beauchamp in *Intruder in the Dust* has a white father but must face the threat of lynching. The white planter, Sutpen, in *Absalom, Absalom!* marries a woman who passes as white in Haiti, and does not discover that she is of mixed blood until their son is born. Race appears again and again as the "unsurpassable point of reference,"[26] thrusting the idea of a white genealogy under threat. All this is due to the original sin: the violence committed by whites on Indians and blacks. The presupposition of Faulkner's narration, Glissant concludes, is therefore the "illegitimate foundation of the South,"[27] about which whites are solely responsible.

Faulkner's South is in this way linked with the Caribbean and Latin America by "the damnation and miscegenation born of the rape of slavery."[28] Contrary to his public stance on the race question, Faulkner obliquely writes into his narratives the history of settler colonialism and slavery and compels us to consider it as an ethical demand, that is, as Glissant puts it, "the recognition of the other as a moral obligation" and "an aesthetic constituent."[29] In other words, responsibility to the other is constitutive of a poetics where descent is impure, linearity is lost, and entanglements are supreme, leading to a "post-identitarian poetics"[30] that is also the poetics of Relation, both in terms of history and in terms of literature-qua-literature. Secrets are revealed in a painstakingly slow manner; hence the narrative tempo moves hauntedly and hauntingly along countless deferrals. Character psychologies are as confused as the intensely wrought and baroque prose, with words going around in circles, "listing, accumulating, repeating" (194), constituting his particular modernist style that has influenced writers all across the Americas and has reached the East Indies.

To the East Indies, Creolization

The legacy of the plantation system at the edge of the Borneo rain forest in Chang Kuei-hsing's Sinophone novel *Monkey Cup* (Houbei, 2000), as in Faulkner's South, is the irreparable damage done to the line of descent due to an original sin, which Chang calls "one hundred years of filth."[31] Here the planters and settlers acquire land and property illegitimately, exploit the trafficked laborers (Chinese coolies) and indigenous people (Dayaks), commit rape and pillage, and encroach upon the oldest rain forest in the world, earning an original condemnation on the succeeding generations of descendants. The planters, or rather their executors, are the Chinese settlers who acquire their derivative power from the British colonizers and essentially function as what I call "middleman settler colonizers,"[32] constituting the middle layer in a colonial system structured by race and class in a hierarchy in descending order: white European colonizers, Chinese middlemen settler colonizers, Chinese coolies, and indigenous Dayaks. As there is no English translation of this Sinophone novel, I offer a summary of the plot first below.

Told in a mix of temporalities traversing a span of about one hundred years, the narrative of *Monkey Cup* begins, in chronological terms, in the year 1882,[33] when a Chinese foreman boldly recommends himself as the substitute planter for a coffee plantation after the British founder in 1860 was killed, a murder that turned out to be staged to look like it was done by the Dayaks, by none other than the ambitious foreman himself. This foreman-turned-planter is Great-grandfather and patriarch of the Chinese Malaysian Yu family. The British governor-general is impressed by this man's silent and able demeanor, with a body that is as tall as the British, "without [such physical deficiencies as] foul smell from the body and the mouth, heat rashes, athlete's feet, tuberculosis, and papaverine-deprived shiftless eyes." They are especially impressed by his multilingualism:

He spoke ten languages: Malay, Indonesian, and Dayak pickled with rice wine, spices, and red pepper; Mandarin, Cantonese, Hakka, and Hokkien filled with the fishy flavors of tree barks, grass roots, and mud; English and Dutch mixed with the flavors of cigar, alcohol, and lead.[34]

In economical prose, Chang imbues the languages listed with specific, racialized characteristics associated with the people who speak them as mother tongues in colonial taxonomy: the foods they eat (for the native races), the settlers' ability to endure hardship (for Chinese Malayans who speak a variety of Sinitic languages), and colonial products and articles of consumption (for the European colonizers). His multilingualism is first of all the crucial skill needed for his middleman colonizer position, but it points also to an incredible mix of cultures on the ground, as this mixture does not merely affect the relationship between Great-grandfather and others but seeps integrally into the interaction among the Yu family members. If multilingualism initially served as a strategy of domination and control, it gradually also becomes a condition of existence for the Chinese Malaysian descendants.

With his multilingualism and cunning, the scheming Great-grandfather, to lease the plantation, secretly presents the British governor-general with a dozen bricks of gold stolen from the gold mine in western Kalimantan where he had been a coolie. Once he gets the plantation, he adds tea, pepper, rubber, and opium poppy to the existing crops of coffee and tobacco and builds a lumber factory. As soon as he accumulates enough wealth, he buys out the plantation from the British colonial government and starts running a gambling den, an opium den, and a prostitution house on the land.[35] In the next ten years, he uses all possible means of deceit and cruelty to acquire a second plantation on the lower reaches of the Baram River, then buys weapons from the British military to protect his plantations against "barbarous natives, poisonous snakes, and fierce beasts."[36] The gambling and opium dens are there to snare the eight hundred or so coolies he employs into addiction, so that they will be entrapped in their work and the plantations will never lack an exploitable labor force. When their debts exceed what they can possibly earn, they would then be forced to sell their daughters as prostitutes to pay off their debts, thus completing a cycle of debt, entrapment, and ruin for the coolies, ensuring the perpetual prosperity of the plantations. Great-grandfather personally imprisons and rapes the women to be forced into prostitution before sending them to his prostitution house, shoots anyone who enters his plantations without permission, and drives away the Dayaks in close-quarter combat, including one battle that results in the deaths of over 130 Dayak men and thirty Chinese coolies. His relationship with the Dayak women predictably mimics the "sex safaris" or "sex peditions" favored by the British, American, and Australian tourists who take them into the rain forest.[37]

Had there been no Japanese invasion and occupation of Borneo during the years between 1941 and 1945, Great-grandfather's plantations might have been handed down to Grandfather, to Father, and then to our protagonist with the English name Teddy Yu. While the Japanese rape and pillage not only the Dayaks but also the Chinese Malaysians, murder all infants in the hospitals in the most gruesome manner (cutting off the penises of the male infants and piercing the vaginas of the female infants), and extract lumber from the rain forest with abandon, Great-grandfather continues to expand his plantations by selling out his compatriots, neighbors, and even his own relatives to the Japanese. The neighbors whose house and land Great-grandfather covets are gruesomely murdered by the Japanese upon his cooked-up charge that they supported anti-Japanese resistance.

But the Japanese could not possibly allow the existence of such a powerful planter, and they eventually force Great-grandfather to dissolve his plantations. At this point, all his past sins begin to catch up with him and his family. The violence he initiated produces a cycle of violence from which there is no escape; the life of ruin he instituted through gambling, opium smoking, and prostituting also catches up with him and his descendants: they die gruesome deaths, all described in Chang's unyieldingly graphic prose. Great-grandfather and Grandfather die of decapitation by the Dayaks who live in the rain forest. Grandmother, bitten by poisonous scorpions released onto the property by the family's enemies on her wedding night, was maimed in one leg and is later killed by the nameless, gigantic beast that Grandfather keeps to protect the remaining gold bricks; her body is pierced by its horn from the back of her anus to the front of her breasts. Father abandons the family and disappears into the rain forest to join in the communist anti-Japanese resistance, his pregnant lover later brutally raped and murdered by the Japanese—betrayed by none other than Grandfather—her unborn fetus and her entrails disemboweled and exposed in broad daylight. Teddy, advised to escape to Taiwan to avoid the curse on the family, ends up committing an unspeakably shameful act of pedophilia there and is forced to return to Borneo. Narrowly escaping a plot on his life thanks to the ingenious plans of a Dayak woman, Teddy eventually plans to marry her, which brings a semblance of truce at least between the Chinese Malaysians and the Dayaks after the departure of the Japanese. If Great-grandfather, the Kurtz-like figure in the heart of darkness that is the Borneo rain forest, can be compared to Faulkner's Sutpen, Teddy confronts his illegitimacy as well as the original sin of his family by mixing with the indigenous people through marriage. As an avid reader of both Conrad and Faulkner, this is Chang's answer to Kurtz's and Great-grandfather's colonial mentality and to Sutpen's inability to confront the reality of mixedness, all through the "vertigo of a word," as Glissant would put it.[38]

In the meantime, nature gradually engulfs the plantations with force and vitality, returning them to their original state. Indigeneity takes over in the vertigo of words, listing, whirling, repeating:

At dusk, Teddy climbed up to the top of the kampung house with a wooden ladder and scanned the surrounding area while standing on zinc metal plates still hot from the heat of the sun. He saw short trees joggling in the wild family land, brushes sinking and surfacing, the river water undulating, grey dust rolling, fallen leaves, rotten grass, and dusty sand brimming, evening cloud stirring, monsoon wind malodorous, centipede-colored moon cracked like a tortoise shell into the shape of waves, a torrent of view-blocking stream in the wild weaved by locusts and preying mantises, there in the monkey farm emerging a series of small outbursts of commotion, chickens, ducks, geese, and pigs withdrawing, eagles flying high and low, their tongues and claws shimmering, vultures with rumbling stomachs bubbling their heads, while several Jackson-style guns are aimed at the silk floss tree.[39]

Here, one gets a sense of Chang's protean imagination and baroque prose, which infuses the 317-page novel without a moment of respite, just as the wild nature gradually and inevitably swallows up the plantations. This entire passage is in fact only a portion of one long sentence in the original Sinophone text, where the full stop is not reached until about ten lines later. The majority of the action that happens in the narrative present is that of Grandfather and Teddy, armed with guns and Malay daggers, fending off the invasion of thousands of giant lizards that attack humans and domestic animals and threaten to take over the house. As they fight the losing battle against the numberless giant lizards, we readers struggle through the suffocating density, ornateness, and violence of Chang's prose, as if under a nameless spell. Chang willfully invents new words and creates new combinations of words and phrases intricately wrought together like the dense rain forest, creolizing the various languages on the ground, like the various plants and animals populating the rain forest all leaving their distinct imprints on the land and the people. This prose disregards the boundaries between time past and present, between exterior and interior realities, between the rain forest and the non–rain forest, between the animal and the human, altogether producing a world that is perhaps more bizarre and more suffocating than Faulkner's South.

The dynamics of the Chinese plantations in Borneo may be historically specific to Borneo, but the plantation system leaves similar legacies as those in Faulkner's South, having been cursed with an original damnation that would carry through generations. As mentioned above, in Chang's Borneo, there seems to be a possibility for redemption, a solution that Faulkner's white southerners refused to take: a willing mixing with the native Dayaks and a surrender to the rain forest.[40] In Chang's novel, it is through affinity and kinship with the Dayaks that our locally born, fourth-generation protagonist is able to arrive at some sort of reconciliation. The rain forest may be the heart of darkness, the tourist mecca, the site of sex safaris for others, but it is also where the logic of the plantation system can be reversed through the process of mixing, leading to unpredictable, unexpected, but diverse and rich possibilities for something new. This is Glissant's world of creolization.

From the West Indies, Reciprocity

Before Chinese coolies were brought to the East Indies, they were brought over to the Caribbean as early as 1806 in the earliest experiment with coolie labor during the time of slavery, but the most concentrated period was between 1852 and 1866, after the abolition took place in various

Caribbean islands. As contracted (but essentially indentured) laborers, the Chinese coolies were often treated as de facto slaves, governed by inhuman laws and regulations and imprisoned in their plantations to the extent that a former chief justice of British Guiana published a report entitled *The New Slavery: An Account of the Indian and Chinese Immigrants in British Guiana* in 1871. The book detailed deception at the point of contract, arbitrary wage delays and deductions, physical abuse, extortion, and imprisonment in jails.[41] As in the East Indies, however, once arrived, they managed to survive the indentured labor contract and gradually emerged "as a 'classic middleman minority,' a small ethnic group carving out a niche in the shopkeeping sector."[42]

By the late 1930s, Jamaica had the second-largest Chinese community in the Caribbean, second only to Cuba. It is to this Jamaica that the young, female protagonist arrives from China in Patricia Powell's *The Pagoda*, which fictionalizes the history of Chinese coolies and shopkeepers in postabolition Jamaica. Escaping from an arranged marriage, the protagonist cross-dresses as a man and steals away on a ship bound for the Americas, not knowing that it is a ship carrying a load of coolies chained under deck. Discovered by the coolie trader, she is raped by him but kept safe from all the other men on board. The coolie trader, who turns out to be an ex–slave trader using an erstwhile slave ship as a coolie ship, keeps her as a mistress and sets her up as a shopkeeper in Jamaica, where she has to masquerade as a man to avoid being devoured by men black, white, or yellow in the postabolition Jamaica of rampant unemployment, labor unrest, and economic depression. When she bears the coolie trader a child, he sets up for her a fake marriage with a white woman who also harbors a secret identity. The Chinese woman's masquerade as Mr. Lowe is the ultimate enigma of the novel, just as her sexuality is to herself, both secrets gradually revealed in a skillful process of unfolding as the readers get more and more glimpses into her past. In the meantime, the racial tension among the Chinese shopkeepers and the continuously dispossessed blacks erupt into the looting and burning of Chinese shops, a fate that Mr. Lowe's shop could not escape, even though she/he as the shopkeeper has painstakingly made efforts to get along with the black community:

> Yes, he'd come to catch his hand, to make something of his life. But he was no poor-show-great. He didn't see himself better than them. Above them. But now they had burned [the shop] down. Flat. Flat. He was there only on sufferance. Himself and the other five thousand Chinese on the island. He realized now how the Negro people must have secretly despised him for being there . . . And the whites didn't give one blast if the others burned it down. So long as their houses were untouched. Their daughters. Their wives and the plantation equipment.[43]

Besides being a livelihood, the shop was also a sanctuary and the embodiment of hope for the Chinese coolies:

> The shop had been for . . . the Chinese who had escaped the sugar estates with broken backs from working twenty hours a day for close to nothing. They came with hands twisted and chewed from water pumps, scarred by deep grooves left over from cane leaves that cut like knives. They came with spit bubbling with blood, asthmatic and tubercular chests from the dust. They came without flesh, with holes in the skin, half starved from inferior food, lashed and mutilated by overseers under the muscle of plantation owners. The shop was there so if they wanted they could come and apprentice with him, till they'd pay off their contracts and with a small loan open up a little shop, selling half flash of rum, a stick of cigarette, big gill of coconut oil, two inches of tobacco, quarter pound of rice, repaying monthly and with interest.[44]

Soon, we learn more of how the coolie trade operates: the abduction of the Chinese forced into becoming coolies, sold like pigs by crimps, drugged and tortured, chained to iron railings below decks on slave ships with only one third surviving the passage on average, sold in the "man markets" while stripped naked upon arrival, and emblazoned with the initials of plantations on their skins by the planters who bought them. Powell's narrative voice is imbued with empathy toward the Chinese coolies and shopkeepers in Jamaica, calling their passage from China, as mentioned above, their own "middle passage." Instead of accusing the Chinese as the middlemen who helped the European colonizers further oppress the blacks, Powell depicts them as having been equally abused by the whites, explicitly making historical connections between slavery and coolie trade. We find out later that black neighbors and customers did not burn down Mr. Lowe's shop.

In the end, Mr. Lowe's secrets are revealed: she is a woman and a lesbian. The secret of Mr. Lowe's white wife is also revealed; she is a fair-skinned mulatto passing as white, and is now living on the lam. In order to conceal her racial identity, she murdered her first (white) husband who discovered their newborn child's dark skin. If placed in Faulkner's novel, she would have been Sutpen's mulatto wife, to whom Powell is possibly making a specific reference. Through all the secrets, Mr. Lowe's half-white, half-yellow daughter grows up and marries a black man who is a labor activist, gives birth to children who are mixtures of all three races, and Mr. Lowe can no longer speak either of the two Sinitic languages, Hakka and Cantonese, without lapsing into "island speech." Unbeknownst to her, creolization has already taken place. Her "West Indianisation"[45] is inevitable, just as creolization is irrevocable.

The history of Manhattan, Jamaica, is as enmeshed in the history of slavery as Faulkner's South, and as enmeshed in the history of Chinese coolies as Chang's Borneo. Here, however, it is not the perspectives of the white or Chinese planters that are captured, but the perspectives of coolies, shopkeepers, mulattos, ex-slaves, and labor activists that are all woven into a deeply moving tale spun by a black Jamaican writer. From a shared and interconnected fate so empathetically depicted—the slavery and coolie trade—emerges an ethics of reciprocity, which the process of creolization makes possible and will further disseminate. The opposite of competitive victimology that seeks and competes for confirmation by the colonizers and powers that be, the ethics of reciprocity practices a kind of minor transnationalism that extends horizontally.[46] After all, Powell seems to be telling us, we all live in Relation or, in the language of the integrative world historians, in an interconnected world inflected by power relations. Amid these power relations, she actively chooses an ethics of reciprocity among the oppressed, rather than a competition for recognition by the powers that be.

From the West Indies to the East Indies and back, the constellation of literary works along the postslavery plantation arc examined in this essay traverses seemingly discreet but in fact interconnected geographical places, peoples, languages, and cultures. The interconnectedness of the world in turn compels us to consider world literature and comparative literature not in terms of juxtapositions but in terms of a network of horizontal and vertical relations, which comparatists have so far consistently ignored due to various vested interests. If Patricia Powell's choice to establish a reciprocal affinity between the histories of slavery and the coolie trade appears to be unique and even counterintuitive, it is because there are certain interests being served by the suppression of this affinity. Coolie trade as a continuation of slavery in a different form and with variation deepens the original sin that Glissant pointed out for Faulkner's American South, now equally implicating the European colonizers in the West Indies and the East Indies. Even as it points to reciprocities and affinities, Relation foregrounds the complex operations of power. Hence the coolies and ex-slaves may find affinity in Powell's Jamaica, but the coolies-turned-settlers in the Borneo rain forest are as capable of oppressing the indigenous peoples as the British colonizers. Relational comparison confronts power as it is, without apology.

With this model of relational comparison, I also hope to build on Glissant's notion of Relation as a verb to suggest that relational comparison is an act, that it takes work, and that it can be further broken down to a specific set of action items, depending on the particular objects that enter into a given relation. These action items would have to include archival and other research work on the texts in question to understand their relationalities in historical contexts, especially the suppressed relationalities that uphold the status quo. The action items would also include close readings of both the content and form of the texts, not only to understand their interconnectedness but also to experience the singularity of each text. The stylistic affinity and thematic parallel in Chang's *Monkey Cup* with that of Faulkner's southern novels is then no longer about the canonical metropolitan writer's influence on a practically unknown writer in the West, but about interconnectedness along the postslavery plantation arc in world history where each literary text's singularity stands out. Chang's work may be as deserving of the Nobel Prize, but relational comparison is not so much interested in metropolitan consecration as in fundamentally short-circuiting those technologies of recognition that tautologically reconfirm the center.[47] Relational comparison is not a center-periphery model, as the texts form a network of relations from wherever the texts are written, read, and circulated. In its singularity as text and interconnectedness in history, we may say, lie a literary work's literariness and worldliness.

NOTES

1   Janet Abu-Lughod, *Before European Hegemony: The World System A.D. 1250–1350* (Oxford: Oxford Univ. Press, 1991), 4.

2   André Gunder Frank, *ReOrient: Global Economy in the Asian Age* (Berkeley: Univ. of California Press, 1998), 5.

3   Frank, *ReOrient*, 226.

4   John M. Hobson, *The Eastern Origins of Western Civilization* (Cambridge: Cambridge Univ. Press, 2004), 22.

5   Micol Seigel, "Beyond Compare: Comparative Method after the Transnational Turn," *Radical History Review* 91 (Winter 2005): 78.

6   Franco Moretti, "Conjectures on World Literature," *New Left Review* 1 (January–February 2000): 54–68. Since publication of this essay, Moretti's new editing efforts present a more diffusive model. See *The Novel*, vol. I of *History, Geography and Culture* (London: Verso, 2007) and *The Novel*, vol. II of *Forms and Themes* (London: Verso, 2007).

7   Pascale Casanova, *The World Republic of Letters*, trans. M. B. DeBevoise (Cambridge, MA: Harvard Univ. Press, 2005).

8   David Damrosch, *What Is World Literature?* (Princeton, NJ: Princeton Univ. Press, 2003), 4.

9   Édouard Glissant, *Poetics of Relation* (Poétique de la Relation, 1990), trans. Betsy Wing (Ann Arbor: Univ. of Michigan Press, 1997), 173, 32.

10   Glissant, *Poetics of Relation*, 94.

11   Glissant, *Poetics of Relation*, 137.

12   Jonathan Culler, worrying that relativism haunts comparative projects, would rather hold onto his sense of judgment by asserting that Western and non-Western texts are "less comparable" than those between Western texts. See his "Comparability," *World Literature Today* 69, no. 2 (Spring 1995): 268–70.

13   Glissant, *Poetics of Relation*, 135.

14   Glissant, *Caribbean Discourse* (Le Discours Antillais, 1981), trans. J. Michael Dash (Charlottesville: Univ. of Virginia Press, 1989), 66.

15   "Continents and Archipelagoes: From *E Pluribus Unum* to Creolized Solidarities," *PMLA* 123, no. 5 (October 2008): 1508–9.

16   David A. B. Murray, Tom Boellstorff, and Kathryn Robinson suggested this in "East

Indies / West Indies: Comparative Archipelagos," *Anthropological Forum* 16, no. 3 (November 2006): 219–27. But, again, their method is a juxtapositional comparison of similarities and differences, or the application of Caribbean theory to Southeast Asia, not a relational method.

17 Murray et al., "East Indies / West Indies," 222.

18 Glissant, *Poetics of Relation*, 45.

19 Glissant, *Poetics of Relation*, 63.

20 See Walton Look Lai's *The Chinese in the West Indies, 1806–1995: A Documentary History* (Kingston, Jamaica: Univ. of the West Indies Press, 1998) for a documented account of the importation of Chinese coolies from China and Southeast Asia.

21 For a visual map of these routes, see Arnold J. Meagher's *The Coolie Trade: The Traffic in Chinese Laborers to Latin America, 1847–1874* (Lexington, KY: Xlibris, 2008), 151.

22 Patricia Powell, *The Pagoda* (New York: Harcourt, 1998), 75. See my analysis of Powell's novel below.

23 Quoted in J. Michael Dash, "Martique/Mississippi: Édouard Glissant and Relational Insularity," in *Look Away! The U.S. South in New World Studies*, ed. Jon Smith and Deborah Cohn (Durham, NC: Duke Univ. Press, 2004), 95.

24 Édouard Glissant, *Faulkner, Mississippi*, trans. Barbara Lewis and Thomas C. Spear (Chicago: Univ. of Chicago Press, 1999), 104.

25 Glissant, *Faulkner*, 23, 30.

26 Glissant, *Faulkner*, 59.

27 Glissant, *Faulkner*, 139.

28 Glissant, *Faulkner*, 88.

29 Phrases used to describe the work of Victor Segalen in Glissant, *Poetics of Relation*, 29.

30 Dash, "Martinique/Mississippi," 104.

31 Chang Kuei-hsing, *Monkey Cup* (Houbei) (Taipei: Linking Books, 2000), 35. All translations from the Sinitic texts in this essay are my own.

32 See my "Theory, Asia, and the Sinophone," *Postcolonial Studies* 13, no. 4 (2010): 465–84.

33 Incidentally, 1882 is the year the first of the Chinese Exclusion Acts was passed in the United States.

34 Both quotations are from Chang, *Monkey Cup*, 179.

35 It is interesting to note that these three types of businesses were the "three voices" of San Francisco Chinatown as seen by outsiders at the turn of the nineteenth century, which Marlon Hom notes was typical of frontier towns in general. See Marlon Hom, "An Introduction to Cantonese Vernacular Rhymes from San Francisco Chinatown," in *Songs of Gold Mountain* (Berkeley: Univ. of California Press, 1987), 3–70.

36 Hom, "An Introduction," 181. Note how the natives are placed on the same list with snakes and beasts, as is typical of settler colonial mentality.

37 "Sex safaris" and "sex peditions" originally in English in Hom, "An Introduction," 244.

38 This is Glissant describing Faulkner's prose style in *Faulkner*, 105.

39 Glissant, *Faulkner*, 262.

40 Brian Bernards therefore rightly argues that the logic of the plantation and the logic of the rain forest in *Monkey Cup* are diametrically opposed. See his "Plantation and Forest: Chang Kuei-hsing and a South Seas Discourse of Coloniality and Nature," in *Sinophone Studies: A Critical Reader*, ed. Shu-mei Shih, Chien-hsin Tsai, and Brian Bernards (New York: Columbia Univ. Press, 2013).

41 Lai, *The Chinese in the West Indies*, 1–20.

42 Lai, *The Chinese in the West Indies*, xiii.

43 Powell, *The Pagoda*, 13.

44 Powell, *The Pagoda*, 15.

45 Lai, *The Chinese in the West Indies*, 19.

46 See "Introduction: Thinking through the Minor, Transnationally," in *Minor Transnationalism*, ed. Françoise Lionnet and Shu-mei Shih (Durham, NC: Duke Univ. Press, 2005), 1–23.

47 See my "Global Literature and the Technologies of Recognition," *PMLA* 119, no. 1 (January 2004): 16–30.

CHAPTER SIX

On Comparison:
Who Is Comparing What and Why?

Walter D. Mignolo

COMPARISON IS MINIMALLY A TRIANGULAR BUSINESS. There are two entities (processes, events, texts, signs, cities, stories, etc.) to be compared, plus the subject who performs the comparison. When someone buys a car, for example, that person goes through a lengthy comparison of two or more options before making the final decision. All living organisms, plants, and animals need to compare what among all the options of the environment is convenient to their survival—comparing is then knowing, and knowing is living. "Comparison" in this regard is a field of investigation into the neurology of cognition. What is of interest here is when and where such a basic foundation of life and survival was conceptualized as "comparison" and systematized as a method in the natural and human sciences. Although living organisms, and not just humans, "compare" to survive, a particular species of living organisms that in the vocabulary of Western languages has been rendered as "human" or "human beings" invented comparative methods

Comparative methodology was invented in nineteenth-century Europe, and there was obviously some need for it. Two purposes come to mind. The first was to systematize in the nineteenth century what had been a European concern since the sixteenth century: when Christians debated the "humanity" of New World Indians, they invented "comparative ethnology." In that genealogy of thought, "comparative ethnology" in the sixteenth century mutated into "Orientalism" in the eighteenth century, when Spaniards were no longer facing the Indians, but the French, German, and British were facing China, India, and what is today the Middle East. The same logic, the logic of the coloniality of knowledge, was reproduced. Only the contents and the imperial control of the enunciation have changed. The other need for comparative methodology was internal to Europe: after the Treaty of Westphalia, Europeans felt the need to unify under differences while at the same time establishing differences between the heart of Europe and the South.[1] Comparative methodology contributed to that goal. In the first case, it served to define Europe's external others: Indians and Orientals. In the second case, it defined Europe's internal others: the south of Europe, the Catholic and Latin countries.

Beyond comparison for survival and for political reasons, there is another distinction to be made: comparing to buy or to endorse (e.g., Democrats or Republicans) and comparing to know and to understand. Comparative methodology was invented to regulate procedures of knowing and understanding "scientifically." Let's think about what sociologists and literary scholars do when they compare. Sociologists who compare countries or social organizations, unlike car buyers or voting citizens, do not have to choose which of the two or three compared entities they have to buy or endorse. Sociologists—if they are not building a political cause and not being "scientifically correct"—compare to correct existing views in the discipline or to influence votes or public policies. Literary scholars, like sociologists, compare to know, understand, and advance or update the discipline. (For example, two or three decades ago the focus was on comparing national literatures; now comparative work has to be articulated with globalization). Unlike sociologists, the main aim of literary scholars is not to influence public policies to improve literature, but to improve the understanding of poetry, fictional narrative, the work of two or three authors, or the trajectories of a literary genre.

Scholars in comparative literary studies, like sociologists, can compare two or more literatures that are alien to their own languages or society (for example, a Nigerian scholar comparing French, Italian, and Bambara literature). However, even in cases in which comparing subjects (sociologists or literary critics) belong to one of the societies or literary languages that is their own, they proceed as if they were detached from the societies or literatures being compared. The comparative scholar mutates into the observer of Western scholarship: objective, neutral, and detached. Western scholarship is characterized by a strong belief in the detached observer who is uncontaminated by whatever is being compared. As such, the observers, who are always located within one or at most two national languages and literatures, are also located in a specific genealogy of scholarship from which they observe and compare the literatures of the world. But what for? Comparative methodologies, including comparative literary studies, carry the weight of their imperial formations. Here I approach the topic of this volume—the theories, approaches, and uses of comparison—both as a scholar in comparative studies (comparative literature, comparative area studies, comparative religion, comparative linguistics, etc.) and as a decolonial scholar and intellectual. Decolonially, I attempt to delink from the disciplinary regulations described above. My aim is not to deny the right or the need to do comparative studies. My goal is to identify instances in which comparative studies, because of the imperial traces it carries within, does more harm than good (not always intentionally).

Comparative Methodology and Its Critics

The legacy of comparative methodology is currently undergoing two types of critique. One is inscribed in the same genealogy of thought in which comparative methodology was born and flourished, and it has its major institutions (departments, magazines, journals, fellowships) in Western Europe and the United States, as well as in global extensions of European and U.S. institutions. I do not know if the term has been used yet, but I will suggest that this critique leads to "postcomparative practices." The other critique comes not from Euro-American scholarship but from scholars in the (non-European) "third world," who see that in comparative studies their literatures do not have the same rank as the literatures that correspond to the main languages of comparative methods themselves. The first critique emerged in the cultural, national, and epistemic territories where comparative methods originated. The second critique emerged from the epistemic consequences of comparative methods, particularly when the comparisons are made between European events, texts, and practices and non-European ones that carry the colonial stigma of being "less than." In this essay I develop the second type of critique, which I describe as "decolonizing comparative studies." Decolonizing comparative studies should lead to an-other order of thinking, an-other option for literatures and cultures that both focuses on and is existentially nourished by the colonial (not the imperial) side of the borders.

The two trajectories are not, however, worlds apart. The "method" (e.g., the way) that corresponds to decolonial options is border thinking or border epistemology. Why? Because it is thinking and dwelling in the border(s), not just studying border cultures but also dwelling in them (see "zero-point epistemology" below). In other words, border thinking dwells in the border of imperial/colonial formations. For comparative scholars, the border is not a question. It requires entities being compared to be independent of each other, and it requires the scholar to be detached from both entities being compared. Border thinking as a decolonial methodology works differently. Decolonial scholars look not for similarities and differences between two or more entities or texts but attempt to understand their location in the colonial matrix of power, an issue to which I will return.

The "Comparative" Question

The history of comparative methodology in the human sciences points toward its origins in comparative philology. The "origin" in standard histories of the method hides their "geopolitical point of origination," Western

Europe. The method consisted of identifying languages with common roots and then comparing features identified as units of comparison. Attention was paid first to the complexity and diversity of European languages. For example, comparison among Romance languages consisted of grouping Western Romance (from Gallo-Italian to the West), Balkan Romance (from Gallo-Italian Italy), South Romance or Italo-Romance, Island Romance (Corsica and Sardinian), and Ibero-Romance (Spanish and Portuguese). Comparison distinguished itself from the historical reconstruction that focused on the origin and unfolding of one single language. In that context, the idea of comparative literature materialized as a need to complement the idea of national languages and literatures with the idea of world literature launched by Goethe. And at that point, European imperial nations (Spain, Portugal, Holland, France, and England) had already expanded, conquered, commercialized, and colonized a significant part of the world. Goethe's concept of "World Literature" (1827) is often taken as a point of reference for the origin of comparative literature. There was renewed interest in translation, revitalizing the work begun in the sixteenth century, when Spanish missionaries translated Indigenous languages (Maya-Quiche, Náhuatl, Aymara, and Quechua) to European languages (Spanish, Portuguese, and Latin). "World Literature" continued the legacies of early missionary work. For proponents of world literature, translation was always centripetal, whether they were translating the world into European languages and cosmology or translating European ideas to Christianize and civilize the rest of the world.[2] Translation and comparative methodology largely contributed to imperial epistemology and the making of colonial (e.g., European and indigenous or African languages) and imperial (e.g., European and Chinese, Japanese and Arabic languages) differences. Border epistemology today is a response to and an attempt to delink from imperial epistemology, an issue to which I will frequently return. Goethe foresaw the limits of national literatures at the time Europe was, literally, all over the world.[3] It was a self-serving project in which Germany was concerned with building the idea of the nation that was taken—then and today—as the natural point of arrival of the universal history that Hegel had already mapped in his lessons on the philosophy of history.[4]

There you already have the colonial and imperial differential at work—the centripetal directions of translation when it involves "literatures" (oral and written texts in non-European languages, transliterated into alphabetic writing, or translated from a non-Latin alphabetic system) from the non-European world. And, at that time, it implied also the self-inflicted imperial difference within Europe itself, avatars that in the present erupted in the crisis of Europe's South (Greece and Italy and the Iberian Peninsula, Portugal and Spain). The self-inflicted imperial difference created the South of Europe, the Catholic and Latin South seen from the Anglo-German Protestant North. Whatever it was,[5] an unmistakable meaning of the expression the "heart of Europe" (Germany, England, and France) was already deep into its global imperial imaginary, which included the marginalization of its own south.

The self-inflicted imperial difference encroached upon linguistics and literary hierarchies: Castilian language lost its Renaissance allure in relation to the languages of the heart of Europe (French, English, and German) and—from the enunciation of the heart of Europe—Galdós came in second place after Balzac and Dickens. I deny neither France's impact in the sphere of knowledge and aesthetics, nor England's intellectual contributions to political economy and political theory, nor Germany's monumental taking over of Western philosophy. Goethe was thinking and writing in that context.[6] It was in that atmosphere that comparative methodology emerged during the nineteenth century in Europe, erasing the memory of comparative ethnology in the sixteenth century. At the time of Goethe, Spain had fallen off the train of modernity, which was driven by Northern countries, where comparative methodologies emerged: political theory, political economy, literature, aesthetics, and the human sciences, as Dilthey was to theorize at the end of the nineteenth century. Theology, at that time, solidified the edifice of Western knowledge and began the disqualification of all non-Western epistemologies. As the reader may realize, I am not moving toward potential comparative analysis but toward unveiling interconnectedness—the relations and hierarchies of the colonial matrix of power.

What all this means is that comparative method in philology and literature in nineteenth-century Europe had one historical foundation (comparative ethnology since the "discovery of America") and three major consequences. First, some 150 years after Westphalia, comparing was convenient and helpful for the consolidation of Europe into a conglomerate of nation-states. That is, comparative methodology connected major European languages and literatures and showed the similarities and differences among national languages. Second, it became a common language for interdisciplinary conversations because disciplines beyond philology adopted the comparative method.[7] Third, comparative methodology interconnected the major countries of Western Europe (France, England, Germany, and—because of Renaissance legacy—Italy) at the same time that the difference with the South was created. It was not the southern countries that invented and promoted comparative methodology. It was invented in the leading imperial countries of the time, where scholars and institutions of learning (museums and universities) were most productive in terms of literature and sciences.

The forces of history in the first decade of the twenty-first century brought refreshing changes to the surface of comparative literature departments, although their Euro-centered foundation had not been shaken up. Globalization changed the old criteria, and the field of comparison expanded. In order to maintain control of literary knowledge, the discipline, the institutions, and the actors had to change, but not the principles and categories of knowledge. Change takes place in the enunciated, not in the enunciation. For that reason, a great deal of attention is being paid to China and East Asia. The goals of comparative literature move according to the changing winds of the economy: imperial Europe in the nineteenth century; East Asia and the Middle East with globalization and after 9/11; East Asian literatures with the rise of the East. "Who is comparing what and why?" is a question whose answer changes with time, for sure. But the point is not that it changes with time, but which factors motivate the changes. The changes, however, are in the rhetoric of modernity and modernization, not in the logic of coloniality. Comparative methodology in the *sciences humaines,* like translation since the sixteenth century, remains unidirectional.

Overall, the major implicit motivation behind comparative methodology (natural history and the emerging human sciences) was to consolidate Europe, in the line of the Renaissance and the Enlightenment, as the epistemic center of the world. In that genealogy we encounter today not only comparative literary studies, as in the 1970s to the 90s, but also the construction of the Republic of Letters and of the literary world system.[8] That means that while comparative philology and literature secured the locus of comparison (the locus of enunciation) in Western principles of knowledge (i.e., it was not founded in Mandarin, Arabic, or Aymara categories of thoughts), Goethe's "World Literature" in the nineteenth century and Pascale Casanova's "Republic of Letters" at the beginning of the twenty-first century presuppose the same epistemic foundation. The "literary world system" that forms the Republic of Letters does not operate by itself. It is managed by a center of enunciation, once again, by actors, institutions, and categories of thought ingrained in the making of Western civilization. Comparative philology and literature were born, after all, within the frame of France and England's global civilizing mission, of which "Orientalism" was one manifestation. World system analysis in literature or political economy as well as the Republic of Letters is addressed to the enunciated, but not the site of enunciation. The enunciation is always located where comparative literature emerged: institutions, languages, and categories of thought of European modernity.

Comparative methods, in other words, served well the self-definition of European identity and as such worked simultaneously in two complementary directions. One direction was self-referential and built upon

Europe's own local history. Hegel's lessons on the philosophy of history are clear in this respect: he defined the heart of Europe (France, England, and Germany), the South (the Latin and Catholic countries), and the Northeast (Poland and Russia). The second direction built on Europe's "exteriority" invented through imperial and colonial differences. We found the blueprint for this construction in Kant's *Observations on the Beautiful and the Sublime* (1764). In his section 4 you have it all: first the construction of Europe's interiority (England, France, and Germany); then the European imperial difference within Europe itself (e.g., the South of Europe, so visible today in the European Union, where the debtors' countries are Greece, Italy, Spain, and Portugal); and, finally, the colonial and imperial differences that start with "the Arabs" (cf. Muslims of the sixteenth century became Arabs in the eighteenth; the imperial difference mutated into colonial difference), then with "Chinese and Indians," then "Africans" and the "Native Americans." When you consider colonial and imperial differences in their complexity, comparative analysis becomes more problematic. This consideration demands that comparison focus on the power differentials that simultaneously unite *and* divide the entities being compared.

Barbados writer George Lamming always disobeyed and refused to be co-opted into a global history of the literature whose enunciation was on the side of the English rather than of the Caribbean novel. He suggested that English critics shift the geography of their reasoning and multiply the loci of enunciations:

An important question for the English critic, is not what the West Indian novel has brought to English writing. It would be more correct to ask what the West Indian novelists have contributed to the English reading. For the language in which these books are written is English—which, I must repeat—is a West Indian language; and in spite of the unfamiliarity of its rhythms, it remains accessible to the readers of English anywhere in the world. The West Indian contribution to English reading have been made possible by their relations to their themes, which are peasant. This is the great difference between the West Indian novelist and the contemporary English novelist.[9]

Lamming expresses an underlying discomforting feeling in this quotation—basically, that "literature" is not a universal concept but a European one. The discomfort began when it was necessary to accept that world literature (or the Republic of Letters) is also a regional concept with global and imperial ambitions that hide its pretense to universality. It expresses a totality that is at the same time half of the story: it is in reality a totality in the enunciated (it embraces the world), but the enunciation is one among many (just European, neither global nor universal). The enunciation "appears" as universal because imperial knowledge has been able to silence, appropriate, assimilate, or give credit to non-European enunciations building their own totality. The epistemic, political, and ethical task is to reduce both the enunciation and the enunciated to size. That is the discomfort in Lamming's statement. For this reason, whatever you compare within the system is always half of the story. The discomfort has several faces and several phases. While writers from the "third world" (in that location or as migrants in Europe and the United States) are writing to be "recognized" in the mainstream literary world, writers like Lamming are doing something else: appropriating the genre to delink from the very bourgeois foundation of the genre itself. At this point, literature becomes decolonial. "Postcolonial literature" can be decolonial, but it can also be a postcolonial effort to be recognized and accepted by actors and institutions that are in a position to recognize and accept. The decolonial analytic is always attentive to the colonial aesthetics and epistemic differences and to the need to delink, to think in terms of options rather than presupposing one single option (universal). The task of decolonial thinkers is not to claim recognition or to be included, but to shift from the one to the many, from a universal option to pluriversal options.

The "Literature" Question

The very concept of "literature" is as centered in European history as the "comparative method."[10] Properly speaking, there is no such thing as literature in ancient Greece before eighteenth-century Europe; there is no such thing as literature among the Aztecs before the nineteenth century and the formation of the modern/colonial republic, and there is no literature in millenarian China before its clash with the British in the first half of the nineteenth century. This is not to say that non-modern civilizations are "lacking" something that makes them inferior. It is to say that they did not have the Western concept of "literature," a concept that is irrelevant to non-Western cultures. And it means that the invention of the concept of "literature" allowed Western scholars and institutions to colonize oral and written expressions of other civilizations. If "literature" is a universal concept, forever there in space and time, then "the world is flat" and unidimensional, and everyone has to submit to universal concepts (be they "literature," "democracy," "freedom," or "development"). However, "literature" (and other concepts of seemingly universal values) and its genres have also been serving decolonial writers and decolonial scholars well.

Chinese and Aztec civilizations created their own writing systems and figured out what to do with oral-body expressions when they were not for everyday life but for what today we describe as "aesthetic performances" and "religious rituals." "Literature" in the Middle Ages referred to everything written in alphabetic writing: "literal locution" was Bartolomé de Las Casas's expression in the Renaissance, to name his own tradition. In the eighteenth century, the concept of "literature" mutated and became part of the emergence of philosophical aesthetics. Aristotle did not write a text called *Literature or Literary Theory* but *Poetics*. And he did not use the concept of "aiesthesis" in his *Poetics* but "mimesis," "poiesis," and "catharsis." To trace the beginning of "literature" in Greece is a regional habitus of Western scholars, a tendency to manage knowledge through a single story.[11] A single story may include many "literatures" in the enunciated, but the enunciation is not diverse: the very concept "of literature" is a monologic concept that reduces the diversity of the world to a single story. By making this argument, I am delinking myself from that single story.[12] There are also conceptualizations that contributed to the colonization of knowledge by forcing verbal practices beyond Western civilization to be conceived as "literature." Chronologically, there was no "literature" in the sixteenth and seventeenth centuries, either—the general concept was "poetry," and it was applied to prose and verse. Lessing's aesthetic treatise, *Laocoon* (1768), was about the "limits of painting and poetry," not about "literature." To project current Western concepts of "literature" onto Lessing would erase differences in the history of Western thought and a slant toward homogeneity and universality coinciding with neoliberal global designs.

If "literature" was not an existing concept in the scholarly traditions of many nonmodern (I do not say premodern to underline that modernity is not a period of universal history but a European fiction to describe its own present and justify its own imperial future) civilizations like the Chinese, Islamic, Mayan, Persian, Turk, Indian Benin Kingdom, and so on, then the concept of "literature" also needs to be—like comparative methodology—decolonized and reduced to size. Let's take an example from Mesoamerican (Aztec) verbal and written expressions. If, for example, we translate Náhuatl expressions such as in *xochitl, in cuicatl* (flowers and songs) as "literature," we reproduce the colonial differential and ignore that the reverse is also possible: that "literature" in eighteenth-century Europe could be translated into in *xochitl, in cuicatl*, as Europeans did not have "flowers and songs." "Literature" came chronologically after. But the faith of modernity is that what came last disqualifies what was there before. That is why it is so important to be *numero uno*: no one will erase you. Consequently, "literature" should be translated into the Náhuatl concept and not the other way around. If we take for granted that "literature" is a universal concept and therefore it shall absorb *in xochitl, in cuicatl*, thereby losing its singularity, we continue to hide how coloniality of knowledge and of being works. The coloniality of knowledge works precisely by disavowing and absorbing differences. The fact is that "literature" and in *xochitl, in cuicatl* are both entangled, and it is precisely the entanglement that poses serious questions to both the universality of the concept of literature and to comparison between it and *xochitl, in cuicatl*. Focusing on the entanglement means the retention of the actuality of in *xochitl, in cuicatl* in the past and in the present; it also means a focus on relations, on encroachment and power differentials.

You could compare and elaborate on the meaning of *xochitl, in cuicatl* among the Aztecs and "literature" in Europe since the late eighteenth century, but you could not silence one in the name of the other. As you can guess, we (you, the reader, and I) are here in the thick of a decolonial work. And you could ask why the Náhuatl language needed a rhythmic expression (try to pronounce out loud, accentuating the *in*: *xochitl, in cuicatl*), while in vernacular and modern European languages they need one noun ("literature" or "poetry" not in the restricted sense of versification, but in the Aristotelian sense). Suppose that someone writes a book on "global *xochitl, in cuicatl*" and includes Shakespeare in one chapter. You may feel surprised. And, if you are British, you may even feel offended. Well, why are you not surprised at the possibility of inverting the terms of the conversation, why do you think that if *xochitl, in cuicatl* is included in "literature," then Náhuatl speakers should be thankful and happy for the recognition? The word and concept of "literature" in Europe comes from "letter," which in the European imaginary refers to alphabetic writing. Imperial differences began to take shape in the making of comparative ethnology and the supremacy of Western alphabetic writing.

Comparison had a very clear and distinctive purpose (the "why" question): comparison was needed to build the imaginary of the European self in contradistinction with the non-European other. The purpose is not fixed in stone, but it has been defined in relation to the overall epistemology of the single story and the centrality of the enunciation that manages the single story. The challenge today is to decolonize the historical foundation of comparative methodology and the concept of literature; only then may the purpose of comparative work shift the geography of reasoning and embrace the geopolitics of knowledge. Decolonizing the legacies of comparative methodologies and literary studies and engaging in a decolonial analytic require, first of all, the unveiling of the imperial connotations of key concepts such as literature, comparison, aesthetics: the entire Euro-centered vocabulary of literary and aesthetic scholarship. In a nutshell, they require the decolonization of knowledge that includes in this case the comparative method and the concept of literature.

A history of Náhuatl "literature" (the language of the ancient Aztecs) was published in the mid-twentieth century, and a history of Persian "literature" is in the process of being composed.[13] They focus on "one" literature (Náhuatl or Persian). However, framing Náhuatl and Persian verbal expressions as "literature" makes visible the colonial epistemic and aesthetic difference and the acquiescence by the scholars doing the job to the universal value of a regional (in space and time) concept. Although these are not explicitly comparative works, the acceptance of the word "literature" in the title introduces comparison by the wayside. Let's explore this issue in more detail by examining two remarkable books that bring it back home.

Dennis Tedlock's *2000 Years of Mayan Literature* and Sheldon Pollock's edited volume, *Literary Cultures in History: Reconstructions from South Asia*, offer us much to think about as well as opportunities to delink from the imperial chains of comparative methodology.[14] What do we learn from them in terms of comparative methodology in the study of literatures? The title of Pollock's edited book indicates a discomfort with the concepts of history and literature. In the introduction, he undermines the universality of both literature and history, and he examines "culture" to look at them from a distance. "Culture," however, belongs to the same family as "literature" and "religion," to the same civilization that invented the three concepts. As a matter of fact, "culture" became, in the eighteenth century, the term used to build communities of birth (nation; i.e., *natio*) and to displace the term used to imagine communities of faith (religion; i.e., *religare, relegere*). National languages and literary "cultures" served nation-states to create communities of birth and to displace the Christian monopoly on building communities of believers. All that was a problem for Europe only, not for China, Islam, or India before the British dismantled the Mughal Sultanate. Taking the step that Pollock took allows for a preliminary distance, if not delinking, from history and literature. Something has to stay. But that two main key concepts (literature and religion on the one hand and literature and history on the other) have been called into question is enough to alert us to follow suit and to call into question "culture," too, but I will not go there at this point. I appreciate the step taken by Pollock, but we cannot do everything at once.

Pollock reminds us of the word *vānmāya*, which he translates as "things made of language." In *Local Histories/Global Designs*, I recast the Western concept of "literature" in the larger and decolonial concept of "languaging," a term I borrowed from Chilean philosopher and neurophysiologist Humberto Maturana. Maturana's "languaging" is already a concept that delinks from the logic of Western thought.[15] Although derived from Latin roots and transmuted into several modern European

languages, the transformation of a noun into an action, languaging
(doing things with language as thinking is doing things with thoughts)
introduces the necessary break-up and wake-up call. Maturana doesn't
work so much with categories of non-Western cultures; his decolonizing knowledge comes from his shifting the way Western sciences have
understood and built the concept of "representation." Starting from the
premise that living is knowing and knowing is living, he has made of a
noun the central concept in the philosophy of language and dispensed
with "representation": languaging focuses on the enunciation and not
on the enunciated. Interestingly enough, languages of Mayan roots—like
Tojolabal—do not have a third person in their pronoun system. In that
language it is difficult to come up with the concept of "representation."

In many Amerindian philosophies, the future is on your back (because
you cannot see it), while the past is at your front (because you can see
it). In that cosmology, it is difficult to come up with the concept of
"progress and development." That is why Michel Foucault felt discomfort
at the essential relations of words and things that Jorge Luis Borges had
previously ridiculed with his notes on the strange classificatory logic of
a certain Chinese encyclopedia. As you may have noticed, my argument
is built on unveiling the entanglement rather than on comparing the
entangled entities; by so doing, I attempt to unveil the logic of comparative methodology. My point is not whether we should defend comparative
studies or get rid of it, but that disciplinary methodologies invented by
human beings at a given point in time and space (e.g., nineteenth-
century Europe) and within specific overarching systems of ideas, beliefs,
and "structures of feeling" were built on the experiences and needs of
European intellectual elites at the time that Europe was affirming itself
as Europe and as the center of the world.

"Things made in language" runs parallel to the Náhuatl expression *in
xochitl, in cuicatl.* When Mexican scholar Angel María Garibay wrote the
"history of Náhuatl literature," he meant all "things made in languages,"
via the mouth and by the extension of the hands (painting codex with
black and red ink). But he did not have a concept other than "literature."
"Languaging" instead of "literature" brings forward "things made with
language" no matter which civilization we are discussing. It functions as a
connector and not an abstract universal, as does "literature." At the same
time, "languaging" brings the subject, the knower, in close relation with
the events or the text. "Languaging" captures not only "literature" but
"comparative methodology," as well (because comparing is something
carried out with language). It dissolves the distinction between literature
as art and comparative studies as scholarship. It delinks from the ontology of the essence (which always directs us toward the enunciated) and
introduces a relational ontology in which the subject is part of the event

being described. As such, "languaging" runs parallel to the relational ontology at work in Native American and other indigenous philosophies.

So if one asks, comparatively, "What were the things made in language that Europeans engaged in?" or "What did Europeans do to bring 'flowers and songs' together and to combine 'the red and the black ink'?," a conclusion could be reached, according to which Europeans did not have concepts such as "things made in language" or *in xochitl, in cuicatl* or *in tlilli,* in *tlapalli.* Europeans were indeed deficient. They used instead concepts such as "poetry or/and literature" to name activities and entities similar to the ones ancient civilizations in South Asia and Mesoamerica conceived differently. But the coloniality of knowledge made us believe that "literature" superseded *in xochitl, in cuicatl* when, decolonially speaking, it did so only for Europeans and for all those who consent to European perspectives. But—as was always obvious, though forgotten or ignored, and even more so today than in the past five hundred years—the majority of the world does not consent to this single story. As you can see, I am not acquiescing with, but delinking from, the universality of the concept of "literature," and of "comparative methodology." Imperial discourses tend to erase nonimperial memories and reproduce forgetting. Decolonizing knowledge means to uncover erased memories. In so doing, my aim here is not only to analyze and report on the concepts of "comparative methodology" and "literature" but also to delink from what I analyze and report on in the very act of reporting and analyzing.

Let's now turn to Tedlock's *2000 Years of Mayan Literature.* Tedlock's study, although using the concept of "literature" in the title, shows that "literature" is a misnomer and an imperial Western appropriation of Mayan oral and graphic expressions. For the attentive reader, Tedlock dismantles careless Western imperial uses of "literature" as a universal concept. Two thousand years is a long time, going back to the beginning of the Christian era. However, Tedlock goes back even farther, to the earlier remains of Mayan writing, several centuries before Christ, even before Greek philosophy, tragedy, and narrative. I am not European but of European descent in the Americas, where Maya, Aztecs, and Incas are to the Americas what Greece and Rome are to Europeans. Why should I take for granted that the Western concept of "literature" is what I want and need? I could only do so on the condition of blocking my lived experience and accepting the principles and categories of imperial knowledge.

Tedlock's first chapter is of enormous interest in exploring civilizational entanglement as well as the scholar's and the intellectual's location in that entanglement. The chapter is titled "Learning to Read." It may sound offensive, or it may make you think of Wolfgang Iser. Its raison d'être, however, is not related to "reader response criticism": "Standing at the core of the Mayan writing system are the signs for dates from a divinatory calendar that was shared with the rest of Mesoamerica. Each date combines a day number, taken from a repeating series that runs from one through thirteen, with a day name, taken from a series of twenty names that run concurrently with the numbers. Because thirteen and twenty have no common factor, there are 260 possible combinations of number and names."[16]

Now, the two thousand years of Mayan literature began to be stretched to 700–500 BC, when the Mayan calendar had been dated. But this is numeracy, not literacy, and literature is a question of literacy, not numeracy. This is an assumption, not a "fact" that comes from the facts themselves. Certainly, from numeracy we could derive "numerature" as we derive literature from literacy. But it could be hard to understand numbers as letters and literature made of numbers. We now face three problems. The first is the ontic dimension of entities and/or events being compared (e.g., "literary" works, "literary" or "artistic" events). The second is that "literature" is universal only from the Western perspective and after the eighteenth century. The third is the ontological question that asks for the condition under which it is believed to be universal (e.g., the belief that Greeks, Chinese, and the Mayans have "literature"). For all three cases we shall keep in mind that, while for the Greeks writing was alphabetic, for the Chinese and Mayans it was not. That is, there were no "letters" from which to derive "literature."[17] By accepting "literature" and at the same time questioning its conceptualization, both Tedlock and Pollock open up the ontological deuniversalizing of Western universals. We are in a position now to argue for the decolonization of comparative methodology.

Decolonizing (Comparative) Methodology: From Critical Theory to Decolonial Thinking

Mainstream comparative studies in any discipline presuppose the ontic dimension of the events, texts, processes, and so forth, being compared. But what if, in trying to *compare* two or more entities, we attempt to *relate* them? What would be the consequences of *relating* instead of *comparing*? The obvious first consequence is that we move from an ontology of essence to a relational ontology. I argue that one way of delinking from comparative methodology is to move from an ontology of essence to a relational ontology.

The first case is Max Horkheimer's distinction between "critical and traditional theory." It was an important step within European epistemology to show the limits of the epistemology of essence (i.e., knowledge about entities that have mass and occupy space, that have an essence, a gist, a "heart"). Although Horkheimer doesn't refer to comparative methodology, it is evident that at the time the method was founded it was inscribed in the frame of traditional theory. Horkheimer uses the expression "traditional theory" descriptively. It means a way of theorizing that already has a tradition, one based on the assumption that the objects of traditional theories are substances inhabited by an essence. Traditional theory starts from the given, and as such it is the philosophy behind empiricism. "Critical theory" instead starts from the assumption that what is to be known is always a construction of the knowing subject. The ontology of the essence is called into question. First, Horkheimer's critical theory is the first step to call into question the foundations of comparative methodology, which assumes the essence of entities being compared. Second, by bringing the knowing subject to the forefront, Horkheimer moves away from an epistemology in which knowing subjects are transparent observers of entities independent of them to a relational ontology in which knowing subjects are constituted as knowers in the process of constituting what is to be known and understood. The ontology of essence goes hand in hand with a zero-point epistemology: the detached observer who describes and explains. Comparative methodology was founded on those assumptions.

Horkheimer's concerns were those of a European philosopher and intellectual dealing with issues and problems relevant to Europe. His concerns were also his limits. The knowing subject of critical theory is an abstract subject, a subject without gender, race, geohistorical location. Consequently, his important conceptualization of critical theory that shows the underpinning of traditional theory (and of comparative methodology) has serious limitations for decolonial thinking. Decolonially, the knowing subject is never abstract, and the same is true of Horkheimer's knowing subject. Horkheimer was European, German, and Jewish. His article was written in 1937. I am neither European (German or Jewish) nor U.S. born and educated, but an American Catholic from Argentina who became a Latino after I arrived in the United States in 1974. Decolonial thinking, then, introduces a third layer after traditional and critical theory, a layer in which the knowing subject and the known object or processes are configured at the crossroads of racial and geohistorical colonial frames. Consequently, relational ontology in decolonial thinking is not the same as the relational ontology in the frame of Western modernity with which Horkheimer was operating.[18]

What other options are available beyond comparing? The answer, I elaborate, is "relating." But the question now is not just that of relating but the frame in which decolonial scholars and intellectuals operate. The answer is that decolonial thinkers are interested in uncovering hidden connections and relations between events, processes, and entities in the colonial matrix of power.[19] The colonial matrix is a structure of global management that came into being during the sixteenth century—a complex structure to manage the economy, authority, gender, sexuality, ethnicity, and, above all, knowledge. It is the control of knowledge that holds the different domains of the matrix together. Because the management of knowledge is what makes the world move—that is, allows the colonial matrix to operate—we are all in the matrix. The matrix cannot be observed from outside because the knower and the known are not only mutually constituted as Horkheimer argued for critical theory, but they/we are also both constituted in and by the colonial matrix. In this case, zero-point epistemology doesn't obtain, and both traditional and critical theory are decolonially called into question.

The colonial matrix is at once a structure of management and the frame of a cosmology. As such, it is an option between other coexisting cosmologies: religious, scientific, and ideological (by which I mean a secular system of ideas, parallel to a religious system of ideas). Comparative methodology, both in its ethnological enactment and methodological institutionalization, presupposed the ideological/religious frame of the Enlightenment; that is, it is limited in space and time to how Europeans imagined themselves, how the world was created, and what the future they envisioned would be. This—the frame of modernity, the belief in the progress of history, of Spirit as Hegel had it, marching from east to West, overcoming previous historical periods in which Spirit did not yet enjoy the Freedom it will find in nineteenth-century Europe and Germany—is where comparative methodology was founded. Invisible behind the march of the Spirit and the triumph of the Enlightenment were already three centuries of coloniality that was being reorganized in nineteenth-century Europe. In Europe, only modernity was visible, not coloniality. That is why the colonial matrix of power was made visible not by Europeans but by non-European decolonial leaders and scholars-intellectuals-activists (like Gandhi or Fanon). Once we move from critical theory within the European frame of modernity, and from modern or postmodern to decolonial relational ontologies, a different landscape opens up. Decolonial projects are not interested in similarities and differences but above all in the mechanisms and strategies that, within the colonial matrix of power, create similarities and differences and maintain relations and hierarchies between entities, regions, languages, religions, "literatures," people, knowledges, economies, and the like. Decolonial thinking briefly delinks from both traditional and critical theory and underlines knowledge as geopolitically and corpopolitically constituted within the colonial matrix of power. The goals, concerns, and interests of decolonial thinkers (intellectuals, activists, scholars) could be compatible but are harder to combine with those of modern and post-modern scholars.

Let me be more specific—as the second case to be examined—by reflecting on the process of coauthoring a book, *Learning to Unlearn: Decolonial Reflections from Eurasia and the Americas,* with Madina Tlostanova.[20] While the subtitle may suggest a comparative project, the argument de-links explicitly from both area studies and comparative area studies: two imperial framings that disavowed thinking in and from those areas being studied and compared. Tlostanova and I did not build the argument on comparison, as if Eurasia and the Americas were two independent entities that can be compared, but instead we tried to explain their place and respective entanglement with the European/U.S. imperial ordering of the world and, therefore, the ways in which the Americas and Eurasia (and we, the authors, as well) are entangled in the colonial matrix of power. Explicitly we delink from "comparative" methods and specifically with comparative area studies. Our goals were to understand how these two entities have been invented, described, classified, and allocated a distinctive place in a global order that has formed since the sixteenth century, a global order that was constructed on the bases of making and transforming colonial and imperial differences that involve us, the authors, in the present. Comparison was not the point; instead, it was the respective locations and relations of Eurasia and the Americas in the modern/colonial world system. And so the focus was not on two assumed autonomous entities to be observed and compared, but on the effort to understand the entanglement, in which we, as scholars, are also intellectually implicated.

For example, within the larger concept of "Eurasia," Central Asia and the Caucasus are—in relation to Russia, the Soviet Union, and the Russian Federation—geohistorical and geopolitical configurations similar to South America and the Caribbean in relation to the United States in the larger frame called "the Americas." To grasp why this is so, it was necessary to go into the history of the modern/colonial world and to understand the secondary role that Russia began to play in relation to European empires, contrary to the leading role that the United States assumed after the decay of European empires at the end of World War II. In turn, Central Asia and Caucasus, on the one hand, and South America and the Caribbean, on the other, became regions dependent on the two major formations that clashed during the Cold War. You can perhaps argue that what we are doing here is comparing, but I should remind you that what Tlostanova and I analyzed are the entanglements that ensnared us, not the entities. Furthermore, the analysis and arguments were not written from the perspective of the United States or Russia/Soviet Union/Russian Federation, but from the perspective of the history of Central Asia/Caucasus and South America/Caribbean. The entanglement of the entities and the entanglement of the knowing subjects with geopolitical entities ranked in the global order through colonial differentials are embedded in the argument.

You may ask, And how do you achieve that? This question could also be asked of someone who claims that her perspective is that of the United States or Russia, or for that matter of someone who claims that his perspective is neutral, that it is above the domain being investigated. How do you assume a neutral or a U.S. or a Russian perspective? The bottom line for decolonial scholars and intellectuals is how to detach from zero-point epistemology (the belief in the detached neutrality of the observer) and one of its surrogates, the nationality of a given subject. Entangled subjects dwelling in the border of colonial and imperial differences have the option of either blocking the experience of the border and assuming the neutrality of the knowing subject, or translating such living experiences into border thinking, a form of decolonial epistemology. The answer is that you engage in the latter when you are aware that your identity and experience are always already sociogenetically overdetermined by the coloniality of knowledge (the crucial sphere of the colonial matrix of power), and when from that awareness you embrace the history and the genealogy of thoughts of your own assumed living experiences, instead of assuming a genealogy of thought that is not embedded in your own living and assumed experience. It is from our respective experiences in Eurasia and the Americas that Tlostanova and I worked out a "relational ontology" (rather than a comparative methodology) that has more in common with Native Americans' epistemology than with Western responses to "de-notative ontology."

Conclusion

I have argued that comparative methodology was founded on the epistemology of the zero point that presupposes a detached observer comparing two independent entities and looking for similarities and differences. I have also argued that comparative methodology as such was an invention of nineteenth-century Europe at the height of its consolidation as Western civilization and as world imperial power. For that reason, comparative methodology was naturalized as a method across disciplines in the social sciences and humanities whose field of investigation was on the one hand the society, economy, and histories of Europe and on the other European society, economy, and histories compared with the non-European world. Eurocentrism (and its extension to the United States) has been called into question for some time now, but there is still a lot of work ahead of us. While recognizing the significant contributions that Western civilization, the last such civilization to appear on the planet, made to the diversity of the human species, today the imperial assumption that the last is the first and the entire planet must bend to its will is not acceptable.

The geopolitics of knowing, sensing, and believing is assumed by scholars and intellectuals all over the world, recognizing that their cultures, societies, economies, knowledges, linguistics, and visual creativity were part of what Europe wanted to know, at the same time that non-European knowing was either ignored or degraded to myth, folklore, folk art, inferior religions, and certainly not sustainable knowledge. Given that the control of knowledge is at the same time the control of being, a means to colonize knowledges and beings (manifesting itself in many ways, from education to the justification of war, exploitation of lands, geopolitical rape and murder), the task ahead for decolonial scholars and intellectuals is to work toward the decoloniality of knowledge and being. This call originated in the ex–third world (Asia, Africa, South America) as well as (more specifically) among Native Americans and First Nations in the heart of the United States, Canada, and Australasia. While comparative methodology and the concept of literature originated in Europe and gained global currency, decolonizing methodology originated in the non-European world and is now gaining global currency. The main goal is not to improve or change the discipline, but to generate knowledge and understanding for epistemic and political liberation as well as for the ethical foundation of knowledge and politics.

Finally, I argue that decolonial scholars and intellectuals do not compare but look at the sites of entanglements—not any entanglements, but those articulated by the "/" of modernity/coloniality. Decolonial thinking presupposes that the domain to be investigated and thought through is first and foremost the location of modern/colonial entanglements defined by colonial and imperial epistemic/ontological differences, a location which the knowing subject cannot escape. That is why border thinking presupposes indigenous (and other nonmodern) relational ontologies rather than substantial Western ontologies, for which modern/colonial entanglements are out of sight. Substantial ontologies are basically modern and territorial. And that is also why decolonial thinking requires delinking from zero-point epistemology, where comparative methodology has been founded, and delinking from the already-made entities such as the ideas of "literature" and of geohistorical entities like "Europe," "Eurasia," or "America." Delinking means unveiling the processes of how such entities came to be, rather than accepting them as already-constituted entities.

NOTES

1   Franco Cassano, *Southern Thoughts and Other Essays* (New York: Fordham Univ. Press, 2011); Walter D. Mignolo, *The Idea of Latin America* (London: Blackwell, 2005).

2   Elizabeth Mudimbe-Boyi, ed., *Beyond Dichotomies: Translation/Transculturation and the Colonial Difference* (Syracuse, NY: Syracuse Univ. Press, 2002), 251–86. I explored some of these issues with Freya Schiwy in "Beyond Dichotomies: Translation/Transculturation and the Colonial Difference," in *Beyond Dichotomies.*

3   Hendrik Birus, "The Goethean Concept of World Literature and Comparative Literature," *CLCWeb: Comparative Literature and Culture* 2, no. 4 (2000): http://docs.lib.purdue.edu/clcweb/vol2/iss4/7.

4   Johann Gottlieb Fichte, *Address to the German Nation, 1807*, trans. R. F. Jones and G. H. Turnbull (Chicago: Univ. of Chicago Press, 1922), 136–38, 143–45.

5   David Damrosch, *What Is World Literature?* (Princeton, NJ: Princeton Univ. Press, 2003).

6   I will refer to a non-German scholar making such assessments. See, for instance, Marshall Berman, "'Goethe's Faust': The Tragedy of Development," in *All That Is Solid Melts into Air: The Experience of Modernity* (New York: Simon & Schuster, 1982).

7   "Discipline" during the Renaissance (as defined by Luis Vives, *The disciplinis*, 1531) was redefined during the Enlightenment (Immanuel Kant, *The Contest of Faculties*, 1798). That became "disciplinary regimes" at the end of the twentieth century (Michel Foucault, 1986) "Disciplinary Power and Subjection," in *Power: A Radical View*, 2nd ed., ed. Steven Lukes (Oxford: Blackwell, 2004), 229–42.

8   Franco Moretti, *The Novel: History, Geography and Culture*, 2 vols. (Princeton, NJ: Princeton Univ. Press, 2006–7) and *Modern Epic: The World System from Goethe to Garcia Marquez* (London: Verso, 1996); Pascale Casanova, *The World Republic of Letters*, trans. M. B. Deveboise (Cambridge, MA: Harvard Univ. Press, 2004). What Moretti and Casanova have in common—beyond Immanuel Wallerstein's frame of world-system analysis—is the Western bent toward the universalization of Western concepts (literature, novel, Republic of Letters). I would include Damrosch, as well, although his approach remains more without the confines of literary "history" rather than literary "system."

9   George Lamming, "The Occasion of Speaking," in *The Pleasure of Exile* (Ann Arbor: Univ. of Michigan Press, 1960), 44.

10 Alain Viala, *Naissance de l'ecrivain, Paris: Minuit, 1985, La culture litteraire* (Paris: Press Univ. de France, 2009).

11 I allude here to Chamamanda Adichie's influential "The Danger of a Single Story," presented at Oxford University, July 2009, available at http://www.permaculture.co.uk/videos/chimamanda-adichie-danger-single-story.

12 I examined this issue in detail in my first book, *Elementos para una teor'ia del texto literario* (Barcelona: Editorial Grijalbo, 1978), and in a later series of articles.

13 *A History of Persian Literature.* At this point, two of the projected twenty volumes have already been published: J. T. P. de Bruijn and Ehsan Yarshater, *General Introduction to Persian Literature*, vol. I (London: I. B. Tauris, 2008); *Mohsen Ashtiany and Ehsan Yarshater, Persian Poetry in the Classical Era, 800–1500*, vol. II (London: I. B. Tauris, 2012). Jose María Garibay, *Historia de la literature Náhuatl*, 2 vols. (México: Editorial Porrúa, 1943–46).

14 Dennis Tedlock, *2000 Years of Mayan Literature* (Berkeley: Univ. of California Press, 2010); Sheldon Pollock, *Literary Cultures in History: Reconstructions from South Africa* (Berkeley: Univ. of California Press, 2003).

15 For more details about my use of Maturana's concept (and reference to his arguments), see "Bilanguaging Love: Thinking in between Languages," in *Local Histories/Global Designs: Coloniality, Subaltern Knowledge and Border Thinking* (Princeton, NJ: Princeton Univ. Press, 2000), 250–77.

16   Tedlock, *2000 Years of Mayan Literature*, 13.
17   Elizabeth H. Boone and Walter D. Mignolo, eds., *Writing without Words: Alternative Literacies in Mesoamerica and the Andes* (Durham, NC: Duke Univ. Press, 1994). Several of these issues are explored in *Writing without Words*.
18   I leave for another occasion the elaboration on the concept of "relational ontology" in indigenous and Western epistemology. For the first, see Shawn Wilson, *Research Is Ceremony: Indigenous Research Method* (Halifax: Fernwood, 2008) and Margaret Elizabeth Kovach, *Indigenous Methodologies: Characteristics, Conversations and Contexts* (Toronto: Toronto Univ. Press, 2010); for the second, see Mustafa Emirbayer, "Manifesto for a Relational Sociology," *AJS* 103, no. 2 (1997): 281–317.
19   I have explained the concept in detail in several publications, chiefly, *The Darker Side of Western Modernity: Global Futures, Decolonial Options* (Durham, NC: Duke Univ. Press, 2011) and "Coloniality: The Darker Side of Modernity," Museo de Arte Moderno de Barcelona (2009), available at http://www.macba.cat/PDFs/walter_mignolo_modernologies_eng.pdf.
20   Walter Mignolo and Madina Tlostanova, *Learning to Unlearn: Decolonial Reflections from Eurasia and the Americas* (Columbus: Ohio Univ. Press, 2012).

CHAPTER SEVEN

Transnationalizing Comparison: The Uses and Abuses of Cross-Cultural Analogy

Robert Stam and Ella Shohat

I N THIS ESSAY, WE EXPLORE the role of comparison within the race and colonial debates as they play across various national and cultural zones—American, French, and Brazilian. Any discussion of these national zones is haunted by a discursive history of comparative dichotomies within situations of assymetrical empowerment: Europe and its others; the West and the rest; Global North and Global South. How should we analyze the rubrics, keywords, and evaluative repertoires in which debates about race and cultural difference are conducted in these diverse sites? What happens in the movement of ideas from one geographical space and cultural semantics to another, and how does that impact the rhetoric of comparison? Here we will deploy a relational and transnational method that seeks to eludicate the insights and blind spots and aporias of diverse comparative approaches and frameworks.

Poststructuralist approaches to translation and adaptation figure in our discussion to the degree that they challenge a moralistic and dichotomous idiom of fidelity versus betrayal, as, for example, in the discussion of filmic adaptations of novels that assumes the possibility of one-to-one adequation between the cultural/textual worlds of original and copy.[1] In terms of cross-cultural translation and adaptation, we prefer to speak not of adequate or inadequate copies of cultures seen as originary and normative, but rather of an unending process of reciprocal transtextuality. Our stress, therefore, is on the interactive and recombinant dialogism evoked by terms like revoicing, reaccentuation, indigenization, and mediation. At the same time, these dialogical mediations are shaped and produced within specific cultural contexts that imply a situated "take" on the act of comparison itself. And just as adaptation theory tries to avoid the axiomatic superiority of one medium (for example, literature) over another (for example, cinema), or of the novel as original and the film as a definitionally inadequate copy, so cross-cultural comparison risks surreptitiously inscribing one cultural or national zone as original and the other as copy, one culture as ontological real and the other as phenomenal imitation, one culture as substance and the other as accident, one culture as normative and the other as aberrant. Here we will be especially critical of comparisons that operate through colonialist, reductivist, culturalist, or essentialist grids that assume linear and dichotomous axes of "foreign"/"native," "export"/"import," "inside"/"outside," "transmitter"/"receiver," "origin"/"copy."

Asymmetries of power, meanwhile, impact the discourse and rhetoric of comparison. Thus cross-cultural comparisons can be reciprocal or unilateral, multidirectional or unidirectional, dialogic or monologic. The question, then, becomes: Which ideas transit easily, and which face obstacles at the border? What are the "social conditions" of what Pierre Bourdieu called, in the title of the last article he ever published, "the international circulation of ideas?"[2] In what ways do national interests, cultural institutions, and global socioeconomic alignments mark the itineraries of "traveling theories" (Edward Said)? How are comparisons shaped by infranational, national, and supranational exceptionalisms, narcissisms, and disavowals? How is national memory narrated and instrumentalized within cross-national comparison? What anxieties and hopes, what utopias and dystopias, are provoked by a comparative treatment of such issues as "race," "colonialism," and "multiculturalism" in diverse sites? Why does cross-national comparison provoke defensive objections along the lines of: "But our situation is completely different; it is simply not comparable"? Here we will examine a few examples of the rhetorics of comparison, some embedded in cultural-essentialist assumptions, while others are mobilized in the critique of such assumptions.

The operative terms of comparative debates sometimes shift their political and epistemological valence in diverse national zones. What, then, are the *blocages symboliques* which prevent comparabilities from being recognized and translated, or, conversely, how do certain taken-for-granted frames of comparison actually impede transnational analysis? How do key terms crystallize identity in ways that prevent the recognition of commonalities? Why, for example, is the concept of *la République* so central to debates in France but not in the United States or Brazil, even though all three are republics? Why is miscegenation a constant theme in Brazil but not in France or the United States, even though all three countries are, in their own way, miscegenated? Why does the term "communitarianism" carry such a powerful negative charge in France yet seldom figure in the debates in Brazil and the United States? In sum, the unpacking of the transatlantic traffic of race/colonial debates requires a relational analysis of knowledge production and dissemination.

How, then, have cross-cultural and transnational comparisons been instrumentalized? What does comparison illuminate or fail to illuminate? Is national or ethnic narcissism inevitable, or can it be transcended? By transnationalizing the debates, we hope to scrutinize what might be called cross-border looking relations. What are the grids, prisms, tropes, and even fun-house mirrors through which comparisons are established? How does cross-national comparison intersect with other modalities of comparison, such as metaphor, simile, and allegory? Along which vectors does comparison take place? What is the cognitive value of cross--national comparison? Does comparison   assume a prior assumption of an illusory coherence on both sides of the comparison? How does comparison change when we move from comparing two entities (with the concomitant danger of reified binaries) to comparing three or more entities (with the danger of a dizzying proliferation)? Or is comparison always in search of a third entity, Aristotle's *tertium comparationis*, and is it a sideways-glancing utterance that is addressed to a third party, which also implies the transcendence of binarism? Is comparison necessarily premissed on overly neat national and geographical boundaries?

Nation as Comparison

Nation-states define themselves with and against other nations in a diacritical process of identity formation. The "fictive we" of the nation is forged with, through, and against other nations, often through a rhetoric of (sometimes invidious) comparison, a specular play of self and other. For example, France has historically defined itself against the Muslim world (Charles Martel, the Crusades, *El Cid*), then against England and Germany, and now, at least in political terms, against the U.S. hyperpower. The United States has defined itself with and against Native Americans internally, and externally against Great Britain (the Revolutionary War), Spain (the Spanish-American War), Germany and Japan (the two World Wars), the Soviet Union (the Cold War), and now Islamic fundamentalism (the "War on Terror"). American neoconservatives, meanwhile, have tried to define the perennial ally, France, as an enemy. Brazil, too, has defined itself vis-à-vis various colonizing or neocolonizing powers— Portugal, France, Spain, Holland, Great Britain, and the United States. Thus ego-reinforcing national narration is always already engaged with national others. It is not only a question of how a nation projects itself but also how it projects others within these mutually shaping projections.

Exceptionalist mythologies in the United States, meanwhile, have tended to stress the ways that the United States is *not comparable* to European nations, for example, that it has never been a colonial or imperial state, even though the United States colonized indigenous America, came to imperialize Latin America, and has indulged in various neoimperial binges and surges. French exceptionalism, by the same token, edits out France's massive participation in the slave trade in the

Caribbean. The structure of these amnesiac denials of commonalities recalls that of the "denegations" (*je sais mais quand même* or "I know, but still . . .") theorized by psychoanalysis. The perpetual temptation, given that nation-state histories always have an element of the sordid and the violent, is to project repressed historical memories onto the screens of other nations and to search for comparisons that flatter rather than those that shame or embarrass.

Exceptionalist discourses often go hand in hand with cultural essentialism and national characterologies, whether mobilized to celebrate (or on occasion denounce) one's own nation or denounce (or celebrate) another nation. American exceptionalism promotes the idea of the United States as uniquely democratic and destined to exercise wonder-working benevolent power in the world. Within the American exceptionalist view, the United States accumulates a series of "firsts"—and "firsts" are simply the chronological version of comparison—premissed on U.S. narcissistic advantage. The United States is proclaimed to be the first "new nation," the first modern constitutional democracy, the first immigrant "nation of nations," and the only country based on opportunity for the individual. Blessed by Providence with a unique purpose and fate, the United States, in comparison to others, avoided their petty foibles and thus transcended the gravity and "downers" of history as that which hurts. U.S. exceptionalism promotes the myth of innocence through tropes of prelapsarian "American Adams"—again, innocent in comparison to postlapsarian European others—wandering in a virgin paradise.

Exceptionalism, whether in the American "Beacon-to-the-World" form or in the French *mission-civilisatrice* form or in the exceptionalism-light of the "we-are-all-mixed-and-tolerant" Brazilian form, is comparison in the superlative mode, with each nation proclaiming itself to be the "greatest" in some respect, whether in terms of political model or cultural expression or popular practices. Exceptionalism forms part of the standard rhetoric of American politicians from both parties who constantly embroider their speeches with ritual references to "this great land of ours," "the greatest nation in history," and the "greatest democracy on the face of the earth." Exceptionalism, in this sense, consists in the *refusal to compare*, in the tendency to find one's own nation peerless, beyond compare. Yet this exceptionalism is rife with aporias. How can a nation-state that regards itself as exceptional demand that others follow in its tracks, if those tracks have already been defined as exceptional? The discourse is inherently paradoxical: while seeing itself as exceptional, the United States also declares itself as a norm to be diffused and emulated, thus containing its own aporia and potential dissolution as it moves from exception to norm.[3] But the United States is not exceptional in its exceptionalism; nationalism, in general, shapes fictions of unsullied virtue and seamless unity and coherence, yet the very foundations of modern nation-states forcibly entail the monopolization of violence, the repression of difference, and the mandatory forgetfulness of originary crimes.

Cross-national comparisons are equally imbued with affect, fears, vanities, desires, and projections. They can idealize the "home" country or denigrate it, just as they can idealize the "away" country or denigrate it, or they can seek broad relationalities, which deconstruct nation-state thinking by discerning commonalities, thereby bypassing the border police. U.S. pro-American exceptionalism is sometimes countered by the negative exceptionalism of its homegrown American critics who fail to see the embeddedness of the United States within broader historical patterns of pan-European hegemony. French anti-Americanism also rests on a tacit comparison: American imperialism in the present is worse than ours in the past.[4] American anti-Americanism, or negative exceptionalism, meanwhile, offers the upside-down narcissism of superlative badness: "Our own imperialism is the absolute worst; no one is as breathtakingly evil as we are."

Cross-cultural and transnational comparisons serve myriad purposes. Negotiating constantly between the facile universalism which denies difference ("We're all human beings!") and the bellicose stigmatization of difference (good versus evil; us versus them), comparison at times can trigger, as we shall see, a salutary deprovincialization and mutual illumination. Variously emphasizing contrasts, similarities, or complementarities, comparisons can move along a spectrum that goes from a maximalist differentialism ("We have nothing in common with them!"), to a paternalistic top-down "good neighborism" ("We have everything in common but do not forget you're subordinate"), to a quasi-masochistic self-denigration ("We will never be as good as you!"). Nations can project their own worst tendencies onto alter-ego nations, imagining in others their own most ignoble traits. Or they develop a resentful discourse of victimization that remains narcissistic because the aggrieved victim nation retains the psychic capital of its own professed innocence. Or dissident minorities and "internal émigrés" can endow other nations with utopian possibilities, seeing them as the sites of hope in a situation of despair.

Sometimes comparisons get mapped onto stagist teleologies, which inscribe countries into larger, global temporalities that project some nations as comparatively "ahead" or "behind" on an imaginary timeline of progress. Stagist theory within Europe goes back to the Enlightenment as a secularization of the teleologies of Divine Providence. According to the modernizing discourse of a G. W. F. Hegel or a Max Weber, South nations like Brazil were seen as "behind" the North. But recently, we have seen a number of historiographical reversals, whereby Latin Americanists stress that Latin America historically preceded Anglo-America by almost a century, and even that most of North America, as evidenced in state names such as Florida and California, was Latin before it was Anglo. The ethnocentric provincialisms of the West, from the Enlightenment to twentieth-century modernization and even, ironically, to postmodern theory, have tended to cast non-European cultures and regions as "allochronic" (Johannes Fabian) or "behind" in the race for progress.

Comparison as Ethnic Ranking

Nationalist and panethnic exceptionalisms sometimes go hand in hand with an especially invidious form of comparison: ranking. We find an example in Hegel's *The Philosophy of History* where every attribute of Hegel's personal identity becomes associated with supreme rank: Germany is the best country, Europe the best continent, Christianity the best religion (and Protestantism its best incarnation). Eurocentric/racist discourse, meanwhile, classically took the form of ranking the higher and lower forms of civilization and comparing the glorious achievements of the "West" to the allegedly paltry achievements of "the rest." In *The Philosophy of History*, Hegel contrasts the Northern Hemisphere, characterized by republican constitutions, Protestantism, prosperity, and freedom, with a Southern Hemisphere characterized by authoritarianism, Catholicism, militarism, and unfreedom. "While South America was conquered," Hegel wrote, "North America was colonized."[5] In terms of relative prosperity, historians might correct Hegel to say that in the early Iberian stage of colonization, which Karl Marx sarcastically called the "rosy dawn of capitalist accumulation," it was South America that was actually wealthier than the North. The European domination of the Americas, moreover, usually involved *both* conquest and colonization

Despite its problems, Hegel's overdrawn North/South schema became hugely influential. The North was erected as the model for the South, just as the West was inscribed as the model for the East. Both Brazilian and American commentators stressed that the countries of South America were less prosperous and dynamic than the United States and that this difference was rooted in national character. Many negative views of Latin American character, both from within and from without, also betray the influence of Max Weber, whose work might be described as an exercise in comparative characterology. The narcissistic question that orients ("occidents?") Weber's *The Protestant Ethic and the Spirit of Capitalism* is how to explain something Weber takes to be axiomatic—European superiority. Why did Europe develop industry, science, and liberal institutions, Weber asks, while the "rest of the world" did not? For Weber, European advantages were not the result of massive appropriation of the land, resources, and labor of the Americas, Africa, and Asia but rather the product of a superior cultural personality, a conflation of ethos (character), ethnos (people), and religion whereby Europeans, and especially Protestant Europeans, were seen as uniquely rational, inquisitive, and ethical.

There are also internal differentiations within Eurocentric thinking, to wit, the familial quarrel between the Anglos and the Latins. The conventional wisdom would place two of the three nation-states in our trilateral comparison (that is, France and Brazil) on one "Latin" side of a cultural divide and the third (the United States) on the "Anglo-Saxon" side. Thus our discussion is always already haunted by a perennial binarism that constructs a strong cultural divide between two transnational panethnic groups. What we have observed time and time again, however, is that the twinned terms "Latin" and "Anglo-Saxon," especially when deployed as part of strongly drawn and reified dichotomous comparisons, betray a retreat into tired paradigms, a confusion of levels, which has hindered the thinking of transnational relationalities.

The two terms "Latin" and "Anglo-Saxon" have to be thought (and unthought) in relation to each other, especially since the two categories were largely constructed in mutual opposition and antipathy. The two terms give expression, we would argue, to regional variants of that larger form of self-love called Eurocentrism.[6] Thus one form of European ethnic/cultural exceptionalism—which we will call Anglo-Saxonism—is associated with Northern Europe and its expansion into the Americas and around the world. As we have noted, figures such as Hegel and Weber gave expression to that form of exceptionalism. The other form, which we will call "Latinism," meanwhile, is associated with France and Southern Europe and its expansion into the Americas. It was formulated as a means of lateral differentiation from the "Anglo-Saxons" and vertical differentiation from non-Europeans in the Americas. Paul Adam, the French author of a 1910 book about Brazil (*Les visages du Brésil*), gives expression to this form of narcissism when he speaks of the "miracle" produced by the Latins who accomplished in the New World what the "Mediterraneans" had begun earlier in Europe: "How is it possible to ignore the continuity of this unilateral evolution . . . navigation, steam, electricity, aviation, Hertzian waves, all that is the work of elites of Mediterranean origin."[7] Adam's account echoes the Hegelian and Weberian discourse of European superiority, but in its warm-water Mediterranean current. But Adam goes on to lament that Latinity has been historically defeated by a "feudal, iconoclastic, disciplinary" Protestantism opposed to "Catholic, sensual, iconolatrous mores."[8]

Of course, if one takes a Native American or an Afrodiasporic "view from below," these differences become largely immaterial, mere nuances within European whiteness. Indeed, many of the debates about race, colonialism, and imperialism revisit, sometimes without acknowledgment, enmities rooted in interimperial wars and debates. For centuries, the Spanish, the Portuguese, the British, the Dutch, the French, and the Americans all vied for domination and influence around the world in a situation where all parties were convinced that their particular form of imperial domination was well intentioned and beneficial, and that all their defeats were tragic misfortunes. It is a case of what Freud called the "narcissism of minor differences," in this case the differences between various European (and Euro-American) forms of imperialism.

The overdrawing of the line between Latin and Anglo imperialisms in the Americas forgets that the two were initially linked through envy and emulation. Spanish and Portuguese colonialism preceded that of the Dutch and British and French. In the early stages of "discovery," the two Iberian powers dominated most of the Americas until challenged (and imitated) by the other powers. The various "latecomers"—such as the British and the Dutch—admired Spain for having transformed itself from a relatively poor country into a major European puissance through the infusion of wealth from its New World possessions. In their own New World endeavors, the British often attempted to emulate the triumphs of the Spanish. Britain's late entry into the sweepstakes meant that it could hope only for the "leftovers" of Spanish conquest, often swept up by English "pirates of the Caribbean."

Our research has led us to a vast corpus of texts, which directly or indirectly assert either a "hard" Anglo-Saxonist and imperialist form of superiority or a "soft" Latin, colonial superiority. Countless texts, for example, contrast the racially phobic and segregationist Anglo-Saxons (whether operating in the U.S. South or in British colonies) with the more open, assimilationist, and tolerant Latins. This binarism haunts even contemporary French books that engage sympathetically with postcolonial theory. A 2002 book by Jacqueline Bardolph on *Études postcoloniales et littérature* calls for a study of "different colonial imaginaries, for a study of the way in which French history, marked by Catholicism and the spirit of the Enlightenment, might offer a less hierarchical vision of non-European peoples than the British imperial vision."[9] Thus old Anglo-French rivalries become embroiled in a new rivalry within postcolonial studies about the relative humanity of variant forms of colonialism. Writers end up parroting the ethnonationalist exceptionalist narratives articulated in schools, history books, museums, and colonial expositions, now voiced by progressive intellectuals supposedly speaking on behalf of the colonized subaltern. What we have, then, are latter-day expressions of narcissistic nationalism, which historically generated claims that our conquest was more gentle than yours, our slavery more humane, our imperialism more cultivated.

The panethnic rivalry between "the Latins" and the "Anglo-Saxons" also had implications for how histories of conquest and slavery were represented through culturalist comparisons. The advocates of Latinidad promoted the myth of a benevolent Catholic conquest and slavery. What especially interests us here is the role of multilateral comparison, as occurs, for example, when a French commentator on Brazil compares race relations in Brazil and in the United States. The Frenchman Joseph Burnichon summarizes the contrast between two forms of colonization from a "Latin" perspective: "The Anglo-Saxon represses the indigenes and ends up annihilating them [while] Spain and Portugal, the Latin colonizers, mix with the so-called inferior race . . . resulting in new peoples, with their own originality and their own value."[10] Such a contrast between Brazilian racial harmony and North American hostility is a frequent leitmotif in French and Brazilian commentary on Brazil.

At the same time, the positions on these issues cannot be predictably aligned with ethnicity or nationality. Some "Latins" preferred the "Anglo-Saxon" approach, and vice versa. Writing in the 1920s, a French visitor to Brazil, Abel Bonnard, lauds the Anglo-Saxon defense of "racial purity," arguing: "We know how stubbornly North Americans, to this day, have preserved the purity of their blood and for our part we will never stop repeating that in so doing they fulfilled their primary duty and thus rendered an uncommon service to humanity . . . The foreigner who sees the variety of colors in the pedestrians of Rio or Bahia can have no doubt that the true tragedy of Brazil lies in its mixture of races, in this sinister struggle where the different spirits of humanity get coiled together like serpents."[11] The Latinists, interestingly, constructed a different, but in some ways equally arbitrary, hierarchy, which acknowledged the material, technological superiority of the "Anglo-Saxons" but asserted the spiritual/intellectual superiority of the "Latins." But all of these comparisons take place between elites; they center on "whose slavery is worse" or who has better treated "our" Indians and "our" blacks. They have little to do with the placing in relation of subaltern perspectives or with mobilizing comparison to critique colonial formations or discover different modes of resistance to slavery and dispossession.

The Ambivalence of Comparative Identity

An ill-formulated injunction suggests that we should not compare apples and oranges, but in fact one can pursue comparison in many directions and for different ends. Even apples and oranges, after all, are comparable as fruits, and for that matter, one can compare fruits and vegetable as foods, or compare one's beloved to a summer's day.

The point of the "oranges and apples" dictum is that one should not compare objects that are too dissimilar, yet a poetics of improbable comparison (*discordia concors*) has catalyzed major artistic schools, from John Donne and the metaphysical poets to the paintings of the surrealists, to the films of Jean-Luc Godard. Jorge Luis Borges's heterotopic Chinese Encyclopedia might be absurd from the standpoint of logic, but its exploding the ground of commensurability has been productive from the standpoint of aesthetics.

One finds a kind of productivity in the vast cross-national corpus of comparative writing that focuses on Brazil and the United States or on France and the United States. The sheer volume of this comparative corpus, which swells with every passing year, is remarkable. For various reasons, intellectuals from these three countries have found the other countries "good to think with." Comparisons usually operate on the basis of what semioticians called "principles of pertinence." The comparative writing treating France and the United States, for example, tends to spotlight the two countries' rival revolutions and discrepant social mores. In Bourdieu's evocative phrase, the United States and France represent "two imperialisms of the universal." One result of this competition over this shared revolutionary heritage is a perennial love-hate relationship between the two countries, accompanied by the emotions associated with sibling rivalry.[12] In the case of Brazil and the United States, the comparisons do not have to do with comparative revolutions—since Brazil, unlike other Latin American nations, did not have a revolution leading to independence—but rather with the two countries' shared status as settler states in the Americas whose histories have both been marked by European colonialism (British and Portuguese), by slavery, abolition, and immigration.

Henry M. Brackenridge was perhaps the first American writer, in 1817, to intuit the need for a systematic comparison between the two countries. While recognizing that limiting the comparison to the present would be to compare a "young giant" with a "mature dwarf"—Brazil, after all, had not even achieved independence at that time—Brackenridge emphasized that it was necessary to imagine what the two nations would become in the future. Contrasting the stormy disunity of the Spanish-speaking nations in Latin America with "the unified and indivisible" Brazilian nation, Brackenridge concludes that "given the vast capacities and resources of Brazil, it is not to be a visionary to foresee that this [Brazilian] empire is destined to rival our own."[13]

In the case of Brazil, comparisons with the United States have been unending, forming an integral part of a specular and reciprocal process of self-definition. Although cross-national comparisons are often narcissistic, in the case of Brazil they have just as often been self-deprecating, whether about Brazil's supposedly derivative culture or about its inadequate political institutions. In Brazil, comparison has often been wielded to the detriment of Brazil by Brazilians themselves. Indeed, playwright Nelson Rodrigues famously called Brazilians "upside down Narcissists" who spit on their own mirror image. The process is similar to any situation of stratified and unequal power—as instantiated in the internalized male gaze analyzed by feminism, for example—by which one group is prodded to see itself from another perspective deemed to be superior. The dominated, whether among nations or within nations, are those who are obliged to compare themselves to a partly imaginary yet empowered form of normativity.

As Brackenridge predicted, both Brazil and the United States consolidated their territories and grew from strength to strength over the course of the nineteenth century. National identity became crystallized in cliché metaphors. Brazil became known as the "Minotaur of South America," and the United States as the "Colossus of the North." These comparisons are asymmetrical and power laden, of course, since Brazilians make the comparison from a position of relative geopolitical weakness, while Americans have made their comparisons from a privileged position of taken-for-granted empowerment. Sociologist Jesse Souza articulates this comparative obsession with the United States very well, noting: "We do not compare ourselves with Bolivia, Guatemala, or even with Argentina. We compare ourselves obsessively with the United States. In fact, explicit or implicit comparison with the United States is the central thread in practically all of the twentieth-century interpretations of Brazilian singularity—because we perceive that only the United States is as great and influential as we are in the Americas."[14]

In Brazil, furthermore, such comparisons are made not only in scholarly texts but also in everyday Brazilian discourse, while in the United States the comparisons tend to be limited to specialists or those Americans who happen to come into contact with Brazil. There is both pathos and grandeur in this generally unreciprocated Brazilian penchant for comparison; on the one hand, it represents a desire to see oneself as equal to the most powerful (and an implicit disdain for one's weaker neighbors); on the other, it constitutes a cry of despair and anger. In its rightist version, the cry was, "how can we ever be equal when you are so great?" and in the leftist version, it was, "how can we be equal to this imperialist giant when the game is rigged and you oppress us?" Needless to say, this power dynamic has shifted significantly with the economic crisis in the United States and the rise of Brazil and other powers from the Global South such as India and China.

Much of the comparative historical work bears on the role of the frontier in the two countries. The question of territory and expansion was essential in both Brazil and the United States. While Brazilians spoke of the *Marcha para Oeste* (the march toward the West), the United States spoke in more grandiloquent and messianic terms of "manifest destiny." In the United States, we encounter Frederick Jackson Turner's "frontier hypothesis," presented to the American Historical Association in 1893, around the time of the official "closing" of the frontier. At the same time, if Brazil has no "frontier hypothesis" à la Turner, there is nonetheless a pervasive discourse of another frontier, that of the Amazon Basin as a reserve of hope and social mobility and supposedly inexhaustible resources, a discourse which, if not identical to the American frontier, nevertheless serves a similar function.

The classic comparative work on the role of the frontier in the two countries, Vianna Moog's *Pioneers and Bandeirantes* (1954), revolves around what seems like a rather humiliating question: why did the United States become so successful and a leading power in the world, while Brazil remained so poor and weak? (A more flattering question for Brazil—and some cultural nationalists have come close to this formulation—might reverse the terms: why did the United States become so bellicose, and imperialistic, and Brazil so cordial?) Indeed, the comparison to the United States is never far away whenever Brazilians talk about their own history or national character, as we see in the work of such major theorists of Brazilian identity and character as Gilberto Freyre, Sérgio Buarque de Holanda, Raimundo Faoro, Roberto DaMatta, and Dante Moreira Leite. What varies is the question of who or what is blamed for Brazil's supposed failure. For Buarque de Holanda, Brazil's comparative disadvantage derives from the negative legacy of Portugal, a backward country where the Enlightenment, the Reformation, the French Revolution, and industrial capitalism had little impact, and where authoritarian personalism reigned. Thus a fatalistic causality, rather like original sin, marks this vision of the history of Brazil. For lawyer, philosopher, and literary critic Raimundo Faoro, in his 1959 book *Os donos do poder: Formação do patronato político brasileiro*, the villain is the patrimonial state, again derived from Portugal (although the concept of "patriominalism" is derived from Weber). What Jesse Souza calls the "sociology of inauthenticity" and a "logic of deficit" portrays Brazilian historical becoming as a case of aborted Western development. In a strategic move parallel to that which sees "counter" and "para" Enlightenments as opposed to a single Enlightenment, Souza switches the terms of comparison by seeing Brazil as a case not of failed but rather of selective modernization, existing not in opposition to the United States and Europe but rather as one point on a modernizing spectrum.[15]

Cross-national comparison is often instrumental in shaping the self-perception of nations. In the case of Brazilian thinkers like Freyre,

Buarque de Holanda, Moog, and DaMatta, comparisons to the United States have often come close to the very heart of debates about *Brazilian* identity. As intellectual popstar Caetano Veloso put it, "Brazil is the other giant of the Americas, the other melting pot of races and cultures, the other paradise promised to European and Asian immigrants, the other. The double, the shadow, the negative of the great adventure of the New World."[16] While in no way identical, then, various Brazilian and American thinkers have seen the two countries as eminently comparable. Within a fraught dialectics of attraction and repulsion, even strong and reiterated statements of difference have historically been addressed to a privileged interlocutor. For many Brazilian intellectuals (as for many American Brazilianists), the "natural" and inevitable historical comparison, for Brazil, has not been to the mother country Portugal, or to a European country like France or even to a Spanish-speaking neighbor like Argentina, but rather to the United States. The issue is not one of identity but of relationality; similar historical elements exist in both countries, but they are reshuffled. Major chords in one country become minor chords in the other. But this penchant for nation-based comparisons remains power laden and overdetermined. The comparisons themselves depend on who is doing the comparing, in relation to which social groups, along what axes, and to what ends.

The Pitfalls of Comparison

One of the most influential and widely cited contemporary theorists of Brazilian national identity against a comparative U.S. backdrop is Brazilian anthropologist Roberto DaMatta. Often insightful and entertaining, DaMatta's writing proliferates in brilliant aperçus which highlight what he sees as the quotidian cultural contrasts between the two countries. His omnivorous and all-encompassing analytical method turns almost any social event—a birthday party, a soccer game, a chance encounter in the street—into material for comparative analysis.

One of DaMatta's books engaging the U.S./Brazil comparison bears the title (quite significantly for our trilateral comparative purposes) *Tocquevilleanas: Noticias da america* (Tocquevilliana: News from America). One essay, called "Images of Brazil and the U.S. in Popular Music," compares three songs that explicitly address the issue of national culture: "The House I Live In [What Is America to Me]" by Earl Robinson and Lewis Allan; Ary Barroso's "Watercolor Portrait of Brazil" (popularly known as "Brazil"); and Jorge Ben Jar's "Pais Tropical." The American song, for DaMatta, defines the collectivity as sharing a modern, civic faith, a belief in freedom and equality as values. The Brazilian songs, in contrast, define Brazil not in terms of its universal political creed but according to its generous, paradisal nature and the seductive, rich, beautiful, and inviting culture that goes with it. DaMatta sums up the difference: "To be American, it is enough to be governed by external rules. But to be Brazilian, one has to samba, wiggle, mix, drink, sleep and sing, in a word, to be, rather than, as in the American case, to belong. Do I exaggerate? Without a doubt, but that is exactly what the songs express."[17] DaMatta is not anti-American; indeed, his writing reveals a good deal of affection for U.S. culture—especially popular music—and his generalizing contrasts are often overly generous to the United States, as when he associates it with "equality before the law." At the same time, DaMatta is especially adept at formulating what might be called "the Brazilian difference," that is, particularly sympathetic aspects of Brazilian behavior and attitude. He accounts very well for the different feeling generated by Brazilian versus American styles of life, at least in the dominant mainstream versions of both cultures.

However, whether speaking of Brazil or of the United States, DaMatta almost always thinks from an unacknowledgedly white-dominant perspective. In this sense, DaMatta offers a slightly revised version of the Anglo/Latin dichotomy, which contrasts the personalities of two dominant elites—one *branco-branco* (white-white), the other *branco-moreno* (white-dark). But the idea that some ideal Anglo "type" has persisted unaltered through centuries of U.S. history implies that the non-Anglo elements have not inflected the national character. This view quietly encodes a neo-Hegelian "triumph of the North European spirit" version of the history of nations, whereby Protestant whiteness inevitably prevails over its non-Protestant, nonwhite others. (Samuel Huntington is deeply Hegelian in this sense.) This view, problematic even in its own terms, is unduly static. The idea that the Protestant work ethic dominates the United States overprivileges New England as the primordial source of American culture, while also ignoring the substantial part of the population that is not Protestant or even Christian and other differentiations within a complex and heteroglossic society.

Although DaMatta's analysis of Carnival is indebted to Mikhail Bakhtin's, his analyses of the United States bypass Bakhtin's preferential option for alterity and multiplicity (crystallized in such Bakhtinian neologisms as "heteroglossia," "polyglossia," "pluristylism," "double-voiced discourse," "polyphony") in favor of variations on a single number—one. For DaMatta, the United States has one language, one ethos, and one style of life. He writes like an anthropologist who claims to have cracked the code of a tribal society, discerning a system unknown even to the "tribals" themselves. Such an approach, already problematic in relation to a well-defined object of study such as a small group of the same origins in a single location, leads to an analytic aporia when applied to "multitribal" peoples and polyethnic states like Brazil and the United States.

The problem, then, is a methodological one, to wit, the reciprocal reification of differences, and the erasure of commonalities, between nations. "Ideal type" generalities homogenize very complex and variegated national formations while denying common features. In a bipolar method of comparison, all individuals line up in conformity with a set of a priori characteristics: on one "Latin" side, openness, sensuousness, syncretism, and hybridity; on the other "Anglo" side, closedness, puritanism, segregationism, and exclusivity. DaMatta's comparisons leave both Brazilians and inhabitants of the United States locked up in a monolithic identity in which there is no room for contradictions and anomalies. His dichotomies make one wish for a comparative anthropology/sociology of exceptions, focusing not on taken-for-granted typicalities but rather on Brazilians who hate soccer and samba, Americans who love Carnival, and so forth. Such analyses would at least have the virtue of unpredictability, of not leaving us incarcerated in the prisons of national stereotype. Such binaristic comparisons, in sum, delineate overdrawn dichotomies rather than differentiated commonalities, resulting in the "ontologization" of cultural difference.

Race through a Comparative Prism

Much of the comparative reflection on Brazil, France, and the United States explores the "touchy" subjects of slavery and race. Cross-national race-related comparisons have been instrumentalized in extremely diverse ways, emphasizing contrasts, similarities, or complementarities.[18] Comparison has been deployed by American blacks (or progressive whites) to needle the white-dominated United States, as when American blacks exalted France's relatively benign domestic model, or Brazil's apparent lack of racial tension and prejudice, as a way of shaming a segregated white America. At times we find what Bakhtin calls "double-voiced discourse," as when African Americans praise Brazil's miscegenated cordiality in order to criticize white racism in the United States but confide to fellow blacks that the situation in Brazil is less than ideal. Or comparison can be used in the reverse direction, by Brazilian blacks to needle the white Brazilian elite, as if to say: "Look at those American blacks, unlike we Brazilian blacks, they've gained real status and power! They have generals and mayors and intellectuals and celebrities and they're constantly visible in the media, and now they have a black president!" Or comparisons can be instrumentalized by the white Brazilian elite, as if to remind black Brazilians that they are lucky to be in Brazil and how much worse off they would be over there, in the racist United States. And comparison can be wielded as a conservative warning, as when white Brazilian (or French) opponents of multiculturalism or affirmative action in Brazil or France argue that it will bring U.S.-style tensions and even segregation.

African Americans have historically looked both to France and Brazil as models of nonracist societies. Many Brazilian blacks, conversely, have pointed to the African American civil rights movement as a model of activism and pride. Already in 1918, a writer for the black journal *O Alfinete* exhorted fellow blacks to "strive to eradicate our illiteracy and see whether or not we can imitate the North American blacks."[19] And in 1933, another black Brazilian writer praised the "confident and self-possessed" African American who "lifts up his head," arguing that the Brazilian model is more devastating for blacks even than the brutal American model: "The Americans lynch fifty Negroes a year. We kill the entire Brazilian Negro race."[20] At times, North American comparative commentary conveys an ethnocentric and subalternizing stagism, the idea that Brazilian blacks need to "catch up" with American black achievements.

Although intellectuals in all three countries have engaged in comparative scholarship concerning slavery and discrimination, the debate often operates within nationalist boundaries whereby scholars ignore the "family resemblances" to be found in the countries of the Black Atlantic. National narcissism sometimes leads intellectuals from the nation-states of the Black Atlantic to project racism as characteristic only of "other" nations, as if conquest and slavery-spawned oppression were a monopoly of only one country. French commentators sometimes like to forget France's massive participation in the slave trade. Popular mythology in the United States, meanwhile, claims that it, unlike European nations, is not a colonial or imperial nation.

Just as narcissism sometimes lies at the core of cross-national comparison, so can it be found at the core of official versions of the history of slavery. Thus some nationalist historians in the United States, France, and Brazil offer prettified versions of their country's relation to slavery, downplaying the cruelty or longevity of the institution, or its continuing traces in the present. In the United States, slavery, even though it lasted for centuries, is sometimes treated, in school textbooks for example, as an early and temporary glitch in an overarching narrative of progress. It is presented as the exception to the rule of democracy, when in fact slavery and segregation have been more the rule, and freedom and equal rights more the exception. In Brazil, some historians argued for another version of "exceptionality," in the guise of a suave version of slavery in the past, and a cordiality and lack of conflict in the present, a relative benevolence variously explained by the heritage of Portuguese flexibility and racial tolerance or by Catholicism's more inclusive and corporative embrace or by widespread mixing and miscegenation.

For many scholars, the two situations offer variations on a theme of racial hierarchy: the differences have to do with the specific modalities of domination. One staple contrast in the scholarship is between the virulent and phobic racism typical of the United States, especially in the past, and the more camouflaged, paternalistic, and "cordial" racism more typical of Brazil. But another position argues that precisely because racism in the United States was so virulent, blacks were more motivated to struggle against it; African Americans had no illusion of an easy assimilation. Brazil, in contrast, seems at first glance to present a situation of "racism without racists" where there is no Ku Klux Klan, no lynching (except of "marginals" who just "happen" to be black), and where politicians seldom make racist statements, yet where black people are constant victims of informal discrimination and are even more disempowered politically, in some ways, than they are in the United States. Race, in this sense, is both a kind of salt rubbed into the wounds of class, and a wound in itself.

After more than a century of comparative studies of slavery, race, and discrimination in the United States and Brazil, scholars are beginning to pursue comparative analyses of race and racism in France and Brazil. Alexandra Poli, for example, compares the dominant racial mythologies of the two countries, noting that the myth of racial democracy in Brazil seems at first glance to be the polar opposite of the French myth of the République. While one common Brazilian line sees the harmonious racial relations created by miscegenation as the key to Brazilian democracy, the French republican myth preaches the refusal of cultural particularism in order to assure equal treatment for all citizens. Meanwhile, the critics of this latter position argue that the impossibility of taking into account differences related to the body, to origin, to ethnicity, or religion—and even the absence of race-based statistics—prevents a realistic assessment of the contours of racial discrimination.

Despite the clear differences, the two models share, according to Poli, their denial of the experience of victims oppressed by racism and discrimination who are expected to keep quiet in the face of the aggressions they have suffered. Thus "racial democracy" in Brazil and "republican values" in France constitute the ideological background for any discussion of racism in the two countries: "The expressions 'country of the rights of man' and 'the country of the mixture of races' serve to reinforce the unity of the people and exclude from the outset any discussion of racism."[21] Yet in both France and Brazil, citizens have protested discrimination and asserted their ethnic, cultural, and religious "right" to difference in such a way as to bring the issue of racism and discrimination back to the table, bypassing narcissistic discussions of "who is less racist?"

While comparison can become an instrument of placing nations or cultures in a rigid hierarchical paradigm, or for establishing rigid and reified contrasts, it can also serve as a trampoline for epistemological leaps and dialogical interventions. It is in this context that we will draw attention to a specific stream of cross-cultural comparative writing concerning the European indigenous encounter, to wit, an ongoing intertext of French writing about Brazil, and specifically about the Brazilian Indian and about Afro-Brazilian culture. While cross-cultural comparisons tend to treat the two societies in question in their hegemonic forms, this has not always been the case. French commentary on Brazilian Indians, for example, goes back to the travel writings of the early sixteenth century, beginning with French captain Paulmier de Gonneville's "relation" to the French authorities about his 1503–5 voyage to Brazil, just three years after Pedro Cabral's "discovery."[22] A number of sixteenth-century texts—notably André Thévet's *Les singularités de la France Antartique* (1557) and *Cosmographie universelle* (1575), Jean de Léry's *L'Histoire d'un voyage à la terre du Brésil* (1578), and the German Hans Staden's sensationally titled *Brasilien: Die wahrhaftige Historie der wilden nacken, grimmigen Menschenfresser-Leute* (1557)—emerged out of an aborted French attempt to found a colony near present-day Rio de Janeiro, called "France Antartique," which lasted from 1555 until 1560.

　　Sixteenth-century cultural differences not only between Europeans (French versus Portuguese; Protestant versus Catholic; Christian against Jew) but also between Europeans and native Brazilians (the misnamed "Indians") shaped how the various groups conceptualized the Tupi peoples, the native group that the French, in this case Protestant French from Normandy and Brittany, came to know with a greater intimacy than did the conquering Portuguese. This encounter became an exercise in comparative cross-cultural projection between the French Huguenot minority and the indigenous Tupi peoples in Brazil. Just as the native peoples projected their cosmologies and assumptions onto the Europeans, different European groups projected their ideologies onto the Tupinamba.

　　These differential readings by Christian factions become evident in their treatment of the Tupinamba leader Cunhambebe, the leader of the Federation of the Tamoios, an aggregation of native groups fighting Portuguese colonization. Although Cunhambebe was a French ally, the Catholic Thévet and the Protestant Léry do not portray him in the same way. The official cosmographer Thévet sees Cunhambebe as comparable to a French king; as Frank Lestringant points out, he royalizes Cunhambebe with exuberant eulogies to the "King of Ubatuba"; he turns the cacique into a French-style monarch.[23] The Huguenot Léry, meanwhile, deeply skeptical toward any monarchy reminiscent of the one that practiced such cruelty against his coreligionists in Europe, resents any authority incarnated in a single person. He therefore mocks Thévet's royalization of Cunhambebe and sees him instead as comparable to the leader of a closely knit, ideal Protestant-style *communitas*. The factual attributes of Cunhambebe, in short, are less important than the discursive and ideological grids through which the comparison is seen. Both Thévet and Léry offer a positive image of Cunhambebe, but Thévet sees him as incarnating a divinely sanctioned hierarchical society, while Léry sees him as the communal avatar of a Protestant leader of an egalitarian community.

In *L'Histoire d'un voyage à la terre du Brésil* (1578), Léry described his experience, some two decades earlier, of being captured by Brazilian Indians and welcomed into the Tupinamba community while waiting for his own ritual deglutition. Léry used comparison as a didactic device to explain Tupi culture to French readers. Claude Lévi-Strauss hailed Léry's history as "a masterpiece of anthropological literature," while Michel de Certeau called Léry's account seminal for historiography and ethnography, the equivalent of a "primal scene in the construction of ethnological discourse."[24] By defending what he sees as the gregarious cultural values and practices of his captors, Léry uses comparison both to explain Tupi customs—for example, by making analogies to French customary practices—but also to point out the relative humanity of the natives when compared to a Europe scarred by wars of religion. Léry contrasts the cruelty of the French Admiral Villegagnon, who denied his companions nourishment, with the open-handed generosity of the Tupinamba. The Indians walk around naked, Léry tells us, but only to avoid having to constantly change clothes in a hot climate.[25] Anticipating Jean-Jacques Rousseau's ideas about child rearing, Léry proposes the practical Tupinamba manner of nursing and caring for children as a superior model for French parents. When Léry explains the European custom of saving up money to leave an inheritance for the children, an elderly Tupinamba ridicules the idea since "the same earth that feeds the parents will feed the children."[26]

In contrast to the later European naturalists, who compared the fertility of Europe to the supposed sterility of the Americas as a place of stunted growth and degeneration, Léry described a robust Tupi society where people were stronger, fitter, and less prone to disease than Europeans, and where everything that was planted grew. Léry draws contrasts between the two groups—native nudity / European dress; native festivity / European productive labor—but he avoids ranking the two cultures. One might object that Léry is actually ranking the two cultures and finding the Tupi superior to the Europeans, but this is not exactly the case. First, Léry points out many negative features of Tupi life as well, their penchant for cannibalism, for example, and their perpetual small-scale wars.

He does not applaud cannibalism, but he points out that it had been seen in Europe as well during the religious wars. Second, he does not "go native"—he remains a believing Protestant Christian, and more precisely a Huguenot. Third, he generally speaks not of morally superior and inferior *people* but rather of better and worse *practices,* such as child rearing, that can be adopted by any group. He does not make his comparisons in order to assert superiority but rather in the interest of finding pragmatic benefits in the practices of another culture.

After Thévet and Léry, this strain of thought entered the European Renaissance more directly and dramatically with Michel de Montaigne. As an early exponent of what would later be called cultural relativism, Montaigne takes from Léry the emphasis on primitive communalism, the absence of laws of inheritance, and so forth. Montaigne met three Tupinamba Indians in 1562, at the court of King Charles IX, and the memory of the encounter followed him throughout his life. By Montaigne's account, the Tupinamba engaged in a comparative critique of French society based on their own axiomatic principles of consensus rule and equal sharing; they wondered why tall adults could bow down to a small boy (the regent), why some people ate well and others ate barely at all, and why those who barely ate did not strangle those who were eating well. Two centuries before the French Revolution, Montaigne relayed and ventriloquized the Indian voice to criticize European civilizational hierarchies. Here, too, it is easy to say that Montaigne was simply turning the usual rankings upside down, but that is again not quite true: rather, he is deploying a comparison in order to question the conventional assumption of superiority of his own culture.

Montaigne practiced a rhetoric of chiasmus or civilizational reversals by arguing that the violence of Tupinamba cannibalism paled in comparison to that triggered by religious wars in Europe, where people were drawn and quartered and tortured in the name of a religion of love. With their irreverent questions and their implied comparisons, the Tupinamba, at least as Montaigne presents them, demolished with a few probing questions the prestige of the hereditary monarchy and the class system. Centuries later, Lévi-Strauss went out in search of "Indians," writing consciously in the tradition of Léry and Rousseau, whom he called "the most ethnographic of the philosophers." We discern here a different modality of comparison, in the form of quasi-allegorical identifications and investments operating across time as well as space, with Lévi-Strauss stressing his strong sense of identification with Léry and praising the generic traits and formal qualities of the *Voyage* as a model for an ethnological essay.

On some levels, one might argue that Lévi-Strauss deploys a technique of reverse ranking, lauding Indian social life as an alternative and even superior social model. While Western culture, as Lévi-Strauss put it in

The View from Afar, "isolates man from the rest of creation and [defines] too narrowly the boundaries separating him from other living beings," native culture sees all of life on a continuum. While the Biblical tradition sees human beings as lords of creation, native thought sees them as collaborators rather than dominators of nature.[27] Given his insider-outside perspective on a Europe about to slaughter its "internal others," Lévi-Strauss perhaps found in the gentle ways of the "external others" of Europe an alternative to what John Murray Cuddihy calls the ordeals of European "civility."[28] One might accuse Lévi-Strauss's praise of the Indians as "Rousseauiste," and a simple reversal of valence, but there are two important differences: 1) Lévi-Strauss, unlike Rousseau, had detailed and intimate knowledge of the Nambiquara and the Bororo and made precise observations about them. And 2) given what was happening in the Europe of the Shoah, he had every reason to cast doubt on any pretension to ethical superiority on the part of Europe. But beyond that there is an important difference between a civilizational ranking that merely resembles and consolidates the preexisting hierarchical power arrangements between peoples and a sympathetic view of an alien culture, which challenges at the same time those dominant powers and the conceptual models deployed in the conventional ranking. Lévi-Strauss deploys comparison as a critique of Eurocentric ranking; his praise of the lifeways of the Nambiquara is not designed to consolidate privilege but rather to undermine it.

Comparison as Excess Seeing

In the case of the French polymath Roger Bastide (1898–1974), the foreigner's "look from afar" (Lévi-Strauss) illuminated Brazil even for Brazilians themselves. The French anthropologist lived in Brazil for sixteen years, teaching sociology at the University of São Paulo where he took over an academic chair first occupied by Lévi-Strauss. In a sense, Bastide prolongs the tradition going back to Jean de Léry, but he identified less with indigenous people than with black Brazilians, or more precisely, with Afro-Brazilian culture. While the official representatives of France were glorying in a "Latinité" shared by Brazilian and French white elites, Bastide discerned the cultural agency of a socially despised, déclassé, black Brazil.[29]

Bastide exemplifies a kind of transnational gnosis. Born a French Protestant, he draws variously on African religion, Brazilian literature, French anthropology, North American sociology, and Chicago School anthropology along with many other currents, becoming a transcultural "medium" who spoke through and to these various voices. To borrow a comparison from Afro-Brazilian religions, he was the "horse" who was "mounted" by diverse methodological "spirits." At the same time, he can also be compared to the "ethnographic surrealists" of whom James Clifford speaks, that is, the French writers who orchestrated an encounter between artistic modernism—in this case, not only French but also Brazilian modernism—and the socioethnography of African and Afrodiasporic culture. Bastide offers a signal instance of the power of what we have elsewhere called, paraphrasing Raymond Williams, "analogical structures of feeling" as a key to transcultural comprehension.[30]

In his studies of the possession religions of Bahia, Bastide broke with the dominant views of African-derived religions as pathological or irrational, appreciating them on their own terms and merits. Most visitors, whether French or American, were inclined to see little more than superstition or animism in the West African religions as practiced in Brazil. Bastide's project was to show that these religions were not "superstitious, quasi-demonic cults but rather legitimate belief systems which embraced a cosmology, a psychology, and a theodicy; and that they express an African thought that is erudite and deeply cultivated."[31]

Long before authors such as Clifford and George Marcus spoke of reflexive anthropology, but very much alongside and in dialogue with the ethnographic surrealists, Bastide developed an "anti-ethnocentric method" with quasi-mystical overtones: "It is a matter, for the sociologist, of not placing oneself outside social experience but rather of living it . . . we have to transform ourselves into that which we are studying, into the multitude, the mass, the class, or the caste . . . It is necessary, as in the act of love, to transcend our own personality in order to join ourselves to the soul linked to what is being studied."[32] Here, ethnography itself becomes a kind of trance, the trigger for a transformation of identities that recalls the scrambled analogies, the exchange of identities, literally "at play" in *candomblé*, where the medium becomes the saint, where male can become female, the adult a child, and so forth.

Bastide suspended the usual ideal of scientific distance and famously declared *Africanus sum* (I am African), a formulation that ironically mingles complete identification with Africa with a Latin language redolent of cultural capital and quintessential pan-Europeanness. Coming up against the limits of Eurotropic analogies, Bastide acknowledged that three centuries of rationalist Cartesianism had blinded him to the complexity of African religion, speaking of the "subtle philosophy" of candomble. Bastide believed in "immersion" (*mergulho*) in the culture being studied, while also practicing a certain reflexivity about his own methods and limitations. He practices both identification and exotopy, the trance and the distanced analysis performed subsequent to the trance. He was also careful not to fall into the trap of Negritude-style (and later Afrocentric) essentialism about Africa, aware of the gap between the "real" Africa and the Africa reinvented in Brazilian *terreiros*. At the same time, his descriptions are marked by a vitalism that runs the risk of reproducing a gendered dichotomy of rationality versus intuition that at times fails to grasp the semiotic complexity of *candomblé* as a living, changing form of religious practice.

For Bastide, the recognition of incommensurabilities and even the limits of cross-cultural comparison triggered an epistemological leap beyond the confines of one's own axiomatic culture. Unlike many anthropologists, Bastide recognized the limitations of the a priori systems and discourses and other cultural baggage that he carried to Brazil, not only in anthropology but also sociology. The Brazilian experience, then, sensitized Bastide to the epistemological limitations of Eurotropic modes of comparative analysis. Rather than force those modes and conceptual categories onto an experience that escapes and resists them, and rather than rank religions in an order of superiority and inferiority, Bastide opened himself up to new modes, including poetic modes, of apprehension. But unlike other writers, Bastide does not Orientalize Brazil as a place where European categories do not work because of its putative irrationality. Rather, he discerns the inadequacies of the categories themselves and pleads for new paradigms worthy of a complex culture that is not inferior but only different.

The Misrule of Metaphor

In this essay, we have seen comparison deployed as an exercise in ranking and civilisational superiority (Hegel, Weber), as a narcissistic fantasy (the diverse national exceptionalisms), as a binarist essentializing of complex cultures (DaMatta), and finally (in Léry, Lévi-Strauss, and Bastide) as an instrument for discerning comparabilities within and between in other ways incommensurable societies. While our text explores three national zones, we have also tried to transcend nationalist framing. We address cross-national and transnational comparisons in order to perform an analytical dislocation by constructing and deconstructing, threading and unraveling, the tangled webs of ideas and practices that constitute complicated national relationships. It is not a question of merely juxtaposing three national histories, then, but rather of exploring their interrelations and linked analogies within a global system of power. Indeed, part of the methodological/theoretical thrust of our project is to stress the interstitial connections and interwoven strands that make up all national formations, which binaristic cross-cultural comparisons have often failed to capture.

Much as Paul Ricoeur in *The Rule of Metaphor* deems metaphor to be a cognitive instrument, so the more general phenomenon of comparison can also be seen as a perennial model of cognition that seeks out and delineates analogies and disanalogies in the search for cross-cultural precision and comprehension. In this sense, we are also interested in the role of metaphor in actively reshaping conceptualizations of academic disciplines and the relations between them. We are struck, in this sense, by the emergence of certain types of tropes within scholarly trends that seek to go beyond the nation-state as the primary unit of analysis. Manifest in such prefixes as "trans" and "cross" and "inter" and "meta," and in the profusion of terms like "transnational," "diasporic," "trans-cultural," "exilic," and "globalized," this trend often appeals to oceanic imagery. The phrase "Black Atlantic" (R. F. Thompson, Paul Gilroy) and coinages such as "circum-Atlantic performance" (Joseph Roach) and "planetary currents" (Peter Linebaugh and Marcus Rediker) and "tidalectics" (Edward Kamau Brathwaite), and even emerging subfields like "oceanic studies" and "island studies," form part of this tendency. Within a poetics of flows and eddies and currents, aquatic imagery is deployed as a dissolvent of borders and binarisms, all part of a search for a more fluid idiom for addressing transnational circuitries of ideas.

Transnational studies also deploy tropes of color to speak both of racialized societies and of a historicized grid of analysis. While the "Black Atlantic" evokes the Middle Passage and the chronotope of the ship, an ancillary concept like the "Red Atlantic" would conjure up canoes and kayaks, the Conquest, and the Trail of Tears.[33] "Red" and "Black" and "White" do not refer to isolatable and unchanging "races"—first, because no one is literally black, white, or red. English colonists, for example, reported that the native peoples of North America were of white complexion, while French and Portuguese colonists said that the native peoples of Brazil were of the same color as the Iberians. Here we intend tropes of color not to refer to distinct races but rather as positions on a spectrum, as an experimental method, a way of casting a certain blackish or reddish light on history to see what becomes visible when we see the history of the "spectral" Atlantic as Black or Red or White or all at the same time. Our assumption, shaped by critical race, intersectional-feminist, and postcolonial cultural studies, is that such demographic/symbolic tropes as blackness and whiteness and redness are overlapping and relational; they take on meaning only in reference to one another, as part of a mobile, ever-changing configuration striated by power and inequality.

Our study of the role of comparison in the Red, Black, and White Atlantic in three zones echoes the triangular traffic by which Europe sent manufactured goods to Africa, African slaves to the New World, and raw materials back to Europe in an unending and lucrative cycle of exploitation. The metaphor of "currents" is especially suggestive in that the Atlantic Ocean is swept by vast circular "rivers" and "streams"— a northern circle running in a clockwise direction from its southern beginnings, and a southern circle flowing in a counterclockwise direction, in a swirling movement evocative of the trade of ideas and goods back and forth between Africa, Europe, and the Americas.[34] Given these liquid transfers and "trade winds"—an expression that goes back to the slave trade—the issue becomes one of discerning the common currents running through the various zones, the ways that histories and texts and discourses mingle and interact within situations of unequal liquidity.

All national comparison takes place on transnational territory. We have proceeded from the assumption that all nations are, on one level, transnations and that all cultures are transcultures, which cannot be seen as monolithic or as congruent with the boundaries of nation-states. While nation-states exercise political and to some extent economic sovereignty—and while some regimes have brutally demonstrated the horrific damage wreaked by nation-states—nations are still sites of perpetual contestation, not reducible to single ideologies. Culture, furthermore, does not conform to neat political boundaries or obey the mandates even of the most authoritarian regimes. National cultural fields are dynamic, heteroglossic, impure, dissensual, and internally differentiated. Cultures are not comparable in the form of a stable set of unchanging properties or a static list of traits. France is not eternally Cartesian; Brazil is not perpetually Carnivalesque; the United States is not unfailingly puritanical. Although cross-border comparisons have often conjured up the image of nations as coherent, consistent, and hermetically sealed units, our emphasis has been on the contradictions, gaps, and fissures within a transnational perspective. We have called attention, in this sense, to what Édouard Glissant calls "transversalities," that is, the comparisons and dialogisms taking place across fluid transnational spaces—not between nation-states but rather between "nation-relations."

NOTES

Some of this material is drawn from the manuscript of *The Culture Wars in Translation* (forthcoming). The project of the book was outlined in preliminary form in Robert Stam and Ella Shohat, "Traveling Multiculturalism: A Trinational Debate in Translation," in *Postcolonial Studies and Beyond*, ed. Ania Loomba, Suvir Kaul, Matti Bunzel, Antoinette Burton, and Jed Esty (Durham, NC: Duke Univ. Press, 2005), 293–316.

1   For an extended elaboration of this idea in relation to film adaptations of novels, see Robert Stam, *Literature through Film: Realism, Magic, and the Art of Adaptation* (Oxford: Blackwell, 2005).

2   Pierre Bourdieu, "The Social Conditions of the International Circulation of Ideas," in *Bourdieu: A Critical Reader*, ed. Richard Shusterman (Oxford: Blackwell, 1999), 223.

3   Some forms of American-style exceptionalism could be called solipsistic ethnocentrism, taking the form not of explicit claims of superiority but rather of a lack of interest in other nations, even those in which the United States is intervening. The U.S. educational system has become more nation centered, with less space for geography and world history, while the U.S. media increasingly limit their foreign coverage to spectacular catastrophes or direct challenges to U.S. interests. U.S. exceptionalism has recently morphed into the idea that the United States makes exceptions for itself when it comes to international law and human rights. See Michael Hardt and Antonio Negri, *Multitude: War and Democracy in the Age of Empire* (New York: Penguin, 2004), 8–9.

4   In our book *Flagging Patriotism: Crises of Narcissism and Anti-Americanism* (New York: Routledge, 2007) we support political anti-Americanism that critiques American social systems and foreign policy but reject culturalist forms of anti-Americanism that based their arguments on supposed ethnic "traits."

5   G. W. F. Hegel, *The Philosophy of History* (New York: Colonial Press, 1899), 84.

6   We explore the subject of national narcissism and exceptionalism at greater length in *Flagging Patriotism*.

7   Paul Adam, *Les visages du Brésil* (Paris: P. Laffitte, 1910), 150–51. Unless otherwise noted, all translations from French and Portuguese are our own.

8   Adam, *Les visages du Brésil*, 165–66.

9   Jacqueline Bardolph, *Etudes postcoloniales et littérature* (Paris: Champion, 2002), 17–18.

10   Joseph Burnichon, *Le Brésil d'aujourdhui* (Paris: Perrin, 1910), 77.

11   Abel Bonnard, *Ocean et Brésil* (Paris: Flammarion, 1929), 76–77.

12   Pierre Bourdieu, "Deux imperialismes de l'universel," in *L'Amérique des Français*, ed. Christine Faure and Tom Bishop (Paris: Francis Bourin, 1992), 149–55.

13   See Henry M. Brackenridge, *Voyage to South America, Performed by Order of the American Government in the Years 1817 and 1818, in the Frigate Congress*, 2 vols. (London: John Miller, 1820), 1:128–29. Cited in Denis Rolland, ed. *Le Brésil et le monde* (Paris: L'Harmattan, 1998), 25–26.

14   Jesse Souza, ed., *A invisibilidade da desigualdade brasileira* (Belo Horizonte: Editora UFMG, 2006), 100.

15   See Jesse Souza, *A modernizacao seletiva: Uma reintrpretacao do dilema brasileiro* (Brasilia: UnB, 2000).

16   See Caetano Veloso, *Verdade tropical* (São Paulo: Companhia das Letras, 1997), 14.

17   Veloso, *Verdade tropical*, 118

18   For an illuminating critique of comparison as a method, see Micol Siegel, *Uneven Encounters: Making Race and Nation in Brazil and the United States* (Durham, NC: Duke Univ. Press, 2009).

19   A. Oliveira, "Aos nossos leitores," *O Alfinete*, September 3, 1918; cited in Siegel, *Uneven Encounters*, 190.

20   Jose Correia Leite, "O grande problema nacional," *Evolucao*, May 13, 1933; quoted in Siegel, *Uneven Encounters*, 202.

21   Alexandra Poli, "Faire face au racisme en France et au Brésil: De la condamnation morale à l'aide aux victimes," *Cultures and Conflicts* 59 (2005): 11–45.

22   See Binot Paulmier de Gonneville, *Le voyage de Gonneville (1503–1505): Et la decouverte de la Normandie par les Indiens du Brésil*, with commentary by Leyla Perrone-Moises, trans. Ariane Witkowski (Paris: Chandeigne, 1995).

23   See Frank Lestringant, *Le huguenot et le sauvage* (Paris: Klincksieck, 1999), 26.

24   Michel de Certeau, *The Writing of History*, trans. Tom Conley (New York: Columbia Univ. Press, 1988), 211.

25   Here we find a clear contrast with Robinson Crusoe who, after many years on his tropical island, is obsessed with remaining clothed, even though he is alone. Crusoe's wealth, incidentally, is generated by a sugar mill (*engenho*) in Bahia, Brazil.

26   The 1989 documentary *Kayapo: Out of the Forest* (Granada Television, 1989), which concerns the well-publicized protests of a coalition of indigenous groups against the construction of a hydroelectric, features similar dialogues between the protestors and the representatives of the energy corporation Eletronote.

27   Todorov argues that Lévi-Strauss, who claims to be a cultural relativist, ultimately "finds Indian culture superior," thus still falling into the trap of ranking and mere binary reversal. Tzvetan Todorov, *On Human Diversity: Nationalism, Racism, and Exoticism in French Thought*, trans. Catherine Porter (Cambridge, MA: Harvard Univ. Press, 1993), 60–89.

28   See John Murray Cuddihy, *The Ordeals of Civility: Freud, Marx, Levi-Strauss and the Jewish Struggle with Modernity* (Boston: Beacon, 1974).

29   Bastide ultimately wrote thirty books on an astonishingly wide variety of topics, ranging from psychoanalysis (*A psicanalise do cafune*, 1941), to literature (*A poesia Afro-Brasileira*, 1943), to mysticism (*Imagens do nordeste mistico em branco e preto*, 1945), to racial relations (*Relacoes entre negros e brancos em São Paulo*, 1955), to folklore (*Sociologia do folclore brasileiro*, 1959), to Afro-Brazilian religions in general (*As religiões africanas no Brasil*, 1971). His work transgressed diverse frontiers: those between disciplines; those between the "high" and "low" arts; those between class and racially defined groups; and those between the sacred and the profane. By mingling the social sciences with artistic analysis, Bastide anticipated what would later be called "cultural studies."

30   See our *Unthinking Eurocentrism* (London: Routledge, 1994), 351.

31   Roger Bastide, *O candomblé da Bahia* (São Paulo: Companha Editora Nacional, 1978), 10–11.

32   Roger Bastide, "Macunaima em Paris," in *O Estado de São Paulo*, February 3, 1946; quoted in Fernanda Arêas Peixoto, *Dialogos Brasileiros* (São Paulo: Ediora da Universidade de São Paulo, 2000), 16.

33   The trope of the "Red Atlantic" is explored in Robert Stam's essay "The Red Atlantic: Tupi Theory and the Franco-Brazilian-Indigenous Dialogue," presented at the Shelby Cullom Davis Center for Historical Studies at Princeton University, April 17, 2009. This concept will also form part of our *The Culture Wars in Translation*.

34   See Jack D. Forbes, *The American Discovery of Europe* (Urbana: Univ. of Illinois Press, 2007), ch. 2.

CHAPTER EIGHT

Race and the Possibilities of Comparative Critique

Ania Loomba

IS IT POSSIBLE TO USE comparative methods to "provincialize Europe"? Recent debates in several disciplines have made it abundantly clear that comparison, as a perspective and a method, has historically served to shore up Eurocentric and discriminatory ideologies and practices. The most productive potential of comparison is that it can establish connections and relations across seemingly disparate contexts and thus challenge provincialism and exceptionalism. But it is precisely this potential of comparative thought that has fed into the development of "global" or "universal" paradigms that posits a hierarchical relation between the entities being compared or simply exclude large chunks of reality from its domain. In other words, the perspective remains narrow while claims are enlarged.

The possibility of alternative methodologies, of course, has been the focus of recent debates within comparative literature and political science, both of which have historically claimed that they can address the "global."[1] As a host of recent comparative projects begin to shift the angle of vision to the global South and decenter Europe (but without denying the power and legacy of colonial-capitalist modernity) it sometimes appears that the Eurocentric roots of comparative methodologies are so deep that it is impossible to denaturalize the habits of mind that have emerged from them.[2] In this essay, I want to explore the possibilities of a comparative critique of racial ideologies across temporal and spatial boundaries. At first sight, such a project would seem particularly problematic, given that the "development" of racial ideologies in the West depended upon making particular kinds of comparisons between women, non-Europeans, blacks, religious minorities, the poor, sexual "deviants," and animals in order to deepen, broaden, and fine-tune the idea of a "natural" hierarchy between peoples and groups.[3] Such comparison was foundational to disciplines such as anthropology, but more broadly to religious, literary, and cultural discourse. It was also an essential part of the very development of racial "science"—analogies and "metaphor [otherwise regarded as antithetical to the method of science]" became "part of the logic of science itself."[4] To write the history of racism thus necessarily involves a study of the work done by comparative thinking. Might such a history also allow us to turn comparison on its Eurocentric head and reveal the global connections that have shaped racial histories in different parts of the world? Or would it be like trying to use the master's tools to dismantle the master's house or to curse in the colonizer's tongue?

At the most fundamental level, the activity of comparison is an outcome of any process of categorization, which is one of the fundamental forms of knowledge production. As Geoffrey C. Bowker and Susan Leigh Star remind us, "sorting things out" into groups may be a necessary part of making sense of the world, but it is crucial to understand the ways in which this work of classification happens—in the sciences, in the social sciences, in the humanities, and indeed in everyday life. Who decides what count as categories, and the lines between them? How are such categories institutionalized so that they become received knowledge? Because over time we learn to take classificatory schemas for granted, they get naturalized and then exert a huge power over us to the point where the line between what is natural and what is socially constructed is obfuscated.[5] These insights can be directed to the work of comparison itself: who decides how categories are to be constructed or which categories can be compared or which comparisons are legitimate and which not? Today we might ask, under what conditions can we denaturalize existing comparative methods and perspectives? In addition, we might ask: is comparison a *necessary* corollary to the work of categorization? On the other hand, can we make use of the comparative method to question these categories themselves?

Comparisons between the racial ideologies of different historical periods, between race and class, between racial and religious difference, and most crucially, between racial formations in different parts of the world are often undertaken by deploying dominant understandings of race, which are themselves colored by the perspectives and methods normalized in and through racial histories. So, for example, theorists and historians of race have widely worked with the assumption that "race" is a "modern" European ideology crafted in the crucible of Atlantic slavery and anchored in the belief that there are "biological" differences between groups of people.[6] The comparison of premodern with modern European ideologies of difference, and of different racial formations across the world, is often shaped by these assumptions. To take two very different instances that will concern me in this essay: it is still common to hear that it is anachronistic to identify racism in the premodern European world because, at that time, human differences were understood to be rooted in "culture" rather than in "nature." For similar reasons, caste exploitation in India has also been excluded from discussion as a form of racism. Strikingly, and not accidentally, this

> "Clash of civilizations"

understanding of "caste" also travels to Latin America, where also it is routinely contrasted with "race."[7]

In this essay, I will briefly discuss both these instances of "premodern" difference, suggesting that we revisit their relationship to the supposedly "modern" forms of racism with which they are routinely contrasted. This exercise allows us to see what is common to these two otherwise diverse histories, and helps us articulate the politics of comparison as a method, *and* to intervene in theoretical and political discussions about the histories and present forms of "race." In both cases, religion is the central issue that seems to cloud the discussion. Religious difference is understood to be rooted in culture, affiliated to discourses of faith and belief rather than those of the body, and therefore, at least theoretically, less rigid. But the history of racial formations testifies not to a neat separation between these categories but to their deep interconnection; without such interconnection we cannot understand the very development of what is now referred to as "scientific" racism. Indeed, "biology" itself has a history, and one that is profoundly shaped by the history of racial ideologies. The separation of "biology" from "culture" is the outcome of this very history. A mechanical and historically uninflected understanding of "biology" obscures the complex contours and genealogies of racial ideologies and reinforces the divisions between "culture" and "nature," which were not established in an earlier period and should not be understood as absolute in our own. Indeed, comparing earlier histories of race with later ones, or European histories with non-European ones, illuminates why concepts such as "biology" and "culture" should be understood as terms whose meaning fluctuates contextually and in relation to one another.

Shu-mei Shih rightly suggests that "the colonial turn" is crucial for understanding racisms in the contemporary world, and for connecting the apparently different forms taken by racism in the "metropole" and the "colony," but this move is not enough.[8] We also need to be able to situate "the colonial turn" itself in a wider and longer history and to understand how the forms *it* took were shaped by precolonial and non-European ways of thinking. We can then revisit more clearly the complex legacies that colonialism has spawned—legacies that cannot be understood through conventional, and still dominant, ways of categorizing racial formations.[9]

In medieval and early modern England, religious outsiders, minorities, as well as people from a vast spectrum of non-European lands were routinely described in terms of color; so in writings of these periods, we get black Jews, black Saracens (or Muslims), black gypsies, and black Indians, just as we get black devils and black evildoers. For some writers, blackness became synonymous with particular geographies—thus, in 1559, George Abbot writes: "The men of the south part of India are black, and therefore are called men of Inde."[10] Blackness was a condition of the lack of Christianity—the English term "blackamoor" fused blackness with Moor (a term that originally meant Muslim). A reverse logic is also visible, as when the seventeenth-century Dutch traveler Jan Huyghen van Linschoten writes about "the black people or Caffares of the land of Mozambique" drawing on the Arabic word "kaffir" meaning "unbeliever" to describe blacks.[11]

Medieval texts often feature the conversion and consequent whitening of such folk: thus, upon conversion, black Moors fantastically become white, and unbelievers find their deformed offspring transformed, as in the thirteenth-century *Cursor Mundi* or the early fourteenth-century *The King of Tars and the Soudan of Damas*. While such transformations can be legitimately interpreted as the sign of a somewhat fluid notion of identity, at another level they can also be seen to tighten the association of particular skin color and bodily attributes with particular faiths or moral qualities, which is a central feature of racial ideologies. The equation between a particular kind of body and a particular kind of religious belief is underlined when a black Muslim is depicted as being transformed into a white Christian. Indeed, it is often *through* such transformations that medieval texts imply that black and white cannot easily mingle; in the thirteenth-century German romance *Parzival*, for example, the child of a black Moorish woman and a white Christian man is born "dappled"— the black and white parts of his skin remain separate and attest to the difficulty of such mixing.[12]

It is often suggested that it was the medieval and early modern belief in monogenesis—the notion that all human beings were, in the words of St. Augustine, "Adam's progeny [*protoplastos*]"—that more readily admitted the possibility of the conversion of non-Christians to Christianity than the later theory of polygenesis, which was itself shaped in and through colonial history, especially the discovery of the New World, and that made possible the conception of different human groups as distinct species.[13] But, although monogenesis *theoretically* facilitated the possibility of conversion, its actual possibility was severely limited by several prejudices and practices. One was the belief about the fixed moral being of non-Christians, especially Jews and Muslims, and their inability to change. This fixity was routinely compared to the indelibility of blackness, as in the 1560 Geneva Bible's lines: "Can the black Moor change his skin or the leopard his spots? *then* may ye also do good, that are accustomed to do evil."[14] The comparison between faith (an inner, unseen quality, and one which is theoretically changeable) and color (a visible marker, supposedly fixed) is reinforced in many medieval and early modern texts— both literary and nonliterary—that convey the difficulty of converting unbelievers by drawing upon the image of an "Ethiope," "Man of Inde," or "blackamoor" who cannot be washed white. Thus, black skin is fixed as permanent by comparing it to the "indurate heart of heretics," but the comparison in turn anchors the heart of the unbeliever as also unchangeable. We see this in an emblem called "AEthiopem Lavare" in England's earliest emblem book, Thomas Palmer's *Two Hundred Poosees* (1566), where the following lines accompany a picture of two white men washing a black man:

> Why washest thou the man of Inde?
> Why takest thou such pain?
> Black night thou mayest as soon make bright
> Thou labourest all in vain . . .
> Indurate heart of heretics
> Much blacker than the mole;
> With word or writ who seeks to purge,
> Stark dead he blows the coal.[15]

A long tradition of describing both non-Europeans and non-Christians in similar terms was continually reshaped by early modern and then modern discourses.[16] Thus, in 1566, Jean Bodin, the French jurist and political philosopher who is often given the dubious distinction of being the first to articulate modern categories of race, asserted that "Asiatics and Africans, unless indeed by miracles from heaven or by force of arms, do not abandon the religion they once adopted" and immediately proceeded to write about Jews in similar terms: "Certainly that race could never by any reward or punishment be enticed from its doctrines and, dispersed over the whole world, alone it has vigorously maintained its religion, received three thousand years ago."[17] The following passage from a Spanish biography of King Charles V makes the logic of the comparison explicit: "Who can deny that in the descendants of the Jews there persists and endures the evil inclination of their ancient ingratitude and lack of understanding, just as in Negroes [there persists] the inseparability of their blackness. For if the latter should unite themselves a thousand times with white women, the children are born with the dark colour of the father. Similarly, it is not enough for a Jew to be three parts aristocratic or Old Christian for one family-line alone defiles and corrupts him."[18] Written in the context of the anxieties over the conversion of Muslims and Jews to Christianity in Reconquista Spain, comparison in this passage hinges on the specter of sex across accepted lines of community borders in order to render both Jewishness and blackness congenital.

Several critics suggest that it was the *possibility* of religious conversion in Iberia, the fact that millions of Muslims and Jews did convert to Christianity, which heightened anxieties about the nature of Christian

identity—posited increasingly as the necessary requirement of a national identity—and catalyzed the development of biological notions
of race.[19] Such anxieties were in part provoked by the fact that Iberian
Jews, Christians, and Muslims were *not* usually physically distinguishable
from one another. Hence the need to find a distinction that lay deeper
inside, or a "purity of blood," which in this case corresponded exactly
to a supposed "purity of faith." In 1480, the Inquisition had formalized
the correspondence between the two by proclaiming that religious faith
was manifested in "purity of blood" (*limpieza de sangre*). Thus differences
of faith indicated different interior essences, and faith was not a matter
of individual choice.[20]

These histories are not obscure, but their implications continue to be
sidelined by many modern theorists and historians of race who invoke
comparisons across historical periods or geographic spaces only in order
to assert qualitative *differences* between premodern and modern ideologies of race. Thus, one critic working with the assumption that modern
racism is a specifically Atlantic discourse born of black slavery insists
that the blood test in Inquisition Spain was related to the "genealogical
context of families" and not "a belief that Jewishness actually resides in
the blood. It reflected the jural dimensions of structured kinship *rather
than* the fact of biological connection, the significance of the *pater* rather
than the *genitor*."[21] But surely what these blood statutes sought to codify
was the *connection* between "pater" and "genitor"—it was precisely the
genealogy of particular families that shaped the classification of larger
religious and increasingly racialized groups. "Blue blood," or *sangre azul*,
was claimed by several aristocratic families who declared they had never
intermarried with Moors or Jews and hence had fair skins through which
their blue blood could be seen—indeed this context is the origin of the
English phrase "blue blood," which now indicates class status rather than
race but actually rests on the connections between the two. The point
I am making is that comparisons between that moment and ours can
illuminate crucial historical connections that can help us understand
many of our present discourses of race. More specifically, the possibility
of religious conversion did *not* testify in some simple way to a "cultural"
and benign notion of difference but was a contradictory and variable
discourse in which we can detect the development of ideas about inheritance, or what we now call "biology."

The relevance of early modern Iberia to "modern" and American forms
of racism has been acknowledged, but Iberian histories are not sealed
off from those of other European countries at the time because of the
transnational connections between early modern nations and shared histories of slavery. Hence when Elizabeth I of England tried to expel "the
great numbers of Negroes and blackamoors" from her realm, authorizing

a slave trader to take possession of them, she also called them "infidels having no understanding of Christ or his Gospel" who had "crept" into her realm from Spain, implying that they were Spanish Muslims.[22] But such people would not have necessarily been dark skinned; Elizabeth's terminology appears contradictory and hard to interpret unless we keep in mind the overlaps between the discourse of faith and that of the body. The history of English slavery is testimony to such overlaps and contradictions. Precisely because of the conviction that Christians should not be enslaved, the practice of slavery often retarded the possibility of conversion. In 1555, Andrew Boorde's "Book of Knowledge" articulated this through the voice of a slave:

> I am a black More born in Barbary,
> Christian men for money oft doth me buy,
> If I be unchristened, merchants do not care,
> They buy me in markets be I never so bare.[23]

A century later, when Richard Ligon spoke to a plantation owner in Barbados concerning the request of a slave to be converted, he was told that "the people of that island were governed by the laws of England, and by those laws we could not make a Christian a slave." Ligon clarified that "[m]y request was far different from that, for I desired him to make a Slave a Christian. His answer was that it was true, there was a difference in that: But, being once a Christian, he could no more account him a Slave, and so lose the hold they had of them as Slaves, by making them Christians; and by that means should open such a gap as all Planters in the island would curse him. So I was struck mute, and poor *Sambo* kept out of the Church."[24] At the same time, of course, the possibility of conversion was continually invoked as a *justification* for English slavery: "It being a means to better these people, and likewise have influence on these they sell as slaves to the English to persuade them, that by their slavery, their condition will be bettered by their access to knowledge, Arts and Sciences."[25] It is hardly surprising that "An Act against Carnal Copulation between Christian & Heathen," passed in Antigua in 1644, uses the terms "white" and "Christian" interchangeably, as it does "heathen" and "black."[26] Some decades later, the Anglican clergyman Morgan Godwyn, who was forced to flee Virginia because he advocated the conversion of slaves, concluded that "bondage is not inconsistent with Christianity," noting that just as "Negro" and "slave" had "by custom grown homogeneous and convertible," so too "Negro and Christian, Englishman and heathen, are by the like corrupt custom and partiality made opposites."[27] Later, the English parliament was enjoined to proclaim that Africans and indigenous Americans were part of God's plan for salvation and should receive baptism and thus formally abandon "the traditional view that Christians cannot enslave Christians, affirm the property rights of the slave-owners, and destroy any possibility of freedom achieved through baptism."[28]

To recover these histories is also to understand better the connections between what are often treated as divergent histories of colonialism—the Spanish and the Anglo-American—as well as past and present configurations of racial formations. In recent years, antiracist work has been confronted with a "culturalist" discourse, which is often regarded as a new development because it posits uncrossable boundaries between different groups even while unyoking their identities from a biological essence. In a suggestive essay written some time ago, Etienne Balibar suggested that modern "neo-racism" or "racism without race," which "does not have the pseudo-biological concept of race as its main driving force," illustrates that today "culture can also function like a nature," becoming an uncrossable barrier between "us" and "them."[29] It is significant that Balibar compared these new forms of racism, directed at largely Muslim immigrants in Europe, to the anti-Semitism of Reconquista Spain—a comparison that subsequently allowed many early modernists, including myself, to analyze earlier forms of discrimination and to make the connection between anti-Semitism and Islamophobia. It also allowed us to make the point that these "new" forms of racism drew upon long and continuing histories. Contrary to the assertions of many analysts of new racisms, it is not the case that religion is a preracial form of difference or the "latest" form of racism or the form of difference confined to the Global South; rather, religion has been central to the development of modern forms of racism all across the globe, and in ways that we need to engage with today.

Balibar's phrase for neoracism—"racism without race"—is now sometimes imported into early modern studies in order to highlight crucial dimensions of earlier histories of difference.[30] But helpful as Balibar's work is for a conceptual reorientation of our understanding of race, this phrase can reconfuse matters by continuing to equate the term "race" with ideologies of difference that center around color or pseudobiological classifications. As a result, a theological or culture-centered notion of difference becomes a special kind of racism—early modern racism, neoracism, but not racism per se.[31] Instead, I am suggesting that early modern histories of difference, by illuminating the centrality of religion and culture to the development of the idea of race, can help us retheorize the idea of racial difference in a much more radical way. We need to adopt a complex understanding of the relationships between the so-called social and the so-called biological discourses that are marshalled by racist discourse and practice. They underscore the point that the biological

discourse of race was never really biological and that its categories were
in fact always cultural, just as, on the other hand, in "premodern" racial
discourse, as Robert Bartlett suggests, the vocabulary deployed was biological ("blood," *gens*, etc.) but the categories it indicated were cultural.[32]
    Comparing "then" and "now" helps us question rigid divides between
"periods," which have been formulated according to a Eurocentric conception of history in the first place, as well as interrogate the usefulness
of making the "culture" versus "biology" distinction the basis for our
understanding of the history of racism.[33]

    I now want to turn to the distinction between "culture" and "biology"
as it surfaced in a public controversy a few years ago, following the plea
of Dalit groups in India that casteism is a form of racism and should
be discussed at the 2001 United Nations Conference against Racism in
Durban.[34] Taking place as it did in a city, which had witnessed the launch
of Mahatma Gandhi's anticolonial campaign, as well as bitter struggles
over apartheid, the conference was an appropriate venue for raising
fundamental questions about forms and legacies of racism—not only
caste (dubbed a "hidden apartheid" by Human Rights Watch in 1999),
but also the question of Zionism, and of reparations for colonialism and
slavery, were brought to the table. Although Balibar rightly notes that
the event signaled "the urgent necessity to question afresh what exactly
we call racism, why we do so, and what kind of political and intellectual tradition we are continuing by using this terminology," it is telling
that his discussion resolutely remains within the confines of European
histories, relegating caste, quite explosive at the conference, to a small
footnote.[35] The three issues—caste, Zionism, and reparations—led to
global solidarity between the various activists raising them at Durban as
well as global alliances between the governments who were seeking to
disallow them as legitimate issues for the conference. Thus, whereas in
1975 India had voted in favor of the United Nations General Assembly
resolution naming Zionism as a form of racism, at Durban it joined
hands with the governments of the United States and Israel on Zionism
as well as the demand for reparations.
    All three issues, particularly caste, highlight the need to rethink the
connections between the different legacies of race and colonialism,
which are lost without some attempt to think comparatively. While I am
mindful of warnings, such as Stuart Hall's against "extrapolating a common universal structure to racism" and his reminder that "it is only as
the different racisms are historically specified—in their difference—that
they can be properly understood,"[36] I am suggesting that, at the same
time, we also need to interrogate the intellectual and political pitfalls
of a mechanical insistence on the uniqueness of different racial forma-

tions. If a certain Atlantic exceptionalism has operated in large sections of Western race theory, then, on the other hand, a colonial and Indian exceptionalism has insisted that caste is sui generis, that it cannot be compared to other discourses of difference because it is quintessentially and uniquely Indian (and the move also conflates "Indian" with "Hindu").

The best-known articulation of this exceptionalism has been Louis Dumont's *Homo Hierarchicus*, which projected caste as *the* symbol of community in India, a community that had been lost in the West with the rise of individualism.[37] Different versions of this approach were also espoused by dozens of other commentators, ranging from nationalist figures such as Jawaharlal Nehru to anticaste activists such as Bhimrao Ramji Ambedkar.[38] Oliver Cromwell Cox's book *Caste, Class, and Race* argued strenuously that the comparison would abstract race from capitalism and render it timeless—the assumption being that *caste* is static and can be abstracted from capitalism.[39] Indeed it is this exceptionalism of caste that was invoked by the Indian government in the Durban debates: "Communities which fall under the definition of Scheduled Castes and Scheduled Tribes are unique to Indian society and to its historical process" and so caste discrimination is an internal matter for the Indian government and Indian people to deal with.[40] An extreme version of this argument was the view that the Dalit desire to go to international forums like the World Conference against Racism showed a neocolonial mentality, or worse, was a product of the "temperament of liberalization"; a well-known academic wrote: "We have ceded knowledge advantage to the West on one front after another—beginning with economic, then flowing on to the political, and now we need tips on how to handle cultural discrimination as well."[41] Some of the most conservative Indian voices piously suggested that bringing caste into the picture would mean that racism would not receive proper attention.[42] Coming from a different direction was the argument that to discuss caste as race was to follow an agenda set by the new American empire: "One of the dangers of US imperialist hegemony is that the global anti-imperialist agenda may also end up being set in US anti-imperialist terms . . . Race, then, as a central category for the struggle, may be self-evident in the US context, but not as useful in other settings."[43] To confine racism to the United States is even more myopic than equating it with oppression against blacks. As I will argue, it is this very narrow understanding of race that has structured much of the denial of comparison between race and caste across the political spectrum in India, just as it has also stymied the understanding of the history of race.

Finally, the case against caste being discussed at Durban was articulated both by the government of India (then formed by the Hindu right-wing Bharatiya Janata Party), as well as several respected academics by reverting to the terms of colonial anthropology. Thus the well-known sociologist Andre Béteille cited long-discredited colonial scholarship on race, arguing that anthropologists had "established conclusively . . . the distinction between race which is a biological category with physical markers and social groupings based on language, religion, nationality, style of life or status . . . If discrimination against disadvantaged castes can be defined as a form of racial discrimination . . . Muslims and other religious minorities will claim that they too, and not just backward castes, are victims of racial discrimination."[44] Dalit activists argued that not only is caste, like race, a hierarchy based on lineage and descent, but it also involves a particular construction of the Dalit body and mind. Dalits were regarded as so polluted that even their shadows were understood as contaminating those they fell upon; even today, Dalits (by some calculations about one hundred and eighty million people) are often debarred from eating, praying, or studying with upper-caste individuals, from marrying outside their caste groups, as well as drawing water from a common well, or dressing above their station. Despite the fact that many Dalits are prominent in public life, the reality for most remains that those who are perceived as transgressive regularly meet with violent hostility, murder, and lynching. Despite the fact that Mayawati, a Dalit woman, is currently the chief minister of India's largest state, and projected by her party as a potential prime minister, Dalit women remain especially vulnerable to rape and sexual assault.[45] Such contemporary realities anchored the Dalit activist position demanding consideration at Durban.[46]

Some theorists have specified the perniciousness of anti-Dalit feelings by contrasting them with religious prejudices. The philosopher Akeel Bilgrami writes: "When I think sometimes about caste in India—without a doubt the most resilient form of exclusionary social inegalitarianism in the history of the world—it's hard to avoid the conclusion that even the most alarming aspects of religious intolerance are preferable to it. To say 'You *must* be my brother,' however wrong, is better than saying, 'You will *never* be my brother.'"[47] Bilgrami is right in theory, but in practice the difference is not absolute. As I discussed in the previous section, the discourse of religious conversions in early modern Europe embodied *both* these attitudes—Jews, Muslims, and blacks were simultaneously invited to convert *and* imagined as unable to fully do so. Moreover, it was the *combination* of these two apparently contradictory positions that catalyzed racial thought. I want to suggest that an analogous—though not identical—contradiction underpins the discourse of caste in India. On the one hand, it is true that in the ideology of casteism, the hierarchy is regarded as fixed. Those Dalits who convert to Christianity and Islam cannot rid themselves of the taint of caste; that is the basis on which many once-Dalit Christians, for example, continue to argue that affirmative-action provisions for Dalits should be extended to them. But, at the same time, it is precisely the place of lower castes within the Hindu religious and social hierarchy that guarantees the stability of the whole, which is why a belonging of sorts—oppressive, unequal, but nevertheless a belonging—is demanded of the Dalits by upper castes and particularly right-wing Hindu ideologues. Thus it is that V. D. Savarkar insisted that "some of us are Brahmans and some Namashudras or Panchamas [untouchable castes]; but . . . we are all Hindus and own a common blood."[48] Thus, too, Hindu conservatives are bitterly opposed to religious conversions.[49] It is on the supposed basis of the "belonging" of Dalits and lower castes to a Hindu whole that right-wing Hindu groups have also embarked on the aggressive wooing of Dalits and Adivasis, which has resulted in complicated new political alliances in various parts of India, but also resulted in the participation of these groups in right-wing organized violence against Muslims.[50]

As early as 1612, the Portuguese observer Diogo de Couto articulated the view that it was the caste order which prevented the conversion of Hindu elites to other religions: "The great impediment to the conversion of the Gentoos is the superstition which they maintain in relation to their castes, and which prevents from touching, communicating, or mingling with others, whether superior or inferior; those of one observance with those of another."[51] The idea that caste kept the Hindu order as a whole from disintegrating was put forth with increasing sophistication during the colonial period. At the end of the eighteenth century, Abbé Dubois insisted that the caste system had guaranteed Indian civilizational achievement; such ideas simultaneously preserved the *difference* of India from the West and made clear the value of a hierarchical order, which could work as a universal model of sorts. This is not to suggest that an unchanging *religious* order demanded this "fellowship"—on the contrary, caste hierarchy is always political and social, and its contemporary forms have been forged in and through particular colonial and postcolonial histories. Nicholas Dirks has argued that "under colonialism, caste was . . . made out to be far more—far more pervasive, far more totalizing, and far more uniform—than it had ever been before, at the same time that it was defined as a fundamentally religious social order" (*COM*, 13). Just as colonialism reshaped other social relations, such as those of class and gender, so also was it the case with caste, although it is important not to see this as a simple imposition by British colonialists but a process involving the active participation of local elites.[52]

Moreover, the histories of Western racial formation and those of caste are not isolated from one another. While there has been extensive writing on the relationship of caste and race, and whether these are analogous or different, scholars have yet to fully explore how European ideologies of race drew heavily upon caste divisions, which European travelers, merchants, and colonists observed in Indian society, and how these borrowings help us think about analogous problems in racial formations in different parts of the world. The Portuguese word *casta* (first used in the Indian context) was used to indicate not just these divisions, but also all kinds of other groupings based on color, class, and religion precisely along the lines that the word "race" was used in early modern English.[53] Often the two were made explicitly interchangeable, as in a decree issued by the Sacred Council of Goa in 1567: "In some parts of this Province (of Goa) the Gentoos divide themselves into distinct races or castes (*castas*) of greater or less dignity, holding Christians as of lower degree, and keep these so superstitiously that no one of a higher caste can eat or drink with those of a lower."[54] Thus, while in the sixteenth-century Europeans felt that they were equated with the lower castes in India, colonial anthropology shifted the alignments to posit an equation between Europeans and indigenous higher ranks.

The term *Arya* (which means "aristocratic" in Sanskrit) was appropriated as "Aryan," a term with biracial connotations in European discourse, and which in turn shaped the ideologies of caste and regional affiliation, as well as Hindu supremacy, in colonial India. In 1786, the British Orientalist William Jones argued that all speakers of Indo-European (or Indo-Aryan) languages belonged to the same racial group and were essentially derived from "a race of conquerors" who migrated from west Asia to various places, including India, a view that was picked up by the German philologist Max Müller.[55] While this argument allowed the theoretical possibility that Indians were of the same race as Europeans, it simultaneously divided Indians into superior Aryans, who were supposed to have moved into the region from the North, and inferior Dravidians, or the original inhabitants of the land. The racial classification of Indians was based on the supposition that the northern or "martial" peoples of India were largely Aryans who developed the caste system as a way of preventing miscegenation with the Dravidians and aboriginals.[56] At the end of the nineteenth century, as Nicholas Dirks has detailed, when race had become the primary mode of classifying humans into hierarchical groups in the West, caste was used to categorize Indians. The census commissioner H. H. Risley was "confident that he could actually test in India the various theories about race and the human species that had been merely proposed on speculative grounds in Europe" (*COM*, 15, 84). According to Dirks, he "fashioned a peculiar symbiosis between the racial anxieties of imperial Britain, and the ritual anxieties of Brahmans and other higher castes at the turn of the century" (*COM*, 224). This symbiosis is evident in a range of British literary texts of the period, such as Rudyard Kipling's novel *Kim*, where caste, region, and race dovetail to produce a taxonomy of "types," such as the fiercely honest and martial Afghan, the Sikh soldier loyal to the British, the effeminate but clever Bengali "Baboo," and so on. Susan Bayly points out that if colonialists interpreted caste through the lens of race, this means that they were in fact *not* regarding India as unique, but trying to fit it into what they saw as universally applicable biological hierarchies.[57]

Such views about the overlap of caste and race are still in circulation— in 2001, precisely at the time when Dalit groups were lobbying to take their case to Durban, a study published by the journal *Genome Research* argued that "the upper castes [in India] have a higher affinity to Euro-peans than to Asians, and the upper castes are significantly more simi-lar to Europeans than are the lower castes."[58] Ironically, of course, the findings of the *Genome Research* study could be cited in *support* of Dalit organizations' plea for thinking about caste as race! That is why, histori-cally, movements against caste oppression seized upon this analogy. In the mid-nineteenth century, Jyotiba Phule argued that Brahmans were colonists who subjugated the native inhabitants: "The cruelties which the European settlers practised on the American Indians on their first settle-ment in the new world had certainly their parallel in India in the advent of the Aryans and their subjugation of the aborigines [that is, Dravidians] . . . This, in short, is the history of Brahman domination in India . . . In order, however, to keep a better hold on the people they devised that weird system of mythology, the ordination of caste."[59] To Phule, caste was "*slavery*, as vicious and brutal as the enslavement of the Africans in the United States, but based in India not only on open conquest and subordination but also on deception and religious illusion."[60] Phule built his views precisely on the same theory of the Aryan race which was used by colonialists and Orientalists, but, as Gail Omvedt argues, he "turned it on its head, in a way somewhat akin to Marx standing Hegelian dia-lectics on its head" (19). Phule emphasized the violence inherent in this process.

Throughout the early part of this century, non-Brahman and Dalit movements were to seize and invert the racialized logic of caste domi-nation, laying claim to being the original inhabitants or *adi-vasis* of the land.[61] Ambedkar, one of the most important Dalit leaders as well as a major interlocutor of Gandhi and other nationalist leaders, was to critique this view, arguing that the Aryans were not a race and that "to hold that distinctions of caste are really distinctions of race . . . is a gross perver-sion of facts."[62] But he nevertheless thought about the relation between *casteism* and *racism*, writing to W. E. B. Du Bois that there was "so much similarity between the position of the Untouchables in India and the position of Blacks in America" and that he "was very much interested to read that the Blacks of America have filed a petition to the UNO.

The Untouchables of India are thinking of following suit."[63] Du Bois mentioned Ambedkar's letter when he expressed his own concern about the narrowness of the Human Rights Charter; later, he also critiqued the American Jewish Committee's "Declaration of Human Rights" for having "no thought of the rights of Blacks, Indians and South Sea Islanders."[64] The name of the radical Dalit Panther party, formed in 1972, is in obvious dialogue with the Black Panther movement.

These historical conversations are still in the process of being fully documented, and they indicate that Dalit thinkers and activists have consistently connected with other antiracist movements globally not in order to *conflate* caste with race, but to highlight their plight, to indicate the overlap between these forms of oppression, and to draw attention to their situation globally. When they raised the question of *comparison*, the dominant academic and governmental response was to construct their argument as one predicated upon a claim of *identity*. Thus, neither critiqued the colonial "science" that had in fact frequently employed the comparison of caste and race, even as they deployed the categories of this very science to lock both race and caste into discrete compartments.

The Durban controversy reminds us that both race and caste are highly malleable categories, which have historically been deployed to reinforce existing social hierarchies and create new ones. Like race, caste overlaps with, but is not identical to, class, and both are deeply entwined with gender oppression. Both demand an engagement with questions of culture and ideology, as well as with questions of the economy. But they also demand that we go further than that, and question the *politics* of theory. As Shiv Viswanathan observed, the answer is to be found "not at the level of concepts but at the level of *the politics of knowledge* . . . The worry about the 'conceptual inflation' that will follow if casteism is recognized as racism arises from an academic debate that is more concerned about the violation of disciplinary categories than with 'atrocity as violation.'"[65]

The comparison of caste and race, or that of older forms of racism with contemporary variants, I have suggested, allows us to track the *politics* of comparison, and the politics of the *denial* of comparison. What is evident in both the cases I have discussed is the persistence of the conflation of race with color that has been especially pernicious in constructing an artificial divide between "scientific"/"biological" and "cultural"/"religious" discrimination. It is this division that has erected an unsustainable divide between historical periods—premodern versus modern—and between different geographical locations. The histories of anti-Semitism, Islamophobia, and caste prejudice cannot then be fully connected to those of slavery, bonded labor, plantation labor, and color prejudice. Thinking across periods, and across regions, allows us to understand better *why* colonial race ideologies took the form they did, and how they drew from other forms of oppression globally.]

There is, of course, brilliant scholarship that has made visible the importance of thinking comparatively and globally in terms of nineteenth- and twentieth-century histories of racialization. Aamir Mufti's work showing why "the crisis of Muslim identity" in modern India "must be understood in terms of the problematic of secularization and minority in post-Enlightenment liberal culture as a whole and therefore cannot be understood in isolation from the history of the so-called Jewish Question in modern Europe" is a case in point. Mufti yokes two histories in order to "resituate the . . . problematic of Jewishness within an extra-European, global frame" and to make this speak to postcolonial debates about secularism and minority culture.[66] But important as it is to connect the histories of Jews and Muslims, European and postcolonial discourses about "minorities," it has been harder to think across the supposed divide between a process of minoritization that rests on *religious* difference and another, which seems to center on discourses of *color* and the *body*.

Even scholars who are otherwise committed to making visible international histories of cross-cultural contact and antagonism find it hard to cross that barrier. For example, Amitav Ghosh seeks to challenge the silence of Indian historians on the subject of race, which he rightly thinks arises out of an overemphasis on the differences between colonial ideologies and practices in different continents; he argues, instead, that the same pernicious forms of racialization that are evident in Africa or the Americas were in fact used by the British in governing India. Ghosh is right that because Indian historiography has worked largely with notions of cultural domination, of "persuasion" rather than "coercion," it has been blind to certain aspects of colonial rule in India: "The truth is that India was to the late 19th century what Africa was to the 18th—a huge pool of expendable labour . . . I believe that it is because we South Asians fundamentally misrecognize racism that we are not able to give it its proper place within the history of colonialism."[67] But for him, making such a connection requires that we *distinguish* between "scientific" and other forms of racism:

Racism . . . is an ideology that is founded on certain ideas that relate to science, nature, biology and evolution—a specifically post-Enlightenment ideology in other words . . . Generally speaking, Indian communalists recognize that their conflicts are located in the social domain: I do not think they put a biological or scientific construction on them.

Similarly racism and caste: you will perhaps remember that Louis Dumont distinguished between them in an appendix to *Homo Hierarchicus* . . . It has taken me a long time to understand that racism is comparable to casteism and communalism only in that it has the same murderous effects: its internal logic is quite different. (158–59)

But the place of racism in "liberal" Enlightenment thought cannot be understood by taking *its* own divisions between culture and biology, or indeed the supposed "internal logic" of either caste or race as *our* analytical categories, not only because, as history tells us, this logic changes and transforms, but also because it does so at least partly in relation to histories that are not as distinct as they have become in our postcolonial analysis.

Take the case of the term "caste" as it traveled to the colonial Americas. Although its histories there are distinct and can hardly be conflated with those on the South Asian subcontinent, there is a striking resonance between their relation to race *as a conceptual problem*. Writing in relation to early colonial Peru, Irene Silverblatt points out that in Latin America as well, "caste is understood to be a legal or social (as opposed to biological) construct at heart" whereas "race emerged as a dominant account of social differentiation in the West's 'modern,' liberal age." She goes on to suggest that we deploy the concept of "race thinking" to cut across this divide, not in order to assert an identity between them but to grasp "what the race-caste division hides: that race and caste were not separate systems but interpenetrating. Race thinking helps us understand how race and caste might, chameleon-like, slip in and out of one another."[68]

Some of these slippages are evident, as I have suggested, in the history of caste in India. It is also painfully evident that European racial categories have patently influenced "communalist" views about the differences between Hindus and Muslims.[69] The language of Hindu fundamentalism, like that of Reconquista Christianity, increasingly draws upon notions of "cultural difference" *as well as* pathology—Muslims breed more prolifically than others, Muslim men are inherently violent, they always desire Hindu women, all Muslims are conservative—and it does so precisely for the same reasons that Reconquista Christian discourse did, because there is no *visible* physiological difference between Hindus and Muslims in India.

Today, "race" has become a term that functions as the universal marker of discrimination *even as it is often* understood in narrow ways that obscure its longer and global histories. I have suggested that a cautious comparativism can make these histories visible, and conversely, careful attention to these histories reveals both the political utility, and the limits, of comparative methods. Systematic analyses of the histories of racial thinking allow us to push at the limits of our understanding of the very grounds of cultural comparison and of knowledge production. For instance, we might ask how our understanding of the histories of racial

thought might change if we think of comparing the historical development of race to the history and structure of caste formations (instead
of the other way around). This history should push us beyond simply
debating whether caste can legitimately be compared to race. Why is it
that we cannot even imagine reversing the terms and comparing race
to caste? The irreversibility of comparative terms is itself shaped by a
Eurocentric view of history, and of what we regard as universal and what
as particular. To push the comparison in this way is to challenge such a
view and make available more complete intersections than have hitherto
been visible.[70] The analytical priorities of that comparison will open up
a different set of global intersections altogether—such as those between
South Asia and Latin America—and thus productively interrupt, reorder,
and fill gaps in our understanding of histories of race.

NOTES

Many thanks to Ashley Cohen, Chris Taylor, Suvir Kaul, Sanjay Krishnan, Jed Esty, the Race
and Empire Reading Group at the University of Pennsylvania, as well as Rita Felski and
Susan Stanford Friedman for their incisive comments on this essay.
1   See, for example, Gayatri Spivak, *Death of a Discipline* (New York: Columbia Univ. Press,
2003); Rey Chow, "The Old/New Question of Comparison in Literary Studies," *ELH* 71
(2004): 289–311; Aamir Mufti, "Global Comparativism," *Critical Inquiry* 31, no. 2 (2005):
472–89; Pheng Cheah and Jonathan D. Culler, eds., *Grounds of Comparison: Around the Work
of Benedict Anderson* (New York: Routledge, 2003).
2   See especially Partha Chatterjee, "Anderson's Utopia," *Diacritics* 29, no. 4 (1999):
128–34, and Shu-mei Shih, "Global Literature and the Technologies of Recognition,"
PMLA 19, no. 1 (2004): 19.
3   See Ania Loomba and Jonathan Burton, eds., *Race in Early Modern England: A Documentary Companion* (New York: Palgrave, 2007).
4   Nancy Leys Stepan, "Race and Gender: The Role of Analogy in Science," in *The Anatomy
of Racism*, ed. David Theo Goldberg (Minneapolis: Univ. of Minnesota Press, 1990), 38–57.
5   Geoffrey C. Bowker and Susan Leigh Star, *Sorting Things Out: Classification and Its
Consequences* (Cambridge, MA: MIT Press, 1999), 1, 319.
6   Joyce Chaplin, "Race," in *The British Atlantic World, 1500–1800*, ed. David Armitage and
Michael J. Braddick (New York: Palgrave, 2002), 154–72; Kwame Anthony Appiah, "Race,"
in *Critical Terms for Literary Study*, ed. Frank Lentricchia and Thomas McLaughlin (Chicago:
Univ. of Chicago Press, 1990), 274–87; Paul Gilroy, *Against Race: Imagining Political Culture
beyond the Color Line* (Cambridge, MA: Harvard Univ. Press, 2000), 31; Roberto Bernasconi
and Tommy Lott, *The Idea of Race* (Indianapolis, IN: Hackett Publishing Company, 2000);
Brian Niro, *Race* (New York: Palgrave, 2003).
7   See Irene Silverblatt, "Modern Inquisitions," in *Imperial Formations*, ed. Ann Laura Stoler,
Carole McGranahan, and Peter C. Perdue (Santa Fe, NM: School for Advanced Research
Press, 2007), 282–83. I came across this essay when this one was being revised so can only
draw attention to ways in which its argument is productively resonant with mine, as I will
do below.
8   Shu-mei Shih, "Comparative Racialization: An Introduction," *PMLA* 123, no. 5 (2008): 1352.
9   It is a measure of the problem I am trying to highlight that the otherwise useful
special issue of *PMLA* on Comparative Racialization (123, no. 5 [2008]) has practically
no discussion of either caste or early modern racial histories.

10   George Abbot, *A Brief Description of the Whole World* (first published 1599) (London, 1664), 106. In this essay I will consider mainly English histories as well as the Iberian ones, which were so consequential for shaping European colonial ideas.

11   "John Huighen van Linschoten His Voyage to Goa, and Observations of the East Indies, abbreviated," in *Purchas His Pilgrims*, ed. Samuel Purchas (London: William Stansby, 1625), 1752, 1753, 1756–57, 1760, 1762–67. Arabs themselves had used the word to describe *both* Christians and blacks.

12   Wolfram con Eschenbach, *Parzival*, trans. Helen M. Mustard and Charles E. Passage (New York: Vintage, 1961). For a discussion of the dappling, see Lisa Lampert, "Race, Periodicity, and the (Neo-) Middle Ages," *MLQ* 6, no. 3 (2004): 391–421.

13   Augustine writes, "if they be definable to be reasonable creatures and mortal, they must be acknowledged to be Adam's issue." St. Augustine, *Of the Citie of God*, trans. John Healey (London: George Eld, 1610), 580–82.

14   Jeremiah 13: 23–25. The later King James Bible substitutes "Ethiopian" for "Blackamoor."

15   John Manning, ed., *The Emblems of Thomas Palmer: Two Hundred Poosees* (New York: AMS Press, 1988), 56. This idea derives from one of Aesop's fables entitled "The Moor or Ethiopian" and is echoed by the Bible as well as many early modern writings.

16   For an extended discussion, as well as complication, of the materials I discuss here see Loomba and Burton, *Race in Early Modern England*. There, other histories such as those of Ireland, Scotland, and Wales are also brought in, which this short essay cannot consider.

17   Jean Bodin, *Method for the Easy Comprehension of History* (first published 1566), trans. Beatrice Reynolds (New York: Columbia Univ. Press, 1945), 127.

18   Quoted by Jerome Friedman, "Jewish Conversion, the Spanish Pure Blood Laws and Reformation: A Revisionist View of Racial and Religious Antisemitism," *Sixteenth Century Journal* 18, no. 1 (1987): 3–29, 16–17.

19   The importance of early modern Spain to the development of what we recognize as race is explored by George Mariscal, "The Role of Spain in Contemporary Race Theory," *Arizona Journal of Hispanic Cultural Studies* 2 (1998): 7–23; James Sweet, "The Iberian Roots of American Racist Thought," *William and Mary Quarterly* 3rd ser., 54, no. 1 (1997): 143–66; Deborah Root, "Speaking Christian: Orthodoxy and Difference in Sixteenth-Century Spain," *Representations* 23 (Summer 1998): 118–34; Friedman, "Jewish Conversion"; Andre Hess, *The Forgotten Frontier: A History of the Sixteenth Century Ibero-African Frontier* (Chicago: Univ. of Chicago Press, 1978).

20   For a development of this argument, see Loomba, *Shakespeare, Race and Colonialism* (New York: Oxford Univ. Press, 2002), 24–27, 67–70.

21   Audrey Smedley, *Race in North America*, quoted by Vijay Prashad, *Everybody Was Kung Fu Fighting* (Boston: Beacon Press, 2001), 15 (emphasis added).

22   43 Elizabeth I (1601), in P. L. Hughes and J. F. Larkin, *Tudor Royal Proclamations* (New Haven, CT: Yale Univ. Press, 1969), 3: 221.

23   Andrew Boorde, *The Fyrst Boke of the Introduction of Knowledge* (London: W. Middleton, 1555), I 2 ᵛ.

24   Richard Ligon, *A True History of the Island of Barbados* (London: Peter Parker, 1657), 15.

25   This anonymous document in the papers of the scientist Robert Boyle is quoted by Cristina Malcolmson, "Biblical Monogenesis: Race and Gender in the Early Royal Society," in *Race, Religion, and Science in the Works of Robert Boyle and Margaret Cavendish* (Florida: Ashgate, 2009).

26   An Act against Carnal Copulation between Christian & Heathen, Antigua, 20 November 1644, "Lawes, Regulations and Orders in Force at the Leeward Islands from 1668 to 1672," 49–50, Colonial Papers CO 154/1, Public Record Office, Kew. Thanks to Carla Pestana for this reference.

27   Morgan Godwyn, *The Negro's & Indians Advocate, Suing for Their Admission into the Church: Or, A Persuasive to the Instructing and Baptizing of the Negros and Indians in Our Plantations* (London: J.D, 1680), 142, 155.

28   Cristina Malcolmson, "Biblical Monogenesis."

29   Etienne Balibar, "Is There a Neo-racism?" in *Race, Nation, Class: Ambiguous Identities*, ed. Etienne Balibar and Emmanuel Wallerstein (London: Verso, 1991), 23.

30   See, for example, Sweet, "Iberian Roots," 165.

31   Goldberg has recently argued that the "concept of *racisms without racism*" is "the peculiar expression of neoliberalizing globalization." "Racisms without Racism," *PMLA* 123, no. 5 (2008): 1712–16. See also Goldberg, *The Threat of Race: Reflections on Racial Neoliberalism* (Malden, MA: Blackwell, 2009).

32   Robert Bartlett, *The Making of Europe: Conquest, Colonization and Cultural Change, 950–1350* (Princeton, NJ: Princeton Univ. Press, 1993), 197–99.

33   One example of a Eurocentric periodization is the fact that non-European places are understood as "medieval" before their contact with Europe. Thus India is called "medieval" until the beginnings of the British Empire in the eighteenth century, and there can be no "early modern India," which is contemporaneous with, say, "early modern England."

34   Dalit literally means "broken" or "ground down" and was adopted as a term of self-definition by oppressed caste activists; the so-called lower castes were previously called "untouchables." Gandhi called them "Harijans" or "people/children of God." For a discussion of the politics of naming see Anupama Rao, "Who Is the Dalit? The Emergence of a New Political Subject," in *Claiming Power from Below: Dalits and the Subaltern Question in India*, ed. Manu Bhagvan and Anne Feldhaus (New Delhi: Oxford Univ. Press, 2008), 11–27. For a useful summary of the contemporary status of Dalits, see N. Paul Divakar and Ajai M., "UN Bodies and the Dalits," in *Caste, Race and Discrimination: Discourses in an International Context*, ed. Sukhdeo Thorat and Umakant (New Delhi: Indian Institute of Dalit Studies, 2004), 4 (hereafter cited as *Caste*).

35   Etienne Balibar, "Racism Revisited: Sources, Relevance, and Aporias of a Modern Concept," *PMLA* 123, no. 5 (2008): 1630–39, 1632.

36   Stuart Hall, "Race, Articulation and Societies Stuctured in Dominance," in *Black British Cultural Studies, A Reader* ed. Houston A. Baker Jr., Manthia Diawara, and Ruth H. Lindeborg (Chicago: Univ. of Chicago Press, 1996), 16–60, 51.

37   Louis Dumont, *Homo Hierarchicus: The Caste System and Its Implications* (Chicago: Univ. of Chicago Press, 1980). The original French edition was published in 1966.

38   See Nicholas Dirks's excellent commentary in *Castes of Mind: Colonialism and the Making of Modern India* (Princeton, NJ: Princeton Univ. Press, 2001), 4–6 (hereafter cited as *COM*).

39   Cox also argued that premodern interactions between peoples were *not* marked by racial antipathy. Oliver Cromwell Cox, *Caste, Class and Race* (Garden City, NY: Doubleday, 1948). Later, the book was retitled *Race: A Study in Social Dynamics*.

40   Thorat and Umakant, *Caste*, xxiii.

41   Dipankar Gupta, "Caste Is Not Race: But, Let's Go to the UN Forum Anyway," in *Caste*, 53–54.

42   Jaswant Singh on February 7, 2001, cited by Vijay Prashad, "Cataracts of Silence: Race on the Edge of Indian Thought," in *Claiming Power*, 134.

43   Prashad, "Cataracts of Silence," 135–36.

44   Andre Béteille, "Race and Caste," *The Hindu*, March 10, 2001, http://wcar.alrc.net/mainfile.php/For+the+negative/14/.

45   For an easily accessible profile of Mayawati, see http://news.bbc.co.uk/2/hi/south_asia/1958378.stm.

46   Many of the pieces published at that time, including Béteille's, are included in Thorat and Umakant, *Caste*.

47   Akeel Bilgrami, "Gandhi's Non-violence: The Philosophy behind the Politics," presented at the MLA Annual Convention, New Orleans, December 29, 2001.

48   Quoted by Christophe Jaffrelot, "The Idea of the Hindu Race in the Writings of Hindu Nationalist Ideologues in the 1920s and 1930s," in *The Concept of Race in South Asia*, ed. Peter Robb (Delhi: Oxford Univ. Press, 1995), 334.

49   See, for example, "A Swami's Open Letter to Pope," *The Times of India*, November 6, 1999.

50   See Anand Teltumbde, ed., *Hindutva and Dalits* (Kolkata: Samya, 2005) for an excellent review of this development. See also Tariq Thachil and Ron Herring, "Poor Choices: Dealignment, Development and Dalit/Adivasi Voting Patterns in Indian States," *Contemporary South Asia* 16, no. 4 (2008): 441–64.

51   Quoted by Henry Yule and AC Burnell, *Hobson-Jobson: A Glossary of Colloquial Anglo-Indian Words and Phrases* (New Delhi: Munshiram Manoharlal, 1984), 171. Dirks, *COM*, sees this attitude as a product of later colonial and missionary views.

52   See Susan Bayly, "Caste and 'Race' in the Colonial Ethnography on India," in *The Concept of Race in South Asia*, 168.

53   In the nineteenth century, W. Hamilton was to suggest that the term had been taken from the term "*Kayastha*," which described a particular caste grouping; see Yule and Burnell, *Hobson-Jobson*, 171.

54   *Archivo Portuguez Oriental* quoted by Yule and Burnell, *Hobson-Jobson*, 170–71.

55   Romila Thapar, *Early India: From the Origins to AD 1300* (Berkeley: Univ. of California Press, 2004), 12–13.

56   See also Tony Ballantyne, *Orientalism and Race: Aryanism in the British Empire* (Basingstoke: Palgrave, 2002).

57   Bayly, "Caste and 'Race,'" 168.

58   Michael Bamshad et al., "Genetic Evidence on the Origins of Indian Caste Populations," *Genome Research* 11, no. 6 (2001): 994–1004, 991.

59   Quoted by Gail Omvedt, *Dalit Visions: The Anti-caste Movement and the Construction of an Indian Identity*, Tracts for the Times series no. 8 (New Delhi: Orient Longman, 1995), 17.

60   Omvedt, *Dalit Visions*, 18.

61   Hindu fundamentalists are caught in the contradictions of this discourse, laying claim, on the one hand, to being Aryan and, on the other, to also being the only original inhabitants of India. See, for example, *The Organizer*: http://www.organiser.org/dynamic/modules.php?name=Content&pa=showpage&pid=257&page=27. A good discussion of some of these contradictions is provided by Jaffrelot, "The Idea of the Hindu Race."

62   Quoted by Omvedt, *Dalit Visions*, 49.

63   Quoted by Thorat and Umakant, *Caste*, xxix.

64   Thorat and Umakant, *Caste*, xxix–xxx.

65   Shiv Visvanathan, "Durban and Dalit Discourse," *Caste*, 272.

66   Aamir R Mufti, *Enlightenment in the Colony: The Jewish Question and the Crisis of Postcolonial Culture* (Princeton, NJ: Princeton Univ. Press, 2007).

67   Amitav Ghosh and Dipesh Chakrabarty, "A Correspondence on Provincializing Europe," *Radical History Review* 83 (Spring 2002): 146–72, 152–53, 160.

68   Silverblatt, "Modern Inquisitions," 282–83. See also note 13 above.

69   While Chakrabarty rightly makes similar points in his response to Ghosh, he hesitatingly conceded the need to distinguish between scientific racism and what he thinks is "prejudice."

70   I would like to thank Chris Taylor for this point.

CHAPTER NINE

The Material World of Comparison

Pheng Cheah

THE INTENSIFICATION OF GLOBALIZATION in the past two decades has led to debates about reenvisioning and reinventing the discipline of comparative literature in a manner that is ethically sensitive to the cultural differences and geopolitical complexities of the contemporary age. The task of reinvigorating comparative literary studies has been so successful that Haun Saussy begins his 2004 report on the state of the discipline by declaring its intellectual triumph, adducing as evidence the widespread diffusion of comparative methods and approaches to all corners and sectors of U.S. universities.[1] But despite this success, comparative literature remains a specific application of a method, perspective, or approach, which it shares with other forms of comparative study such as comparative politics, comparative sociology, or comparative history, as opposed to a clearly delimited field with established aims and objects of study. Hence, even if comparison is crucial to the formation of a critical consciousness and the improvement of knowledge production by giving an area of knowledge greater range and depth, it remains essentially a technique to be wielded by intellectual consciousness in its various projects and endeavors. The question that has almost never been asked is this: if comparison is a fundamental activity of human consciousness, then what is it that makes us compare? Is it something that is internal to consciousness or the human spirit or something that comes from the external or objective world?

The essay has two aims: it traces the genealogy of the idea that comparison is an activity that forms consciousness in some canonical texts of modern philosophy and the elaboration of this idea into a stimulus for the awakening of anticolonial consciousness in radical postcolonial nationalist literature. It then argues that in contemporary globalization, comparison is no longer a critical activity but a material infrastructure that undermines the formation of a shared world even as it makes us more connected in unprecedented ways. What are the implications of this material world of comparison for the struggles for freedom of peoples in the postcolonial South in the current global conjuncture?

Comparison and the *Bildung* of Humanity

The connection between comparison and the formation of the mature consciousness of a social being lies in the fact that comparison is an activity that consciousness undertakes when it encounters something foreign or other to itself. Jean-Jacques Rousseau's thought is exemplary because he suggests that comparison is a fundamental psychological mechanism in the human species's passage from a state of nature to social existence and further distinguishes between a salutary form of comparison that is the necessary precondition of our knowledge of ourselves as members of humankind and a defective, pernicious form of comparison that is the origin of social ills and inequality. Rousseau elaborates on the first kind of comparison in the *Essay on the Origin of Languages*.

Reflection is born of the comparison of ideas, and it is their plurality that leads us to compare them. Whoever sees only a single object has no occasion to make comparisons. Whoever sees only a small number and always the same ones from childhood on still does not compare them, because the habit of seeing them deprives him of the attention required to examine them: but as a new object strikes us, we want to know it, we look for relations between it and the objects we do know; this is how we learn to observe what we see before us, and how what is foreign to us leads us to examine what touches us.[2]

When something foreign or unknown enters our perceptual field, we begin to observe it closely, form conceptions of it, and compare these to what is familiar to us. Hence, the experience of alterity, the presence to consciousness of a *plurality* of objects, stimulates knowledge of what immediately surrounds us. What is emphasized here is the force of the foreign as it breaches the world we are accustomed to and moves the mind to compare.

Rousseau associates this force not with violence but with sociability and humanity. The knowledge formed from comparison enables us to imagine the experiences of others and to identify with them, thereby leading to the development of social affections such as pity, and eventually to knowledge of ourselves as members of a common humankind.

The social affections develop in us only with our knowledge [*lumières*]. Pity, although natural to man's heart, would remain eternally inactive without imagination to set it in motion [*en jeu*]. How do we let ourselves be moved to pity? By transporting ourselves outside ourselves; by identifying with the suffering being. We suffer only to the extent that we judge it to suffer; *we suffer not in ourselves but in it*. Think how much acquired knowledge this transport presupposes! How could I imagine evils of which I have no idea? How could I suffer when I see another suffer if I do not even know that he suffers, if I do not know what he and I have

in common [*de commun entre lui et moi*]? Someone who has never reflected cannot be clement, or just, or pitying, nor can he be wicked and vindictive. He who
imagines nothing feels only himself [*sent que lui-même*]; in the midst of mankind
[*genre humain*] he is alone.[3]

   There are therefore three different moments in the generation of *human* sense, the sense that one shares something in common with others
and is part of a common world of humanity. First, by forming knowledge
about the other, comparison converts the force of the initial shock of
alterity into virtual images. These images operate as a motor force that
transports us beyond ourselves. Second, in the moment of identification,
the self is propelled into the skin of the other. We regard the other as
another version of ourselves, an alter ego, and we feel his suffering as
if it were ours. Third, as a result of this identification, the self becomes
conscious of what is common between itself and the other.
   It is imperative here to distinguish between the common and the
similar or the like. The similar is what is familiar to us because it is immediately around us and habitually present to our sight. It constantly
touches us in its physical proximity, and we relate to it through feeling.
In contradistinction, the common involves a power of abstraction that
only comes about after the foreign has disrupted the familiarity of the
similar. It is both the end result and object of knowledge. Moreover, the
consciousness of what is common enables us to know our true selves *qua*
human beings instead of merely feeling our immediate selves, either as
isolated beings or as members of a family.

Apply these ideas to the first men, you will see the reason for their barbarism.
Never having seen anything other than what was around them, they did not
know even it; they did not know themselves. They had the idea of a Father, a
son, a brother, but not of man. Their hut held all those who were like themselves
[*semblables*]; a stranger, an animal, a monster were all the same to them [*étaient
pour eux la même chose*]: outside of themselves and their family, the whole universe
was naught to them [*ne leur était rien*].[4]

Because it enables the conceptualization of the idea of man as that which
is common to the self and others, the imagination's abstractive power
generates the knowledge that one belongs to a common humanity. Without this power, we simply cannot distinguish others in any meaningful
sense that will lead to the establishment of relations based on what we
share in common. Whatever lies outside our immediate family circle is
simply a homogeneous mass that does not exist for us. Hence, without
the imagination, we will only have an impoverished sense of ourselves
that is limited to the ties of blood and kinship. We will not be able to
"see" (that we are part of) humankind.

But comparison is also a double-edged process. In the *Second Discourse,* Rousseau suggests that the comparative gaze sets off the development of *amour propre* (vanity) in the human person and that it is also the first step toward inequality and vice in nascent social life. As is well known, *amour propre,* as distinguished from the natural sentiment of *amour de soi-même* (love of oneself) that is directed at self-preservation, is a social passion. *Amour de soi-même,* when regulated by reason and tempered by pity for the suffering of others, "produces humanity and virtue."[5] As we have seen, the identification with the suffering of others that is crucial to the activation of pity requires comparative activity. In contradistinction, the genesis of *amour propre* involves a different kind of comparative gaze. Here, one does not step into the other's skin and identify with him, but instead gazes at oneself through the other's eyes. The self sees itself as an object of possible disapprobation or admiration, disrespect or esteem, in the other's eyes and thus *desires* to be highly regarded or valued.

Amour propre is only a relative sentiment, factitious, and born in society, which inclines every individual to set greater store by himself than by anyone else, inspires men with all the evils they do one another, and is the genuine source of honor.

[I]n the genuine state of nature, Amour propre does not exist; For, since every individual human being views himself as the only Spectator to observe him, as the only being in the universe to take any interest in him, as the only judge of his own merit, it is not possible that a sentiment which originates in comparisons he is not capable of making, could spring up in his soul. (*FI* Note XV [1–2], 218; 219)

Here, the introduction of otherness in the self does not lead to the productive disruption of the familiar by difference that brings about the construction of a common human world. Alterity is now a threat since the other occupies the position of a judge that can devalue the self and undermine its security. Hence, observing the other does not lead to the appreciation of its differences, the identification with its suffering, and the knowledge of myself as human through the grasping of a common humanness. Instead, the self imagines how it is observed by this interloper and seeks to aggrandize itself in front of the other to defend against the other's judgment. There is no breaching of the circle of familiarity and sameness, no establishment of the larger circle of the common. Instead, the circle of sameness is reinforced through an oppositional, competitive relation to the other. *Amour propre* is a relative sentiment: it is a sense of self that can never be fully centered in the self but is always derived in relation to the other and therefore involves the permanent unease of competition.

Accordingly, selfhood and reflection have entirely negative connotations. Reflection does not lead to identification with the other. It is instead a movement of turning back on oneself in a way that rigidifies the self's boundaries, thereby blocking the identification with the other that defines pity.

Now this identification must, clearly, have been infinitely closer in the state of Nature than in the state of reasoning. It is reason that engenders amour propre, and reflection that reinforces it; *reason that turns man back upon himself, reason that separates him from everything that troubles and afflicts him*: It is Philosophy that isolates him; by means of Philosophy, he secretly says, at the sight of a suffering man, perish if you wish, I am safe. (*FI* I.37, 153; 155–56)

Instead of transporting the self beyond the limited circle of the same so that it can arrive at a sense of its own humanity, reflection here generates an impoverished, atomistic self that is imprisoned within this circle. The more educated one is, the less one identifies with the sufferings of others because one acts according to selfish calculations of prudence.[6]

Moreover, the pernicious modality of comparison leads to forms of hierarchy at the level of social life. In a presocial stage, human interaction with natural forces leads to the determination of relations to the outside world in quantitative terms such as greatness, strength, speed, et cetera. The human ability to master nature through prudential calculation gives the person a sense of the human species's superiority. The development of the same comparative activity in social relations with other human beings leads to individual pride, social hierarchy, and the vices that accompany property and civility.

Everyone began to look at everyone else and to wish to be looked at himself [*Chacun commença à regarder les autres et à vouloir être regardé soi-même*], and public esteem acquired a price. The one who sang or danced best; the handsomest, the strongest, the most skillful, or the most eloquent came to be the most highly regarded, and this was the first step at once toward inequality and vice: from these first preferences arose vanity and contempt on the one hand, shame and envy on the other. (*FI* II.16, 166; 169–70)

[C]onsuming ambition, the ardent desire to raise one's relative fortune less out of genuine need than in order to place oneself above others, instills in all men a black inclination to harm one another, a secret jealousy that is all the more dangerous as it often assumes the mask of benevolence in order to strike its blow in greater safety: in a word, competition and rivalry on the one hand, conflict of interests on the other, and always the hidden desire to profit at another's expense, all these evils are the first effect of property, and the inseparable train of nascent inequality. (*FI* II.27, 171; 175)

This is precisely the unfolding, at every stage of social life, of the pernicious modality of comparison found at the heart of *amour propre*, where the self views itself competitively through the other's eyes.

Let us sum up Rousseau's views about comparison. First, the distinction between the salutary and defective forms of comparison and reflection is essentially a distinction between a relation to alterity where the other is integrated into the self through identification and the difference is overcome through the establishment of what is common, and a relation to alterity where difference is seen as a threat that has to be contained by reinforcing the self's boundaries through withdrawal, self-aggrandization, and competition. Second, in the "good" kind of comparison, there is an initial recognition of qualitative differences between self and other that are resolved by identification, which establishes a complete symmetry, substitutability, and equality of self and other. Ideational work raises up difference into what is common and shared, to a larger communal self. In contradistinction, comparison-as-competition is essentially a quantitative relation between different magnitudes, a matter of more or less. The relation between self and other is here structurally asymmetrical and unequal since the self always desires to be greater than the other in power or force. Third, comparison is primarily a matter of the subject's desire. It may open up a common world or obstruct such an opening, but comparison remains a dynamic of the subject rather than an objective worldly structure.

German idealist philosophy resolves the contradiction between the two modalities of comparison by means of a teleology of history in which conflict and antagonism are regarded as the motor of human progress toward a telos that has universal validity for all individuals and peoples within the human species. Kant called the good type of comparison "pluralism," which he defined as the opposite of egoism, the attitude in which consideration is given only to one's viewpoint in matters of logical judgment, taste, and morality. Comparison is primarily a rigorous testing of the self's presumptions by means of the perspectives of others and it leads to the formation of a collective subject, humanity, in which the self strikes down its own egoism by acknowledging that it exists with others within a larger whole, that is, a plural world. Pluralism, Kant writes, is "the way of thinking in which one is not concerned with oneself as the whole world, but rather regards and conducts oneself as a mere citizen of the world [*Weltbürger*]."[7] The optimal cultivation of this intellectual perspective in individuals can only be attained in a world federation that secures the highest state of peace.

But, paradoxically, human beings are motivated to establish a cosmopolitan federation by the competitive kind of comparison. Because of our egoistic nature, human beings are pulled by two conflicting tendencies. On the one hand, we desire to be isolated individuals because we want the world to operate according to our selfish wishes. But, on the other hand, we also desire to be in society because egoism finds its highest expression in the desire for power, wealth, and honor. These are social phenomena because one can only aggrandize oneself and have status in the eyes of others. "Through the craving for honor, the craving for domination, or avarice, he is driven to seek status among his compeers, whom he cannot bear, yet cannot leave alone [*getrieben durch Ehrsucht, Herrsucht oder Habsucht, sich einen Rang unter seinen Mitgenossen zu verschaffen, die er nicht wohl leiden, von denen er aber auch nicht lassen kann*]."[8] Kant calls this constitutive feature of human life "unsocial sociability" (*ungesellige Geselligkeit*).[9]

Social existence thus involves a physics of mutual attraction and repulsion. Since each person will try to resist the inclination of others to bend him to their will and is also aware that this resistance is mutual, he must develop his natural predispositions so as to enable him to resist the will of others, as well as skills, taste, and social graces to attract others and reduce their resistance to being bent according to his will. Competitive comparison is crucial to human progress. "Nature should thus be thanked for fostering social incompatibility, enviously competitive vanity, and insatiable desires for possession or even domination [*Herrschen*]! Without these desires, all man's excellent natural predispositions [*Naturanlagen*] would never be roused to develop."[10] A similar competitive dynamic is repeated at the level of interstate relations. States seek to aggrandize themselves in each other's eyes in terms of cultural achievements because this is a way to influence other states. "The mutual relationships between states are already so sophisticated [*so künstlichen*] that none of them can wane (or slacken) in its internal culture [*in der inneren Kultur nachlassen kann*] without losing power and influence in relation to the others."[11] Such competition can lead to war, which itself can be an incentive "for developing to their highest degree all the talents that serve for culture [*die zur Kultur dienen*]."[12] Rivalrous comparison, however, gives way when states reach a point where they realize that a cosmopolitan federation provides the optimal conditions of security for the development of culture and the moral cultivation of their citizens.

Hegel's philosophy of history takes the generative character of the comparative gaze's competitive aspects to its extreme. Because Hegel rejects the possibility of a cosmopolitan federation as an empty utopian dream, he views the totality of world history as a process of successive struggles between national spirits (*Volksgeister*) to assume the mantle of the world spirit (*Weltgeist*). As universal spirit, world spirit can only exist in the particular shape of a national spirit.[13] Hence, in any given epoch it is vested in only one state, whose actions will have universal normative force. A given state's eligibility to assume the mantle of world spirit in a given epoch depends on its national spirit's historical achievements as manifested in the quality of its political institutions and spiritual-cultural products and the eternal contribution they make to world history. This confers to a given nation its right to be recognized as the dominant nation in a given stage of world history. World history is thus the ultimate forum of judgment of the actions of particular nations and individuals. But the universality of its judgments exceeds the sphere of mere morality or justice. It metes out undying fame. Its judgment and recognition are neither tolerant nor benevolent. To the contrary, they legitimize the violence and domination suffered by nations that do not embody the world spirit as being favorable to universal progress.

It is through this dialectic that the *universal* spirit, *the spirit of the world*, produces itself in its freedom from all limits, and it is this spirit which exercises its right— which is the highest right of all—over finite spirits in *world history* as the *world's court of judgment* [*Weltgericht*].[14]

In contrast with this absolute right which it [the dominant nation] possesses as bearer of the present stage of the world spirit's development, the spirits of other nations are without rights [*rechtlos*], and they, like those whose epoch has passed, no longer count in world history.[15]

Two points are important for present purposes. First, because of the importance Hegel gives to spiritual-cultural forms as a measure of the contributions of a national spirit to world-historical progress, world history's court of judgment—the forum that *is* world history—is a theater of comparison for cultural forms. World history is the objective condition of possibility of art, religion, and philosophy, the three shapes of absolute spirit. We can only recognize these forms as expressions of absolute spirit *after* we understand the place of their respective national spirits within the chain of world history. Because art, religion, and philosophy are recognized as such only after the judgment of the world, the study of these forms is necessarily comparative and must range across different cultures and periods. Second, Hegel's comparative gaze places the spiritual products of each people within a (Eurocentric) developmental hierarchy or teleology of the progress of universal spirit, where the cultural forms produced by previously dominant nations are judged as defective in comparison with those of the now-dominant Europe in terms of the development of universal reason's consciousness of the concept of freedom and how it is expressed in individuals.

In all world-historical nations, we do indeed encounter poetry, plastic art, science, and even philosophy. But these differ not only in their tone, style, and general tendency, but even more so in their basic import; and this import involves the most important difference of all, that of rationality . . . For even if one ranks the Indian epics as highly as Homer's on account of numerous formal qualities of this kind—greatness of invention and imagination, vividness of imagery and sentiments, beauty of diction, etc.—they nevertheless remain infinitely different in their import and hence their very substance.[16]

The comparative gaze of world history produces the Eurocentric characterizations of non-Western art that abound in Hegel's *Aesthetics,* for instance, the judgment that the failure of the Egyptian, Indian, and Persian peoples to grasp the true nature of the absolute leads to the production of bizarre and grotesque objects whose phenomenal forms are forced to express a higher meaning inappropriate to their shape, whereas classical beauty is only achieved in the Greek world.[17] We can call this world history from the present of (nineteenth-century) European hegemony. It looks at the past in a way that affirms Europe as the teleological model by which to judge all other nations as wanting and thus elevates Europe into a developmental standard toward which all other nations ought to aspire.

Postcolonial Literature and the Revolutionary Politicization of Comparison

These philosophical ideas about the constitutive nature of comparison foreshadow key motifs in our contemporary discourse concerning the ethics and politics of comparison. For example, how is the advent of the other and the comparison it stimulates beneficial to the development of consciousness and, indeed, even constitutive? How does identification across difference lead to the formation of a common human world? Conversely, how does comparison as a type of competitive relation to the other undermine the establishment of humanity? We are reminded that comparison always involves relations of power. We also see two different solutions to the conflict between a hospitable and a competitive relation to alterity: the gradual achievement of a pluralistic universalism in which we test our assumptions by including other perspectives after a historical process of antagonisms (Kant), and the generalization of conflict into a hierarchical economy of domination that operates in the entire span of history where difference is subordinated to a developmental standard (Hegel). Finally, we also see the importance of the imagination in establishing a relation to otherness in the form of either the role of identification in building a common humanity or the optic that places all peoples and their cultural products within the forum of world history.

These ideas have left a lasting imprint on the way we think today. Indeed, even the Eurocentric comparative gaze of Hegelian world history has been influential as a catalyst for the decolonizing nationalist imagination. Here, the imposed developmental hierarchy is exposed as Eurocentric and even racist, and the energy of that critique then fuels the educated native's desire that his people not be left out of world history. The struggle to assume the role of an autonomous agent in world history is precisely the political project of anticolonial revolution: the destruction of the colonial world where natives cannot be at home and cannot develop as autonomous subjects, and the creation of a new common world where they can.[18] I discuss two examples of this revolutionary politicization of comparison from the literature of decolonizing and postcolonial space.

José Rizal's *Noli Me Tangere* (1887) is a novel written by an *haute bourgeois* Filipino colonial subject in Spanish (published in Berlin) that is widely regarded as an important literary inspiration of the revolt against Spanish colonialism in the Philippines. The book's protagonist, Juan Crisóstomo Ibarra, the scion of a wealthy mestizo family, has, like the book's author, returned to Manila after several years of study and travel in Europe. As he reacquaints himself with the colony's urban landscape, he feels the haunting shadow of Europe in everything he sees. The most notable features in this landscape, such as the tobacco factory and the botanical gardens, are copies of European phenomena and are made largely for the consumption and enjoyment of the Spanish colonizers and wealthy mestizos. Ibarra feels what Frantz Fanon calls the belatedness of the colonial world. He cannot help but compare the colony with Europe.

At the end of the bridge the horses broke into a trot, heading toward the Paseo de la Sabana. On the left, from the Tobacco Factory of Arroceros he could hear the roar of cigarette makers pounding the leaves. Ibarra could not help but smile at the memory of the overwhelming odor that had permeated the Puenta de Barcos at five each afternoon and made him queasy when he was a boy. The lively conversations and joking automatically carried his thoughts back to, among other things, the Lavapiés section of Madrid with its cigarette-vendor riots, so fateful for the unfortunate cops.

The botanical garden drove away these delightful memories and the devilry of comparison [*el demonio de las comparaciones*] placed him back in front of the botanical gardens of Europe, in those countries in which one needs a great deal of will and even more gold to bring forth a leaf and make a flower open its calyx, even in these colonies, rich and well tended and open to the public. Ibarra looked away, to the right, and there saw Old Manila, surrounded still by its walls and moats, like an anemic young girl wrapped in a dress left over from her grandmother's salad days.[19]

In this narrative construction of the psychological development of the imperative to revolt against colonialism, what strikes the reader first is the automatic nature of comparison, which the narrator refers to as a demon.[20] When Ibarra recalls his childhood, the chattering cigarette makers transport him back to the prototypical scene in Madrid. The moving carriage then brings up another Manila landmark, the botanical gardens, which is a colonial project. Ibarra is transported yet again to the "original" versions in Europe, about which the narrator reminds us that much effort and money is needed to make flowers bloom compared to the lush tropics. But his next glance brings to view the degradation of Manila, which despite the conduciveness of its warm climate to health is figured as a pale waif in hand-me-down clothing, a human life whose vitality is stifled by colonial rule.

At this point of the novel, the political meaning is still subconscious, but the demon of comparisons has laid the ground for Ibarra's gradual realization that the basic human freedoms of the Enlightenment available *over there* in the Europe he idealized as a student are not available *here* in the Philippines because of the anachronistically repressive colonial regime. This endless comparison of *here* and *there* and the conclusion that *here, in the colonial present,* there is only a dead end without any future of a common humanity finally leads Ibarra to the resolution to revolt: "Now I see the horrible cancer gnawing at this society, rotting its flesh, almost begging for violent extirpation . . . For three centuries we have held our hand to them, asked them for love, eager to call them brothers, and how do they answer us? With insults and mocking, denying us even the status of human beings. There is no God, no hope, no humanity, nothing more than the rights of power!"[21]

My second example comes from Pramoedya Ananta Toer's *Buru Quartet*. Its third volume, *Footsteps* (Jejak Langkah, 1985), was published almost a hundred years after Rizal's *Noli*, but it is set in the Dutch East Indies of the early 1900s, the years of the rise of anticolonial sentiment and protonationalist political organizations. The decade or so separating this from the time of the *Noli* has seen rapid technological change. These innovations have transformed the demon of comparisons into an objective world of comparison where the emergence of a more readily accessible world of print, especially in the vernaculars of colonized peoples, has made them increasingly conscious of progress in the outside world and the role of colonialism in perpetuating their stagnation. One no longer needs to be educated abroad like Ibarra to be possessed by comparison since the entire world of comparison—events occurring not only in Europe but also the rising tide of anticolonial movements in other parts of Asia, such as the successful Philippine revolution against Spain (1896–98), the Republican movement in China that led to the downfall of the Ching dynasty on February 12, 1912, and the Japanese defeat of Russia in the Russo-Japanese war (1904–5)—can come to the educated native through newspapers and other forms of printed knowledge.

The phrase "world of comparison" (*alam perbandingan*) appears in an episode where the protagonist, Minke, a Javanese aristocratic youth who has been educated in the exclusive Dutch colonial school system, becomes possessed by an anxious restlessness as a result of his awareness that his people have been subjected to a foreign people because of their backwardness. He contrasts this restlessness to the stagnant tranquillity and childlike ignorance of "traditional" communal life in the villages and points out that they remain stagnant because they are not part of the world of comparison.

I began to observe more closely the life of the village. I clearly could not ask its inhabitants to discuss the issue of modern organisation. They did not possess any knowledge of their own country. Most probably, they rarely left their own village. They have never read a book. Illiterate.

. . . A large number of [the small village children playing] will die due to a parasitical disease . . . And if they survive, if they manage to overcome the parasitical diseases, is their condition any better than the time of their childhood? They will continue to live within their narrow destiny. Without ever having any comparison. Happy are those who know nothing. Knowledge, comparison, makes people aware of their own situation, and the situation of others, there is dissatisfied restlessness in the world of comparison [*gelisah dalam alam perbandingan*].

. . . The people around me have never known what I know . . . They do not know anything except how to make a living and reproduce themselves. Oh, creatures like herded cattle! They do not even know how lowly their lives are. Nor do they know of the monstrous forces [*kekuatan raksasa*] in the wider world, which grow and expand, gradually swallowing everything in their way, without being satiated. Even if they knew, they would not pay any heed.

Within these surroundings, I felt like an All-Knowing god, who also knew their fate. They would become the prey of both criminals and imperialists. Something had to be done [*Sesuatu memang harus dikerjakan*].[22]

This is the catalyst for Minke's organizational activity as a radical nationalist. In the previous volume, *Child of All Nations* (Anak Semua Bangsa, 1981), the world of comparison had led him to identify with the frustrations of the Chinese youth movement:

[The backwardness of my people was] [s]hameful. But not only that. I became incensed because of my powerless awareness [*kesadaran yang tidak berdaya*] . . . And Maarten Nijman wrote: "The Chinese Young Generation of intellectuals are envious of Japan's progress . . . Envious! Also furious and incensed because they are aware but powerless." *Just like me.*[23]

More and more, we see that comparison is something that comes upon and constitutes the reflective self rather than something that it wills or decides to do. It is less a function of human psychology in Minke than it was in Ibarra. Comparison is no longer a matter of memory but of the inescapable force of what is read. It stems from the disquieting aware-ness of material forces at work in the wider world, especially forces that circulate knowledge and information, which disrupt our nonreflective intimate relationship with our immediate social surroundings. As was the case with Hegel's teleology of world history, comparison is an economy for the formation of the consciousness of peoples. But here it is the consciousness of a revolutionary subject who seeks to overturn Hegel's Eurocentric hierarchy.

As in Hegelian world history, in these novels about the rise of revolution-ary anticolonial consciousness, comparison is a field of conflicting forces that is appropriated by the reflective consciousness of the subject that it forms. In the final instance, comparison, even though it is no longer a merely subjective technique but has become an objective structure, always returns back to the subject. Whatever disruption, anxiety, or competition it brings, it is an economy that ultimately serves the development of the human spirit and the establishment of the common good. This is why we have always understood comparison within the horizon of ethics. It is always a matter of the relation of a self to the other and how the self responds to, acts toward, or seeks to know the other.[24]

Infrastructural Comparison and Biopower

We would be mistaken if we regarded the two modalities of compari-son I have discussed above as being in a simple relation of opposition or contradiction that can be resolved by the regulation of competitive strife by ethical ideals of common humanity. The ethical relation to the other, indeed, ethics in general, is always a matter of power because it involves the capacity or ability to act or to do: to be generous, gracious, respectful, tolerant, or accepting of differences. This ability is coextensive with the strength of the self, computed in terms of its intellectual and material resources in specific contexts. This is evident in Hegel's developmental narrative and its reversal in anticolonial and postcolonial literature in a colonized people's revolutionary desire to develop itself. Indeed, the emergence of comparison as a material or objective structure—a world—in Pramoedya's *Buru Quartet* suggests that the ethical modality of comparison is premised on a more fundamental modality of comparison.

The emergence of comparative studies in Europe followed the discovery of the New World and the increased contact with non-European peoples that led to nineteenth-century colonialism. This gave rise to the need for the production of knowledge about these "others" within unequal power relations, especially those "others" with great civilizations and cultures that could be museumized. The critique of the complicity between colonialism/neocolonialism and anthropology's construction of the other is representative.[25] The ethical imperative to relate to the cultural other in a nonreductive, humane manner that informs current reflections on the comparative enterprise and also all of postcolonial theory is part of this epistemic formation. It seeks to reverse the epistemic violence inflicted on the cultural other that has resulted from the complicity between knowledge production and colonial/neocolonial domination. Edward Said, the founder of postcolonial theory and an eminent comparatist, offers this exemplary comment: "History is made by men and women just as it can also be unmade and unwritten, always with various silences and elisions, always with shapes imposed and disfigurements tolerated, so that 'our' East, 'our' Orient becomes ours to possess and direct."[26]

However, if we understand comparison only as a subjective technique that can be corrected or reformed through the raising of consciousness by means of an ethical dialectic of self and other, we obscure more fundamental processes of comparison that create the material conditions of the capacity for ethical comparison. These processes are concerned with the quantification and calculation of the conditions of human life in order to increase life as a resource. They are material processes in several senses. First, they are technologies directed at the material conditions of life that directly impact the population instead of individual consciousness. Second, they are deployed by states in order to enhance the material well-being of a society or nation by maximizing its resources. Third, they create a milieu in which the material existence and corporeal needs and capabilities as well as intellectual abilities of individual subjects as members of the population are crafted. Consequently, comparison becomes an ongoing material activity, an objective motor or operational infrastructure that shapes every aspect of human life. It conditions, influences, and shapes any intellectual consciousness that is engaged in ethical comparison and, thus, also exceeds and circumscribes such endeavors.

Adam Smith elaborates on this modulation of comparison from a technique of consciousness in the production of knowledge into a process that shapes a society by means of policies that improve its wealth. *An Inquiry into the Nature and Causes of the Wealth of Nations* (1776) is a veritable machine of comparison that engages in comparison and makes it the motor of healthy societies. It begins by using comparison as a mode of philosophical analysis in the study of economic phenomena, for example, the comparison of wealthy and poor nations in terms of different plans in increasing productivity and the different theories of political economy these plans generate. But since these theories exert influence on policy makers and can have an enormous impact on the economies of nations, comparative knowledge is also indispensable to policy makers. Comparison should, therefore, be the operational basis of any healthy political economy and be built into the science of political economy and its institutionalized policies and technologies.

Though those different plans were, perhaps, first introduced by the private interests and prejudices of particular orders of men, without any regard to, or foresight of, their consequences upon the general welfare of society; *yet they have given occasion to very different theories of political economy* . . . Those theories *have had considerable influence*, not only upon the opinions of men of learning, but upon the public conduct of princes and sovereign states. I have endeavoured . . . to explain, as fully and distinctly as I can, those different theories, and *the principal effects which they have produced* in different ages and nations.[27]

Comparison is, moreover, central to human existence at another level: the practices of individuals in daily life. According to Smith's philosophical anthropology, exchange and trade are innate human propensities.

In civilised society he [man] stands at all times in need of the co-operation and assistance of great multitudes, while his whole life is scarce sufficient to gain the friendship of a few persons. In almost every other race of animals each individual, when it is grown up to maturity, is entirely independent, and in its natural state has occasion for the assistance of no other living creature. But man has almost constant occasion for the help of his brethren, and it is in vain for him to expect it from their benevolence only. He will be more likely to prevail if he can interest their self-love in his favour, and show them that it is for their own advantage to do for him what he requires of them . . . We address ourselves, not to their humanity but to their self-love, and never talk to them of our own necessities but of their advantages.[28]

Cooperation in the interests of self-love involves comparison. It requires a temporary coincidence of advantages arising out of plurality. Such coincidence is brought out by comparative activity that shows the other that his advantage coincides with my needs. This is an a priori form of exchange, an ontological reciprocity, if you will. Because we always need help from others, we must identify a synchronicity across all our differences of needs and advantages. This synchronicity then leads to actual exchanges, which gradually develop into the division of labor. Smith calls such comparison a "trucking disposition." "As it is by treaty, by barter, or by purchase, that we obtain from another the greater part of those mutual good offices which we stand in need of, so it is this same trucking disposition which originally gives occasion to the division of labour."[29]

The modality of comparison Smith outlines is distinguishable from the ethical dialectic of self and other in two respects. First, although it involves the identification of similarities, the common does not refer

strongly disagree

to attributes of an ideal humanity. Smith explicitly rejects any appeal to a common humanity to facilitate cooperative exchange in favor of shared needs and interests. Since needs and interests change with the development of society, this commonality itself is inherently plastic and a product-effect of material changes. Second, the development of a society is furthered by technologies of comparison at the level of government that have become institutionalized. This means that the technologies that productively shape human life are detached from and exceed individual intellectual consciousness.

Indeed, this infrastructural form of comparison is the necessary backdrop for the emergence of what Michel Foucault calls biopower, a positive or productive modality of power that takes as its targets and objects of investment the life of the population. States, Foucault argues, begin to treat their populations as a resource because the post-Westphalian system of competitive relations between multiple absolute state units gives rise to a new principle of political power that is concerned with the maximization of the state's forces—its natural resources, commercial possibilities, balance of trade, and quality of its population. It is only within a framework of comparison between states that "we enter a politics whose principle object will be the employment and calculation of forces."[30] Henceforth, states attempt to organize production and commerce with the interrelated aims of enriching themselves through financial accumulation, strengthening themselves through increasing population, and maintaining themselves in a state of "permanent competition with foreign powers."[31] They also establish technologies of internal management (policing) so that they can develop their forces while preserving internal order (*STP* 313). Initially, in the seventeenth century, the population is regarded as a productive force and power (*qua* discipline) is directed at individual bodies (*STP* 69). However, from the eighteenth century onward, with the rise of biopower proper, the population is regarded as a set of biological processes that are dependent on a series of variables that need to be managed "at the level and on the basis of what is natural in these processes" (*STP* 70).

For present purposes, two features of this new modality of power arising from infrastructural comparison are important. First, power is primarily affirmative and productive rather than prohibitive and repressive. It invests in the population in order to enhance and maximize the positive aspects of the population as a force. Second, it does not operate by directly impacting on the consciousness or even the psyche of its targets, that is, the collective will of the population or the individual wills of its members. It acts instead on a range of factors and elements that are remote from the population and its immediate behavior but have a fundamental impact on shaping the population because they constitute the physical-material milieu or environment for the biological existence of the population. Biopower is therefore a form of structural causality that works with natural processes to shape the milieu within which the biological well-being of the population and, therefore, their material needs and interests, can be formed and altered. It does not repress and manipulate what is spontaneous in individuals, namely, desire, but encourages their free play in order to achieve the general interest of the population.[32] Simply put, biopower does not affect individuals as a set of juridical subjects capable of voluntary actions that are restricted by sovereign legal command. Its object is "a multiplicity of individuals who are and fundamentally and essentially only exist biologically bound to the materiality within which they live" and it works by positively shaping this material milieu (*STP* 21).

Today, this biopolitical infrastructure of comparison operates at every level of human life and organizes human existence as such. The health of national economies is continually measured through quantitative comparison, and states carefully monitor and act on the constantly fluctuating diagnoses. The mass media keenly report this information, and it affects the lives and interests of households and individuals, primarily in the form of national stock exchange indices and currency exchange rates, mechanisms that most immediately indicate a country's healthy economic activity and purchasing power. For example, a recent newspaper article berates American consumers for living beyond their means in tough economic times.

Year after year, the United States bought more from the rest of the world than it sold as foreign nations cranked out shipload after shipload of goods destined for American consumers . . . It was only thanks to the kindness of strangers that such a drain of dollars was able to continue. Every year, overseas investors poured hundreds of billions of dollars into U.S. stocks, bonds, real estate and other assets, largely offsetting our taste for imported goods . . . Foreigners have become wary of underwriting the U.S. standard of living. The flow of outside investment is slowing.[33]

The economic rise of China is repeatedly characterized in terms of the usurpation of the United States' rightful place as the world's father figure.[34] Anxious, inflammatory, pseudo-Hegelian pronouncements about the beginning of a perverse world-historical stage also abound in the opinion pages of leading Western newspapers. A regular opinion columnist in the *International Herald Tribune* screams: "The baton passes to Asia."

Every now and again, an ice cap the size of Rhode Island breaks off. The breaking sound right now is that of the end of the era of the white man . . . The West's

moment, I thought, is passing. Money and might are increasingly elsewhere . . .
Come to Asia and fear drains away. It's replaced by confidence and a burning
desire to succeed. Asian business leaders are rock stars. The culture of education
and achievement is fierce. China is bent on beating the U.S.A. What you feel in
Asia, said Claude Smadja, a prominent global strategist, is "a burst of energy, of
new dreams, and the end of the era of Western domination and the white man."[35]

But any resemblances to Hegel are fundamentally misleading. The
divisive kind of comparison denounced by Rousseau that surfaces here
is not generalized into an economy for the development of the human
spirit or the establishment of a common good or pluralistic universal
across qualitative differences. The comparison is not about quality but
quantity. It is about the increase of resources by better management
and the securing of more advantageous terms of exchange. It points to
a certain "common," but this is not humanity as an ideal project to be
actualized across qualitative differences, an end to which one strives to
move upward, but the lowest common denominator of consumption and
production for all human beings that a nation-state needs to increase
within its borders in order to be "better" than others. It is concerned
with a subject of biological needs. Such newspaper articles are not intended to foster the kind of critical revolutionary consciousness that
will overthrow a system of unbearable domination we saw in Rizal's and
Pramoedya's novels. They are concerned with maintaining current consumer standards of populations in the West. They express the anxiety
that the West will be outdone by Asia in consumption with the hope of
instilling this anxiety in their readers. Comparison is not a process of a
critical consciousness but something that occurs so effortlessly and obviously as part of the biopolitical infrastructure of comparison that we no
longer think about it.

What happens to critical or revolutionary consciousness in this material world of comparison? I end by briefly discussing Michelle Cliff's *No
Telephone to Heaven* (1987), a novel that dramatizes the tragic implications
of comparison as a material infrastructure for a nation in the contemporary postcolonial South. Clare Savage, the novel's female protagonist,
is a Jamaican from a privileged Creole clan. At sixteen, she is uprooted
when her family migrates to America. After experiencing racist discrimination in America and the "mother country," England, where she
attends university, she returns to Jamaica and joins a guerrilla movement
to fight against the degradation of her country and her people by the
global capitalist transformation of Jamaica into a destination for luxury
tourism and an exotic location for films. Clare is the contemporary Caribbean counterpart of Ibarra and Minke. The demon of comparisons
has ignited her patriotism. After decolonization, the revolution's target

is the postcolonial state, the collaborator with global capital. Clare is instructed by the guerrilla leader to revolutionize her consciousness: "Perhaps you will go further . . . sometimes it is the only way. We are not thugs, you know . . . You speak of the knowledge of resistance . . . the loss of this knowledge. I ask you to think of Bishop. Rodney. Fanon. Lumumba. Malcolm. First. Luthuli. Garvey. Mxembe. Marley. Moloise. Think of those who are gone—and ask yourself how, why?"[36]

In the novel's final chapter, the guerrillas attack the site of a film about Jamaican history. This incident is framed by a thematization of the extent of Jamaica's degradation by global capital. A fictive excerpt from the *New York Times* sells Jamaica as a beautiful film location, noting among other things that "it also has a racially mixed population of many hues and ethnic distinctions, which . . . includes a number of people willing to serve as extras."[37] The narrative then cuts to a scene where two film industry people scouting for locations crudely discuss the prostitution of Jamaica. "You can't beat the prices. And, besides, they need the money . . . real bad. They'll shape up . . . they have to. They're trapped. All tied up by the IMF."[38] "Jamaicans will do anything for a buck . . . Everyone from the hookers to the prime minister, babe. These people are used to selling themselves. I don't think they know from revolution."[39]

People can only sell themselves and a state can only sell its people if human life is viewed through the quantitative measure of growth. The promise of growth is also a trap, the IMF trap where inflows of foreign capital through tourism are viewed as the optimal basis for Jamaican national development. The novel's ending is appropriately ambiguous. The film shooting is a trap set for the guerrillas who are killed by fire from Jamaican army helicopters. On the one hand, Clare is repatriated. In her death, she has become part of her native soil. On the other hand, the popular nation, personified by the guerrillas, is betrayed by the Jamaican state, which appears to have arranged the ambush. But more importantly, it is unclear whether their deaths are also recorded as part of a filmic retelling of the suppression of resistance in Jamaican history to give the film even greater realism. In the earlier conversation, one of the film producers boasts that he has rented soldiers from the Jamaican army complete with helicopters. The narrative therefore dramatizes the snuffing out of revolutionary consciousness by the material world of comparison.

The more sobering point, however, is this: even if a revolution is successful, successful government would require increasing resources and enhancing means so as to best satisfy the needs and interests of the population. The quantification of human life would necessarily inform and shape the values and principles of actors pursuing the common good. We remain part of the material world of comparison insofar as calculations concerning resources, means, and capabilities cannot be absolute. They are always relative and competitive, always a matter of more or less in comparison to whom.

The implications for rethinking comparison are several. First, the fact that power is not primarily directed at consciousness but works through infrastructural comparison and political technologies that shape the milieu affecting populations in order to craft bodies and material interests severely qualifies the preoccupations of an ethics of comparison. Such an ethics attempts to rectify the exclusion of the other through repressive discursive representations that distort and reinforce qualitative differences. There are undoubtedly instances of Orientalist stereotyping in economic processes, for example, to justify the exploitation of cheap overseas labor or the mistreatment of migrant workers. There are also discriminatory practices targeting minority groups within populations that should be resisted. But the current emphasis on repatriating jobs and creating new ones in the North Atlantic in times of economic distress indicates that power's primary focus is to incorporate bodies and enhance the population by accommodating the needs and interests of its members. The competition between populations is a dynamic internal to the quantification of life. Even though it produces and reinforces effects of domination, the original impetus of the quantification of life is not the will to dominate others but the inclusion of others. The reduction of human beings to the same lowest common denominator of basic needs and interests that are calculable makes us all intrinsically interconnected because it facilitates the formation of tighter and, in principle, optimal relations of mutual advantage. Accordingly, free trade is seen as friendly competition and all developing countries want friendly inflows of foreign capital. Just as Marx inverted Hegel and argued that the various shapes of spirit were epiphenomena of a material infrastructure, just as he argued that world literature is generated from a material world of production, I am suggesting that the figures of comparison that preoccupy humanities scholars today and the current reinvigoration of comparative intellectual activity are the epiphenomena of infrastructural processes of comparison premised on the quantification of life. An ethics of comparison is too easily integrated into this infrastructure as a form of cultural capital that bespeaks the intellectual superiority of national academic institutions capable of cultivating such an ethics.

Second, it would be sentimental and nostalgic to counter this material world of comparison by lamenting the degradation of the human spirit by calculation and quantification and calling for a reaffirmation of humanity and its rights, or better yet, to make claims on behalf of both a degraded humanity and its excluded others. The Frankfurt School's critique of instrumental reason also contained a critique of quantification.[40] But because it remained within a Marxist framework of alienation and preserved the priority of human critical consciousness, it foreclosed the fact that humanity itself and all its capacities, needs, and interests are produced by these calculative technologies. This means that all claims in the name of humanity are necessarily imbricated in and circumscribed by these technologies. For example, much is made of the importance of education in fostering socially responsible and humane development. But in the final analysis, education is about the enhancement of human capital so that a given country can be comparatively stronger than others in this most valuable of resources.

Third, one vocational task of literature in this world of comparison is to provide an aesthetic-cognitive mapping of how the mechanisms and technologies of infrastructural comparison work in specific locations and their negative, coercive effects. But literature is also part of the postindustrial comparison machine, which conjures up new forms of comparison where cultural production is indispensable. To take the most obvious example, in the endless search for new opportunities in global markets, there is intense competition among cities outside the top tier of global cities (New York, London, and Tokyo) to join the ranks of the second tier in order to be better equipped to attract transnational capital and gradually ascend the international division of labor. Culture is an important variable in ranking global cities. A city with a vibrant cosmopolitan culture and built environment that can serve as symbolic markers of global city status is more attractive to foreign talent. Aspiring global cities around the world have organized culture festivals, film festivals, art biennales, and literature festivals to demonstrate the presence of a critical mass of cultural capital. Committed literature can outline the limits of the world of comparison and point to a world to come. But like the ethics of comparison, it is also implicated in the processes of infrastructural comparison.

NOTES

1   Haun Saussy, "Exquisite Cadavers Stitched from Fresh Nightmares," in *Comparative Literature in an Age of Globalization*, ed. Haun Saussy (Baltimore: Johns Hopkins Univ. Press, 2006), 3.

2   Jean-Jacques Rousseau, *Essay on the Origin of Languages*, in *The Discourses and Other Early Political Writings*, ed. and trans. Victor Gourevitch (Cambridge: Cambridge Univ. Press, 1997), 268, translation modified where appropriate; *Essai sur l'origine des langues: Oeuvres complètes*, ed. B. Gagnebin and M. Raymond (Paris: Pléiade, 1995), 5:396.

3   Rousseau, *Essay on the Origin of Languages*, 267–68, emphasis added; 5:395–96.

4   Rousseau, *Essay on the Origin of Languages*, 268; 5:396.

5   Jean-Jacques Rousseau, *Discourse on the Foundations of Inequality among Men*, in *The Discourses and Other Early Political Writings*, ed. and trans. Victor Gourevitch (Cambridge: Cambridge Univ. Press, 1997), Note XV [1], 218 (hereafter cited as *FI*); *Discours sur l'ori-*

gine et les fondements de l'inégalité parmi les hommes: *Œuvres complètes*, ed. B. Gagnebin and M. Raymond (Paris: Pléiade, 1959) 3:219.

6   Rousseau notes that during a riot, the uneducated rabble prevents combatants from killing each other whereas the prudent man withdraws (I.37, 153–54).

7   Immanuel Kant, *Anthropology from a Pragmatic Point of View*, ed. and trans. Robert B. Louden (Cambridge: Cambridge Univ. Press, 2006), 18.

8   Kant, "Idea for a Universal History with a Cosmopolitan Purpose," in *Political Writings*, ed. Hans Reiss, trans. H. B. Nisbet, 2nd ed. (Cambridge: Cambridge Univ. Press, 1991), 44, translation modified; "*Idee zu einer allgemeinen Geschichte in weltbürgerlicher Absicht*," in *Schriften zur Anthropologie, Geschichtsphilosophie, Politik und Pädagogik I, Werkausgabe*, ed. Wilhelm Weischedel (Frankfurt am Main: Suhrkamp, 1968), 11:31–50.

9   Kant, "Idea for a Universal History," 44; 37.

10   Kant, "Idea for a Universal History," 45, translation modified; 38.

11   Kant, "Idea for a Universal History," 50, translation modified; 46.

12   Kant, *Critique of the Power of Judgment*, ed. Paul Guyer, trans. Eric Matthews (Cambridge: Cambridge Univ. Press, 2000), 300; *Kritik der Urteilskraft, Werkausgabe*, ed. Wilhelm Weischedel (Frankfurt am Main: Suhrkamp, 1968), 10:392.

13   See G. W. F. Hegel, *Lectures on the Philosophy of World History: Introduction*, trans. H. B. Nisbet (Cambridge: Cambridge Univ. Press, 1980), 52–53.

14   G. W. F. Hegel, *Elements of the Philosophy of Right*, ed. Allen W. Wood, trans. H. B. Nisbet (Cambridge: Cambridge Univ. Press, 1991), §340, 371.

15   Hegel, *Elements of the Philosophy of Right*, §347, 374.

16   Hegel, *Lectures on the Philosophy of World History*, 143.

17   G. W. F. Hegel, *Aesthetics: Lecture on Fine Arts*, trans. T. M. Knox (Oxford: Clarendon Press, 1998), 1:77.

18   For a fuller discussion of decolonization as a form of *Bildung* and the striking privileging of the Bildungsroman in the literature of revolutionary decolonizing nationalism in Asia and Africa, see Pheng Cheah, *Spectral Nationality: Passages of Freedom from Kant to Postcolonial Literatures of Liberation* (New York: Columbia Univ. Press, 2003), 235–47.

19   José Rizal, *Noli Me Tangere*, trans. Harold Augenbraum (London: Penguin, 2006), 54.

20   Benedict Anderson has translated the phrase *el demonio de las comparaciones* as "the spectre of comparisons." This passage from Rizal's novel is crucial to Anderson's own formulation of a non-Eurocentric method of comparison in which Europe is viewed from the standpoint of Southeast Asia as through an inverted telescope. See Anderson, *The Spectre of Comparisons: Nationalism, Southeast Asia and the World* (London: Verso, 1998), 2. For a more sustained discussion, see Pheng Cheah, "Grounds of Comparison," in *Grounds of Comparison: Around the Work of Benedict Anderson*, ed. Pheng Cheah and Jonathan Culler (New York: Routledge, 2003), 1–20. My analysis of Rizal has benefited from conversations with Anderson.

21   Rizal, *Noli Me Tangere*, 400–401.

22   Pramoedya Ananta Toer, *Jejak Langkah* (Kuala Lumpur: Wira Karya: 1986), 170–71, my translation. For a more detailed discussion of how the world of print generates a comparative gaze in Pramoedya's tetralogy, see Cheah, *Spectral Nationality*, 273–80.

23   Pramoedya Ananta Toer, *Anak Semua Bangsa* (Kuala Lumpur: Wira Karya: 1982), 46, my translation.

24   The ethical relation to the other can be radicalized (à la Levinas) to the point that even in the "good" kind of comparison, the establishment of a common world and of humanity as the measure of what is common to self and other involves the domestication of alterity insofar as otherness is brought back into the self by identification and is seen as comparable to the self because it is an other self, an other that is like the self. The self is elevated into a communal self at the expense of the other.

25   See Johannes Fabian, *Time and the Other: How Anthropology Makes Its Object* (New York: Columbia Univ. Press, 1983); and Edward Said, "Representing the Colonized: Anthropology's Interlocutors," *Critical Inquiry* 15, no. 2 (1989): 205–25.

26   Edward Said, *Orientalism*, twenty-fifth anniv. ed. (New York: Vintage, 2003), xviii.

27   Adam Smith, *An Inquiry into the Nature and Causes of the Wealth of Nations*, ed. Edwin Cannan (Chicago: Univ. of Chicago Press, 1976), 3, emphasis added.

28   Smith, *Wealth of Nations*, 18.

29   Smith, *Wealth of Nations*, 19.

30   Michel Foucault, *Security, Territory, Population: Lectures at the College de France 1977–78*, ed. Michel Senellart, trans. Graham Burchell (Basingstoke: Palgrave Macmillan, 2007), 295 (hereafter cited as *STP*).

31   Foucault, *The Birth of Biopolitics: Lectures at the College de France 1978–79*, ed. Michel Senellart, trans. Graham Burchell (Basingstoke: Palgrave Macmillan, 2008), 5.

32   See Foucault, *Security, Territory, Population*, 73; and *Birth of Biopolitics*, 44–45.

33   Sam Zuckerman, "Lifeline in Sea of Debt," *San Francisco Chronicle*, April 27, 2008, A1, A8.

34   Roger Cohen, "The Fleecing of America," *New York Times*, September 22, 2008; and Jane Perlez, "China Competes with West in Aid to Its Neighbors," *New York Times*, September 18, 2006.

35   Roger Cohen, "The Baton Passes to Asia," *International Herald Tribune*, March 31, 2008: 6.

36   Michelle Cliff, *No Telephone to Heaven* (London: Metheun, 1987), 196.

37   Cliff, *No Telephone to Heaven*, 200.

38   Cliff, *No Telephone to Heaven*, 201.

39   Cliff, *No Telephone to Heaven*, 202.

40   See Herbert Marcuse, *One-Dimensional Man*, 2nd ed. (Boston: Beacon Press, 1991).

CHAPTER TEN

Chomsky's Golden Rule:
Comparison and Cosmopolitanism

Bruce Robbins

NOAM CHOMSKY, ARGUABLY THE MOST cosmopolitan of American intellectuals, is also a conspicuous practitioner of comparison. This is natural enough, for comparison is often associated with cosmopolitanism and indeed is sometimes taken as its signature operation. For some critics, this is a decisive argument against both. In demanding an ever-increasing inclusiveness, cosmopolitanism is held to produce the illusory spectacle of the world as a whole. This spectacle was and is a product of imperialist violence, so the argument goes, and that violence is repeated in the everyday act of comparison. Comparison presupposes common norms; common norms, which by definition impose sameness on difference, presuppose a view from outside or above; the view from outside or above presupposes that the viewer is a holder of power. Thus both comparison and cosmopolitanism can be assimilated to capitalist globalization, which is understood to rule by reducing difference to homogeneity.[1]

It is no surprise to find this line of argument popular within literary studies, where it of course repeats the discipline's self-defining reverence for the unique, the particular, and the incomparable while making it seem that the discipline itself is anti-imperialist by its very nature. By the same token, however, there is a certain interest in following out the relations between cosmopolitanism and comparison in Chomsky, who is second to none (not even the literary left) in his denunciations of imperialism, yet who could not be less "literary" either in his writing or in his philosophical premises. That is the task of the present essay.

"The average life expectancy of a species," Chomsky writes on the first page of his book *Hegemony or Survival*, "is about 100,000 years." With the help of evolutionary biology, which routinely counts in units of hundreds of thousands of years, Chomsky sets himself up to take a very long view of "America's quest for global dominance"—that's the book's subtitle—and of everything else.[2] One page later, as if the biologist's perspective were not distant enough, Chomsky evokes humanity's capacity for self-destruction by adopting an even more distant viewpoint: that of "a hypothetical extraterrestrial observer."[3]

It does not seem accidental that Chomsky should appeal in this way to a "hypothetical extraterrestrial observer." In a sense, the extraterrestrial observer is his tutelary spirit. Chomsky has arguably become the most famous and most cosmopolitan public intellectual in the United States in large part because his viewpoint so successfully mimics that of a visitor to Earth from outer space. When we read him, whether we are Americans or not, we feel at least momentarily as if we ourselves were aliens, spectators looking down from a great height on the bad behavior of our fellow earthlings. This alienness gives a distinctive kind of rhetorical pleasure, and it has a distinctive kind of political force. The pleasure and the force come together to define Chomsky's distinctive version of cosmopolitanism, which allows readers not only to take a giant step backward from the United States' assumptions about the essential rightness of its habitual ways of thinking, but also to enjoy the experience. I insist on the enjoyment because cosmopolitanism is so often represented as aridly intellectual, abstract, and detached, empty of such potentially compromising creaturely delights. And I insist on the rhetoric because as I will propose, it is his rhetoric that allows us to see where, politically speaking, Chomsky belongs.

It needs to be stressed that the hypothetical extraterrestrial observer is indeed a rhetorical figure. Such figures are not easy to spot in Chomsky. His writing is unusually bare of metaphor, wordplay, tonal variety. If he has a rhetorical signature, it is perhaps the refusal of any and all rhetorical eccentricity or creativity. He seems to compose as if expecting at any minute to be stopped in order to be translated and as if any stylistic embellishment on his part could only be expected to get in the way of that process. Both expectations are entirely reasonable. As Franco Moretti has noted, the narrator's voice is the element of literary structure that is most anchored in its locality. As opposed to plots and character types, which are readily borrowed, voice has much more trouble crossing national and linguistic borders.[4] Chomsky's prose, on the other hand, is remarkably efficient at crossing borders. *Hegemony or Survival* has already been translated into forty-six languages. In this sense too, Chomsky must be considered a cosmopolitan. By offering a minimum of resistance to translation, his prose makes a visible effort to approach as closely as possible to extraterrestrial universality, to be as little marked as possible by the accidents of his birth in a particular nation and his being raised in a particular language.

If Chomsky is trying to be transparent and universal, it follows that in attributing rhetoric to him, I will appear to be arguing with him—arguing at least with his implicit claim to be a universalist or cosmopolitan in the strongest sense. Rhetoric, as I understand it, is an inevitable sign of partiality or belonging. To be shown to be using rhetoric undercuts the cosmopolitan's claim to exist in a state of pure extraterrestriality or detachment. This argument does not count as a crippling critique, however, if one believes, as I do, that there is no such thing as cosmopolitanism in the strongest sense—that all cosmopolitanism involves some mode or degree of belonging, however minimal or reluctant. But if the critique is not damning, neither is it trivial. If no cosmopolitanism is pure, this doesn't mean that all cosmopolitanisms are equal. My purpose here is the delicate one of beginning to distinguish among unequal cosmopolitanisms, searching for significant differences in their ways of inhabiting the paradoxical condition of detachment and belonging, and ways of judging those differences.

Rhetorically speaking, the key component in Chomsky's cosmopolitan voice is the act of comparing, or, more precisely, an unrestricted, uninhibited practice of comparing. Chomsky draws comparisons without concern for anyone's tender sensibilities, especially not those of his compatriots. To make one's country and countrymen freely available for comparison seems to be, for him, the fundamental moral gesture. Though the following is as he says a "moral truism," it is nonetheless a useful one: "The standards we apply to others we must apply to ourselves."[5] The slogan sounds a lot like the Golden Rule, and that is no doubt one reason why it travels so well. At any rate, Chomsky has gotten a lot of mileage out of it. Consider how often he makes the same exact move in his comments in January 2009 about the Israeli invasion of Gaza, which was then in process, and the heavy civilian casualties it was inflicting. When an Israeli journalist speaks of "the price the inhabitants [of Gaza] will have to pay" in order for Israel to achieve order and security, Chomsky sarcastically inserts the statement into an unpleasant series of analogies: "The problem has been familiar to Americans in South Vietnam, Russians in Afghanistan, Germans in occupied Europe, and other aggressors." (Sarcasm is one rhetorical mode that, perhaps because it is relatively unambiguous, seems to translate pretty well.) Again: "*Times* columnist Thomas Friedman explained that Israel's tactics both in the current attack, as in its invasion of Lebanon in 2006, are based on the sound principle of 'trying to "educate" Hamas, by inflicting a heavy death toll on Hamas militants and heavy pain on the Gaza population.' That makes sense on pragmatic grounds," Chomsky notes drily. "And by similar logic, bin Laden's effort to 'educate' Americans on 9/11 was highly praiseworthy, as were the Nazi attacks on Lidice and Oradour, Putin's destruction of Grozny, and other notable attempts at educational exercises."[6] That which we criticize in others we must also remember to criticize in ourselves and our allies. If we disapprove of the attacks of 9/11 or the Nazi massacre of civilians in retaliation for acts of resistance, we must also disapprove of the Israeli devastation of Gaza. We cannot assume that the United States and its most reliable ally are somehow magically protected from the judgments that are routinely brought to bear upon nonallies—Russia bombing the population of Grozny, al-Qaeda flying planes into the World Trade Center, or whatever.

Thomas Friedman is an easy target, yet he takes for granted nothing more than what most of us take for granted most of the time: that it is as natural and normal to root for our country as to root for our team, that where national belonging is concerned, it is natural and normal to apply a double standard. It's this simple, shockingly pervasive assumption that Chomsky quietly withdraws. And with that foundational premise gone, various ideological edifices crumble. Comparison liberated from this premise—an unshackled, free-range comparison that almost looks like a different species from the domesticated variety we thought we knew—is the hero of Chomsky's cosmopolitanism.

Following his vigorous version of the Golden Rule, Chomsky specializes in asking whether the United States has done unto others what it would like done unto it. He compares the actions of the United States with the actions of other countries, especially those of whom the U.S. government and media express their strongest disapproval, so as to make the point that the United States itself has been either as bad or worse. For example: "the US itself is a leading terrorist state."[7] Or: "the US, in fact, is one of the most extreme religious fundamentalist cultures in the world."[8] Apropos of the U.S. "drug war" in Colombia, he writes: "Imagine the reaction to a proposal that Colombia or China should undertake fumigation programs in North Carolina to destroy government-subsidized crops used for more lethal products."[9] Bush's policy of "anticipatory self-defense" in Iraq resembled the Japanese policy at Pearl Harbor.[10] And so on. These are all great lines. One would like to see more students trained to feel their force and sent out into the world prepared to deliver lines like them. Hearing calls to boycott the 2008 Beijing Olympics in the name of Tibet, I naturally asked myself what Chomsky would say. Why didn't the U.S. media see fit to add, I thought, that if the Olympics had been happening in an American city, the war in Iraq would offer much stronger moral grounds than Tibet for Americans to boycott a U.S.-based Olympics?

Chomsky clearly goes well beyond the now-customary celebrations of cosmopolitanism as diversity. If some of the celebrants have forgotten to ask whether cosmopolitanism helps persuade Americans to adopt a relation to the rest of the world that would make them less likely to bomb, invade, occupy, or otherwise mistreat the rest of the world,

Chomsky has clearly not forgotten. His voice demonstrates the moral power of rising above loyalty to one's homeland, tearing free of its peculiar cultural assumptions, and looking at it with an alien's eye. At the same time, however, this is not cosmopolitanism in a pure or absolute sense. (Here my argument makes a turn.) It is not a view from nowhere. True, Chomsky blames the United States as if he did not belong in any way to the United States, and as if his readers didn't either. When we Americans read Chomsky, we feel at least momentarily as if we ourselves were extraterrestrials, looking down on the misconduct of others. It's not *our* misconduct; we're from another solar system. Reading him is pleasurable the way certain works of science fiction are. We are visitors from another world, taking in the bizarre customs. We are confident at every instant that they are not our customs. Yet on second thought it is strange that we are so confident, because if we are Americans, they *are* our customs, at least in a sense of "our" that remains to be specified.[11]

Chomsky's practice of comparison tries hard to escape the constraint of national belonging. But that constraint reasserts itself, so to speak, negatively. The United States is criticized in almost all of Chomsky's comparisons. But that makes it the one fixed point of those comparisons. In other words, Chomsky puts the United States at the center of virtually all his judgments. It occupies a negative, devalued, nonhonorific center, but a center nonetheless. This means that other things are, as the saying goes, marginalized or excluded. The one consistent principle that is followed in his commentaries is that what the United States has done or is doing is wrong. No other principle gets more than the briefest recognition. Though Chomsky sounds like a universalist, his practice of national self-blaming is not in fact universalistic, therefore, unless you are ready to count the presumptive guilt of the United States in every case under discussion as an example of universalism. Chomsky will compare an action by the United States (say, the claim to "humanitarian intervention" in the 1990s) with an action by another nation (say, the interventions of India in Bangladesh in 1971 or of Vietnam in Cambodia in 1978). He will ask, quite rightly, why the latter did not get described by the so-called international community as humanitarian interventions, though each might be said to have stopped a genocide. But Chomsky does not stop and ask whether the actions of the Indian and Vietnamese governments were actually worthy of approval or not. What were their motives? Were they acting in a more disinterested way than the United States? Does he approve the principle that intervention is acceptable if it does stop a genocide? If so, he might be obliged to praise the United States if and when (perhaps in the former Yugoslavia) it could be established that it did just that. But if not, then he would be obliged to be critical of the Indian and Vietnamese governments and *their* excuses for intervention.

It would seem that he backs off from such criticisms on the grounds that he is not himself Indian or Vietnamese. In other words, here we seem to be in the presence of a double standard based on national identity or location—not universalism at all, but nationalism in reverse.[12]

As someone committed to universal rational principles and the rhetoric of the Golden Rule, Chomsky might be expected to reject any hint of a double standard. The fact that he doesn't do so, that he is so reluctant to consider, say, the opinion of an Indian citizen about the Indian government or the opinion of a Vietnamese citizen about the Vietnamese government, or for that matter the opinion of a *Cambodian* citizen who was perhaps saved by the intervention of the Vietnamese government (you see how this could go on), the fact that no perspectives matter except perspectives about America, as long as they are wholly critical, is the negative sign of a concealed, disavowed Americanness.[13] It indicates that Chomsky's cosmopolitanism is not after all extraterrestrial, but very American.

What difference does it make if we recognize that Chomsky's cosmopolitanism is, in its way, an imperfect, local, Americanocentric cosmopolitanism? My own view, briefly stated, is that there are plenty of things for which one can properly condemn Chomsky, but one can't condemn him simply for being a partial or imperfect cosmopolitan. Partial, imperfect cosmopolitans are the *only* cosmopolitans. A full, absolute, genuinely extraterrestrial cosmopolitanism doesn't exist. There is no cosmopolitanism without some degree or mode of belonging, even if that belonging takes the negative form of shame rather than the positive form of pride. All cosmopolitanism is really "local" or "rooted" or "discrepant," "patriotic" or "vernacular" or "actually existing." Therefore all cosmopolitanism is more or less paradoxical. The question is, what follows?[14] What is the next step? If there is no clean escape from the cosmopolitan paradox, are there at least significantly different ways of inhabiting it?

In moving toward an answer to this question, it needs to be said first of all that Chomsky's negative but intensely possessive mode of belonging to America has certain political disadvantages. One disadvantage is that it makes the rest of the American Left disappear. It's as if he were saying: there can be only one alien, and that alien is me.[15] Michael Bérubé has described this heroically self-isolating pose in a Melvillean phrase: "I only am escaped from America to tell thee."[16] This pose is not helpful, for example, for those interested in encouraging solidarity or building movements. A further and related disadvantage is the series of lapses of political judgment and instances of badly misplaced solidarity into which Chomsky's anti-Americanism has led him. One famous example is his defense of Pol Pot. When the official American discourse was calling Pol Pot a mass murderer, Chomsky compared the Khmer Rouge with the French Resistance to the Nazis. (It's this that he's trying to conceal, I think, with his faint praise of the Vietnamese intervention to stop the Cambodian genocide—he himself was very late in recognizing that a genocide had happened.) Another example is his de facto denial of the Serbian ethnic cleansing of Bosnia and Kosovo and his opposition to any supranational intervention to stop it. Slobodan Milosevic may have been a thug, but so was the United States. What could possibly legitimate the intervention of one thug against another? It's a fair question, but not an unanswerable one. The answer is: when one of them is at the moment in the act of committing genocide. Attacking Milosevic's attackers at that moment had the practical effect of defending both Milosevic and genocide.

Chomsky's objection could have been raised against efforts to save the Jews of Europe from the Nazis, had the Allies made any such efforts. This objection could also have been raised against United Nations efforts to stop the Rwandan genocide, had the Clinton administration permitted the United Nations to act or even to use the G-word. Political action is rarely carried out by the saintly. There is something both irresponsible and extraterrestrial, therefore, about Chomsky's suggestion that he has decided the issue when he declares to all that the United States is a sinner, and at least as great a sinner as any other nation. What the U.S. government thinks or does can't be enough to decide anyone's political judgments or solidarities, whether positively or negatively. This point also applies to those occasions when anyone is tempted to assert that colonialism necessarily remains the sole or prime causal factor in each and every instance of human suffering and injustice in the former colonies.[17] It is possible to recognize the living legacy of colonialism without being quite so provincial, so negatively narcissistic about "the West." Negative narcissism is still narcissism.

The moral to be drawn here might appear to be: do as Chomsky says, not what he does. Apply the same standards to every nation, whether the United States happens to like or hate that nation. On second thought, however, it seems possible that this is not the proper moral after all. Do we believe it is in fact right to apply standards equally to all? The question arises in Walter Benn Michaels' book *The Trouble with Diversity*.[18] It is strange to note that though their political purposes could not be more opposed, Michaels in fact adopts a rhetoric of comparison that closely resembles Chomsky's.

In his brief against identity politics, Michaels rather cleverly compares American political theorist Samuel Huntington with the Aymara Indians of Bolivia. The demand of indigenous peoples that their endangered cultures be protected from the assimilatory pressures of modernization,

Michaels says, is precisely the same demand that Huntington makes when he opposes the cultural and linguistic influence of Hispanic immigrants in order to preserve and defend a distinct American, Anglophone identity. The comparison seems perfect: "What Huntington wants for Americans is what . . . the Aymara Indians want for themselves: to preserve their (and our) identities" (*TD* 148–49). Here Michaels applies precisely the same standard to the United States as to the Aymara Indians. I have no problem with embarrassing Huntington by comparing his own cultural conservatism to the identity politics he despises. Why then do I feel that this rhetoric is less egalitarian than it seems?

The reason for unease becomes clearer when Michaels follows his argument up and away into the imaginative (and equally Chomskyean) domain of the counterfactual—a flight of imagination that is demanded, of course, by the Golden Rule itself. Let us "imagine ourselves," Michaels tells his fellow Americans, "on the losing side of globalization. Imagine the United States fifty years from now—we're so poor that China and India are outsourcing production to the desperate and hence very hard-working masses of Michigan and Ohio" (*TD* 162). This fantasy turns into an argument against Americans hanging on to English: "If we don't learn Hindi, we won't even be able to get the call center jobs that would keep us out of the sweatshops, where all our friends who just speak English work twelve hours a day making athletic shoes to be worn by Asians . . . So when the United States is going to become the place jobs are out-sourced to, I want to be able to speak Hindi or at least make sure that my children do. In a world where economic opportunity depends on the ability to speak Hindi, why would I want them to keep on speaking English?" (*TD* 164–65).

Michaels calls this the "final twist," but it is not where the argument actually ends up. As the counterfactual fades and we return to the world where Americans are on the winning rather than the losing side of globalization and where English is not threatened with imminent extinction, the point of the argument once again becomes the irratio-nality of globalization's losers, who really are faced with the loss of their language and culture and who insist, against the manifest imperative of "economic opportunity," on wanting to preserve both. All of this *jeu d'esprit* comes back to the aim of discrediting the Aymara Indians. And the discrediting is accomplished by none other than Chomsky's Golden Rule. Look, Michaels says, I'm applying the same standard to myself that I apply to others. *I* am willing to give up my language in exchange for further economic opportunity. So why shouldn't *they*? As a reward for my magnanimity, I win the right to say that the third world in general and indigenous peoples in particular must accept whatever deal global capital offers them, even if it means surrendering their languages and cultures. That's what I would do if I were in their place. You've just seen me put myself in their place.

The problem here is not whether the standard is applied equally and reciprocally. The problem is the standard itself. Whose standard is it? For Michaels, the standard appears to be: successful adaptation to global capitalism. This standard assumes an American self that travels light, always remaining itself no matter what it has to jettison. This makes a certain sense (less than Michaels assumes, but that isn't the point here) from the perspective of those who have gotten a relatively good deal from global capitalism. It makes much less sense if, as for the Aymara, jettisoning things like culture and language means that one would no longer *be* oneself. It's not that economic well-being is irrelevant to the Aymara. On the contrary. No moderately interested observer of indigenous struggles to preserve their languages and cultures could miss the fact that language and culture are not merely tokens of identity to be preserved for their own sake; they are also means to an economic end. In the nations and situations where peoples like the Aymara live, securing the right to practice one's language and culture belongs to the larger economic and political enterprise, the effort to seize control over lands, territories, and resources that are at present controlled or severely threatened by foreigners, including multinational corporations. Michaels's solution for the Aymara and other indigenous peoples, conveyed by the call-center analogy, is to submit to the multinationals, exchanging their native languages for "economic opportunity." He does not seem capable of imagining that one might actually contest the claims of the multinationals rather than submitting to them. Nor does he notice that preserving native languages might be a strategy for contesting those claims.

The results of the comparison will of course depend on the standard applied. Michaels's standard of successful adaptation to global capitalism, along with the streamlined self it implies, manifestly pushes the comparison in a different direction than it might have gone had the standard been, say, "economic well-being." The latter might conceivably be embraced by the Aymara themselves. The former probably would not. If the standard of comparison demands a free, presocial individual, imagined to remain itself no matter how much of its cultural and linguistic baggage it throws overboard, then the Aymara are clearly placed at a disadvantage from the outset. Applying that standard allows North Americans who are willing to give up their language to look better and ensures that the Aymara will look worse. Michaels is perfectly willing to apply the same standard to himself that he applies to the Aymara. But it's his standard, not theirs, and thus the comparison plays to his advantage. The same point might be made about Chomsky's Golden Rule. He wants the same standards applied to United States citizens that we apply to others. But he has no means of objecting to standards as long as they *are* applied to us as well, even if the standards themselves favor us, thus winning comparative advantage for us if and when we do apply them both to ourselves and to others.

The reader may already have been speculating about one inequality buried within Chomsky's version of the Golden Rule: the inequality of power between the parties compared. (Indeed, it is that inequality, provisionally removed by means of Michaels's counterfactual, that proves decisive once it is brought back in.) But this inequality seems to work in Chomsky's defense. If he has deviated from true universality by always putting the United States at the center, it might be argued that the United States *belongs* at the center, precisely because it has so much power. The Unites States is, after all, not merely a power but a superpower, and as such it tilts the playing field between nations in its own favor. You cannot judge a small, relatively powerless country by the same standards. Chomsky's practice, which deviates from his Golden Rule, is ethically superior to the Golden Rule.

This comes very close to what Chomsky himself argues when accused of falling away from a universal standard, though he presents his position in terms of another moral universal. "The most elementary moral principles," he writes, "would lead to 'playing up' the crimes of domestic origin in comparison to those of official enemies, that is, 'playing up' the crimes that one can do something about."[19] Principles are relative to responsibility, which is itself relative to proximity. We have more responsibility to criticize that misconduct which lies closest to hand, which we are most causally involved in and/or which we can most easily have an effect on. In this sense, pure universalism would be a moral and political error. Comparisons must, after all, be selective.[20] As Chomsky says, this does seem to be an elementary moral principle. It was the indispensable response, for example, during the recent massacre of civilians in Gaza when Zionists demanded that American critics of Israel spend equal time criticizing Hamas. No doubt Hamas had things to answer for. But we Americans, and especially we American Jews, were ethically obliged to spend greater critical energy on the evils supported by our government and committed in our name.

Still, there is an issue here, that of the relation between cosmopolitanism and power. Chomsky's version of the Golden Rule—"the standards we apply to others we must apply to ourselves"—is so successfully cosmopolitan because it does not seem to represent any one nation at the expense of any other, and thus seems to rise above the power alignments and power imbalances that otherwise structure the world of nations. As we have seen, however, it never completely separates itself from power; even Chomsky's self-defense (the need to "play up" the crimes of one's own nation) assumes a greater power to affect the crimes of one's own nation. It assumes, in other words, that the American cosmopolitan *possesses* a certain power. This point could be made cynically: look, one might say, even the rhetorical figure of the extraterrestrial assumes a degree of power that needs to be spelled out. Like Steven Spielberg's E.T., who could make bicycles fly and perform other neat tricks, Chomsky's extraterrestrial would also have to possess superhuman powers merely in order to have arrived on earth in the first place. Those powers may go unmentioned, but they must be part of what the figure actually means to us. One might argue that in this respect, too, the alien is secretly American. But the point is not merely that Chomsky should confess to the powers he secretly possesses by virtue of being an American citizen. That could be said, and most often *is* said, *as if the only proper position were to be powerless.* It's that position, a position that I associate rightly or wrongly with his anarchism and with the more pervasive antistatism of our historical moment, that I'm arguing against here.

I illustrate from the 2007 book *On Suicide Bombing* by the anthropologist Talal Asad. Asad notes that so-called "legitimate violence exercised in and by the modern progressive state—including the liberal democratic state—possesses a peculiar character that is absent in terrorist violence (absent not because of the latter's virtue but because of the former's capability)."[21] The usual criteria of virtue have been suspended here and replaced by criteria of capability. It's not that terrorist violence is virtuous; it's merely that it has less capability to harm than the violence of the state. True enough. Yet the implication here seems to be that the *lack* of the capability to harm becomes, if not virtue itself, then a new functional *substitute* for virtue, the basis for a new ethics. This new ethics is antinormative because it is assumed that ethical norms have been put in place by the powerful, those who do have the capability to harm. It is anticosmopolitan because the perception that your very survival is threatened—the ultimate degree of powerlessness—justifies, following the logic of Carl Schmitt, an absolute embrace of your nation in defiance of all cosmopolitan universals. And, by the same token, it dispenses you from making moral judgments.

Chomsky specializes in making moral judgments, of course, yet there is a striking overlap between Chomsky and Asad nonetheless. They share a kind of extraterrestriality—an internationalism of the putatively powerless. I elaborate on this point in my conclusion.

Though Chomsky is best known in the humanities as a Golden Rule universalist, whether because of his belief in a biologically based human nature or his famous 1971 debate with Michel Foucault, he often insists on the contamination of supposedly universal standards by unequal power.[22] He has been extremely critical of the selectivity of human rights—so much so as to be taken by some as a simple opponent of human rights.[23] In *Hegemony or Survival,* ethical norms are presented as merely the random ideology of the latest crop of thugs.[24] In the debate with Foucault, similarly, Chomsky notes that "international law is, in many respects, the instrument of the powerful; it is a creation of states and their representatives . . . It's simply an instrument of the powerful to retain their power." Then he adds, however, that "international law is not *solely* of that kind. And in fact there are interesting elements of international law, for example, embedded in the Nuremberg principles and the United Nations Charter, which permit, in fact, I believe, *require* the citizen to act against his own state in ways which the state will falsely regard as criminal."[25] His impulse is to suggest that while much international law, like all domestic law, is a creation of the state, some international law is not, and it's the part of the law that is not produced by the state that's valid. Here we see Chomsky's anarchism, his assumption that whatever is created by states is invalid and must be resisted. (The epigraph to Chomsky's *For Reasons of State* is from Bakunin: "The State is the organized authority, domination, and power of the possessing classes over the masses.") It is this anarchist assumption that seems to underlie his rhetorical opportunism about humanitarian intervention to stop genocide.[26] He cannot come out and say that what the governments of Vietnam and India did to stop genocide should indeed count as humanitarian intervention, because to admit this would be to endorse the action of a state. States are always bad guys, except perhaps when they are in the act of resisting the United States.[27]

Yet the state is precisely what Chomsky does partially endorse—what he can't keep himself from endorsing, I want to say—when he talks about the law. When he's talking about law in general, it's clear that domestic law too has ethical validity in his eyes: "To a very large extent existing law represents certain human values, which are decent human values: and existing law, correctly interpreted, permits much of what the state commands you not to do." The same is of course also true about the parts of international law that he likes: they too are largely if not entirely produced by "states and their representatives."[28] Chomsky cannot sustain his anarchism if he is also going to be a cosmopolitan; he cannot be a cosmopolitan without the state, and the state's power. That power is also his power. Let me put this another way. Here Chomsky is accepting implicitly a series of principles that he absolutely refuses to accept explicitly. First, the principle that cosmopolitan standards he considers valid are produced in part by the power of states, whose authority he rejects. Second, and by extension, the principle that the cosmopolitan standards he considers valid are invested in part with the power of states. Third and more simply, the principle that cosmopolitanism is invested with power. Finally and most simply, the principle that having power is a good thing—a good thing for cosmopolitanism, and a good thing for anyone who wants not just to interpret the world, but to change it.

These principles flesh out Chomsky's self-defense against the charge of selectivity in his comparisons. The states we inhabit are agents over which we can have a certain leverage. In that sense they are proper objects of selective or disproportionate criticism. But they do not merely deserve unequal treatment because they are near at hand, causes of an evil for which we are responsible. This criticism is also merited because they are agents on which we can have an effect. As an anarchist, Chomsky may only want to say that the state can be resisted. But once he opens the door to the possibility of successful resistance, he can't block the possibility of pushing the state to do things he believes in, as it has already done in passing the laws of which he expressly approves. Indeed, he cannot consistently deny that the state has already done things he would have liked it to do. That might mean desegregating the Alabama schools (in Alabama in the 1950s and 1960s, the local meant racism, and the federal government was fighting racism). Or it might mean stopping a genocide, as Chomsky almost concedes the Indian and Vietnamese states did.

In a sense, I am only illustrating here the abstract theoretical point already made. All cosmopolitanism is paradoxical or imperfect in the sense that it involves belonging as well as detachment. Cosmopolitanism and belonging to a nation-state are not always and everywhere antithetical to one another. Usable power is, as it were, the good side of the imperfectness of Chomsky's extraterrestrial detachment, the hidden benefit in a disavowed belonging, a disavowed partiality. The point seems worth insisting on because it undermines Chomsky's anarchism and because anarchism is such a large if only implicit impulse in contemporary celebrations of a supposedly postnational condition. We cosmopolitan humanists do not like to acknowledge that we belong, in the strong sense, to states, though states, when we push them, do the work of guaranteeing human rights and providing welfare as well as (when we don't stop them) making war and keeping out unwanted migrants. Anarchists like to think of themselves as free but powerless. They are neither as free as they think, nor as powerless. Power is not something that belongs only to the bad guys; it's certainly not a way of telling who *is* a bad guy. A better way of inhabiting the cosmopolitan paradox would involve recognizing that we are invested with a certain power, and that despite the threat it brings to our ideal impartiality, we wouldn't mind having more of it.[29]

I want to conclude by returning to the practice of comparison as seen against a troubling background of unequal power. It is of course true that the scale of power matters. Talal Asad's point was made and remade during the Israeli invasion of Gaza. It is grotesque to assume that a few rockets aimed at Israeli civilians by Hamas, however wrongly, can be properly met with the wholesale slaughter inflicted on the Palestinian inhabitants.[30] Any norm that justifies the latter by equating or "balancing" the two, as mainstream American discourse has repeatedly done, deserves to be treated as worthless. But many of us in the humanities generalize this position (mistakenly, in my view), preferring, like Asad, to place ourselves outside norms, thereby evading the supposed arrogance of "speaking for humanity."

In her recent book *Frames of War,* Judith Butler counsels Asad to reject this move. She first makes the Foucaultian point that normativity is indeed interfered with by "the differential of power."[31] The category of "the human," she warns, is already normative in a way that tilts the comparison in favor of some and against others. So yes, "speaking for humanity" is a problem. Yet the refusal to do so is also a problem. When Asad offers an anthropological "understanding" of suicide bombing in place of, and as opposed to, any normative judgment, one might say that he presents himself as a sort of extraterrestrial, looking on with complete detachment from the urgencies of judgment that mere humans feel obliged to respond to.[32] By this account scholarship itself would be a cosmopolitan space in the extraterrestrial sense: ethically speaking, it would be a space of perfect nonbelonging.

This danger is most acute for anyone who depends on a politics of comparison. One who criticizes another nation typically compares that nation with her own but leaves her own nation out of bounds, safely unscrutinized. It's this nationalist habit, particularly obnoxious in the United States, that Chomsky so vibrantly exposes and demolishes. He makes the unmarked term visible again. Yet the same thing can happen when one compares two other nations or situations, and in that case the risk is that the third term, the comparer himself, will become ethically invisible. It's this risk that I think Butler is revealing to Asad, and her warning seems relevant to Chomsky as well.

In the case of the Khmer Rouge, one of the statements that got Chomsky into trouble was an act of comparison between the outrage expressed in the West against Pol Pot and the relative silence that greeted the simultaneous and extremely bloody Indonesian invasion of East Timor in December 1975, which was backed by the United States. "In the case of Cambodia reported atrocities have not only been eagerly seized on by the Western media but also embellished by substantial fabrications," Chomsky wrote. "The case of Timor is radically different. The media have shown no interest in examining the atrocities of the Indonesian invaders, even though in absolute numbers they are on the same scale."[33] Chomsky's defender Milan Rai comments that the focus in this piece is "on assessing the performance of the media—its handling of the evidence available at the time. The focus is not on judging the situation in Cambodia itself." Rai finds it incomprehensible, then, that Chomsky and his cowriter Edward Herman "were harshly attacked for allegedly doubting the facts of the Khmer Rouge massacres." A critic who accuses Chomsky of saying that the Cambodian "executions have numbered at most in the thousands" is reprimanded by Rai, who goes back to the original article. In that article we read: "Such journals as the *Far Eastern Economic Review*, the London *Economist*, the *Melbourne Journal of Politics*, and others elsewhere, have provided analyses by highly qualified specialists who have studied the full range of evidence available, and who concluded that the executions have numbered at most in the thousands." Rai concludes: "Chomsky was not presenting *his* conclusion 'as based on the analysis of highly qualified specialists themselves'; he was presenting the conclusions of the specialists themselves, without comment."[34]

To pretend that you can hide behind the authorities you cite is strange for an anarchist, especially one who is so reluctant to attribute authority to experts or specialized knowledge. To hide behind the authorities is like hiding *between* the two objects of a comparison, such as Cambodia and East Timor: it assumes that the one who is making the comparison is not part of the events that are under analysis, that the speaker citing others need make "no comment" on what is going on. To present the analysis of qualified specialists without rebuttal and without comment is, in effect, to say those words oneself. In this case, it is to radically diminish the Cambodian genocide, even if only in order to prove the existence, in the Western media, of "an appalling double standard regarding Cambodia and East Timor."[35] Ethically speaking, Chomsky makes himself disappear—that is, he claims to be a "hypothetical extraterrestrial observer."[36]

Butler's point about Asad is that his extraterrestrial withdrawal from normative judgment is not wrong (there are good reasons to be wary of norms). Rather, it is weaker than it needs to be: "There is a *stronger* normative position here—a more consequential exploration of normativity—than its author explicitly allows."[37] She repeats the comparative term "stronger." She insists that there is no stepping outside the practice of comparison. Asad's argument that terrorism cannot be considered apart from state violence depends implicitly on "a horizon of comparative judgment," she says, and when Asad is comparative, he is also normative. He is normative despite his attempted refusal of normativity. This is what gives Asad's argument "its rhetorical force." Accepting that he is indeed speaking normatively (presumably even if this entailed making a moral judgment on suicide bombing) would make his argument "stronger."

I read Butler's recourse to the vocabulary of force and strength as also, simultaneously, a way of making a theoretical point about power. I take her to be saying that, however reluctantly, Asad is participating in shared norms and thus in the social power that those norms embody. He seems to prefer imagining himself as outside such norms, hence as powerless. But that is not the case, either for him or for Chomsky, nor should it be what he and Chomsky desire. Both are right to condemn state violence. But they are wrong to condemn the state as (sole) possessor of power, or—what seems to follow from it—to condemn the possession of power as such. State violence cannot be shielded from comparison with so-called terrorism, as it is by the prevailing discourse. But the comparison between the two, once launched, suggests that power can and must be fought with alternative power. A cosmopolitan theory of power must insist, with Foucault, that power is distributed more widely and unpredictably. Power is never absolute, and one can never reject it absolutely. Cosmopolitanism cannot go about acquiring more power unless it begins by admitting that it already *has* some power.

As we have established, the landscape of comparison is always distorted from below by differentials of power. Yet that cannot stop us from practicing comparison, and practicing it both so as to expose the hidden normativity of certain comparisons and to find a normativity that will empower our own countercomparisons. Incomparability and incommensurability, which attempt to escape entirely from norms, cannot determine our goal. The aim, as Butler says, "is not to dispense with normativity, but to insist that normative inquiry take on a critical and comparative form." This measured embrace of comparison is what will make our cosmopolitan arguments stronger, and our strength more cosmopolitan, at a time when we need both more cosmopolitanism and more strength.

NOTES

1   For a nuanced but not unrepresentative version of this argument, see Natalie Melas, *All the Difference in the World: Postcoloniality and the Ends of Comparison* (Stanford, CA: Stanford Univ. Press, 2007). The premise of Melas's book is that it is paradoxically possible to have "a ground of comparison, but no given basis of equivalence"—in other words, a mode of comparison that fully respects "incommensurability" (xii).

2   Noam Chomsky, *Hegemony or Survival: America's Quest for Global Dominance* (New York: Metropolitan Books, 2003).

3   Chomsky, *Hegemony or Survival*, 2.

4   Franco Moretti, "Conjectures on World Literature," *New Left Review* NS 1, (Jan–Feb 2000): 54–68.

5   Chomsky, "Commentary: Moral Truisms, Empirical Evidence, and Foreign Policy," *Review of International Studies* 29, no. 4 (2003): 605–20.

6   Chomsky, "'Exterminate All the Brutes': Gaza 2009," chomsky.info, January 19, 2009, http://www.chomsky.info/articles/20090119.htm.

7   Noam Chomsky, *9-11* (New York: Seven Stories, 2001), 40.

8   Chomsky, *9-11*, 21.

9   Chomsky, *9-11*, 60–61.

10   This is cited from Arthur Schlesinger.

11   Why take for granted that like Steven Spielberg's E.T., an extraterrestrial would be *nice*, that he or she or it would *like* us? If one pays attention to Chomsky's rhetorical figure—never an easy thing to do with Chomsky's rhetoric, which seems designed to look innocent, transparent, not like rhetoric at all—this is exactly what Chomsky does take for granted. His extraterrestrial seems *surprised* by human self-destructiveness. Why so surprised? In its intergalactic travels, did the visitor from space encounter only life forms that were naturally peace-loving and ecologically friendly? One wonders whether this visitor has really done any traveling at all. Perhaps, at heart, the extraterrestrial is really rather provincial—an indignant but basically friendly American human, equipped with the standard set of humane values, and unusual only in its willingness to apply those values to the mystifications and hypocrisies of America's official discourse.

12   See below for further discussion of Chomsky's anarchism, which stops him from seeing the value in state action of any sort.

13   As an astute graduate student at Wayne State University noticed during an earlier version of this paper, Chomsky's rational-comparative view of justice does not demand any response from the subjectivity or opinions of others. This avoids the threat to justice that would arise from recognition of a chaotic swirl of potentially incommensurable subjectivities, but it also closes down any sense of the public sphere as a site where these subjectivities might nonetheless reach some degree of agreement. The distinctive authority of Chomsky's voice comes in part from the premise that he does not have to stop and listen to anyone. On the Americanness of Chomsky's critique, see also Joe Lockard, "Chomsky on 9-11," *Judaism* 51, no. 2 (2002): 249–52.

14   This looser definition presents a more than merely hypothetical danger that soon very little will be excluded from it—that we will approach the fatal indistinction of the formula "*everything* is cosmopolitanism." If some rough distinctions can't be drawn both around and within it, then politically speaking, the term will have been murdered by its success.

15   Note the contradiction between this and Chomsky's other rhetorical effect, which is to suggest that we are *all* aliens. If one reads Chomsky for tone, there is something a little strange about the "visitor from another planet" rhetoric. Chomsky is indignant, of course, but he is also bemused, as if he can't quite believe that people continue doing and saying things that are so obviously counter to justice and common sense. And he does not seem to worry that we might disagree with him. It's as if he imagined himself telling all this to the Martians back home, who could be counted on to chuckle along with him. And it's also as if we were guaranteed to react in the same way as those Martians. Hence the strangeness: on the one hand, there are no Martians, or none we know of. On the other, the Martians are us.

16   Michael Bérubé, *The Left at War* (New York: New York Univ. Press, 2009), 45.

17   This is of course just what the current crop of dictators never tires of saying. It's a betrayal of those struggling against them.

18   Walter Benn Michaels, *The Trouble with Diversity: How We Learned to Love Identity and Ignore Inequality* (New York: Metropolitan Books, 2006) (hereafter cited as *TD*).

19   Quoted in Robert F. Barsky, *Noam Chomsky: A Life of Dissent* (Cambridge, MA: MIT Press, 1997), 178. See also where the ethical emphasis falls on "atrocities for which [one] shares responsibility and knows how to bring to an end, if [one chooses]" (188).

20   Differences of power are also the key to the eloquent critique of comparison in comparative literature in Rey Chow's *The Age of the World Target*. Comparison cannot be the basic ethical act if, as Chow argues, all comparison presupposes norms of comparison which implicitly favor one side over the other. Comparison is grounded, "as the etymology of the word suggests, in the notion of parity—in the possibility of peer-like equality and

mutuality among those being compared" (72–73). Yet the notion that such equal common ground exists in some natural or unproblematic way has been troubled. Chow's citation of Foucault's citation of Lautréamont—"the fortuitous encounter on an operating table of a sewing machine and an umbrella" (76)—makes the act of comparison seem at once random and violating, epistemologically untrustworthy and sneakily aggressive. At the same time, Chow is unwilling to discontinue comparing, and, as I have argued elsewhere, the alternative, self-consciously tentative versions of comparison she offers are probably close to the best practice standard that already exists. Among these alternatives it is, in effect, comparison as the study of the uneven distribution of power that keeps comparison from ever assuming the ideal parity on which it depends, and in that sense keeps it from being what it claims to be. Rey Chow, *The Age of the World Target: Self-Referentiality in War, Theory, and Comparative Work* (Durham, NC: Duke Univ. Press, 2006). See also Bruce Robbins, afterword to "Remapping Genre," special issue, *PMLA* 122, no. 5 (2007): 1644–51.

21 Talal Asad, *On Suicide Bombing* (New York: Columbia Univ. Press, 2007), 3.

22 Compared to Foucault, Chomsky does indeed come off as a stalwart defender of norms. He rejects Foucault's idea that "the notions of justice or of 'realization of the human essence' are only the inventions of our civilization and result from our class system. The concept of justice is thus reduced to a pretext advanced by a class that has or wants to have access to power." Chomsky on the contrary speaks up for "fundamental human rights." If one looks deeper, however, his position is more complicated. Noam Chomsky and Michel Foucault, *The Chomsky-Foucault Debate: On Human Nature*, foreword by John Rajchman (New York: New Press, 2006), 138–39.

23 For reflections on consistency as a criterion in Chomsky and his "mistake . . . that hypocrisy is the principal evil of our time" (534), see Jeffrey C. Isaac, "Hannah Arendt on Human Rights and the Limits of Exposure, or Why Noam Chomsky Is Wrong About Kosovo," *Social Research* 69, no. 2 (2002): 505–37.

24 The rule, Chomsky writes, is "that only the most powerful are granted the authority to establish norms of appropriate behavior—for themselves." The exception (a sarcastic exception) is when this authority is "delegated to reliable clients. Thus, Israel's crimes are permitted to establish norms: for example, its regular resort to 'targeted killings.'" Chomsky, *Hegemony or Survival*, 24.

25 Chomsky and Foucault, *The Chomsky-Foucault Debate*, 48–49.

26 It is this same assumption that seems to underlie his rhetorical opportunism about humanitarian intervention to stop genocide.

27 An interesting alternative to Chomsky on India and Vietnam would be the practice of comparison by Perry Anderson, who refuses to cite authorities whose political credentials are less than impeccable. Since there are few if any such authorities, Anderson could logically find himself being extremely critical of the movement against the Iraq War in 2002–3 on the grounds that the antiwar movement looked to the United Nations or to Europe, each of them compromised in the extreme, as useful counterweights to U.S. militarism. Politically speaking, this takes Anderson out of the game, or at any rate forces him into a posture of analytic spectatorship. It's perhaps worth asking which, Anderson or Chomsky, is the more extraterrestrial.

28 Chomsky and Foucault, *The Chomsky-Foucault Debate*, 47.

29 A cosmopolitan theory of power would have to insist that power is not located in one place. This was Foucault's point about not having cut off the king's head in the domain of political theory, and though Foucault is widely thought of as an antistatist (I've said this myself) looking back to the debate between Foucault and Chomsky makes it clear that of the two, it's Chomsky who is more of an antistatist, and more mistaken, therefore, in his theory of power. No state has all the power. But the all-important corollary to this is that cosmopolitanism also has power.

30 But there is also large, transnational power in the norms by which Israel's slaughter of civilians is condemned around the world—in those voices, like Asad's and like Chomsky's, that gather around those norms and speak them.

31 Judith Butler, *Frames of War: When Is Life Grievable?* (London: Verso, 2009), 77.

32 Chomsky created a great deal of trouble for himself by making a similar move with regard to the French literature professor Robert Faurisson, who was fired from his position on the grounds that he had denied the existence of the gas chambers. Chomsky signed a petition in his defense and wrote the following: "I have nothing to say here about the work of Robert Faurisson or his critics, of which I know very little, or about the topics they address, concerning which I have no special knowledge." Barsky, *Noam Chomsky*, 180.

33 Milan Rai, *Chomsky's Politics* (London: Verso, 1995), 28.

34 Rai, *Chomsky's Politics*, 28–30.

35 Rai, *Chomsky's Politics*, 31.

36 Here one might say it is Chomsky himself who takes the unmarked place of the United States.

37 Butler, *Frames of War*, 151–58.

CHAPTER ELEVEN

Endings and Beginnings:
Reimagining the Tasks and Spaces of Comparison

Mary N. Layoun

'Ὡμως την μαστοριά σου όληνα τη θέμε τώρα.
Σε ξένη γλώσσα η λύπη μας κ' η αγάπη μας περνούν.
Το αιγυπτιακό σου αίσθημα χύσε στην ξένη γλώσσα.
K. Π. Καβάφης,
"Για τον Αμμόνη, που πέθανε 29 ετών, στα 610"

[But we need all of your craftsmanship now.
Into a foreign language our sorrow and our
love move.
Pour your Egyptian sensibility into a foreign
language.
C. P. Cavafy,
"For Ammonis, Who Died at 29 Years of Age,
in 610" (1917)]

Comparison is a specter precisely because it is
a form of inhuman automatism conjured up by
capitalism's eternal restlessness.
Pheng Cheah, "Grounds of Comparison"

Comparative projects are likely to remain driven
by particular interests, animated on the one hand
by singular knowledge, commitments, languages,
and on the other by the general theoretical questions that arise when one reflects on one's interest
in multiple kinds of texts.
Jonathan Culler,
"Whither Comparative Literature?"[1]

"On Comparison" and the Comparative
in the Modern, Again

THOUGH I'M A "PROFESSIONAL COMPARATIST"—that is, my academic
training and paid job are located in the discipline of comparative literature in a U.S. academic institution—I've chosen not to
respond to the intriguing series of questions posed by our editors with

another account of the disciplinary or institutional or historical aspects of comparison.[2] I've written elsewhere about the history and practices of the discipline that I inhabit, suggesting there a comparative process predicated on "relational literacy."[3] And as I will briefly outline below, others have traced with insight and scholarly care the trajectory of disciplines and of philosophical categories of comparison in the modern period—from which work I draw with appreciation. Here though, I will turn to two literary texts as a response not to the question of what comparison or disciplines have been or should be, but to one of our editors' questions regarding "what other methods of comparative thinking we might envision." I am interested in the *literary* instances of the workings of the comparative in a 1917 poem by the Greco-Egyptian Alexandrian poet C. P. Cavafy, "For Ammonis, Who Died at 29 Years of Age, in 610," and the Jordanian born, Iraqi-educated, Saudi-Iraqi novelist Abd al-Rahman Munif's1977 novel *al-Nihāyāt* النهايات (Endings).[4]

In thinking about comparison, each of those literary instances is suggestive in its own right. Both evince a poetic understanding—if we understand poetic in its literal, classical Greek sense as "creative making"—of comparison as created in a matrix of the modern that radically accelerates the juxtaposition of difference both temporally and spatially. And something like this notion of the juxtaposition of what is different or "foreign" or "strange" or putatively "incomparable" and the discerning or distinguishing potentially provoked with and among the juxtaposition of those differences has long seemed to me a more productive way to think about comparison—in listening to, speaking with, and inhabiting diverse communities and a diverse world. (This is the literal meaning of the classical Greek concept of comparison as *synkrisis*—from συγκρίνω: to distinguish or discern [κρίνω/ *krino*]—*with* or *among* [συν/ *syn*]—what is brought together.)

Telling Historical and Theoretical Stories: "On Comparison" and on the Comparative in the Modern

The histories, origins, and modern practices of comparison have been the object of much and welcome scholarly attention in recent years. A striking characteristic of no small part of that scholarly attention has been the effort to redress other accounts and practices of comparison—and of "the comparative" as its adjectival putting into practice—that have forgotten or ignored the nineteenth-century origins of modern comparative thought, that have forgotten or ignored the times and spaces beyond Anglo-Europe, which were constituent components of that comparatist positivism or universalism or imperial triumphalism.[5]

In this context, and because much of the comparative theoretical and historical work I cite below takes a rather more specific focus, it may be worth remembering that, in the broadest sense, comparison is resolutely situated on the ground (political, historical, social) of modernity, occasioned by the very component aspects of that modernity. The massive movements and dislocations of peoples in the modern period, the radical juxtaposition—in metropolitan cities or in colonial centers, for example—of different peoples and ideas and things that were hitherto not colliding with one another in quite the same close fashion, raise an explicitly *modern* question of comparison. What is to be made of the often stark juxtaposition of disparate entities made equivalent or comparable in exchange? Is there a modern imperative to compare in the face of an increasingly fierce network of connection, which depends on unevenness and difference?[6] In the face of the apparent and the less-apparent workings of a world made smaller by technology, by colonial and now late capitalism? Of course, juxtaposed differences, however stark, are not in themselves a comparative act. Yet the recognition of difference is both predicated upon and calls out for a concept of comparison or of comparative acts of one sort or another.

The eighteenth-century British essayist Joseph Addison already recognized the call of comparison in the great jostling of differences in the space and time of the modern as he walked through the British Royal Exchange.[7] His recognition of difference as "an Englishman" is grounded in comparison. "It gives me a secret Satisfaction, and in some measure, gratifies my Vanity, as I am an *Englishman*, to see so rich an Assembly of Countrymen and Foreigners consulting together upon the private Business of Mankind, and making this Metropolis a kind of *Emporium* for the whole Earth."[8]

In Addison's account, it is the trade-regulated juxtaposition of difference that occasions an exultant comparison. The contemporary historian of East Asia Harry Harootunian reminds us of a rather different instance of the comparative mandated by the radical juxtaposition of differences generated by colonialism: "the peoples of the world outside of Euro-America have been *forced to live lives comparatively* by virtue of experiencing some form of colonization or subjection enforced by the specter of imperialism" (emphasis added, 26).[9]

The nearly three hundred years between Addison's and Harootunian's insights have seen the exercise and theorization of comparison as well as its forgotten, ignored, or recalled histories as fraught with what David Damrosch sagely calls, in the context of his own comparative turn to "world literature," "a celebration of new opportunities" but also and more warily "a gallery of cautionary tales" (36).[10] So it is perhaps not surprising that scholarly reexaminations of comparison—and, in the initial examples cited here, reexaminations of the field and discipline of comparative literature in particular—have occurred under the rubric of anxiety or death or crisis.[11] These works, marked in their titles and content more by Damrosch's "cautionary tales" than by his celebratory "opportunities," have produced important and engaging reconsiderations of the comparative. Their reconsiderations offer a productive context in which to situate the consideration of the literary comparative here. And their efforts are conjoined by scholarly work in a slightly different pitch that also seeks to outline a new comparison. Emily Apter's provocatively wide-reaching *The Translation Zone: A New Comparative Literature* suggestively recovers the history of Leo Spitzer's sojourn and extensive work in Istanbul and of his contributions to the comparative field.[12] *The Translation Zone* also attempts to reconfigure "a new comparative literature" in the context of a capacious understanding of translation in the twenty-first century.

If Apter's account looks to the early decades of the twentieth century and to the recruitment of German intellectuals by the new Turkish state as a pivotal influence on the modern comparative literary field, method, and discipline, Natalie Melas begins her inquiry from an earlier moment in the latter half of the nineteenth century.[13] "Grounds for Comparison," the introductory chapter of her *All the Difference in the World*, offers a thoughtful history of modern comparison in general and of comparative literature in particular. There, astutely refusing a myopic either/or of universalizing or relativizing, Melas formulates a concept of "postcolonial formalism" (37) predicated on the "incommensurability" of comparison[14]—that is, a "grounds of comparison" "without basis for equivalence" (31).

Beyond literary studies, there has been much equally suggestive work on comparison and comparative studies, in which fields the relation of comparison to modernity is even more directly invoked. Peter Osborne's "On Comparability: Kant and the Possibility of Comparative Studies" holds out a "global social whole," reengaging the work of Immanuel Kant in a "transcendental analysis of comparability as space, time, and idea." Drawing from Kant to construct "a concept of 'objective comparability'" (4), Osborne situates that philosophical concept in the context of comparative area studies. And drawing from the work of Gilles Deleuze and of Walter Benjamin, he proposes "a conception of global modernity as immanent difference" (18) as crucial to comparative area studies.[15]

Harootunian's "Some Thoughts on Comparability and the Space-Time Problem," a passage from which is cited above, is a wonderfully shrewd intervention in opposition to a comparative approach that emphasizes the spatial at the expense of the temporal.[16] In an intensely suggestive alternative, Harootunian configures Ernst Bloch's concept of "contemporary non-contemporaneousness"—a concept that "allows us to return to the question of temporality and the temporalization of forms

through which it is expressed in those social spaces whose appearance
have been spatialized by the capitalist nation state" (50)—in relation to
Henri Lefebvre's "rhythmanalysis" of the everyday and its concept of the
double but nonidentical measure of internal and external rhythm. And
in that configuration, Harootunian argues for the necessary inclusion of
a differently defined temporality in a comparative understanding of the
modern: "If, in any event, our strategies of comparison are to have any
utility at all, they must be embedded in specific temporal and spatial forms
. . . perhaps as a history of dissonant rhythms, as a continuing and never
completed conjuration of the past in the present" (52). The accounts of
comparison in the nexus of modernity by Harootunian and Osborne, as by
Gayatri Spivak in her *Death of a Discipline*, are explicit reminders of the possibilities and limitations of our individual, as well as collective, scholarly,
and intellectual locations on the landscape. Their cautionary tales—as
Harootunian warns, "comparability is too important a consideration to
be left to disciplines such as comparative literature" (24)—are reiterated
from another academic field in Marcel Detienne's *Comparer l'incomparable*
(Comparing the Incomparable).[17] There he indicts the "customs officers"
(xiii) of classical Greek scholarship who seek to regulate or bar the passage
of research across borders. *Comparing the Incomparable* insistently refuses
the modern history of scholarly fixation on classical Greek singularity with
its own four examples of experimental comparative projects "between
history and anthropology." In something of a contrast to Melas's incommensurability, Detienne's projects seek "a constructive comparativism"
(xiii). Unequivocally situated in the French intellectual and academic
context, Detienne's intrepid call nonetheless resonates beyond France.
In his proposition for a collaborative, transborder comparison, Detienne's "incomparables" are an elegant marker not only of a disputatious
history and practice of comparison but also of alternatives to them.

In spite of their differences from one another, each and all of these
recent reconsiderations of comparison share the crucially *modern* context
of our understandings and practices of comparison, no less in the field
of classical Greek scholarship than in that of the postcolonial or late
capitalism. They suggest the tension between the interests or desires of
comparison and its necessity. They remind us of the juxtaposed differences of the modern—the radical differentials of the capitalist modern—
which our comparisons cannot afford to ignore or forget or efface in
the telling. And Harootunian's caveat notwithstanding, I would suggest
that one place in which we can discern and reflect on the possibility of
the comparative is in the space of literature.

But before turning from this provocative series of theoretical works
to two literary texts, I would cite one additional insight into the configuration of the comparative—here, again, specifically of comparative

literature. That is the shrewd observation in Timothy Brennan's essay on
Edward Said: comparative literature has been "always a response to war"
(29).[18] Brennan situates comparison not only in the modern, in general,
or World War II, in particular, but in the context of modern war. "It has,
of course, been conventional to point out that the modern version of
the field emerged from the crises of World War II, led by mostly German scholars seeking to keep the spirit of Europe alive at the moment
of its near extinction. But it is forgotten that Goethe's *Weltliteratur* was
conceived in the wake of the Napoleonic invasions and flourished again
at the turn of the century on the eve of World War I" (29).

This observation returns us to the tension suggested by the opening
citations from Pheng Cheah and Jonathan Culler. That is, on the one
hand, comparison as an "inhuman automaton" generated by capitalist
modernity—Cheah's astute observation about the work of Benedict
Anderson (though one not limited to Anderson's work as his own and
Harootunian's essay makes clear). Cheah's observation on the "specter of
comparison" as a structurally generated necessity is a suggestive counterpoint to Culler's summary account of comparison as driven by "one's . . .
particular interests." It is to this tension between comparison of interest
and of necessity that the two literary texts below speak most eloquently.

Of course even a cursory reading of the revisionings of the comparative discussed above would find that "one's interests"—gendered, raced,
classed—are scarcely exempt from the historical, political, economic, or
institutional contexts in which they arise. We can understand comparison
as a response of necessity *and* of interest or desire to the juxtaposition
of difference. As such, it is unequivocally underwritten by questions of
situated power and authority. It is always predicated on horizontal and
vertical locations on and relations across a landscape of difference. So
if the juxtaposition of differences in the modern calls out comparison,
what does comparison call out? What are its "ends" (Melas)? National/ist
"satisfaction" (Addison's "Englishman")? Imperial equivalence (against
which Melas proposes a postcolonial formalism and incommensurability)?
Colonial force (Harootunian)? Expansive opportunities and cautionary
tales (Apter or Damrosch)?

Two Literary Texts on Comparison and the
Comparative in the Modern

While responses to the questions above will always depend on the moment, location, and juxtapositions of comparison, on the necessities and
interests at work in the comparative act, literature offers a reasonably
contained landscape in which to think about the question of comparison.

Literary texts are "reasonably contained" or circumscribed in an almost banal, literal sense that, unlike experience or social movements or history, literary texts offer the gift to thought of some sort of demarcated beginning and ending. While scarcely free of the constraints that mark all thought, literature, as imaginative, aesthetic production, can still offer a "bounded" space to think otherwise.

The realm of the aesthetic, as Herbert Marcuse reminded us so many years ago,[19] offers the space of an imaginative freedom for thought. That realm—a translation of the "art" or *Kunst* of his original German title *Permanenz der Kunst*—is "permanent" as a field for thought and understanding. For Marcuse, art is potentially emancipatory for thought and understanding because it is "transhistorical." That is, it is unquestionably located and yet significant beyond the specificity of its historical moment and space of production or reception. In a rather different register, Spivak has proposed that the literary is "learning to learn from the singular and unverifiable."[20] In this configuration, the verifiable repeatability that is a criterion of scientific provability does not inhere in a literary text. Yet in Spivak's "singular and unverifiable" as a cautionary tale and in Marcuse's realm of literature and the aesthetic as opportunity for thought, there remains a provocative space *for* and *in* literature.

In this tension, and in that of the necessity (the automaton) and interest of comparison, I would like to situate the literary examples of comparison at work below: the poem "For Ammonis, Who Died at 29 Years of Age, in 610,"[21] written in 1917 by C. P. Cavafy (1863–1933), and the 1977 novel *Endings* by the Iraqi-educated, Jordanian-born, Saudi-Iraqi novelist Abd al-Rahman Munif (1933–2004).[22] For it seems to me these two literary texts offer a productive response to this tension in their literary mappings of juxtaposed differences, of comparison-in-practice called out by those juxtapositions, and—no less strikingly—of the vexed and uneasy possibilities of comparative relations across difference.

Unquestionably, the tasks and spaces of comparison are multiple and often contradictory—deadly for some, grandly authoritative for others. Yet in the imaginative space of the juxtaposition of difference in the two literary texts below, and in their comparative evocation of other visions of relation, differences are not always necessarily pathological or deadly; there may be other (imaginary) relations of cohabitation possible.

"For Ammonis, Who Died at 29 Years of Age, in 610": "Our Ammonis" and "Our Alexandria"

Cavafy was born in 1863 in Alexandria, Egypt, where his Greek parents had settled in the mid-1850s. On the death of his father in 1870, economic necessity motivated his family's move to England, back to Alexandria in 1877, and in 1882 to Constantinople and mainland Greece.[23] By the mid-1880s, Cavafy returned again to Alexandria, remaining there until his death in 1933. He worked first as a newspaper correspondent, then in the late 1880s as his brother's assistant at the Egyptian Stock Exchange. A few years later, he became a clerk at the Irrigation Office of the Egyptian Ministry of Public Works in Alexandria, where he worked for the next thirty years, eventually becoming its assistant director. In 1933, eleven years after leaving the ministry, he died of cancer.

During his lifetime, Cavafy published little of his work; a short collection of poetry was printed privately in the early 1900s and reprinted with some new poems a few years later. Cavafy chose instead to circulate his verse among friends. Yet from his death in 1933, as Maria Margaronis notes in her review of recent translations of his work,

his sensibility began to color the work of other poets, among them Auden, Brecht, Brodsky, Milosz and Montale, as well as the Americans Robert Hass, Louise Glück, James Merrill, Rachel Hadas and Mark Doty. It was Auden who brought Cavafy's work to a broad American readership by introducing Rae Dalven's translation of the *Complete Poems* in 1961: "I can think of poems," he wrote, "which, if Cavafy were unknown to me, I should have written quite differently, or perhaps not written at all."[24]

Even more than the story of his own life "lived comparatively," Cavafy's elegiac poem "For Ammonis, Who Died at 29 Years of Age, in 610" offers a provocative space of necessary and interested comparison—temporally, spatially, linguistically.[25] Though its characters are imaginary, the historical "present" of the poem is unequivocally located by its title: 610 CE, on the cusp of the short-lived Sassanian conquest of Egypt from the Byzantine Empire, prior to the great Islamic expansion into Egypt. This context is, of course, centuries removed from 1917, the historical moment of the poem's composition. Yet in 1917 as well, Egypt was in the midst of massive changes, "liberated" from a crumbling Ottoman rule by the aggressive, if nominally indirect, British control of a protectorate.

This, then, is the poem's first juxtaposition of difference: the temporal difference between the time internal to the poem (the *then* of 610) and that external to the poem (the *now* of its composition in 1917). (For though few of his poems were published in his lifetime, Cavafy carefully dated each of his poems in his notebooks.) The poem's first implicit comparative turn is evoked by this juxtaposition of temporal difference that invites comparison of—reflection on the differences between—then and now. And nested within the juxtaposition of this then and now, the temporal difference of the pastness of 610 to 1917, is the figure of the beautiful young poet, Ammonis, who has just died. In his name is figured another temporal *and* cultural difference of the past in the present. For as the title of the poem announces from the outset, Ammonis, the young poet whose death has occasioned the request for an epitaph, is an Egyptian. Though "misspelled" by one letter in Cavafy's poem,[26] Ammonis or Amun is the ancient Egyptian god of creative force, and later of fertility, whose name originally meant "hidden from view." Here, too, the juxtaposition of difference echoes in the proper names of the poem as in their introduction of temporal difference. The year 610 CE is precisely the Christian era only a few decades prior to the expansion of Islam into Egypt and centuries from 1917. And the original historical time, at least, of the ancient Egyptian god is thousands of years earlier.

Following on and already suggested by this juxtaposition of temporal and nominal difference, the second comparative turn of the poem is figured in its explicit juxtaposition of a foreign language to a localized sensibility: that is, the repeated reference to Greek as a "foreign tongue" (ξένη γλώσσα)—the language in which, of course, Cavafy's poem is actually written—in juxtaposition to "your Egyptian sensibility" (Το αιγυπτιακό σου αίσθημα). Juxtaposed difference—between language and sensibility, Greek and non-Greek—as the basis for the comparative distinction of relationship is subtly but distinctly connected in more ways than one. It is registered in the command form of the Greek "χύσε" (pour or let flow) in the phrase, "pour your Egyptian sensibility into the foreign tongue [of Greek]." The poetic epitaph itself is to become the relation with and among the differences of sensibility, historical time, cultures, and languages.

The very designation of a "foreign tongue" presupposes the nonforeign, one language implicitly juxtaposed to another. But the explicit juxtaposition here is between a language and a sensibility as the foreign and the local. And while the poem's explicit comparison is of the connection of poetry across those differences, there is another connection of sensual community, bound by language, sensibility, subtle beauty, and longing. The juxtaposition of temporal and linguistic difference in the poem allows a comparative distinction—or *synkrisis* / σύγκριση—of those relations as possibility.

But that possibility is figured as imaginative reality in the direct address of the first and last stanzas of the poem—that is, in the direct address by the poetic I to Rafael, another poet for whom Greek is a foreign language.

> Rafael, a few lines they ask you to compose
> As an epitaph for the poet Ammonis.[27]

And the last stanza opens with a reiteration of this direct address:

> Rafael, your lines should be so written
> As to have, you know, something of our life in them.

Relation of community across the juxtaposed differences of languages and sensibility is not only implicit as noted above. It is explicitly embodied, in the first instance, in this small community of direct address. The relationship between the poetic I and Rafael, which precedes and continues in the aftermath of the death of "our Ammonis" itself bridges the foreign (the Greek language) and the local (an Egyptian sensibility). It bridges perhaps even time and death in the poem. Their small community of two, in the absence of a third, Ammonis now dead, is one of shared languages and sensibilities, of shared sorrow (η λύπη μας) and shared love (κ' η αγάπη μας). The poem iterates and reiterates *our* relationship to a foreign tongue, which, infused with *your* Egyptian sensibility, must speak of *our* love and *our* sorrow—of Ammonis's poetry but especially of his delicate beauty. The poetic I calls for harmonious musicality to honor *our* Ammonis.

In the careful poetic gathering and juxtaposing of these multiple differences, the space of comparison emerges as a community in the face of the "untimely" death of "our Ammonis." And that poetic community, in the concluding lines of the poem, is decisively located in the city of Alexandria. The poem's final stanza employs end rhyme in the first and third lines that explicitly links the injunction "to be written" (να γραφούν) with that "to reveal" or "make apparent" (να δηλούν). Rafael's verse must not only be "so written (να γραφούν) / as to have, you know, something of our life in them" but also "as to have the rhythm and every phrase reveal (να δηλούν) / that an Alexandrian writes for an Alexandrian."[28]

There is yet one further way in which Cavafy's poem offers for reflection the complexity of comparison. In addition to the comparison called out by the juxtaposition of differences noted above, and by the closing invocation of the specifically Alexandrian space of difference and of comparative relation across that difference, a most literal space of comparison is suggested in the use of the "single" language in which the poem is written. This difference is that of the historical-linguistic divide (or diglossia) in modern Greek between the formal (*katharevousa*) and the colloquial (demotic) languages. The nineteenth-century purist construction of *katharevousa* was predicated on the putative recuperation of an uncontaminated classical Greek in opposition to a putatively corrupted demotic or everyday language.[29] But it is not only a combination of *katharevousa* and the demotic that marks the language of Cavafy's poem. Classical and Byzantine Greek and alternate grammar in a richly unique Alexandrian Greek juxtapose the different historical registers of a *single* language far beyond differences between the colloquial and the formal.

For example, the intensely colloquial, "Συ θα μπορέσεις" (you can do it) or "την μαστοριά σου όληνα τη θέμε τώρα" (your skill or masterliness we need all of now) is juxtaposed with a finely wrought sensuality:[30]

> Of course you'll speak of his poetry—
> But speak also of his beauty
> Of his delicate beauty that we loved.[31]

And the casual colloquial tone is punctuated by the use of distinctly less colloquial forms: "ολίγους" rather than "λίγους" for "a few lines," in the use of "λείον"/"λείος" for "smooth" or "unadorned," and "ως αρμόζει" for "as is fitting or harmonious." This later echo of classical Greek presages the characterization, two stanzas later, of Rafael's Greek as "Πάντοτε ωραία και μουσικά" (always beautiful and musical).[32]

Cavafy's poem turns on the distinction and movement between two languages—the "foreign language" of Greek as distinct from whatever is the nonforeign language. It turns as well on the distinction between language itself and nonlinguistic sensibility ("your Egyptian sensibility"/Το αιγυπτιακό σου αίσθημα).[33] And it does this in the multiple historical registers (classical, Byzantine, demotic, literary) of the poetic speaker's "foreign language"— Greek. The poem is composed with and speaks of distinctions that are made possible by the bringing together of differences. And it is those distinctions of memory, sensuality, beauty, language, and sensibility—as the very "epitaph" of the poem itself—which offer a vision of community not only *across* differences but precisely *amongst* them. Here the comparison embedded in Cavafy's lapidary, elegiac poem works to "distinguish with or among" the juxtaposition of what is different or "foreign" or "strange." That poetic comparison suggests the possibility of intimate relationships among and across multiple languages and cultures—even across time. It is a possibility of shared community in the face of difference—even that ultimate but universal difference between life and death.

Endings: "Our ʿAssāf" and "Our al-Tība"

If understanding comparison as the distinguishing of a relationship called out by the juxtaposition of differences is "revealed in the writing" of an early twentieth-century poet writing from Alexandria (Cavafy's cunning να γραφούν / va grafoun, να δηλούν / va deloun of his poem's final stanza), it is also differently "revealed in the writing" in Abd al-Rahman Munif's 1977 novel *al-Nihāyāt* (Endings).

Born in 1933 in Amman, Jordan, to a Saudi father and an Iraqi mother, Munif was raised and educated first in Jordan and then in Iraq and Egypt.

After completing a PhD at the University of Belgrade in the economics of oil, he took up residence first in Lebanon and then, in 1963, in Syria. He worked there for the oil ministry for nearly a decade, publishing his first work—a study of the future of the oil industry—in 1972 in Beirut. Munif came to literature when he was nearly forty, publishing his first novel the following year in 1973. He wrote fourteen more novels from that year until his death in 2004. He was "An Arabian Master," as the distinguished Egyptian literary scholar Sabry Hafez announces in the title of his posthumous tribute to Munif. In that essay, Hafez aptly characterizes Munif as

not only a major Arab novelist but one of the most remarkable figures of contemporary world literature. It is difficult to think of another writer, in any language, whose life experience and literary enterprise has the same kind of dramatic range . . .One of the most advanced and incendiary writers of the Arab world, politically active as militant or technician across five countries, author of fifteen novels—including the most monumental of all modern narratives in Arabic—and another nine books of non-fiction. (39)[34]

Hafez notes that Munif's 1977 novel *Endings*, "in its sharp discontinuity of structure, mosaic use of short stories, and poetic impersonality of tone . . . [is] one of the most advanced fictions in contemporary Arab literature"(50). A prelude of sorts to his great *Cities of Salt* trilogy, *Endings* unquestionably stands as a unique achievement in Munif's oeuvre—not least of all for the reasons Hafez notes above, though I would recast his characterization of the novel ever so slightly. For, I want to suggest, what seems to be its "discontinuity of structure" or "impersonality of tone" is, rather, precisely the workings of comparison in the novel's fierce juxtaposition of differences. And it is not only in the stories told that the novel enacts comparison across and amongst difference. *Endings* structurally embodies this fierce juxtaposition of difference and evocation of comparative possibility in its division into two distinct parts.

At the heart of *Endings* is an untimely death, which recalls that of the beautiful young poet Ammonis at the heart of Cavafy's poem. As in the poem, it is, perhaps, precisely this most radical juxtaposition of difference—between life and death—that allows the comparative relations of *Endings*. In Munif's novel—as implicitly in the temporal difference between Cavafy's poetic imagining of a once-glorious Alexandria juxtaposed with its early twentieth-century present—the slow death of a drought-stricken village at the edge of the desert is thrown into high relief by a sudden and tragic death. Though with profound difference of style, tone, and setting, it is also the tremendous divide of death that provokes the rupture of the novel but at the same time provides an occa-

sion for the possibility of relations otherwise across and amongst difference. Yet if Munif's novel ends structurally with a strikingly experimental
vision of shared community in the face of difference, it also reveals far
more explicitly than Cavafy's poem the brutal ravages of other kinds of
relationship across difference.

The village of al-Tība (الطيبة) that is the locus for the novel stands at
the edge of the desert, not only in immediate and forceful relation to the
harsh natural world, but also in immediate and forceful relation to the
human world of the city—and by extension of the state. If relations with
the natural and nonhuman worlds are those of one kind of geographic
necessity, relations with the human world are predicated on a different
necessity: on the forceful exertion of relationship without reciprocity;
on the imposition of meaning from an urban center that has for generations ignored al-Tība; on the plight of an apparently immutable peasant
patience of the village in the face of that necessity.

The history of such relationships exerted by those with power—economic, political, and social—over those who have less is familiar. It is
worth recalling again in broad outline the example of the rise of the
modern fields of "comparative studies" in nineteenth-century Europe.
Informed by metaphoric categories of familial genealogy, comparative
studies sought to "scientifically" operationalize—to make verifiably
repeatable—those categories. The impetus to locate and hierarchize a
"universal family"—of languages, folktales, anatomy, religions, law, and
literature—was also an impetus to define the European or the "West"
over against what were increasingly apparent as rising challenges to the
imperial domination of that "West."

But this is not exactly the story that the literary works of Cavafy and
Munif tell—however much that history is or isn't a backdrop to their
works. Rather Abd al-Rahman Munif's 1977 novel *al-Nihāyāt* (Endings),[35]
as Cavafy's 1917 poem, suggests in content and in form a comparison
that evokes relations otherwise across and with difference. *Endings*, in
particular, narrates comparative stories of uneasy and violent cohabitation in the face of the juxtaposition of stark differences while pointing
to a distant horizon of cohabitation otherwise.

But if this metareflection is suggested by both poem and novel, their
differences in tone and focus are obvious from the novel's opening
exclamation: "Truly drought. Drought . . . again! And in the season of
drought, life and objects are changed, even human beings (*al-bashr*) are
changed. (v) "[36] It is not only Cavafy's languages or sensibilities or the living and dead poets of a distant past who are gathered and juxtaposed
here in Munif's novel. Every narrative turn of *al-Nihāyāt* pivots on the
stark juxtaposition of differences between city and village, generations,
human and animal life and the inanimate world of objects and ma-

chines, and the landscape as a living entity in its own right. The stories
of these fierce juxtapositions of difference and of the "necessary" relations of comparison across them are told by the novel's unnamed and
initially "detached" (as Hafez characterizes him) third-person narrator.
The first half of the novel is unequivocally dominated by the narrator's
representation of the network of relations in which a particular village
and its inhabitants are caught.

That particular village,[37] al-Tība where the stories of *al-Nihāyāt* unfold, is named but not identifiably located in a specific country, state,
or region.[38] But it *is* clearly topographically located: on the border of
a desert, hours distant by car from "the city," and bereft of any of the
city's benefits that would protect it from the dreaded return of drought,
which opens the novel. But from that opening declaration of recurring
disaster, the narration arrives at the village of al-Tība, and its inhabitants
in particular, only after lengthy generalizing observations on human and
nonhuman responses to drought in the abstract.[39] In this first chapter,
the narrator introduces an inevitability that will seem to govern places,
people, and events as well as his narration in the first half of the novel.[40]
For "this"—the responses of human and nonhuman life and of the
natural environment to drought—is the "fate" (*al-qism*) of "most of the
people in that cruel and long year" (١٢), the narrator intones with grim
detachment. Only as his account of an apparently inexorable network
of relationships governed by "fate" is concluded, seeming to mime in its
movement the abstracted relationship between the city and the village,
does the narration finally arrive at the village of al-Tība.

This arrival at the specific after broad generalities is at first in order to
note, in its persistent if narrow version of comparative analysis, that al-Tība,
"like every town and village in this world," has its own particular habits
and ways of life. The village of al-Tība is—and is not—unique. *Al-Nihāyāt*'s
narrator reiterates an abstraction of oscillating sameness and difference
in relation to the place where his stories unfold in a fascinating example
of comparison of interest. Yet the comparative differences he juxtaposes
in relation to al-Tība are most often those of necessity—the harsh landscape, the distant city, and the "inevitable" exodus of the young to that
city. Though not identifiably of the place he narrates, the clearly informed
narrator knows the local landscape, the village, and its inhabitants well
enough to constantly compare them—if in the conventionally restricted
manner noted above—to those of villages and residents elsewhere. Differences and specificities are juxtaposed only to be repeatedly subsumed
under generalities or nondifference.[41] In the first instance, the comparative
working of *Endings* seems strikingly different from that of Cavafy's poem.

The second chapter opens, then, on this already familiar note. "Al-Tība,
like any place in the world, has things in which it takes pride" (١٥) The

narrator's juxtaposition of the simultaneity of the general and universal ("like any place in the world") with the particular and different (those things in which al-Tība in particular takes pride) forcefully frames not only the stories he tells but the manner in which he tells them.

But it is in the story of the life and death of the strange, stubborn, stalwart villager ʿAssāf that the narrator's comparative frame will meet its match. The story of ʿAssāf's life and death will change more than the villagers' understanding of their "fate." It will become a pivotal instance of a "thing in which it [the village] takes pride." And as it interrupts and transforms their understanding of comparative possibility across and with difference, so will it strikingly interrupt and shift the narrator's detached narration.

ʿAssāf and the one-eyed dog who is his constant companion live on the edge of al-Tība as the village itself lives on the edge of the desert (١٩). Orphaned as a child, ʿAssāf is less proficient with the dictates of human society than with those of the desert and its nonhuman life; he knows the desert better and respects the natural landscape more than any other character in the novel. Alternately disparaged and admired by the villagers for his eccentricities, ʿAssāf is nonetheless their gruff guide to survival—a taciturn but compassionate provider for the village because of his skills as a hunter and his keen knowledge of the desert. And in spite of the narrator's opening exclamation in the novel, it is less the drought itself than virtually everyone in the novel's gross misunderstanding of it that precipitates ʿAssāf's death. For in spite of this most recent drought that has gripped the village and its surroundings, the sons of al-Tība, who have gone to the city for its promises of a better life, return to the village with their urban friends for a desert hunting trip.[42] The villagers, ever the congenial hosts to guests, press ʿAssāf into service as a guide for the hunt, although he is initially fiercely unwilling.[43] A fierce sandstorm arises that kills both ʿAssāf and his dog. Finally recovering ʿAssāf's body, the village sons and their urban friends mournfully return to the village in absolute silence.

It is precisely here in the novel that the narrator's generalizing "detachment" is ruptured. A clearly apt producer of words and explanations himself, he asks plaintively: "How is it that human beings can fall so silent and for such a long time?"; "How can they forget the entirety of the sounds and words they've used since birth?" And then, immediately following these questions, he asks: "How? How can this happen?" (١٠٥) The pronominal referent here is unclear, potentially multiple. Is the "this" a reference to the men's silence? To their forgetting language? To ʿAssāf's death? To the multiple catastrophes in which al-Tība finds itself? This eruption of rhetorical questions marks the profound qualification of the narrator's hitherto apparently detached, "ethnographic" account

of the landscape, region, village, and inhabitants of al-Tība. It marks
as well a challenge to the presumably unquestionable authority of his
comparative method. For his account and its method will be strikingly
countered in the second half of the novel.

That second half of the novel—with its wonder and amazement, its
alternate ways of understanding and its collective telling—occurs over
ʿAssāf's dead body, laid out in the house of the village Mukhtar. Following
on the prescient signal of the narrator's rhetorical questions about meaning, ʿAssāf's wake is the occasion for the transition from the "ethnographic
realism" in the first half of the novel to a kind of "marvelous realism" in
the second half.[44] The transition from one part of the novel to the other
is marked by the nervousness or anxiety or anguish (بعصبية) and anger
(بحدة) of the village men as they agree to spend the night together over
the dead man's body. Here, as in Cavafy's poem, though with a profound
difference, beautifully crafted tone, language, and structural configuration serve to produce the context in which juxtaposed difference can be
distinguished and comparative relations understood otherwise.[45]

It is the village baker, in response to the Mukhtar's anguish (بعصبية) about
the decision to leave ʿAssāf's beloved dog behind in the desert, who introduces the comparative form of the adjective "most amazing" (أعجب) that
titularly divides the two halves of the novel: "Some stories from that
amazing night" (الليلة العجيبة). He explicitly repositions ʿAssāf's untimely
death in relation to the community, observing that:

One of the most amazing (أعجب) things in this world is the bond between
humans and their surroundings, to animals and trees and houses and rivers, even
to the desert which is never far from al-Tība; in them is deliverance. That's why
ʿAssāf went there. He went to save al-Tība . . .' (١١٣).

In the call and response of the villagers' anxious conversation, a man
who had hitherto been silent replies tearfully to the baker: "In al-Tība,
like in any other place in this world, what needs to change is man himself." A very young man, whose presence had gone unnoticed, observes,
"If al-Tība is going to do nothing other than simply wait for rain, everyone will die as ʿAssāf died, perhaps worse" (١١٣). An increasingly angry
(بحدة) and agitated (بعصبية) exchange ensues until a village elder chides
the assembled "sons of al-Tība" to "stop their foolishness and keep
company with the dead man until his burial at the first light of dawn."

This, then, is the climate in the Mukhtar's house, characterized by the
narrator as "fraught with mystery and anger," as the evening vigil begins.
For the narrator, the villagers' uneasy desire here to avoid silence in the
omnipresence of death (unlike the absolute silence of the return to the
village with ʿAssāf's dead body), and his own memory of "that amazing

night," recalls a single thing: "the end." And so his narration "ends" and gives way to a different kind of storytelling and a different kind of story, "hikayat," in the only titular division in the novel:⁴⁶ "Some stories from that amazing night" (اللـيـلـة العجـيبة).

Demarcated by this single titular division in the novel—"Some stories from that amazing night"—a sequence of fourteen tales told by the villagers of al-Tība at ʿAssāf's wake are clearly juxtaposed with the narrator's account that precedes them.⁴⁷ Prior to the collective storytelling session, the narration has been framed and shaped by the narrator's self-confident "ethnography" and its account of the relentless landscape, the stalwart patience of the old peasant generation in the face of one disastrous calamity after another, and the empty promises of the city for change. But as the "stories from that amazing night" begin, they are linked by an alternative reason: a different order of relationship or juxtaposition to one another; a different narrative mode of understanding the human and nonhuman world and their interaction. Each tale, as well, comments on the process of story-telling and the unreliability of proliferating words and stories.⁴⁸ And as the sequence of tales unfolds, each one frames and resituates the tales that precede it as well as the events of the novel and the death of ʿAssāf. In this male "circle of storytelling," the fourteen linked tales reflect and reflect on ʿAssāf's taciturnity, his admonitions against killing for pleasure or from passion, and his injunction to the hunters to stay in a circle and to help one another.⁴⁹

The connections among the marvelous tales of animals, humans, and the environment are wonderfully, poignantly, and often humorously suggestive. They begin with a tale of Al-ʿAnzi, the "crazy" hunter of the village of al-Jawf. Goaded by his pride in his hunting and the challenge of another villager, Al-ʿAnzi accepts a wager that he can kill a wild desert goat with a single rifle shot while riding in a car.⁵⁰ Though he wins the wager, as he walks up to the dying goat, she looks at him with tears in her eyes; he leaves the rifle in the Land Rover and walks away, never to be heard of again.⁵¹ The sixth and the ninth tales are drawn from one of the sources of the rich Arabic narrative tradition: al-Jahiz's ninth-century *Book of Animals*. The fourteenth and final story, the second of only two narrated in the first person, tells of a poor man who finally finds a room to rent. The terms of his reduced rent are that he walk the old landlady's beloved dog twice a day.⁵² As the final tale concludes, there is no clear transition back to the narrator's telling; it simply begins again. But as it does so, his narration in closing is now just one more tale in the sequence of stories that make up the second half of the novel. And as the wake concludes with the approach of dawn, the narrator's story, too, is now one of the amazing or marvelous or parareal. He relates without qualification the apparent madness that seizes the Mukhtar, the magical flight of ʿAssāf's coffin to its final resting place, and the unusual presence and amazing (if to him incomprehensible) dance of the village women at the gravesite.[53]

ʿAssāf is dead and buried—a literal and obvious instance of the novel's titular endings. And there are other endings, as well—for example, the apparently immutable patience of the villagers. For on the road to the city, as the novel concludes, the village Mukhtar lucidly and unequivocally announces that he will return to the village only when the bulldozers come to grade the land for a dam. And there is another ending of sorts, already noted above—that of the relentless oscillation of the narrator's accounts between the general and the particular, between sameness and difference, that marks the first half of the novel. Instead, his narration in conclusion focuses on the villagers' remaking not of their conditions of existence but of the way they understand and respond to those conditions.

That beginnings follow on endings in Munif's novel is most explicit in the Mukhtar's determined final statement and in the rupture of the narrator's detached assurance, and his narration, in the second half of the novel. But the possibility of still other beginnings is there in the silence that punctuates and concludes *al-Nihāyāt*. There is no interrogatory outburst from the narrator at the villagers' silence in conclusion, nor at the vocal and forceful presence of the women of al-Tība at the gravesite, as there was at the "absolute silence" of the return of ʿAssāf's body to the village.[54] And though the women return from their fierce circular dance to their everyday lives in the village, they do so having engaged, however momentarily, in relations otherwise—to one another, to their male cohabitants, to death. *Endings* suggests that beginnings are yet to be forged—including, as least potentially, across and with gender differences.

On Comparison and the Literary Comparative, Again

If Munif's novel and Cavafy's poem are illustrative of something about the workings of the comparative, it is striking that what comparison as *synkrisis* in those two literary texts affords is not the radical transformation of differences juxtaposed, nor is it the subsumption of those juxtaposed differences into a grander order or category or synthesis. In the "small" literary examples of poem and novel, comparison holds out a perhaps far-less-grand proposition of understanding and response otherwise. Its range is not grandly authoritative. It is in this context that I understand the weight and possibility of something like Melas's "postcolonial formalism" or Spivak's vision of a more collaborative and humble discipline or Harootunian's "more modest agenda."

Whether the distinguishing of juxtaposed difference in comparison is based on necessity (Cheah, Harootunian) or on interest (Culler, Apter), comparison itself as distinction or discernment drawn with and among juxtapositions implicates foremost the community of comparatists. Lest this seem like a proposal for intellectual narcissism, let us return for a moment to the space of literature that occasions this speculation.

The untimely death of Ammonis at the heart of Cavafy's poem is not "overcome." He remains dead. And it's not quite clear that Rafael's poetic epitaph will be able to do justice to Ammonis or the community around him, as the poem's speaker requests. Nor is it clear whether the differences between the foreign language of Greek and the local Egyptian sensibility will be bridged—whether that called-for "translation" is in fact possible. Yet Cavafy's poem constructs its own "translated epitaph" in a "foreign language," "pouring" its local Egyptian—but here specifically Alexandrian—sensibility into its comparative effort. The comparative distinction among and with juxtaposed differences implies a modest shift in understanding of relations across those differences. It implies as well the tenuous and fragile creation of connection in the comparative effort itself.

Both the villagers of al-Tība and the narrator who recounts and evaluates their stories come to realize other kinds of relations in which they can engage across the stark human and nonhuman differences juxtaposed in the novel. And, as in Cavafy's poem, the juxtaposed differences in *Endings* remain. They are not resolved or dissolved. What shifts, both explicitly and implicitly, is what is distinguished *with and across* those differences and the possibilities that can perhaps be derived from what is distinguished. What shifts or "begins" is an understanding of and response *otherwise* to the juxtaposition of differences.

Both literary texts are the occasion, too, for the production of exquisite literary language. And in thinking about the history and present of comparison—and about the perhaps eccentrically insistent notion of comparison as *synkrisis*, as a "distinguishing with and among" the juxtaposition of what is different or "foreign" or "strange" from which we might discern something more or else—Cavafy's poem and Munif's novel offer a small, imaginative space for comparative reflection. If the potential of such comparison for a vision of relationship not only *across* differences but precisely *amongst* them is a possibility, it is scarcely a guarantee. That story we know well.

In calling attention to a kind of comparison suggested in these two literary texts, I respond to the purposes and the processes of comparison. Whether the juxtapositions of difference on which comparison is based are of historical necessity or of our own interested making, the comparative effort, predicated on an always partial and incomplete relational literacy, might offer an understanding otherwise—might offer possibilities of relations with and among differences otherwise. It is a comparison committed to the effort to cohabit with, listen to, and consider alternate stories of those who are different—often precisely across the corpse of what the refusal to so engage has wrought.

For Ammonis, Who Died at 29, in 610
C. P. Cavafy

Raphael, they're asking you to write a few lines
as an epitaph for the poet Ammonis:
something very tasteful and polished. You can do it,
you're the one to write something suitable
for the poet Ammonis, our Ammonis.

Of course you'll speak about his poems—
but say something too about his beauty,
about his subtle beauty that we loved.

Your Greek is always elegant and musical.
But we want all your craftsmanship now.
Our sorrow and our love move into a foreign language.
Pour your Egyptian feeling into the Greek you use.

Raphael, your verses, you know, should be written
so they contain something of our life within them,
so the rhythm, so every phrase clearly shows
than an Alexandrian is writing about an Alexandrian.[55]

["Για τον Αμμόνη, που πέθανε 29 ετών, στα 610"
Κ. Π. Καβάφης

Ραφαήλ, ολίγους στίχους σε ζητούν
για επιτύμβιον του ποιητού Αμμόνη να συνθέσεις.
Κάτι πολύ καλαίσθητον και λείον. Συ θα μπορέσεις,
είσαι ο κατάλληλος, να γράψεις ως αρμόζει
για τον ποιητήν Αμμόνη, τον δικό μας.

Βέβαια θα πεις για τα ποιήματά του—
αλλά να πεις και για την εμορφιά του,
για την λεπτή εμορφιά του που αγαπήσαμε.

Πάντοτε ωραία και μουσικά τα ελληνικά σου είναι.
Όμως την μαστοριά σου όληνα τη θέμε τώρα.
Σε ξένη γλώσσα η λύπη μας κ' η αγάπη μας περνούν.
Το αιγυπτιακό σου αίσθημα χύσε στην ξένη γλώσσα.

Ραφαήλ, οι στίχοι σου έτσι να γραφούν
που νάχουν, ξέρεις, από την ζωή μας μέσα των,
που κι ο ρυθμός κ' η κάθε φράσις να δηλούν
που γι' Αλεξανδρινό γράφει Αλεξανδρινός.][56]

NOTES

1   Κ. Π. ΚαβάΦης, *ΑΠΑΝΤΑ I 1896–1918* (Athens: Ikaros, 1982), 79; Pheng Cheah, "Grounds of Comparison: Around the Work of Benedict Anderson," *Diacritics* 29, no. 4 (1999): 2–18; Jonathan Culler, "Whither Comparative Literature?," *Comparative Critical Studies* 3, no. 1–2 (2006): 85–97.

2   I am grateful to Susan Stanford Friedman and Rita Felski for their careful reading and thoughtful comments on an earlier draft of this essay.

3   See, for example, "The Multi-, the Pluri-, the Trans-, and the Marketplace: A few Thoughts on the Comparative and 'Relational Literacy,'" *Passages: A Journal of Transnational & Transcultural Studies* 1, no. 2 (1999): 173–213. Originally solicited and accepted for Charles Bernheimer's collection on comparative literature and multiculturalism in the mid-1990s, it was subsequently rejected by the editorial board of the Johns Hopkins University Press. A singular "honor," it was the only essay in the collection eliminated at that stage of publication. Whether it was the inclusion of comic books, the discussion of Palestine and Israel, an unconventional assembly of texts, or an argument about comparison deemed unworthy, the concept formulated there of the comparative as "relational literacy" is one I would reiterate and to which I will return here in conclusion.

4   Something of Harry Harootunian's necessarily lived comparatism is suggested, ironically enough, in the string of hyphenated trans-national modifiers to their names here. See the passage referred to in footnote 9 below.

5   Nineteenth-century comparative studies—comparative anatomy, law, linguistics, religion—arose and developed as the imperial dominion of Europe was vigorously and, in retrospect, decisively challenged in the colonies. That anticolonial challenge underwrites— or at least is coeval with—the necessity and the desire of nineteenth-century comparative studies.

6   For an insightful account of unevenness and theory, see R. Radhakrishnan, *Theory in an Uneven World* (Malden, MA: Blackwell, 2003).

7   That this "jostling" and juxtaposition of difference in the modern is temporal as well as spatial is indicated in his bucolic opening quotation from Virgil.

8   Joseph Addison & Richard Steele, *The Spectator* 69, May 19, 1711.

9   Harry Harootunian, "Some Thoughts on Comparability and the Space-Time Problem," *boundary 2* 32, no. 2 (2005): 23–52. This proposition of a structurally enforced experience of comparison echoes Cheah's citation of the "inhuman automaton" as the specter of comparison in Benedict Anderson's work.

10 David Damrosch, "Goethe Coins a Phrase," *What Is World Literature?* (Princeton, NJ: Princeton Univ. Press, 2003), where Damrosch frames his twenty-first-century story of world literature as "an essay in definition, a celebration of new opportunities, and a gallery of cautionary tales" (36). See also his subsequent *How to Read World Literature* (Malden, MA: Wiley-Blackwell, 2009). And for an insightful and astute assessment of the comparative, see his "Rebirth of a Discipline: The Global Origins of Comparative Studies," *Critical Comparative Studies* 3, no. 1–2 (2006): 99–112 or "Comparative Literature?," *PMLA* 118, no. 2 (2003): 326–30.

11 For example, Charles Bernheimer, "The Anxieties of Comparison," in *Comparative Literature in the Age of Multiculturalism* (Baltimore: Johns Hopkins Univ. Press, 1994); Gayatri Chakravorty Spivak, *Death of a Discipline* (New York: Columbia Univ. Press, 2005); and

Susan Bassnett's reconsideration in "Reflections on Comparative Literature in the Twenty-First Century," *Comparative Critical Studies* 3, no. 1–2 (2006): 3–11, of the conclusion of her *Comparative Literature: A Critical Introduction* (Oxford: Blackwell, 1993) in the light of Spivak's *Death of a Discipline.*

12   Emily Apter, *The Translation Zone* (Princeton, NJ: Princeton Univ. Press, 2006). See Anthony Pym's review in *Target: International Journal of Translation Studies* 19, no. 1 (2007): 177–83 for an account both appreciative and critical of some of Apter's comparative readings.

13   Natalie Melas, *All the Difference in the World* (Stanford, CA: Stanford Univ. Press, 2007).

14   Melas's postcolonial formalism as a mode of comparison is richly informed, as she notes, by Édouard Glissant's "elaboration of Relation in which . . . the overarching commensuration of imperialism's cultural comparison is overturned and also relayed in the postcolonial condition as cultures come into constant contact without a unifying standard, thus engaging in ubiquitous processes of comparison that are no longer bound to commensuration" (37).

15   Peter Osborne, "On Comparability: Kant and the Possibility of Comparative Studies," *boundary 2* 32, no. 2 (2005): 3–22.

16   Harootunian, "Some Thoughts on Comparability," 23–52.

17   Marcel Detienne, *Comparing the Incomparable,* trans. Janet Lloyd (Stanford, CA: Stanford Univ. Press, 2008).

18   Timothy Brennan, "Edward Said and Comparative Literature," *Journal of Palestine Studies* 33, no. 3 (2004): 23–37.

19   Herbert Marcuse, *The Aesthetic Dimension: Toward a Critique of Marxist Aesthetics* (Boston: Beacon Press, 1978); the title of the German original published a year earlier (1977)—*Permanenz der Kunst*—is rather more indicative than its English translation of the argument therein about the realm of the aesthetic.

20   Though now often cited, including by Spivak herself, this provocative phrase was tucked away in a footnote early in her *A Critique of Postcolonial Reason: Toward a History of the Vanishing Present* (Cambridge, MA: Harvard Univ. Press, 1999), 31.

21   K. Π. Καβάφης, *ΑΠΑΝΤΑ Ι 1896–1918* (Athens: Ikaros, 1982), 79. Though the translation here is my own, see C. P. Cavafy, *Collected Poems,* rev. ed., trans. Edmund Keeley and Philip Sherrard, ed. George Savidis (Princeton, NJ: Princeton Univ. Press, 1992). I've consulted Keeley and Sherrard's distinguished translations with interest and admiration. For a thoughtfully insightful account of Cavafy's life and poetry (as well as his considerable influence on international poetry) by way of a review of two recent translations of his poems by Daniel Mendelsohn, see Maria Margaronis, "Mixing History and Desire: The Poetry of C. P. Cavafy," *The Nation,* August 3, 2009, 27–30.

22   النهايات، عبد الرحمن منيف (Beirut: Al-muassasat al-arabiyyat lid-dirasat al nashr, 1977/ 2007).

23   The period from 1879 to 1882 was one of increasing political foment and peasant and worker protests in Egypt as the `Urabi Revolt against British and French intervention in Egypt and the corrupt Egyptian Khedive organized for and achieved its initial successes. Alexandria was one of the centers of political organizing and actions. By the time the British bombarded Alexandria, the Cavafy family had already left for Constantinople. With the defeat of the `Urabi Revolt, the British occupied Egypt. But Alexandria remained an important center of political organizing and actions. This was the Alexandria in which Cavafy lived and wrote from late 1880s to his death in 1933.

24   Margaronis, "Mixing History and Desire," 27.

25   In K. Π. Καβάφης, *ΑΠΑΝΤΑ Ι 1896–1918,* 79. Please see the entire poem in the addendum.

26   Cavafy writes Αμμόν / Αμμόνης rather than the more conventional Greek rendering of Ammon's name Αμμών.

27   Na synthésēs / να συνθέσεις ("to compose" but literally to bring together, to "synthesize") forms a neat rhyme in the next line with sē tha borésēs / συ θα μπορέσεις ("you will be able"). This is one of the only two irregular end rhymes in the poem and serves as clear emphasis for the content of those lines.

28   Ραφαήλ, οι στίχοι σου έτσι *να γραφούν*
      που νάχουν, ξέρεις, από την ζωή μας μέσα των,
      που κι ο ρυθμός κ' η κάθε φράσις *να δηλούν*
      που γι' Αλεξανδρινό γράφει Αλεξανδρινός (emphasis added).

29   Its literal meaning is "clean-flowing."

30   "Μαστοριά"—of Byzantine origin—is more commonly used to refer to artisanal work than to the creation of poetry.

31   Βέβαια θα πεις για τα ποιήματά του—
      αλλά να πεις και για την εμορφιά του,
      για την λεπτή εμορφιά του που αγαπήσαμε.

32   "Ωραία" here also perhaps refers back to the delicate beauty of Ammon in the conclud-ing line of the preceding stanza. For while "ωραία" does come to generally mean beauty in modern Greek, it is a classical word that links beauty or fairness to timeliness, to something produced in its proper time, in its appropriate season. And while Ammon's beauty and youth were "timely," his death—like that of ʿAssāf below—is anything but "timely."

33   There are numerous example of this "bringing together" (συν) to distinguish (κρινω) in Cavafy's published and unpublished work. See "Επάνοδος από την Ελλάδα" ("Return from Greece") for a striking instance.

34   Sabry Hafez, "An Arabian Master," *New Left Review* 37 (January–February 2006): 39–66.

35   For an excellent translation, which I've consulted with admiration and interest, see Abd al-Rahman Munif, *Endings*, trans. Roger Allen (Northampton, MA: Interlink, 2007).

36   *Al-bashr*/ البشر suggests "humankind" or "human race" rather than a more colloquial "men" or "people" such as *al-nas*, with which the novel refers to "the people of al-Tiba." This signals from the beginning of the novel the significance of the human in relation to the nonhuman—other living things, the natural world, objects—that is persistently distinguished throughout the novel.

37   Perhaps ironically, the name of the village is derived from the root "to be good" or "pleasant" or "agreeable"; the ordinary meaning of *tiba* is goodness or congeniality.

38   As Hafez points out in his essay, "Munif's novels rarely designate the country in which they are set, even where the reference is clear" (42). He then quotes a wonderfully pre-scient observation by Munif from a 1999 interview, "Crisis in the Arab World," in *L'Orient Express*, translated and reprinted in *Al Jadid*, 9, no. 45 (2004).

If, for example, we discuss the political prison in a confined territory such as Iraq or Saudi Arabia, it seems as if we are exonerating other places or as if political prisons do not exist in these places, especially when we know they exist from the Atlantic to the Gulf. *Thus I consider the generalization of this subject is the ultimate specificity* (emphasis added).

39   The narrator's initially broad, generalizing categorization in the novel's opening pages—abstracted or generalized human beings, animals, and things that change as the climate changes—becomes rather more specific and particular in subsequent pages. Peasants, shepherds, merchants, old people, young people, moneylenders, shopkeepers, flocks of birds in general, geese, cranes, or sand grouse are all specified and their diverse behavior in the face of drought noted.

40   The chapters in the Arabic text are unnumbered but obvious from the insertion of blank pages and bold-faced opening words. I've numbered chapters here for ease of reference. Roger Allen's translation notes only the titularly designated "some stories from that amazing night" and designates other breaks only with a few extra lines on the page. Thus, interestingly, the translation reads as rather more continuous and unstructured than the original.

41 Roger Allen's translation eliminates much of what would be repetitive in English translation. Yet in the original, repetition—especially in the speech of the villagers—serves to mark the cyclical or at least repetitive time which the village and its residents inhabit and from which they break in the end. It is implicitly juxtaposed to the time of the city and its unfulfilled promises—for a better life, for roads to the village, for a long-promised dam that would ease the ravages of recurring drought.

42 It is a company clearly gendered male. The presence, knowledge, and behavior of women in the novel are always marked as such and as different than the presence, knowledge, and behavior of men. In fact the narrator of *al-Nihayat* comments repeatedly on the differences of age and gender in shaping what people know and understand and in how they communicate.

43 For, as he angrily protests to the urban hunters later, he hunts from need not from desire for pleasure as they do (٨٩). It is noteworthy in thinking of relations otherwise, that, as ʿAssāf leaves the hunting party at daybreak to set out on foot with his dog, he cautions the men to always stay in a circle—larger or smaller, but always in a circle. And he concludes his mandate of circular connection by advising them "the only thing you have to understand is how to help one another" (٧٩).

44 See Kumkum Sangari's astute reformulation of magical realism and "the real" in her "The Politics of the Possible," in *Theory of the Novel: A Historical Approach*, ed. Michael McKeon (Baltimore: Johns Hopkins Univ. Press, 2000), 900–922.

45 It is the specific construction of that context which allows the *synkrisis* of comparison to occur. And so, unable, I suspect, to assume familiarity with Munif's novel, I briefly specify that context here.

46 The hikāyāt of the subtitle are oral tales, unequivocally distinguished from the stories (قصص) which the visitors tell. (See 47.)

47 "Though the visitors told stories (قصص) that night too, the villagers couldn't understand them very well" (١١٦).

48 And in this, the villagers' tales are scarcely evidence of the "manic illogic" with which the narrator characterizes them (١١٢).

49 See note 43.

50 This mode of hunting is, Al-ʿAnzi ruefully observes, that of "the rich who drive their landrovers around like locusts looking for gazelles to shoot." Of course this is precisely the mode of hunting in which the village sons and their friends from the city have just engaged.

51 In a wonderful elaboration, the second tale responds with an account of the goat, now further identified as a pregnant goat who weeps as she tries to give birth to her offspring before she dies. There are other noteworthy narrative turns. The third tale moves from hunting in the wild to "hunting" in the Agha's garden and an ongoing contest there between a she-dog and two crows that swoop and dive at her—a battle which was the amusement of the residents of the quarter where the Agha lived. When a local policeman shoots the she-dog and her five puppies, the crows hover over the cart with the dead animal bodies squawking and trailing the cart. They disappear and are never seen again by the residents of the quarter. The fourth tale is of a beautiful, cocky male bird that falls in love with a gentle she-bird and dies in grief at her death. And so the tales continue in their suggestive interaction with one another and their reframing of what has come before in the novel and in suggestion of what is possible—reflecting on and poetically suggesting other ways of "comparing" the human and the nonhuman, the living and the inanimate, the natural and the human-made worlds. Each story, in its own way, tells of connection over "disengagement" and conventional domination. The seventh tale introduces the first instance of first-person narration in the novel and in the sequence of tales; it is reiterated in only one other instance—the first-person narration of the fourteenth tale.

52 "The wealthy pay full rent; the poor half."

53 In a formation that echoes ʿAssāf's injunction to the (male) hunters to stay in a circle and to help one another, the women, the narrator notes, "form a circle, combining mournfulness, joy, intensity, pleasure, and anger" (٢٠٩). "Rhythmic and controlled," their increasingly intense and complicated movements are punctuated by a sound (not a word) that "adds a new reality to a particular movement, making it more fiery" (٢١٠). Unable to understand exactly what the women are doing or saying, he *is* able to recognize and point at their amazing (their singular and unverifiable?) formation.

54 "How is it that human beings can fall so silent and for such a long time? How can they forget the entirety of the words and sounds they've used since birth? . . . How? How can this happen?" (١٠٥).

55 C. P. Cavafy, *Collected Poems*, 71.

56 Κ. Π. Καβάφης, *ΑΠΑΝΤΑ Ι 1896–1918*, 79.

CHAPTER TWELVE

Comparison Literature

Rebecca L. Walkowitz

A FAMOUS SOUTH AFRICAN AUTHOR COMPOSES a series of essays in English for publication, first, in German and, later, in French. The essays are to be called "Strong Opinions." However, the author does not simply *write* the essays. Rather, he scrawls a few illegible notes onto a sheaf of papers, dictates into a tape recorder, and then hands both notes and tape to a Filipina-Australian typist, who transfers his words onto computer disks, though not before fixing them up, as she puts it, "where they lack a certain something."[1] These essays come to us, along with the story of their production and circulation, in J. M. Coetzee's most recent novel, *Diary of a Bad Year*, whose *Wereldprimeur* appeared in Holland on August 2, 2007.[2] The book was soon published in Australia, Coetzee's current home, and then in the United Kingdom, Canada, Spain, the United States, Germany, Japan, and France. Fourteen months after its release, Coetzee's novel was available in at least nine national editions and six languages.[3]

Published in multiple languages almost simultaneously and beginning in Dutch rather than in English, *Diary of a Bad Year* does not belong to any one national, ethnic, or linguistic tradition. It is instead a comparative novel, or an example of what I call *comparison literature*. It fits this rubric because of its circulation, to be sure, but also because of its production: formally, the text experiments with comparative structures such as lists and catalogues; typographically, it invokes historical practices of translation that emphasize comparison between source and target; and thematically, it reflects on gestures of ethical, national, and generic comparison. These elements often work together, as when the novel's comparative architecture—almost every page features a public essay interparagraphed with personal diaries—establishes a visual juxtaposition that matches classic modes of interlineal and facing-page translation. We are urged to compare verbally as well as visually: to consider how a word's appearance in a philosophical essay at the top of the page relates to its appearance in one of the diaries printed below, and how the meaning of an idea changes as it moves between the novel's many discursive registers. These registers include academic and popular; public and private;

the geopolitical and the neighborhood; oral, written, analog, and digital; standard and vernacular. Comparison functions, too, as one of the novel's abiding ethical concerns: the text asks whether transnational enlargement in fact enhances—or ultimately thwarts—our capacity for social responsibility and political agency.

By using the term *comparison literature,* I mean to draw our attention to the traditional distinction between a field of national literature, in which scholars typically share a locus of production (a place, a community, a language), and the field of comparative literature, in which scholars typically share a structure of analysis (comparison in its various modes). Whereas British literature, to take one example, points to the study of texts that were made or published in the United Kingdom or by U.K. citizens, comparative literature points to no specific archive.[4] Instead, it designates a repertoire of intellectual strategies that are addressed to multiple literary cultures or language traditions. However, since comparative literature often takes for granted that each literary culture is geographically and politically separate, the distinction between fields is not as sharp as it may at first seem. Both British literary studies and comparative literary studies trade in national categories and assume the ontological integrity of a given text. *Comparison literature* fits uneasily within methodologies, comparative and national, that assign unique locations or unique substance to literary artifacts. It asks us to imagine new geographies of literary production and requires methodologies that understand the history of a book to include its many editions and translations.

Novels such as Coetzee's are part of an emergent genre of transnational fiction whose preoccupation with comparison is stimulated in part by the historical conditions of the global literary marketplace, and in part by several related developments such as the flourishing of migrant communities, and especially migrant writers, within metropolitan centers throughout the world. In addition, comparison literature responds to the ongoing problem of statelessness and post-Holocaust debates about the treatment of minorities. And it joins the renewed effort to imagine transnational and/or cosmopolitan paradigms that offer alternatives to national models of political community. Comparison literature is also part of a general turn to translation that has been crucial to many intellectual projects of the past two decades, including work in political philosophy, literary history, and postcolonial studies. Judith Butler has recently argued that a "non-nationalist or counter-nationalist mode of belonging," a mode of belonging that does not exclude minorities, will require a "certain distance or fissure," which Butler associates literally and figuratively with translation.[5] Instead of "extending or augmenting the homogeneity of the nation," she asserts, genuine equality requires "a collectivity that comes to exercise its freedom in a language or set of languages for which difference and translation are irreducible" (61–62). While Butler has placed translation at the center of a debate about political philosophies of the nation, Susan Bassnett has claimed that the field of comparative literature needs above all to "rethink its relationship to Translation Studies"; in fact, she argues, "as translation studies establishes itself firmly as a subject based in inter-cultural study and offering a methodology of some rigour . . . so comparative literature appears less like a discipline and more like a branch of something else."[6]

However, as Bassnett implies, it is not simply a matter of importing the old translation studies into new transnational contexts. Both Butler and Bassnett are invoking a mode of translation that emphasizes 1) the historical uses of translation in and between cultures; 2) the importance of translation and multilingualism within nation-states; and 3) the ethical and intellectual imperative to keep translation "irreducible," which is to say, visible within collective speech acts (Butler's example is the national anthem) and translated texts. Naoki Sakai, Rey Chow, and Lawrence Venuti, to name perhaps the most well-known advocates for this mode of translation, have all argued that, in Venuti's words, the most responsible translation will actually refuse "the illusion of transparency . . . by deviating from the values, beliefs, and representations that currently hold sway in the target language."[7] Moreover, as Chow argues, it will understand the source language and culture as "comparative" rather than as "monolingual, monocultural, or mononational" (85). In other words, the new translation studies insists on a definition of national languages that emphasizes internal variety and a complex mixing of local, regional, and global idioms. Comparison thus appears as predicate as well as practice. It is this development, above all, that is central to Coetzee's work, in which he considers how transnational comparison shapes the insides of novels, persons, and communities.

Treating comparison at the level of typography, language, genre, and theme, *Diary of a Bad Year* anticipates its own future as a work of world literature. It is therefore a novel that does not simply *appear* in translation but in important ways has been *written for translation*. To adapt Matthew Kirschenbaum's phrase for artworks that begin on the computer ("born digital"), we might say that Coetzee's novel is *born translated* in a diegetic and nondiegetic sense.[8] Before I turn to the way these problems occupy the novel's diegesis, it is worth noting that the novel's many and immediate translations are historically unprecedented, if we consider how quickly *Diary* saturated various national markets across several continents. By saturation of national markets, I refer to the publication of different editions in the same language (for example, Australian, U.K., U.S., and Canadian) and of different editions in different languages (for example, English, French, and Japanese); these editions have appeared in several regions of the globe (for example, Australia/Japan, North America, Western Europe). Of course, long before the twenty-first century, there were literary works that traveled from their first language into multiple languages and national editions. But these travels were relatively slow and initially confined to regional distribution. To take several, well-known examples, the international bestseller *Don Quixote*, noted by Franco Moretti for its exceptionally fast absorption into many language systems, took fifty-one years, from 1605 to 1656, to find its way into six national languages; and it was only in 1769 that the novel was published outside of Western Europe.[9] Isabel Hofmeyr tells us that *Pilgrim's Progress*, first published in 1678, has been translated into more than two hundred languages, including eighty African languages, but it began its migration beyond Europe and the North Atlantic in 1835.[10] And according to Martin Puchner, the 1848 appearance of the *Communist Manifesto* in German was followed by Swedish, English, Russian, Serbian, and French editions in a speedy twenty-four years; the first edition printed in a non-European language was the Japanese translation, published in 1904.[11] Finally, a contemporary example that echoes the expansive geography and in some ways the speed of *Diary*'s diffusion: between July and December of 2005, the phenomenally successful sixth installment of the Harry Potter series, *Harry Potter and the Half-Blood Prince*, entered fifteen languages, including Vietnamese, Afrikaans, and Estonian, though as a result of piracy concerns, the first translation was delayed by two months.[12] In this case, linguistic and economic translatability may have actually hindered the process of translation.

Born-translated novels are designed to travel, so they tend to veer away from the modernist emphasis on linguistic experimentation. In the work of James Joyce and Samuel Beckett and, later, Anthony Burgess and Salman Rushdie, thematic innovation is sutured to the resources of vernacular idiom such that the work becomes, in the words of contemporary novelist and translator Tim Parks, "a thing made of language."[13] In order to find a place in the global marketplace, Parks asserts, books written for translation will need to invent alternatives to the emphasis on idiolect. For better or for worse, he avers, "the writer whose quarrel with language is not manifested in rebellious and provocative events at the narrative level is almost certain to be passed over" (245). Born-translated novels have to be accessible, as Parks suggests, but they need not be obsequious. To accommodate translation, after all, is not only to encourage it. Accommodation may also involve appropriation, opportunism, and innovation. Comparison literature, then, as I imagine it, does emphasize narrative over idiom, but it uses that emphasis to explore the political history of languages in formal and thematic registers that can survive translation. In this way, comparison literature adapts the novel of transnational contact to an age of multilingual circulation.

Any list of novelists whose works are born translated would have to include Coetzee, Kazuo Ishiguro, W. G. Sebald, Tim Parks, Caryl Phillips, and Jamaica Kincaid. We could also point to individual works by David Peace, David Mitchell, the collaborative authors/artists Young-Hae Chang Heavy Industries, Peter Ho Davies, Kiran Desai, and Mohsin Hamid, the author of the bestseller *The Reluctant Fundamentalist.* One can see among these writers the proliferation of what I call "the anthological novel": think here of the geographic sampling and collating we see in Sebald's *The Emigrants*, Phillips's *The Distant Shore*, Ho Davies's *The Welsh Girl*, and Desai's *The Inheritance of Loss.*[14] Comparison literature tends to be written in English, and most works hew to the novel form. Novels travel more easily than other genres, and Anglophone novels travel especially well because English has become the most-read, most-translated language in the world. Yet the hegemony of the marketplace does not guarantee the hegemony of marketplace fiction. Unlike the average international bestseller, translated works of comparison literature confront readers with the history and politics of language, and they do this better than many so-called untranslatable novels that emphasize vernacular culture and idiomatic expression. This may seem counterintuitive, but it makes sense when we consider that a good translation is supposed to pass for a work produced from the start in the target language. To do this, translators will often homogenize regional differences within national languages by simplifying vernacular idioms or exchanging vernacular phrases for standard formulations. Some translators of complex idiomatic works, such as *Ulysses* and *Finnegans Wake*, resist simplification but accept instead that versions in new languages will venture far afield of the original works. Given these practices, novels that treat multilingualism through narrative events, characterization, and structure are more likely than novels that treat multilingualism through idiom to retain in translation an engagement with local histories of language.

Not only for the instrumental reasons detailed above, but also for reasons of political strategy, Coetzee has argued persistently against the assumption that all works in the original give us better or more representative access to local communities than all translations do. In his novels, Coetzee often represents non-English speech or writing, but he avoids stylistic marking such as grammatical inversion or broken diction that would remind readers of a specific original language. There are at least three consequences to this choice. Coetzee's texts can be more easily translated, since there is no dialect to be reproduced in another language. He does not associate the consciousness of a kind of character, where kind is defined by ethnic community or third-world experience, with specific features of language. Finally, he creates a text in which even English readers are blocked from imagining a direct, simultaneous encounter with a language that is their own. This last point is crucial: for Coetzee, it has always seemed inappropriate, both ethically and historically, to suggest that his writing is part of a unique national-language tradition or emerges from a coherent national community. In this way, one could say that all of Coetzee's fiction—not only those works that treat transnational comparison thematically—project comparative beginnings.

We can find this ambivalence about national traditions stated more or less explicitly throughout Coetzee's interviews, criticism, and fiction. "Perhaps—is this possible?—I have no mother tongue," muses the essayist in *Diary of a Bad Year* (195). The essayist implies that his sense of discomfort in any one language, his sense that in his voice "some other person (but who?) is being imitated, followed, even mimicked" (195), can be attributed to the history of colonialism. He imagines that middle-class Indians might experience something similar: "There must be many who have done their schooling in English, who routinely speak English in the workplace and at home (throwing in the odd local locution for colouring), who command other languages only imperfectly, yet who, as they listen to themselves speak or as they read what they have written, have the uneasy feeling that there is something false going on" (197). The falseness that Coetzee hears in his own voice and imagines in the voices of postcolonial readers and writers elsewhere does not represent a failure to use English successfully. To the contrary: it represents the difficulty of registering, as one speaks or writes flawlessly, the history of violence suppressed by fluency and monolingualism. As both a colonial and a postcolonial nation, to use Andrew van der Vlies's helpful formulation, South Africa has continued to struggle over whether national belonging should ever be associated with a single language.[15]

Coetzee's work has internalized many of the strategies of comparison that have transformed the literature disciplines, among them the investigation of transnational and multilingual histories of literary culture, the analysis of how the global dissemination of literature has been tied to institutions of the state and the apparatus of imperialism, and a new focus on technology and translation.[16] *Diary of a Bad Year* exchanges one kind of comparison for another: instead of arranging representative examples from distinct locations, genres, or points of view, the novel places narrative episodes, characters, and historical events into multiple containers. Sometimes it can seem as if there are no containers at all, and this is the central problem that comparison literature poses both for literary history and for models of political community. In the remainder of this essay, I will turn, first, to the extant paradigm we have for literature that solicits comparison—world literature—and then I will take up briefly Coetzee's recent novel, which allows us to consider how comparison literature rejects and in some ways retains national paradigms.

Making World Literature

Recent discussions of world literature have assumed that books begin in one place and then move out to other places.[17] But there are many novels, written by migrants and for an international audience, that exist from the beginning in several places. Of course, the notion that a book could begin in several places complicates traditional models of literary history and political community. Literary critics will need to ask how the multilingualism of the book changes the national singularity of the work. Philosophers of the nation will need to ask how the translation of literary texts, into more languages and faster than ever before, establishes networks of affiliation that are less exclusive and less bounded than the nation's "community of fate." Generally speaking, we can identify two paradigms that influence most contemporary accounts of the relationship between literary history and political community: the paradigm of "possessive collectivism," which has a long history in philosophy, anthropology, and legal theory, and the paradigm of "imagined communities," which Benedict Anderson introduced in 1983, and which has become so influential in history, literary studies, and many other fields that it operates almost tacitly in our ways of talking about the effect of books on political collectivities.[18] Where have these theories brought us, and where might we now go in thinking about literature's engagement with conceptions of the collective?

"Possessive collectivism" extends the idea of possessive individualism to nations and ethnic groups.[19] In Quebecois ideology, the anthropologist Richard Handler explains in a well-known study, the nation was understood as both a "collection of individuals and a collective individual," who/which possesses unique, permanent qualities such as a "soul, spirit, and personality," and who/which has the capacity to exercise sovereignty, free will, and choice.[20] Rosemary Coombe has used Handler's work on nationalist ideology to describe the effects and underlying assumptions of international copyright. In copyright law, Coombe argues, "each nation or group is perceived as an author who originates a culture from resources that come from within and can thus lay claim to exclusive possession of the expressive works that embody its personality" (224–25). Literary works belong to the nation because they are the embodiment of its internal spirit or genius, and we know the nation has a spirit or genius because it has literary works to show for it. This is a feedback loop: nationhood owes its identity to authorship, but there is no authorship without nationhood, since expressivity belongs to unique individuals, who in turn belong to unique groups. Among minorities and colonized subjects, possessive collectivism has had the positive effect of validating intellectual labor and justifying political sovereignty. For our purposes, possessive collectivism is notable because it helps to explain why emphasizing the original production of artworks tends to affirm national literary histories: original art and original nations grow up together. We could speculate, however, that a theory of artworks that understood acts of editing and translating as acts of making might affirm a different norm of literary history and a different conception of the community that literary history helps to justify.

Before I push this speculation further, consider Benedict Anderson's idea of "imagined communities." Rather than rehearse Anderson's now-classic theory, I would like to mark an important difference between his account of literary nation making and the possessive collectivism model. It was Anderson's innovation to argue that the rise of print culture, and especially the rise of novels and newspapers, contributed to the possibility of imagining a nation as a shared, exclusive collectivity among strangers. Print culture contributed to this possibility in two structural ways: by creating the impression of simultaneous reading across space; and by creating the impression, within the novel, of simultaneity among people who never meet—an impression that Anderson memorably calls the experience of "meanwhile" (25). The second impression strengthens the first: if we can perceive the novel as a container for strangers who act together without knowing it, then we can imagine the nation as a container for us, the readers of that novel, who act together in just the same way—simultaneously, collectively, and invisibly. As Jonathan Culler has observed in an essay on Anderson's work, it is not the novel's content or theme but its form, its way of being a container for simultaneity among strangers, that creates "a political distinction between friend and foe."[21] Anderson's model does not imply that the artwork is expressing a repertoire of national characteristics that could be owned; rather, it argues that the novel represents—and generates—a community based on the imagined concurrence of action. If there is a residue of possessive collectivism in Anderson's materialism, it is in his assumption that a text has an original language and that the text's language will coincide with the language of its readers. What happens, we need to ask, when these languages are not the same? Or when there is no original language to speak of?

We can address these questions by returning to Anderson's project. But instead of approaching *Imagined Communities* as an argument, as others have done so well,[22] I want to treat it as an example, since it is as an example of world literature that Anderson's book coincides, historically and formally, with today's traveling novel. Like Coetzee's recent works, *Imagined Communities* stages an encounter between literary history and political theory. And like Coetzee's novels, the study itself functions as a work of world literature both because of its circulation and because of its production. As a text, *Imagined Communities* takes as its subject the effects of print culture on the development of nation-states throughout the world. Individual chapters are devoted to case studies of small countries such as Hungary, Thailand, Switzerland, and the Philippines. As a book, *Imagined Communities* has circulated among many of these small countries, and among many large ones too. It was first published in English in 1983 and has been translated over the past twenty-six years into twenty-seven languages, including Japanese, German, Portuguese, Serbo-Croat, and Catalan. Yet the phenomenal success of Anderson's project has led not only to translation and also retranslation, but also to new production. In 1991 and 2006, respectively, Anderson issued second and third English editions, each of which includes new material that responds to criticism of the work and reflects on the transnational communities that the book's circulation has helped to create.

The third edition adds to the book's subject matter—how print culture contributes to the imagination of community—an account of how the translation and reception of the book we are reading has contributed to the imagination of communities to which the book now belongs. In this account, we learn that the transnational and multilingual circulation of *Imagined Communities* has led Anderson to consider that the global appeal of his argument may have been spurred by its own transnational beginnings—that is, by origins understood not simply as London or the Anglo-American academy, but as a transnational conglomerate, the United Kingdom, in which devolution and multiculturalism offer conflicting models of political history and collective fate. Anderson acknowledges in the 2006 edition that the original rhetoric of the book was borrowed in part from debates about postcolonial migration and the decline of empire that had become especially urgent in the United Kingdom of the late seventies and early eighties. From the perspective of later editions, we see that Anderson's text is rather more transnational than we had at first perceived. Yet what I am calling transnational, the narrative's attunement to histories of devolution and multiculturalism, also remains local in an important sense. Regional, semimetropolitan, Anderson's work shows us that global disarticulation—belonging to nowhere—is not the only alternative to national simultaneity. Moreover, it suggests that the repression of translation may be tied, as it is in Anderson's text, to the repression of transnational impulses within national projects.

There is no chapter in *Imagined Communities* that presents itself as an analysis of the novel today, but the afterword to the third edition is suggestive about translation's effects on literary history. Readers become part of the book's story about how print culture structures imagined communities, and thus the community of the book is shown to exceed the community of the text. In this way, *Imagined Communities* shares its narrative structure with many other contemporary transnational works and also resembles edited and translated works from earlier eras. As Anderson argues, translation can contribute to the imagination of national communities. But as Anderson demonstrates, translation puts pressure on the conceptual boundaries between one community and another and may spur the perception of new communities altogether. To relinquish my initial distinction between Anderson's example and his argument, we might consider those nineteenth-century books such as anthologies, periodicals, and episodic novels in which the experience of a single container is disrupted by the perception of alternative collectivities.[23]

In modernist literature, the apprehension of simultaneity in time and space is regularly breached by free indirect discourse, by the importation of multiple languages, and by multiple frames of narration. In the decades since World War II, with the expansive circulation of Anglophone writing, transnational novelists have developed structures of "meanwhile" that are not only "relative," as Wai Chee Dimock has put it, but recursive and rivalrous.[24] But perhaps the most significant continuity between Anderson's text and those of Coetzee and other comparative writers is their response to new theories and practices of translation. If Anglophone modernists made their novels nearly untranslatable because tied so closely to the idiosyncrasies of English, writers such as Coetzee and Ishiguro (and Anderson) purposefully accommodate translation by encouraging multiple editions of their novels and by designing comparative texts that emphasize networks of collectivity. These developments—a transformation in the time and space of literary production; the rise of migrant writers who address their work to communities of various scales; and a new engagement with translation within literary fiction—have been vital to the emergence of comparison literature.

Diary of a Bad Year

Coetzee's novels offer an opportunity to consider the relationship between the production and reception of world literature because, in addition to circulating widely, they have made practices of circulation a principal concern. Not only do they resist national location in the form of the book, but by beginning in several places and languages at once, they engage with the problem of national location in the form of the text, taking up comparison both structurally and thematically. We see this explicitly in three recent novels: 2007's *Diary of a Bad Year*; 2005's *Slow Man*, which brings together theories of migration and theories of art; and 2003's *Elizabeth Costello*, named for the fictional writer whose experiences on the international lecture circuit are described in many of the chapters. *Slow Man* and *Diary* ask how new technologies of reproduction and prosthesis transform our sense of the enclosed national community. They are testing two of Anderson's central claims: first, that "the book . . . is a distinct, self-contained object, exactly reproduced on a large scale" (34); and second, that the book's self-containment imitates and even stimulates the imagination of a contained, simultaneous collectivity (30). In *Slow Man*, Coetzee considers how different strands of post-1945 migration (from "new" Europe as well as from postcolonial nations) have introduced new agents of Anglophone literary production, how new technologies such as personal computers and digital scanners have altered our understanding of artworks in the world, and how theories of prosthesis (a spare leg or a translated edition) might alter our conceptions of individuality and national belonging. In *Diary*, Coetzee treats these issues by placing a work of world literature—a series of short essays about global politics written in English and published in German—alongside a story about the production of that work and its author's relationship with his typist.

Some readers may have first encountered an excerpt of *Diary of a Bad Year* in a July 2007 issue of *The New York Review of Books*. There, one finds bracing short essays titled "on the origins of the state," "on anarchism," "on democracy," "on Machiavelli," and "on terrorism." Aphoristic in length and style, the essays are interrupted every few paragraphs by a single paragraph, printed in boldface, in which a narrator describes his encounter with a shapely woman in a short red dress, whom he has met in his building's laundry room. The narrator's crass reflections on the shortness of the dress, the shapeliness of the woman, and his own comparative decrepitude provide an odd but welcome contrast to the dour seriousness of the political compositions. As the excerpt ends, it becomes clear that the diary writer is the essay writer, and the shapely woman in the short red dress will be his typist.

The July teaser gives the impression that the longer book will consist of two voices: one impersonal, political, and a little stilted; the other intimate, solipsistic, and a little coarse. But in the novel, there is a third voice—the typist's account of her interactions with the writer—and on almost every page at least two and usually three of these voices appear. Each is separated from the others by a thin horizontal line. At the top, we find the essays; in the middle, we find the author's account of his interactions with the typist; and at the bottom, there is the typist's account of those same encounters. What seems in *The New York Review of Books* excerpt to be a series of political and philosophical essays interrupted by the occasional paragraph of personal diary appears in the novel as a much more balanced structure, or even a rivalry, in which the essays and the two diaries vie for our attention and indeed require us to organize our attention at every turn. While the excerpt implies that the diary exists as light background for the strong opinions, the novel gives greater emphasis to the diary's subject matter: the dictating, the typing, the conversation between author and typist. The novel suggests that those processes inform the essays' models of sovereignty and political action.

It is important to Coetzee's project that the personal essay and the diary are two of the genres we associate most closely with individual voice. *Diary*'s first English edition encourages this association by displaying a manuscript on its cover and typewriter font on its title page—even though neither manuscript nor typewriter appears in the narrative. Both of these technologies promise what Shakespeareans call "character": the character of handwriting, the character of a typewriter's unique impression, the character of an author's expression. But the novel obstructs generic promises of self-revelation by introducing multiple diaries and by making the diaries part of the novel's action. Additionally, the fact that the author's essays have been dictated and then transferred to a computer makes it impossible to establish whether the essays we are reading are the author's words or the author's words altered by the typist's purposeful editing and the computer's automatic interventions. The novel confirms that the essays are collaborative in at least minor ways: for example, the fourth essay begins with a reference to "talkback radio" (17), and many pages later we find out from one of the diaries that the South African–Australian author incorporated this Adelaide idiom at the suggestion of his Filipina-Australian secretary (51). This recursive correction makes us wonder whose sentiments, language, and tone are represented in each section of the novel, and tells us that the apparently distinct voices of personal essay and diary are, in important ways, collective.

We should note that idiomatic distinctions such as "talkback radio" are treated diegetically, allowing the problem of idiom, if not the precise example, to survive translation. And it can be no accident that talkback radio is itself a vernacular technology: a genre which imagines hosts and listeners alike talking and talking back in nonstandard locutions. But the subject of idiom is also addressed by the novel's comparative structure, which asks us to consider that there are several ways to speak, as it were, on any one page, and by the proliferation of diaries, whose addition and revision suggest the social nature of the essayist's individualism. The relationship between language and community is thus treated through reference to vernacular writing, to be sure, but it is also treated through formal patterns of translation and thematic engagement with topics such as interiority, migration, embeddedness, and solidarity.

Apart from representing a collaborative interiority, the proliferation of diaries in the novel has an important generic effect. It shifts the text's emphasis from matters of political theory (global economy, genocide, ethical abstraction, and so on) to matters of social realism (private economy, jealousy, sentiment, and so on) and, at the same time, suggests that social realism, insofar as it emphasizes the embeddedness of social agents, exerts a strong, collective—we might even say, national—pull on the novel's antinational theories. We encounter those antinational theories in both explicit and implicit ways. Implicitly, *Diary* approaches the problem of national containment by invoking the problem of scale: how do we determine the boundaries of a person or a nation? The only pages in the novel that feature a single narrative—the only pages, that is, that display what appears as an individual voice—are those assigned to the essay "On the Afterlife," which focuses on the question of the individual soul. Unsurprisingly, the essayist finds "the notion of an individual afterlife" unconvincing (154). Central to his critique is the changeability of the self and the self's transformation through encounters with other selves. Which version of the individual, the essayist asks, will the afterlife recognize? These observations about the limitations of individuality as a concept are immediately followed by the second part of the novel, in which the essayist tries to revise not only his opinions but also his relationship with the typist. We learn from these later pages that the earlier essays, including the one on the Afterlife, were influenced by the author's conversations with the typist, which were in turn influenced by the typist's conversations with her boyfriend, which were in turn influenced by the boyfriend's surreptitious reading of the author's essays and of the author's computer-born diary. This is all to say that even the pages that seem to feature a single voice and focus on an univocal conception of the self are made to function in the context of other voices: they are not self-contained. If the essays do not support the uniqueness of the individual, either as a concept or as a narrative device, neither do they support the uniqueness of the nation. The writer treats with irony and distaste the assumption "that each person on earth must belong to one nation or another and operate within one or another national economy" (78). His complaint is in part directed at the so-called naturalness of the assumption; and in part it is directed at the national exclusivity and competition that follow.

Yet, for all its rejection of uniqueness in individuals and nations, the text finds room for uniqueness in collectivities such as those formed by the novel's paragraphs and those generated between author and typist by the circulation of those paragraphs. Additionally, Coetzee's affection for social realism—references to Leo Tolstoy and Fyodor Dostoevsky appear throughout the novel—competes with his suspicion of caricature and national containers. The persistence of collectivity becomes increasingly notable in the latter part of the novel, where the essayist is no longer committed to the version of enlargement he had espoused in his initial writings and where he embraces the sentiment and intimacy of realism even though he often disapproves of realism's approach to simultaneous community.

Diary begins with sweeping transnational and transhistorical comparisons: the essayist considers together the U.S. torture of prisoners, South Africa's violent preservation of apartheid, and Britain's imposition of colonial rule (39–45); elsewhere, he moves from the suppression of indigenous populations in Australia to histories of genocide in South Africa and the United States (107–9). But the novel ends with the sense that large-scale comparisons, while ethically necessary, are socially paralyzing. "Moral theory," the essayist opines, "has never quite known what to do with quantity, with numbers. Is killing two people worse than killing one person, for example? If so, how much worse?" (204). He then queries comparisons of quality: "Which is worse, the death of a bird or the death of a human child?" (205). The problem implicit in these questions, a problem that concerns Coetzee in all of his recent world fictions, is not only how to order narratives of violence, but whether there is a single conceptual scale that can comprehend diverse units of analysis. Instead of comparison as a measure of quantity (which is more?) or quality (which is worse?), Coetzee suggests that comparison might function better—more effectively, more sympathetically—as a practice of irreducible translation. In this, he does not evade or even trump the national container. Not really. Aspiring to solidarity without exclusion, agency without possessiveness, works of comparison literature nevertheless make groups of various kinds. For writers such as Coetzee, the principle of comparison guarantees only that those groups will have to be generated over and over again. By creating a novel in which individual voices are modified by circulation, Coetzee suggests that transnational communities—like transnational novels—operate at several scales at once.

Coetzee's comparative approach, in which we are asked to see how the logic of transnational circulation places characters, episodes, and even paragraphs within multiple containers, suggests new directions for literary critical methodology. Historians of the transnational novel will need to analyze how a work participates not only in its first literary system, the literary system of the language in which it was composed, but also in the other literary systems in which it has a presence. Because a text may begin in several places and because it may continue to travel to numerous regions and languages, its location and culture will be dynamic and unpredictable. It is no longer simply a matter of determining, once and for all, the literary culture to which a work belongs. Comparison literature such as Coetzee's implies the intersection of three major methodologies: book history, theories of globalization, and translation studies. Benedict Anderson helped us to see that the history of national literatures requires the history of the book. The history of comparison literature requires the history of many books: excerpts, anthologies, editions, and translations.

NOTES

This essay has benefited from the gracious questions offered by audiences at several universities and conferences. My thanks to all of my hosts and interlocutors on those occasions. I am especially grateful for the intellectual generosity of Rita Felski, Susan Stanford Friedman, and Henry Turner.

1   J. M. Coetzee, *Diary of a Bad Year* (London: Harvill Secker, 2007), 29. Unless otherwise indicated, all future references to the text will refer to this edition.

2   Coetzee, *Dagboek van een slecht jaar* [Diary of a Bad Year], trans. Peter Bergsma (Amsterdam: Cossee, 2007). A sticker affixed to the front cover proclaims the Dutch edition *Wereldprimeur de nieuwe roman van de Nobelprijswinnaar* (a rough translation of which would be "world premier of the new novel by the Nobel Prize winner").

3   In 2007, *Diary* was published in Australia on September 3; the United Kingdom on September 6; Canada on October 23; Spain on October 30; and the United States on December 27. In 2008, the book appeared in Germany on April 1; Japan on September 9; and France on October 1.

4   In his introduction to a special issue on globalization and world literature, Djelal Kadir writes, "comparative literature is neither a subject, nor an object, nor is it a problem. It is a practice." Djelal Kadir, "To World, To Globalize—Comparative Literature's Crossroads," *Comparative Literature Studies* 41, no. 1 (2004): 4.

5   Judith Butler and Gayatri Chakravorty Spivak, *Who Sings the Nation-State? Language, Politics, Belonging* (London: Seagull Books, 2007), 58–61.

6   Susan Bassnett, *Comparative Literature: A Critical Introduction* (Oxford: Blackwell, 1993), 11.

7   Lawrence Venuti, "1990s and Beyond" in *The Translation Studies Reader*, 2nd ed., ed. Lawrence Venuti (New York: Routledge, 2004), 334. For Sakai's and Chow's versions of this approach, see Naoki Sakai, *Translation and Subjectivity: On "Japan" and Cultural Nationalism* (Minneapolis: Univ. of Minnesota Press, 1997); and Rey Chow, *The Age of the World Target: Self-Referentiality in War, Theory, and Comparative Work* (Durham, NC: Duke Univ. Press, 2006).

8   Matthew Kirschenbaum, *Mechanisms: New Media and the Forensic Imagination* (Cambridge, MA: MIT Press, 2008), 114.

9   Franco Moretti, *Atlas of the European Novel, 1800–1900* (London: Verso, 1998), 171–73.

10   Isabel Hofmeyr, *The Portable Bunyan: A Transnational History of the Pilgrim's Progress* (Princeton, NJ: Princeton Univ. Press, 2004), 240–43.

11   Martin Puchner, *Poetry of the Revolution: Marx, Manifestos, and the Avant-Gardes* (Princeton, NJ: Princeton Univ. Press, 2006), 62–65.

12   For details of the *Potter* translation history, see Rebecca L. Walkowitz, "Unimaginable Largeness: Kazuo Ishiguro, Translation, and the New World Literature," *Novel* 40, no. 3 (2007): 5.

13   Tim Parks, *Translating Style: A Literary Approach to Translation—a Translation Approach to Literature*, 2nd ed. (Manchester: St. Jerome Publishing, 2007), 147.

14   I discuss the anthological novel at greater length in "The Location of Literature: The Transnational Book and the Migrant Writer," *Contemporary Literature* 47, no. 4 (2006): 527–45.

15   Andrew van der Vlies, *South African Textual Cultures: White, Black, Read All Over* (Man-

chester: Manchester Univ. Press, 2007), 5. Two of the best recent studies of multilingualism, book history, and the South African context of Coetzee's work are van der Vlies and Rita Barnard, "Coetzee in/and Africaans," unpublished manuscript.

16 For examples of many of these new developments within the field of comparative literature, see Haun Saussy, ed., *Comparative Literature in an Age of Globalization* (Baltimore: Johns Hopkins Univ. Press, 2006).

17 Moretti, "Conjectures on World Literature," *New Left Review* 1 (2000): 54–68; David Damrosch, *What Is World Literature?* (Princeton, NJ: Princeton Univ. Press, 2003).

18 Benedict Anderson, *Imagined Communities: Reflections on the Origin and Spread of Nationalism*, 3rd ed. (London: Verso, 2006).

19 Rosemary Coombe, *The Cultural Life of Intellectual Properties: Authorship, Appropriation, and the Law* (Durham, NC: Duke Univ. Press, 1998), 225. Coombe's use of this phrase is derived from Richard Handler, "Who Owns the Past? History, Cultural Property, and the Logic of Possessive Individualism" in *The Politics of Culture,* ed. Brett Williams (Washington, DC: Smithsonian Institution, 1991), 63–74.

20 Handler, *Nationalism and the Politics of Culture in Quebec* (Madison: Univ. of Wisconsin Press, 1988), 39–41.

21 Jonathan Culler, "Anderson and the Novel," in *Grounds of Comparison: Around the Work of Benedict Anderson,* ed. Pheng Cheah and Jonathan Culler (New York: Routledge, 2003), 50.

22 See Wai Chee Dimock, *Through Other Continents: American Literature across Deep Time* (Princeton, NJ: Princeton Univ. Press, 2006); Jahan Ramazani, *A Transnational Poetics* (Chicago: Univ. of Chicago Press, 2009); and Brent Hayes Edwards, *The Practice of Diaspora: Literature, Translation, and the Rise of Black Internationalism* (Cambridge, MA: Harvard Univ. Press, 2003).

23 On the integration of regional articles within national magazines as a disruption of the homogeneous, empty time/space of national consciousness, see James Buzard, *Disorienting Fiction: The Autoethnographic Work of Nineteenth-Century British Novels* (Princeton, NJ: Princeton Univ. Press, 2005), 172–73.

24 Wai Chee Dimock, "Literature for the Planet," *PMLA* 116, no. 1 (2001): 174.

Part III **Comparison in the Disciplines**

CHAPTER THIRTEEN

Rethinking Comparativism

Gayatri Chakravorty Spivak

WHAT IS IT THAT ONE "compare"-s in comparative literature? Goethe's *Weltliteratur* is usually invoked when talking about the beginnings of a comparative literature. The other story is Leo Spitzer and Erich Auerbach in Turkey. There is also the story of the rise of the discipline of comparative literature to intellectual prominence in the United States in the period following the Second World War, largely as a result of the migration to the United States of a group of noted European comparativists seeking asylum from totalitarianism. This group had a great influence in fostering the theoretical transformation of literary studies and in bringing about fundamental changes in national literature studies. But to think of comparative literature as comparative had something to do with the notion of *la littérature comparée* in France—where comparison implicitly referred to the standards of the French eighteenth century. This attitude is reflected in the fundamental premises of Pascale Casanova's work today.[1] René Etiemble's *Comparaison n'est pas raison* attempted, in 1963, to combat that impulse in a manner that is still favorably comparable to much that goes on in the Euro-U.S. today.[2] But in terms of the questions we are asking, it is still too much within the internationalist side of cold war logic—going no further than the front-line languages of India and East Asia, with a somewhat paternalistic approach. Whatever the outcome of that debate, and whatever the status of the classical traditions of Asia, comparative literature within the United States remained confined to European literary regionalism. After the Cold War, the division between a Eurocentric comparative literature and geopolitically oriented "area studies" seemed to have become less tenable than before. But comparison in favor of the European tradition has remained in place.

Seen another way, comparison assumes a level playing field and the field is never level, if only in terms of the interest implicit in the perspective. It is, in other words, never a question of compare and contrast, but rather a matter of judging and choosing. When the playing fields are not even continuous, the problem becomes immense. Most metropolitan countries acknowledge the problem simply because of the volume of migration in recent decades. There, a certain degree of levelness (entry into the circuit of citizenship, desired when denied) is already established. I, on the other hand, write as I have always written, as soon as I began to publish in the seventies, with a sense of the world rather than the demands of immigrants, in themselves also and of course a powerful disciplinary initiative. I would, however, like to distinguish my position, simply because it does not arise from "the forcing of cultures into greater proximity." Charles Bernheimer wanted comparative literature to include "subaltern perspectives."[3] As I have regularly noted, I am just as regularly asked to help curate shows that will, give or take the culture, "bring the barrio to the museum." This is to misunderstand even the way in which denial/desire/demand work in the establishment of the class-cross-hatched space of migrant generations in metropolitan space. The degree of systemic change necessary for such transference to take place is precisely the issue.

It is absurd to expect a humanities discipline to bring about these changes. The result of the steady influx of people from elsewhere into the metropolis and the attendant demands are reflected in comparative literature in the last few decades in the following way: each literary tradition, tied to a dominant language group, confronts the narratives produced by this Eurocentric history, more or less. Thus we have a confrontation of comparative literature and East Asian languages; comparative literature and South Asian languages; comparative literature and Central/North Asian languages are just stirring. comparative literature and Arabic/Persian/Turkish shades off into Orientalism as such ("a manner of regularized (or Orientalized) writing, vision, and study, dominated by imperatives, perspectives, and ideological biases *ostensibly* suited to the Orient") and, through Bulgarian, into Ottoman studies and Balkan studies.[4] The modern period in each of these language groups relates in a different way to that main tradition, which remains "Europe" as affected by Eastern European theory filtered through France.

We are not speaking of cultural studies here. Very generally speaking, I think it is safe to say that cultural/ethnic studies, generally considered to be the political corrective to Eurocentric comparative literature, legitimizes the implicit comparison by reversal. This is of course too sweeping a generalization and would have to be modified in any extended discussion.

Mainstream comparative literature divided over French theory. It has been touched also by the transformation of German theory through the fall of mere socialism. One consequence of these circumstances was the flight of intellectuals and the rise of comparativism. The much more resplendent social-philosophical consequence of that was Hannah Arendt and the Frankfurt School.

This is the set we consider when we think of rethinking comparativism. When we, the first generation of U.S. PhDs in comparative literature, were graduate students in the sixties, we took a certain pride in asserting that the word "comparative" in our discipline was a misnomer, that the point about comparative literature was that it did not exactly "compare." For the last few years, some of us have been trying to rethink comparativism by pondering how exactly comparative literature does not compare and how that not-comparing can shelter something affirmative.

I think the solution we found in the sixties is not quite right for these times. Those of us who belonged to the U.S. mainstream of comparative literature found affinity among national literatures in place of what the verb "compare" offers: not only the etymological "pairing with" but also some hint of ranking. We found a strong ally in the theory of archetypes, psychoanalytic with C. G. Jung and R. D. Laing, literary-historical with Thomas O. Brown and Northrop Frye. Notions of the collective unconscious allowed us to bypass the problem of comparison and ranking. That line of work has found a strong champion today in my colleague and friend David Damrosch.[5] I admire his work so greatly and so enjoy working with him that I should make clear that in this context, now, my thinking is different from his.

What was especially useful for us in those early days was the study of *topoi*, sets of imageme-narrateme-philosophemes that seemed to travel without either historical or psychic ballast across the history of literatures and cultures that make us code geography, write our world. The Greek god Apollo and the Hindu goddess of learning, Saraswati, share the swan as a familiar. Ernst Robert Curtius was our guide here.[6] In the nineties, I wrote on "Echo" in this manner, finding in the nonagential voicing of the Greek mythological figure a way to think about woman's fate, particularly in postcoloniality.[7] As graduate students, we had been helped by the topological phenomenologies of Gaston Bachelard, Maurice Merleau-Ponty, and Georges Poulet.[8] I still recognize those trajectories in Emmanuel Levinas (though not as a placeholder for comparison) and, of course, in the work of Jacques Derrida, whose brilliant topological slides do indeed teach us to think about relations without relations between diverse European texts.

Encompassing structures and archetypo-topical texture, not strictly polarized, helped us think affinity in place of mere comparison. We know today that those great networks of affiliations work by way of exclusions. Apollo and Saraswati quietly ignore those who have no right to learning. It is perhaps not too contentious to point out also that, in today's divided world, to discover varieties of sameness is to give in too easily to the false promises of a level playing field.

I am standing with my mother in Charles de Gaulle Airport in Paris. For a week we have fed our ears on academic French. Suddenly I hear

an exchange in the harsh accents of upstate New York. I turn to my
mother and say, in Bengali, roughly this: "Hard to listen to this stuff."
And my mother: "Dear, a mother tongue." My mother, caught up as she
was in the heyday of resistance against the Raj, still extended imaginative charity to English.

I have told this story before and will say it again. Today I hold on to the
fact that there is a language we learn first, mixed with the prephenomenal,
which stamps the metapsychological circuits of "lingual memory."[9] The
child invents a language, beginning by bestowing signification upon a
part-object (Melanie Klein). The parents "learn" this language. Because
they speak a named language, the child's language gets inserted into
the named language with a history before the child's birth, which will
continue after its death. As the child begins to navigate this language,
he/she is beginning to access the entire interior network of the language,
all its possibility of articulations, for which the best metaphor that can be
found is—especially in the age of computers—"memory." By comparison,
"cultural memory" is a crude concept of narrative rememorization that
attempts to privatize the historical record.

Comparative literature imagines that each language may be activated in
this special way and makes an effort to produce a simulacrum through the
reflexivity of language as habit. Here we translate not the content but the
very moves of languaging. We can provisionally call this peculiar form of
translation before translation the "comparison" in comparative literature.

This is not to make an opposition between the natural spontaneity of
the emergence of "my languaged place" and the artificial effortfulness of
learning foreign languages. Rather it is to emphasize the metapsychological and telecommunicative nature of the subject's being encountered by
the languaging of place.[10] If we entertain the spontaneous/artificial opposition, we will possibly value our own place over all and thus defeat the
ethical comparativist impulse. Embracing another place as my creolized
space may be a legitimation by reversal. We know now that the hybrid is
not an issue here. If, on the other hand, we recall the helplessness before
history (our own and of the languaged place) in our acquisition of our
first dwelling in language, we just may sense the challenge of producing
a simulacrum, always recalling that this language too, depending on the
subject's history, can inscribe lingual memory—in other words, a sense
of equivalence among languages, rather than a comparison of historico-
civilizational content. Étienne Balibar has suggested that equivalence
blurs differences, whereas equality requires them. Precisely because civil
war may be the allegoric name for an extreme form of untranslatability,
it is that "blurring" that comparative literature needs.

I am not making claims of cultural equivalence or full translatability
—the unexamined, dull anthropologism of cultural relativism. If you

do not assume language to be isomorphic with cultural formation, you cannot move to such convictions. The apparent discrepancies in cultural power, measured on the grid of place to space, are meaningful in terms of the language's relative elaboration and importance. They become a matter of constative historical inquiry and performative resistance in the present, always waiting for what will have happened.[11] This is why we must remain mindful that the assumption of equivalence is upstream from all the historical language battles of postcoloniality and neocolonial power that are still being fought and must continue to be fought. I repeat that this is not nativism; any language or language(s) can perform this function. If in situations of migration, the first language is lost, it is still a loss—not because of any kind of nationalist nostalgia—but because that originary metapsychological constitution of ethical semiosis is deactivated. I think there is some kind of historical process that shifts those mechanisms into the newly chosen "naturalized" "first" language—which operates most successfully in the second generation.

Our rethinking of comparativism starts, then, with the admission that as language, languages are equivalent, and that deep language learning must implode into a simulacrum of lingual memory. We must wait for this implosion, which we sense after the fact, or, perhaps, others sense in us, and we thus enter into a relationship with the language that is rather different from the position of a comparer, a charter of influence, who supposedly occupies a place above the linguistic traditions to be compared. In other words, I have had enough of being told that imperialism gave us the novel.

Comparative literature, then, begins to insist on the irreducibility of idiom, even as it insists on translation as commonly understood. When we rethink comparativism, we think of translation as an active rather than a prosthetic practice. I have often said that translation is the most intimate act of reading. Thus translation comes to inhabit the new politics of comparativism as reading itself, in the broadest possible sense.

In the name of comparativism as equivalence, we are prepared to undertake a serious and continuous undoing of nationalist or national language-based reading. We have not moved too far from the regionalist impulse of the initial vision of European comparative literature. We have simply announced a worldly future. It is our hope that, in this process, the performativity of comparativism will face the task of undoing historical injustice toward languages associated with peoples who were not successfully competitive within capitalism—with the added proviso that these languages attempt to establish an interconnection among themselves through our disciplinary and institutional help. This will take us a step outside the necessarily nation-centered and culture-centered frontiers of the United Nations.

The idea of a subaltern collectivity of languages and literatures outside of national-language restrictions is a difficult one. In order to take the diversified subaltern or less-taught languages out of enclavist or collectivist pedagogy and politics, to save comparative literature from unacknowledged and exclusivist comparison, structural and epistemological changes are required. I will quote some prose here that reflects a long, ongoing effort at institutional change. The implicit terms of resistance—this is against globalization—entrenches comparison beyond the discipline, indeed situates the discipline upon contemporary cognitive topography in a negligible niche. I leave this caution here, proceed to the institutional passages, and close with two readings that can only look forward to the necessary yet impossible institutional guarantee of access to equivalence. Here is the institutional passage, used in a couple of grant proposals:

> Even as we want to include Europe and necessarily the United States in any version of a globalized world, we also recognize that our efforts cannot succeed without a thorough-going program of the less-taught languages of that world . . . This latter group could only be taught for a few semesters, with insufficient quality control, by insufficiently trained instructors, and with no possibility of students moving on to a major or a doctoral track. This lack of parity between established and less-taught languages goes against the very spirit of an enlightened globalization of the curriculum. This is matched by the lack of parity between teachers of language and teachers of literature in all U.S. universities . . . The labor is, of course, immense. It will involve faculty development seminars, postdoctoral fellows, extensive and new recruitment procedures, and the involvement of national professional associations. There must be a consortium, since the less commonly taught languages are many, the need is acute, no single university could hope to cover all bases and, given distant learning resources, the first stages of language learning could easily be shared.[12]

It is in view of the resistance to institutional change that I often speak of the humanities supplementing globalization by providing a world. The worldliness of our new comparative literature could be a key element in this continuing and persistent effort. For, given the differential between the "first" language and others, the equivalence that would formalize our new comparative literature will never be fully established. We must always work in the element of simulacra, putting in place a bond between the world's neglected languages. The literature of Okinawa will then take its place with the wisdom songs of Ghana and the historical fables of the Popol Vuh.

I want to make a methodological point before I conclude. We start from an assumption of linguistic equivalence, which rests on language's capacity to inscribe. Always with one language as accidental standard, we escape national restrictions and create the simulacrum of equivalence

through deep language learning across the spectrum of the subaltern
languages of the world. The diversity and singularity of idiom remain a
constant reminder of the singularity of languages. The absence of material equivalence provokes historical study. Within this procedural frame,
how do we read now as comparativists?

Over the last few years, teaching the introductory course in comparative literature and society to graduate and undergraduate alike, I have
drawn a conclusion: in disciplinary method we remain astute. Attention
to idiom, demonstration through textual analysis, acquisition of expertise
in plotting the play of logic in rhetoric and vice versa. Insofar as our
object of investigation is concerned, however, we acknowledge as comparativist any attempt that the text makes to go outside of its space-time
enclosure, the history and geography by which the text is determined.
Thus disciplinary convention expands toward what would otherwise
escape it, and the field expands greatly, in many ways.

I now test my notion of textual comparativism with a look at Medoruma
Shun's short story translated "Hope."[13]

"Hope" has been called "the first post-colonial work of Okinawan literature."[14] Like all *post*coloniality, it looks forward to an undecidable future.
Its very title, "Hope," out of joint with the narrative content, gives us a
sense of this. How can it help us in the task of rethinking comparative
literature in view of such an undecidable future?

By my disciplinary responsibility I would have to undertake the difficult
journey of entering Japanese idiom and its relationship to the idiom of
Okinawa. I would have to plot the relationships as I would, with appropriate differences, in Ireland or Hong Kong. I am ill prepared for this.
What I can attempt now is the lesson of reading—locating an impulse
toward comparativism in this new sense in the story itself.

The story is about a sacrifice and a suicide. Upon a scene of political
conflict, such a double gesture often reflects a comparativism of last resort: a plea to the political other to recognize equivalence, to respond,
and, finally, to end oppression. I have been long attracted to this species
of comparativism, attempting to go outside of the space-time enclosure,
when that enclosure means oppression, colonial or gendered or both,
undoing history and geography by inscribing the body with death.

I place the story of "Hope" in that genre with "Can the Subaltern
Speak?" with suicide bombing in Palestine, with Viken Berberian's *The
Bicyclist*, with Santosh Sivan's "The Terrorist," a film dealing with anti-
colonial resistance and gender in Sri Lanka.

One of the characteristics of this species of comparativism in extremis
is the double bind between ethics and politics. This too is a theme that
attracts me greatly.

(Comparativism in extremis is not a disciplinary choice of method. It can be located in our objects of investigation if it is represented. Comparativism in extremis is a political gesture when response [perhaps based on that lesson of equivalence in a context broader than our discipline] is denied. I have given above a few examples of such representation, including "Hope." *Bamako*, a film I will discuss at the end of this essay, is a teaching text, not a representation of comparativisim in extremis. The film hopes that its lesson—the difference between resistance and the people—will be learned. Other examples of the representation of comparison in extremis—merely indexed—is a line in Rabindranath Tagore that I have discussed elsewhere. Speaking of the people to whom human rights were denied millennially in India, he writes: "'*mrityumajhe hobe tobe chitabhashshe shobar shoman*'—you [addressing his "unfortunate country"] will then be equal to all of them in the ashes of death, thus predicting the death of a nation." The only thing that will make me equal to you, because you deny response, is a shared death. This is also the theme of Ernesto Cardenal's poem "Prayer for Marilyn Monroe" (1965), made into a film by the Instituto Cubano de Arte e Industria Cinematográfico [ICAIC], where the items of comparison are Marilyn Monroe, with her desperate life on the one hand and the millions of dead children in Latin America on the other, standing in as victims of the U.S. system, a place of no response. Cardenal is a priest, a liberation theologian—for him in death the two sides were equal in God's eyes, comparison as equivalence in extremis. Perhaps it may be said that our lesson of learning equivalence, practicing equivalence, indexing a small epistemic change or shift, may come to facilitate a world where comparison in extremis will no longer be required.)

A double bind, then. Between ethics (I must not kill) and politics (I can have a "response" from my nonrespondent[s] only in a shared death).

To some the double bind seems a dangerous idea. And yet, to deny its pervasiveness leads to failed revolutions. Paradoxically, to acknowledge its pervasiveness does not lead to unqualified success. This is its danger. I have put together a somewhat positive description, which I will share with you today. This by no means exhausts the power and danger of the double bind. The one thing that we can propose is that the fiction and reality of comparativism in extremis often makes visible the double bind between ethics and politics.

Here, then, is my somewhat bland and optimistic account of the double bind, which some of you have already heard:

The double bind can be a general description of all doing, all thinking as doing, all self-conscious living. Contradictory instructions come to us at all times. We learn to listen to them and remain in the game.

When and as we make a decision, we know that we have broken the double bind into a single bind, as it were, and that change will have to be undertaken soon, or, things will change. If we don't know this, our self-congratulation is typically followed by denial or bewilderment.[15]

To put it formulaically, as does the fiction, the political situation requires the violence of sacrifice: "*What Okinawa needs now is not demonstrations by thousands of people or rallies by tens of thousands, but the death of one American child.*"[16] Yet the ethical unacceptability of violence requires the destruction of the political subject or actor. The pull of the ethical is so strong that the political act cannot be described as willed: "Just as fluids in the bodies of a small creature that is frightened suddenly turn into poison, [so] this deed of mine is natural and what had to happen [*hitsuzen*] for this island, I thought." And the pull of the political is so strong that the act representing the ethical is also a sacrifice and a destruction. The impossibility of containing the ethical subject in its worldly envelope is indicated in the text by the management of time:

At the moment that I *reclosed* the trunk, the sun *broke* through the cloud veil that *covered* the sky. I *am* sweating, and I *break out* in goose bumps. I *crossed* the forest on foot . . . and *returned* home . . . The air conditioning *doesn't* work . . . I *lower* the windows but I *pour* with sweat. I *went* up to Naha city . . . I *pour* a bottle of gasoline on my jacket and pants . . . A group of junior high schoolchildren *came* running.[17]

The sweating and sacrificing body breaks through into the present tense as the narrative progresses in the past tense. The body reenters the narrated past as an object before language in the last sentence.

On the side of the dominant, there is the longing for a release from the double bind between nationalism (the political) and responsibility (the ethical). Thus Oe Kenzaburo repeats a phrase in 1969: "Is it possible to change to a Japanese who is not a Japanese?"[18]

The dominant can also refuse this longing and simply deny the double bind. Here is a comment from the staff of the Japan Policy Research Institute: "Americans are likely to be shocked by Medoruma's subject matter and tone." It is a well-meaning comment, for the staff then proceed to list U.S. marine criminal activity against Ryukyuans, especially females. Yet to separate nationalism and responsibility is precisely a denial of the double bind that can reduce resistance to the politically correct.

One of the incidental but altogether astute moments in "Hope" is when the narrator recognizes that every inhabitant of the island is not infected by what I am calling comparativism in extremis—the necessity to call for a response from the colonizer. The first gesture from an islander is the innocent one of joy at seeing a known person on TV! And the last gesture is the equally innocent frivolity of the children kicking the agent reduced to object. Between these two gestures of innocence lies the story, apparently useless. Commemorated in fiction, it becomes useful if we learn how to read as we mark time toward a comparativism of equivalence.

Without this, we cannot pick up the message if an artist points at the distance between protest and the people. Abderrahmane Sissako's film *Bamako* (2006), for example, is regularly read like a documentary of protest by most policy-oriented folks.

The film stages a trial, held in an African compound, by African judges and lawyers, with the participation of two white lawyers on either side, of the World Bank for its crimes in Africa. The trial is contained within fragments of local action and a slim subplot about the death of a charismatic singer's husband.

The new comparativism can read this film as a filmic discourse on epistemic discontinuity in the welding of place. We notice how much of the staging is in terms of a relief map of languages, colonial and local. The trial is framed by a community where only the ones who have graduated into the discursive practice of the good whites are able to "speak the truth." The director took good care to point this out by making the subplot with a very attractive singer, by closing the film with her, focusing on her husband's death, and making clear that it has little to do with the main argument. The high point of eloquence in the film, and deliberately, if you notice the framing, is the good white guy (apparently the director just gave them the parts and said, "now speak")—makes us think precisely about the problem. There are also the moments of grassroots choice when access to the "trial" of the World Bank is turned off by the young men of the village, the real agents of collaboration with the destruction of the country. The bridge agents are a woman who is accused of not fitting the evidentiary structure and, on another level altogether, the traditional healer who utters (apparently in a language not necessarily understood by the "native speakers"). The complexity of the framing is evident also in the presence of the film within the film, an exaggerated eye-catching African Western.

The entire film can be a figuration of why resistance against the transnational agencies misfires. But it is inconvenient and counterintuitive to understand this.

A few images now merely to suggest how the film might figure the separation, indeed the discontinuity, between resistance and the people.[19] It is not without significance, surely, that the World Social Forum had had a meeting in Bamako just before the film's release. I will repeat my earlier points in order to relate them to the images.

We are looking at a symbolic trial of the World Bank, staged in an African compound in Bamako. Sissako places two persons outside the frame: the charismatic female singer who would travel easily into the musical circle of global protest and the traditional healer. The name of the film appears on the screen after those two placings outside of the work.

Figure 1. Singer interrupts film to have bustier laced

Figure 2. Healer leaves trial

Here is the woman singing simply to show her forceful presence in the film. Indeed this bit is used to promote the film—although it is not part of the trial, where the participating Africans have achieved sufficient continuity with the European Enlightenment to be able to criticize its travesty:

Figure 3. Singer's dynamism

Now to images where, in the film, Sissako distinguishes carefully between the difference in the response.

First, the good white guy testifying against the World Bank. He speaks
in metaphors and the audience is shown responding collectively.

Figure 4. Good white guy

Next, the black woman testifying. She is eloquent, speaks more statistics. The response is more singular, less public.

Figure 5. Black woman testifying

Then the traditional healer, who finally intervenes, out of place. This is an undecidable moment, the moment of a double bind. For, if Mamadou Diouf is right, the Africans here do not necessarily understand what he sings. It may indeed be a procedural complaint on his own behalf. The response is mysterious, a pattern of close-ups of individual faces. We contemplate the distinction between singularity—repeatable difference—and the individual subject.

Figure 6. Healer singing

Contrast the much more innocent and open response to the African-Western film within a film. This too is discontinuous from the trial. The African Western, with Danny Glover starring, is a generic opposite from *Bamako*, the film in which it is embedded. That is already a discontinuity. Further, the kind of innocent joy in such bloody mayhem that is portrayed in the mother and daughter is remote indeed from a critique of Western benevolence, from a social position in society within that enclosure, as represented by the "educated" Africans participating in the trial.

Figure 7. Innocent response to African Western

Without overparsing, it remains noticeable that there are no white women in the film, no global feminist solidarity as is evident at the World Social Forum. Gender is the alibi for the entire spectrum of good and bad globalizing intervention. Has a criticism been represented here on the workings of the screen? For, as I have mentioned, Sissako takes good care to present a taxonomy of black women, roughly in terms of distance from the European Enlightenment, if you like. Islam is elsewhere. The "Muslim" woman (presumably the other African women are Muslim too) swears in the home of Allah and disappears from the film. And, at the film's end, an Islamic ritual—the funeral of the man who begins the film—with no more than minimal subtextual development. And yet the implicit possibility of a male solidarity is clearly shown across the color-class line across the line where the black African has achieved rational epistemic continuity with the white European. When Maître Rapaport—incidentally an actual person—interrupts on the side of the prosecution, his white colleague says to him, not waiting for procedure: "Shut up," with a gesture behind his rump.

Figure 8. "Shut up"

When he addresses the court, the men active in the village world of unofficial microgovernance (please contrast this to world governance) disconnect the loudspeaker, also without waiting for procedure.

Figure 9. Africans disconnect loudspeaker

Sessako and I have slipped in the question of gender, bigger than capital, since both sides are caught in reproductive heteronormativity and use gender as an instrument, an alibi—"the surrogate proletariat"; a question that the organized left intellectual, out of touch, expects only women and queers to ask, which is why a feisty philosopher like Agnes Heller, deeply sympathetic to women, says she is "against 'feminism.'"

In conclusion, I quote two paragraphs from my forthcoming book to designate the position from where my stereotype of myself rethinks comparativism.

In 1992, asked to give the first T. B. Davie Memorial lecture at the University of Cape Town after the lifting of apartheid, I suggested that we learn to use the European Enlightenment from below. I used the expression "ab-use," because the Latin prefix "ab" says much more than "below." Indicating both "motion away" and "agency, point of origin," "supporting," as well as "the duties of slaves," it nicely captures the double bind of the postcolonial and the metropolitan migrant regarding the Enlightenment. As such, we want the public sphere gains and private sphere constraints of the Enlightenment; yet we must also find something relating to "our own history" to counteract the fact that the Enlightenment came, to colonizer and colonized alike, through colonialism, to support a destructive "free trade." But "ab-use" can be a misleading neographism and come to mean simply "abuse." That should be so far from our intentions that I thought to sacrifice precision and range and simply say "from below." This too rankles, for it assumes that "we," whoever we are, are below the level of the Enlightenment. A double bind.

The phrase "double bind" comes from Gregory Bateson's *Steps to an Ecology of the Mind*, first published in 1972.[20] To begin with, the double bind was a way for him to understand childhood schizophrenia qualitatively. Bateson was, however, aware that "[b]oth those whose life is *enriched* by trans-contextual gifts and those who are *impoverished* by trans-contextual confusion are alike in one respect: for them there is always or often a 'double take.'" In other words, inhabiting thus the two ends of the spectrum, the double bind could be generalized. In "A Theory of Play and Fantasy," Bateson spelled out the training of the imagination in terms of a mise en abyme, an indefinite series of mutual reflections. This "training," the bulwark of an aesthetic education, habitually fails with religion and nationalism: "Up in the dim region where art, magic, and religion meet and overlap, human beings have evolved the 'metaphor that is meant,' the flag which men will die to save, and the sacrament that is felt to be more than 'an outward and visible sign, given unto us'";[21] it is interesting that Freud mentions the same two items—"Throne and Altar"—in "Fetishism," as the monitors of fetishistic illogic.[22]

A comparativism rethought might restore the metaphor to this white mythology. In Goethe's spirit, we can interminably prepare ourselves to work in the hope of a promise of equivalence to subaltern spaces and times, a hope cradled in despair except when reading flourishes.

Working a century ago, Franz Boas clearly indicated the need for deciding if the cultures of "primitive" places had independent origins or were influenced by transmission. To compare seemed to be the only solution. The time for that initial anthropologistic comparativism is long over for us. Undoubtedly we should not rule out the contrast between historically independent origin and a comparativist study of dissemination from our discipline. In order to be able to do this as part of the discipline, however, we have to take a step back and perform the epistemological difference, looking forward to an epistemic difference "to come": the lesson of thinking the equivalence of language, potentially, in the metapsychological theater.

NOTES

1   Pascale Casanova, *The World Republic of Letters*, trans. M. B. DeBevoise (Cambridge, MA: Harvard Univ. Press, 2004).
2   René Etiemble, *The Crisis in Comparative Literature*, trans. Herbert Weisinger and Georges Joyaux (East Lansing: Univ. of Michigan Press, 1966). Originally published as *Comparaison n'est pas raison* (Paris: Gallimard, 1963).
3   Charles Bernheimer, ed., *Comparative Literature in the Age of Multiculturalism* (Baltimore: Johns Hopkins Univ. Press, 1995), 44.
4   Edward W. Said, *Orientalism* (New York: Vintage Books, 1995, c1978), 202.
5   David Damrosch, *What Is World Literature?* (Princeton, NJ: Princeton Univ. Press, 2003).
6   Ernst Robert Curtius, *European Literature and the Latin Middle Ages*, trans. Willard R. Trask (New York: Harper and Row, 1963, c1953).
7   Spivak, "Echo," *New Literary History* 24, no. 1 (1993): 17–43.
8   For a checklist, one might think of Gaston Bachelard, *The Psychoanalysis of Fire*, trans. Alan C. M. Ross (Boston: Beacon Press, 1964); *Water and Dreams: An Essay on the Imagination of Matter*, trans. Edith R. Farrell (Dallas, TX: Dallas Institute Publications, 1983); *Poetics of Space*, trans. Maria Jolas (Boston: Beacon Press, 1958); Maurice Merleau-Ponty, *Phenomenology of Perception*, trans. Colin Smith (London: Routledge & Kegan Paul, 1962); *The Visible and the Invisible*, trans. Alphonso Lingis (Evanston, IL: Northwestern Univ. Press, 1968); Georges Poulet, *Studies in Human Time*, trans. Elliott Coleman (Baltimore: Johns Hopkins Univ. Press, 1956), *The Interior Distance*, trans. Elliott Coleman (Baltimore: Johns Hopkins Univ. Press, 1959); *The Metamorphoses of the Circle*, trans. Carley Dawson (Baltimore: Johns Hopkins Univ. Press, 1966).
9   Alton Becker, *Beyond Translation: Essays toward A Modern Philology* (Ann Arbor: Univ. of Michigan Press, 1995), 12.
10   "[I]t would be bad natural history to expect the mental processes and communicative habits of mammals to conform to the logician's ideal." Gregory Bateson, *Steps to an Ecology of Mind* (Chicago: Univ. of Chicago Press, 2000), 180.
11   For the structure of constative-performative-attendance, see Jacques Derrida, *Rogues: Two Essays on Reason*, trans. Michael Naas and Pascale-Anne Brault (Stanford, CA: Stanford Univ. Press, 2005).
12   In the hope of increasing institutional attention, I have included these words also in "Translation in the Undergraduate Curriculum," forthcoming in the *ADFL Bulletin*, and will probably continue to recite them indefinitely.
13   For an expert account of the story, see Ikuo Shinjo, "Homoerotikusu no seijiteki haichi to 'reisen': Okinawaeno / kara no manazashi no koso," Frontiers of Gender Studies (F-GENS) Annual Report Number 5 (2005), Ochanomizu University. Presented as "The Political Formation of the Homoerotics and the Cold War: Battle of the Gazes at and from Okinawa," at the American Comparative Literature Association Annual Conference at Princeton University, March 23–26, 2006.
14   Quoted in *JPRI Critique* 6, no. 12 (1999): www.jpri.org/public/crit6.12.html.
15   The pervasive presence of the acknowledgment of the double bind in Derrida's work can allow us to think of deconstruction as a philosophy of (praxis as) the double bind. In

Gilles Deleuze and Félix Guattari's *Anti-Oedipus*, trans. Robert Hurley et al. (Minneapolis: Univ. of Minnesota Press, 1992), the attempt to think schizophrenia in a more general sense leads to the French title (subtitle in the English): "Capitalism and Schizophrenia."

16   Shun Medoruma, "An Okinawan Short Story," trans. Steve Rabson, *JPRI Critique* 6, no. 12 (1999): www.jpri.org/public/crit6.12.html. All quotes are from this translation. Translation often modified.

17   I have emphasized the tensed words to show the play of present and past tenses.

18   Oe Kenzaburo, *Okinawa Notes* (Tokyo: Iwanami Shoten, 1970), 16. I am grateful to Shinjou Ikuo for making this text available to me. I thank Norie Oka for producing a digest at short notice.

19   All images from the film *Bamako* (2006) by Abderrahmane Sissako © Archipel 33 are reproduced by permission.

20   Bateson, *Steps to an Ecology of Mind*, 272.

21   Bateson, *Steps to an Ecology of Mind*, 183.

22   Sigmund Freud, "Fetishism," in *Standard Edition of the Complete Psychological Works of Sigmund Freud*, trans. James Strachey (New York: Norton, 1961, c1930), 21:152.

CHAPTER FOURTEEN

The Uses of Incommensurability in Anthropology

Richard Handler

I N COMMON USAGE, THE VERB "to compare" has two distinct meanings: on the one hand, to liken, to describe as similar; on the other
hand, to note similarities *and* differences. When speakers have the
first meaning in mind, they can assert that because two phenomena
are different, they "cannot be compared" (apples and oranges, as we
say). Such usage shades into a related one that has explicit evaluative
overtones: people say that two phenomena cannot be compared when
they mean to rank one decisively above the other. (For example, "you
can't compare [the quality of] Major League Baseball to [that of] Little
League Baseball.") When people have the second meaning in mind, the
question often becomes: given two similar phenomena, what significance
should we attach to their differences? For anthropologists, this question
(in the study of human culture, what difference does difference make?)
has always been crucial. In this essay, I will explore what I consider to be
the productive use not just of difference, but of *incommensurable* difference.

To study the relationship between similarity and difference entails
consideration of the relationship between apparently discrete phenomena ("things") and the linguistic and cultural categories we use to group
them. Do people group things together because they are similar, or do
they conceive them to be similar because they group them together?
(We can ask the same questions about differences.) More generally, the
question "what is a thing?" has bedeviled modern anthropology and
modern social sciences. In his seminal treatise on method, Émile Durkheim wrote, "The first and most fundamental rule is: Consider social
facts as things." According to Durkheim, social facts should be *considered*
as things since they are external to individual actors. But Durkheim also
knew that social facts are *not* things since, unlike other natural phenomena (such as those of biology), they include, and are in part constituted
by, what he famously called collective representations.[1] As we shall see,
the comparative study of collective representations entails translation,
which in turn raises the issue of incommensurability—the situation of
phenomena that are, ostensibly, impossible to measure or compare in
terms of the same metric.

Comparison in anthropology differs depending on which of two grand epistemological traditions, the positivist and the interpretive (corresponding to Durkheim's emphasis on social facts as things, and on collective representations, respectively), it engages.[2] In traditions we can loosely call positivist, it is thought possible to identify phenomena (from material items like tools to social institutions like "the family" to cultural assemblages like "ancestor worship") that exist in different cultural settings; in other words, classes of things that are in some important sense "the same" no matter the particularities of their historical and cultural context. Typically, in this tradition, analysis of similarity and difference leads to generalizations about causality linked, often, to ideas about human nature or about the nature of culture and society.

In traditions we can loosely call interpretive, objects of study are not considered to be given in advance; rather, they are thought to be constructed in semiotically mediated exchanges between "observer and observed," outsider and insider, anthropologist and "native." In this tradition, the anthropologist starts with concepts or models (like the family or ancestor worship) that orient research, but that cannot be assumed as apt analogues for realities that exist elsewhere. Anthropological research and writing leads to revised understandings of one's initial terms (and the familiar worlds to which they belong) as well as to an emergent understanding of other peoples' worlds. This kind of anthropology aims not for causal analysis, but for comparative reinterpretation of both insiders' and outsiders' cultural worlds.

Anthropologists on both sides of this epistemological divide agree that their discipline is inherently comparative; as Margaret Mead once wrote, "every single statement that an anthropologist makes is a comparative statement."[3] Thus, anthropologists do not speak of "comparative anthropology" as a distinct field or subfield in the way scientists speak of comparative anatomy or humanists of comparative literature. Rather, anthropologists see their discipline as inherently comparative because its fundamental intellectual dilemma is the relationship between human diversity (understood in terms of historical, social, and/or cultural particularity) and human unity (we are all members of the same species). Given human unity (as a species), what difference, anthropologists ask, does cultural difference make? To answer such a question requires comparison of the kind anthropologists routinely call "cross-cultural."

Anthropological cross-cultural comparison is one variety of the type of comparison practiced in the social sciences. In these disciplines, comparison is understood to work across collective kinds, that is, social groups conceptualized, roughly, as species are conceptualized in the natural sciences. Acceptance of an analogy between what we might call naturally and nationally occurring kinds has meant that in the social sciences, comparison has tended to work across such "units" as nation-states, societies, cultures, tribes, or races.

The geographic and temporal range of comparison in anthropology differs from the range of comparison in the other social sciences due to the peculiar history of anthropology as a residual category in the modern curriculum. As George Stocking explains, "as the various human sciences gradually differentiated themselves . . . during the nineteenth century, the peoples who became the primary subject matter of anthropology dropped through the boundary spaces between the gradually separating disciplines." History, for example, had no place for "people whose only records were oral traditions," just as political economy (and ultimately politics and economics) lost interest in "peoples outside the cash nexus." Anthropology became the discipline responsible for all those places, peoples, and epochs that were considered beneath contempt or "without history" by the other disciplines.[4] In contrast to the other social sciences, anthropologists have always struggled to understand what other, non-Western (or nonmodern, or simply "uncivilized") people had to teach them about humanity. To put this slightly differently, for anthropologists, the question of what the human species is "as such" has always been open to dispute in ways it hasn't been for most other disciplines. Responsible within the university for the study of varieties of humanity that held no interest for other scholars, anthropologists included in their cross-cultural comparative studies historic and ethnographic materials that had been deemed irrelevant by the other disciplines. In theory, anthropologists could not presuppose any particular variety of humankind as their disciplinary starting point.

In practice, of course, late-nineteenth-century anthropologists held most of the presuppositions concerning the absolute superiority of Western civilization that all educated Euro-Americans of the time held. As such, the discipline propagated an essentially negative understanding of who its objects of study were. "They" were considered to lack what "we" (modern Euro-Americans) had developed; comparison in professional anthropology was born as invidious comparison. But from the beginning, anthropologists struggled against that legacy. Much of the history of anthropology in the twentieth century has been a struggle to critique and to transcend the racist, socioevolutionary anthropology of the Victorian age. Making sense of incommensurable cultural differences has been, and remains, central to that intellectual project.

The Unit Problem

A recent encyclopedia entry on "cross-cultural research" names Edward B. Tylor's 1888 paper, "On a Method of Investigating the Development of

Institutions; Applied to Laws of Marriage and Descent," as "the first cross-cultural study" in anthropology.[5] The preeminent British anthropologist of the Victorian age, Tylor was concerned to establish anthropology as a natural science, which, for him, meant showing that human civilization had everywhere developed according to the same laws and principles, and following the same stages of growth. In the 1888 paper, he pioneered a statistical method of working out both historical and functional relationships, in order to "demonstrate that the problems of anthropology are amenable to scientific treatment."[6]

Explaining at the outset that he had spent "many years" collecting "evidence found among between three and four hundred peoples, ranging from insignificant savage hordes to great cultured nations," Tylor constructed tables of "adhesions" (or correlations) to show the systematic clustering of customs or culture traits. From such clusters, Tylor inferred both historical sequences (which he presumed to be unidirectional and determined by natural factors) and functional relationships. For example, Tylor argued that the clustering of such traits as in-law avoidance, "residence after marriage" (whether the husband went to live with the wife's people, or vice versa), and teknonymy (a term Tylor coined to designate the naming of parents after their children, as in such appellations as "father of Mary") strongly suggested that matriarchy had preceded patriarchy in the history of civilization. And from the clustering of certain systems of kinship terminology, marriage rules, and the ceremony of "marriage by capture," Tylor argued that the function of exogamy (prescribed out-marriage) is to create political alliances. He conveyed this conclusion in what was to become a famous anthropological aphorism: "Again and again in the world's history, savage tribes must have had plainly before their minds the simple practical alternative between marrying-out and being killed out."[7]

Tylor delivered his paper at a meeting of the Anthropological Institute of Great Britain and Ireland, and one of the oral responses, from the chair of the session, Francis Galton, became famous in the literature as "Galton's problem." Galton thought Tylor's results needed to be screened to eliminate comparisons between apparently independent customs ("found," as Tylor said, among apparently separate "peoples") that were in fact "duplicate copies of the same original."[8] The larger question, debated for decades, concerned the relative place in human history of "independent invention," on the one hand, and "diffusion," on the other. For Tylor, cross-cultural comparison showed the human mind working everywhere in similar fashion and human civilization progressing through orderly stages of development. In this comparative perspective, the appearance worldwide of similar customs testified to a uniform causality underpinning human history. Human rationality responded everywhere in the same way to similar natural conditions. Diffusionists, on the other hand, explained worldwide cultural similarities in terms of borrowing or migration. From their perspective, Tylor's adhesions did not provide conclusive evidence of causal sequences or functional relationships, since any particular assemblage of customs may have moved across space and time as a totality rather than developed independently (in the same causal sequence) again and again.

Anthropologists no longer debate diffusion versus independent invention, but it is remarkable that theorists of globalization in the past two decades have not been more cognizant of the social-scientific history of the issue, nor of the epistemological dilemmas it poses. Galton's problem never went away, and I discuss it here as the unit problem. For present purposes, I am most interested in the epistemological difficulties that ensnare us when we consider two types of phenomena—1) groups of people ("societies" or "cultures") and 2) social institutions or cultural traits—as analogous units readily available (as if they existed in nature) for comparison. It will be convenient to survey the problem as it appears in the work of another anthropological ancestor, Ruth Benedict.

In Tylor's collection of evidence, the basic comparative unit might be termed a person-people report. By this I mean a case study or body of documented evidence constructed by one European "participant-observer" (usually, a missionary, colonial officer, trader, travel writer, or ethnographer, working with unacknowledged "native" intermediaries) focused on a local group of people deemed by the observer to be a distinct society or culture. Such participant-observers have been more or less aware of the formidable difficulties of establishing ethnic, tribal, or cultural units, and in the last half century, anthropologists have increasingly abandoned mid-century notions of social units as neatly bounded, culturally homogeneous entities. But in the early twentieth century, anthropologists of the emergent Boasian school in the United States and functionalist school in Great Britain were more interested in studying the discrete structure and identity of cultures than in questioning the assumptions about boundaries and homogeneity that underpinned their models.

Benedict and her colleagues (first- and second-generation students of Franz Boas, like Mead, Alfred Louis Kroeber, Robert Lowie, and Edward Sapir) were well aware that large societies like the United States contained internal diversities of race, region, religion, and so on. Sapir wrote a series of elegant essays on individual variations within apparently unitary cultures, while Mead wrote about the challenge various kinds of social diversity presented to the anthropologist who would treat large national cultures as units. Interested in civilizational history, Kroeber looked beyond neat homogeneous units in a different way, tracking the development of basic culture patterns over societies, centuries, and continents.⁹ But these anthropologists (with the exception of Sapir) also tended to treat "primitive" or small-scale societies as well-bounded units that could, for anthropologists, take the place of laboratory experiments under controlled conditions. As Benedict wrote: "With their comparative isolation, many primitive regions have had centuries in which to elaborate the cultural themes they have made their own. They provide ready to our hand the necessary information concerning the possible great variations in human adjustments, and a critical examination of them is essential for any understanding of cultural processes. It is the only laboratory of social forms that we have or shall have."¹⁰

Benedict posed an initial question that was not unlike the kinds of comparative questions socioevolutionary positivists like Tylor asked: she wanted to use comparison to separate universal culture traits from those that were local and historically particular. Unlike positivists, however, Benedict assumed that most cultural forms had developed through unique historical processes, not lawlike natural ones. She also assumed there would be very few traits that were so widely shared as to be universal. Moreover, she thought if such traits existed, they were as likely to have arisen from diffusion among early human groups as from universal cause-effect sequences; universality was, in effect, historical, not natural.¹¹

Thus for Benedict, comparison revealed differences, not similarities. Yet with respect to the two aspects of the unit problem sketched above, Benedict proceeded in epistemologically contrary ways. Her work exaggerated the presentation of societies as discrete units, but in her analysis of the internal structuring of such units, she used a configurationalist or gestalt approach in which individual culture traits could be understood only in terms of their relationship to the whole culture. For example, in her famous study of Japan (to be considered below), Benedict showed that the Japanese had repeatedly borrowed Chinese ethical concepts, but "integrated them," over time, into a cultural pattern that was distinctively Japanese. Although one could trace the historical connections between Japanese and Chinese culture traits, historically connected traits were no longer the same thing (or unit) in the two cultures; they became, in effect, incommensurable.¹²

Thus Benedict deconstructed culture traits (which did not, in her analysis, have a transcultural unity or identity) while she simultaneously constructed cultures as bounded groups of people sharing a way of life. George Stocking has described this tension as basic to Boasian anthropology. For Boas, the history of the diffusion of culture traits gave the lie to the evolutionists' theories of uniform cultural development. Human history consisted not of repetitive cause-effect sequences, in which human rationality, responding to the natural world, invented the same things (culture traits) over and over again. Rather, people traveled and borrowed cultural materials, which they then transformed as they integrated them into their local lives. But this model required Boas and his students to conceptualize the social unit—tribe or culture—across which traits diffused and into which they were absorbed. Those social units came to be treated as irreducible cultures, each with its own spirit or *Geist*.[13]

In *Patterns of Culture*, Benedict presented a theory of cultural "integration" that explained the unity of individual cultures, and she illustrated it with three case studies—the Pueblos of New Mexico (where she herself had carried out fieldwork), the Dobuans of Melenesia (studied by Reo Fortune, Mead's second husband), and the Kwakiutl of the northwest coast of North America (studied by Boas). In this book-length treatment of the culture concept for a wide audience, Benedict set up her societal examples to highlight their discreteness. Despite the facts that much of her research before the publication of the book was in the diffusionist vein, and that she had particularly studied continuities and connections as well as discontinuities among American Indian groups,[14] she presented two Indian cultures that were geographically far apart, and between them she introduced an example from the other side of the globe (Dobu was the second of the three case studies). Mead reports that Benedict chose the examples she did because she knew the fieldworkers. In my terms, she felt she could trust those particular person-people reports.[15] But whatever her conscious motives were, the result was that *Patterns of Culture* made it easy for readers to think culture exists in the world primarily in the form of well-bounded packages.

Translating the Incommensurable

Benedict's rather positivist notion of the unity of individual, "integrated" cultures led her, paradoxically, to a second and very different epistemological approach to the work of cross-cultural comparison and translation. Cultures differed, Benedict argued, not only because they contained a bewildering diversity of customs ("self-torture here, headhunting there, prenuptial chastity in one tribe and adolescent licence [*sic*] in another"). More importantly, they differed because they were integrated differently. Over time, Benedict thought, cultures tend to become ever more organized in terms of a central set of ontological values or aesthetic attitudes: the "pattern" or *Geist*. Thus, although customs diffused worldwide and many cultures absorbed the same customs, apparently similar customs took on unique significance once they were integrated into particular cultural patterns. And those historically derived, local culture patterns became, relative to one another, "incommensurable":

"They [individual cultures] are traveling along different roads in pursuit of different ends, and these ends and these means in one society cannot be judged in terms of those of another society, because essentially they are incommensurable."[16]

Benedict's notion of incommensurability has been vulnerable to a common misreading: the idea that cultures cannot be judged and cannot be compared. Each culture, in this view (as expressed by hundreds of my undergraduate students over the years) has the "right" to be the individual that it is. And outsiders to a culture have no right to criticize that culture's values in terms of their own. That conclusion often leads Benedict's readers to a moral relativism that frightens them (usually voiced in classroom discussion with reference to Hitler). Their fear in turn prompts them to retreat to a positivist position from which they can espouse universal values—usually those of consumer individualism, which structured their reading of Benedict in the first place. At the end of these discursive (or sentimental) maneuvers, cultural relativism ends up looking like American individualism in which each person or culture is an irreducible whole with the right to make choices; yet the range of choices my students can imagine reflects a set of values assumed to be universal.

Benedict no doubt facilitated this sort of reading by exaggerating the boundedness of individual cultures and then emphasizing their incommensurability. On the other hand, by illustrating her theory with maximally divergent examples, she was able to show her readers that cultural comparison required sophisticated translation practices that went far beyond the naïve idea that each term, trait, or unit in one culture could be matched to a corresponding term, trait, or unit in another. If *Patterns of Culture* reproduced the unit problem in the discussion of society, culture, and group, it transcended it in its treatment of particular customs or social facts.

The finest example of Benedict's comparative hermeneutics (one of the finest examples of cross-cultural comparison in the entire anthropological literature) is her book-length study of Japan, *The Chrysanthemum and the Sword*. Published in 1946, it grew out of Benedict's work for the Office of War Information during World War II. Benedict described her task (her "Assignment: Japan," as the title of the first chapter put it) as the use of anthropological techniques to elucidate the culture of "the most alien enemy the United States had ever fought in an all-out struggle." This was an enemy whose very definition of war differed from that of the European and North American combatants: "Conventions of war which Western nations had come to accept as facts of human nature obviously did not exist for the Japanese." Thus "we"—Americans and their allies— "had to understand their behavior in order to cope with it."[17]

But to understand and then to cope with Japanese behavior and ideas, it was not sufficient to focus solely on them. American ways of misunderstanding Japan, based on American conceptions of the "facts of human nature," had also to be brought into the picture. This was a fundamental if often implicit attitude among Boasian cultural anthropologists. When Mead asserted that an anthropologist's every statement "is a comparative statement," she was referring not merely to the anthropologist's knowledge of many cultures, gained, presumably, through a standard graduate training program. She was referring as well to the anthropologist's attitude toward his or her own culture, which anthropological training rendered visible as culture, not as human nature. Mead made this clear in the introduction to her own wartime study of a national culture, that of the United States:

Speaking from a platform to a woman's club, if one is merely an experienced speaker at women's clubs, one notices whether the audience is smartly dressed, and how smartly. If one is an American sociologist, one may add observations about the probable class level of the audience and the proportion of professional women—lawyers in sober suits seeking to tone down their sex, social workers in pleasant but serviceable headgear, civil servants with clothes that look like uniforms or clothes that aggressively do *not* look like uniforms. But I never completely lose a still further point of reference—the awareness that my audience wears clothes . . . I do not cease to observe whether this is a patriotic group of women, valiantly and self-consciously wearing last year's hats, or an afternoon group of women who are homemakers, or an evening group of women who, whether they are homemakers or not, don't do homemaking in the daytime—but this other consciousness: "These people are completely clothed," stays with me to widen my perspective.[18]

For their wartime work, then, Mead and Benedict had to undress Americans to reveal their implicit cultural assumptions. Without such a revelation, Americans would project those assumptions onto their enemies and even their allies, and the resulting misinterpretations would in turn lead to strategic and tactical errors in the conduct of the war.

Thus two-way translation is at the center of *Chrysanthemum*, much more explicitly than it had been in *Patterns of Culture*. In the earlier book, Benedict sometimes used the comparative vantage point generated out of analysis of an alien culture to make her Western readers aware of their own foibles. At times Benedict's critique of America became quite sharp, but in general her focus was outward, as she directed her readers to take seriously the reality of other cultural worlds. In *Chrysanthemum*, however, an active focus on Japan had to be constructed in tandem with an active focus on American culture. As Benedict put it, "the question was how the Japanese would behave, not how we would behave if we were in their place." To answer it, Benedict had to bring to her readers' conscious awareness "the premises on which we act as Americans" (5).

The heart of *Chrysanthemum* consists of four chapters on Japanese notions of hierarchy and indebtedness. For egalitarian-minded Americans, hierarchy is one of the most difficult social facts to comprehend, since the American national origin myth is a story in which the "tyranny" of hierarchy must be transcended through revolution before a new, egalitarian social order (at once more natural and more rational than feudal hierarchy) can be established. Benedict's explication of Japanese hierarchy proceeds simultaneously with an explication of American egalitarianism. She begins not with a Japanese aphorism but with an American one: "In the English language we talk about being 'heirs of the ages.'" "Oriental nations," she continues, "turn the coin to the other side: they are debtors to the ages" (98).

There follows an introductory discussion of "ancestor worship," a topic central to any understanding of the influence of the emperor on Japanese war policies. Benedict's discussion points in several directions at once, toward Japanese cultural conceptions and Americans' culturally patterned misinterpretations of them, and vice versa—all of which must be carefully disentangled and explained:

> Much of what Westerners name ancestor worship is not truly worship and not wholly directed toward ancestors: it is a ritual avowal of man's great indebtedness to all that has gone before. Moreover, he is indebted not only to the past; every day-by-day contact with other people increases his indebtedness in the present. From this debt his daily decisions and actions must spring. It is the fundamental starting point. Because Westerners pay such extremely slight attention to their debt to the world and what it has given them in care, education, well-being or even in the mere fact of their ever having been born at all, the Japanese feel that our motivations are inadequate. Virtuous men do not say, as they do in America, that they owe nothing to any man. They do not discount the past. Righteousness in Japan depends upon recognition of one's place in the great network of mutual indebtedness that embraces both one's forebears and one's contemporaries. (98–9)

In the American (and British) use of the term "ancestor worship" to translate Japanese realities, both words are wrong. First, to express indebtedness in "daily decisions and actions" is not worship. Indeed, the English word interjects Christian notions of the appropriate human posture to "God" that have little to do with the fulfillment of social obligations that is foremost in the Japanese attitude. When Americans project this religious posture onto Japanese conceptions of the emperor, they confirm Western stereotypes of Oriental despotism as central to Japanese politics. But, as Benedict notes later in her discussion, the emperor is not a god in the Western sense: "Kami, the word rendered as 'god,' means literally 'head,' i.e., pinnacle of the hierarchy. The Japanese do not fix a great gulf between human and divine, as Occidentals do, and any Japanese becomes kami after death" (127). This passage suggests the second sense in which the phrase "ancestor worship" is wrong. Japanese attitudes toward the dead, toward "forebears," are continuous with their attitudes toward the living. Toward the living and the dead, it is not worship that is appropriate, but the recognition and fulfillment of obligation.

But of course, Japanese also misinterpret Americans. They cannot recognize self-reliance as the American version of virtue. Benedict suggests that Americans are apt to rebel against government and its laws, whereas for Japanese, "obeying the law is repayment" of their debt to the kami (130). The result: "Japanese judge . . . that we are a lawless people. We judge that they are a submissive people with no ideas of democracy" (138). Much of *Chrysanthemum* explicates the kinds of wartime errors of judgment that follow from this mutual misreading of the enemies.

Although Benedict tells us that hierarchy "is the fundamental starting point" of Japanese culture, I would add that it is fundamental from an American point of view, and not just a generic "American point of view" but the particular variant of it that Benedict was motivated to articulate. In Benedict's version of cross-cultural comparison, starting points are generated by the analyst who brings together two incommensurable cultural patterns to force each to reveal, as it were, some (but only some) of the secrets of the other. Since no term from one culture can serve as a direct gloss of any term from the other, there are no shortcuts in the process. Benedict had to find an entry point into the Japanese pattern and then work outward from one "native" concept to the next. And at every step of the way, she had to reflect back on American native ideas or American mistranslations of Japanese ideas. We might almost say that comparative understanding grows from the cumulative force of mutual mistranslations, emended, painstakingly.

The Comparative Study of Modern Individualism

In 1946, *The Chrysanthemum and the Sword* was still atypical for anthropology, focused as Benedict was on a modern nation-state, however "alien" Japan may have been to Americans. Since that time, the discipline has moved inexorably away from its "savage slot" toward the study of interconnected, contemporary peoples in a globalizing world.[19] As anthropologists have engaged increasingly with what we imagine are contemporary issues, we find it ever more necessary to focus critically on modernity and its ideologies and institutions: nationalism, racism, economic development, transnational corporations, international and nongovernmental agencies, et cetera. As we do this work, we find our cross-cultural comparative perspective to be as useful for illuminating the particularities of apparently familiar phenomena as the anthropologists of Benedict's time found it for understanding exotic "primitive" peoples.

But the anthropology of modernity entails a new dilemma (or, perhaps, it renews a long-standing one). The social sciences are themselves part and product of modern ideology. Social scientific assumptions—about nation, race, group, individual persons, and social motivations—cannot easily be disentangled from the political and economic ideologies that are hegemonic in Western democracies and many other nation-states and international bodies. This means that when we as anthropologists turn our attention to contemporary phenomena, we often find ourselves trying to analyze a set of ideas with a conceptual toolkit that has been built out of the same ideas. In that situation, much social scientific analysis becomes a kind of second-order rationalization of native concepts that the analyst presupposes and cannot "see." That is one reason why anthropology's cross-cultural, comparative habits of mind become so useful in the study of modernity: they provide a critical vantage point for the analysis of ideologies that might otherwise be presupposed and then replicated.

To illustrate the point, I turn to my long-standing research on nationalism and the politics of culture in North America. Once the domain of historians and political theorists, the study of nationalism began to attract broader attention in the social sciences after World War II, as decolonization led to the emergence of the so-called new nations.[20] In retrospect, we can see political scientist Benedict Anderson's *Imagined Communities* (1983) as the work that cemented the new paradigm in the social scientific study of nationalism, much as Ruth Benedict's *Patterns of Culture* did for Boasian cultural anthropology. For anthropologists studying nationalism, the work of Louis Dumont was as important as that of Anderson, although Dumont did not achieve the same interdisciplinary prominence. Both Dumont and Anderson constructed their analyses of nationalism by way of comparison with "traditional" hierarchical societies: India (Dumont) and Java and Southeast Asia (Anderson). And both saw modern individualism as the ideology which underpinned political and cultural nationalisms.[21]

Dumont's formulation neatly captures the relationship between nationalism and individualism: in nationalist ideology, the nation is conceived both as a "collective individual" and a "collection of individuals."[22] In this world view, "the individual" is understood to be the building block of nations (a basic premise of all Western political theories that begin with the notion of a social contract). The nation is thus a collection of individuals. At the same time, nations, as the most encompassing social units, are imagined as collective individuals: nations vis-à-vis one another are individuals, and, as collections of individuals who are imagined to share a national essence or personality, these nations are collective individuals (personified by such figures as Uncle Sam).[23] Crucially, in such a system, solidarity is imagined as "horizontal," as Anderson put it;[24] the social glue that holds society together is the similarity (or shared essence) of the equal individuals who make up the society. In principle, no individual is better than any other, and hierarchy based on social privilege, or on a theory of different kinds of persons bearing relatively more or less social value, is disallowed. Both Dumont and Anderson explicated this principled denial of hierarchy in modern nationalism by way of comparison to societies that are structured hierarchically, societies that valued hierarchical relationships between persons defined as having greater or lesser autonomy, completeness, or purity.

A key question for analysts of nationalism (and of modernity more generally) thus becomes: what is the cultural definition of an individual in these systems? For anthropologists, an enormously productive approach to this question is the cross-cultural, comparative study of personhood. Dumont distinguishes between the "empirical agent" or person, present in all societies, and persons understood as rational, equal individuals, which is an ideological construct of the modern West.[25] In the modern conception, individuals are unitary and discrete—that is, the boundaries between individual persons, and between persons and society, are onto-logically clear. Closely connected to this idea is the idea that individuals are homogeneous within their boundaries; that is, they have a distinctive identity (often imagined as an inner essence) that distinguishes them from all other individuals. (In nationalism, the individuals that make up the collectivity share an essence or identity, which in turn character-izes the collective individual.) Individuals, by nature, are self-interested; self-interest expresses itself through the accumulation of private prop-erty. Modern individualism has been called "possessive individualism," referring to this tight linkage between identity and possessions. This is especially salient in nationalist ideology, in which culture is imagined as property, and the nation is said to possess the cultural property that gives it its unique identity.[26]

These features of modern individualism can be brought into view when one compares this system of thought to others. For example, the idea that individuals are well bounded makes little sense in many places where persons are imagined to participate in the personhood of the people around them. To give one striking example, in her comparative analysis of Wintu (Northern California) and English grammar, Dorothy Lee remarks, "the Wintu conceive of the self not as strictly delimited or defined, but as a concentration, at most, which gradually fades and gives place to the other." Thus, for example, Wintu do not use the conjunction "and" when referring to related individuals; when English speakers would say "he and his sister," Wintu say "the two who sibling-together." More generally, Wintu do not conceive of society as a collection of individuals: "For the Wintu, the individual is a delineated part of society; it is society that is basic, not a plurality of individuals." So thorough is their sense of living together that it extends to phenomena English speakers would consider private property. In Wintu, the speaker does not assert aggressive action against things we consider property (in the final analysis, in our philosophy, things "wrested" from nature). "The term for what is to us possession or ownership is formed by means of [a] suffix, from the three kinds of *to be*: in a standing, sitting or lying position. *I have a basket* means really *I live with* or *I sit with a basket*."[27]

Lee wrote a series of elegant essays comparing modern American individualism to Native American societies that she found to be at once more collective and more individualistic than we are.[28] Far more common in work that deconstructs modern individualism by way of comparison are studies like those of Benedict, Dumont, and Anderson, which use hierarchical societies as their comparative reference. At the fount of this tradition is Alexis de Tocqueville's *Democracy in America* (1835–40). For Tocqueville, the European aristocratic order was a lived reality, in comparison to which his experiences of American democracy in the 1830s must have been particularly significant.[29] While the first volume of *Democracy in America* is a treatise on political history and institutions, the second volume strikes me as anthropological in its attention to what Clifford Geertz called "common sense as a cultural system,"[30] as revealed in seventy-three chapters (some of which are no more than a page) devoted to the details of daily life.

For present purposes, I want to note just two strands in Tocqueville's comparative analysis of American individualism. First, he saw (more clearly than most analysts who came later) the cultural relationship between individualism and anonymity. Anonymity was not a dysfunctional or pathological side effect of modern individualism; as Tocqueville saw it, it was integral to the cultural formation. The central feature of individualistic ideology is that all individuals are equal, and all are alike; a differentiation of the cosmos into different kinds of persons, unequally valued, is in principle taboo. Yet their very equality and similarity make individuals insignificant and weak, anonymous faces in the crowd (from which observation Tocqueville went on to his famous analysis of the importance of voluntary organizations, or interest groups, in American society). Second, so great is their faith in the principle of equality that Americans tend not to recognize the real inequalities of condition that separated rich and poor (not to mention slave and free) in a society of

unprecedented social and economic mobility. "It is in vain," wrote Tocqueville, "that wealth and poverty, authority and obedience, accidentally
interpose great distances between two men; public opinion . . . draws them
to a common level and creates a species of imaginary equality between
them, in spite of the real inequality of their conditions."[31]

I want now to illustrate how an anthropologist's comparatively informed awareness of these features of modern individualism can lead
to productive research questions. Between 1989 and 1991, Eric Gable,
Anna Lawson, and I carried out field work at Colonial Williamsburg,
the famous outdoor history museum of revolutionary-era America. We
were interested in the ways in which a large nonprofit corporation (the
Colonial Williamsburg Foundation) constructed national history for a
mass public; in particular, we wanted to study the impact the "new social
history" of the previous two decades may have had on the telling of the
American story at a site renowned as a patriotic shrine, yet a site where
slavery was an important, if often unacknowledged, part of that story.[32]
As we carried out our work, we became intrigued by the dilemmas that
historical and present-day social hierarchies presented to the managers
of a site dedicated to the celebration of egalitarian individualism. On the
one hand, there was the ongoing struggle over the inclusion of African
American history. On the other hand, there was a constant tension between workers and management, often negotiated on the backs of the
visitors, who were considered (ambivalently) at once as an unruly mass
to be managed and as special "guests" to be treated like VIPs.[33]

An important part of our fieldwork was a consideration of foundation
documents, and I spent many hours in the corporate archives reading
through the *Colonial Williamsburg News*, an in-house newspaper that has
been published since 1948. There I found a recurring story about what
we might call milestone rituals, enacted on the person of the one-, two-,
three-, et cetera millionth viewer of the museum's orientation film, *The
Story of a Patriot*. Shot in Technicolor and directed by George Seaton of
Paramount Pictures, the film debuted on April 1, 1957, in the museum's
orientation center, where it has been shown ever since to arriving visitors,
for whom it depicts colonial life on the eve of the American Revolution.[34] News stories about the x-millionth viewer were no more (or less!)
intriguing than the scores of other items I reviewed. But I had the sense
that the concept of an x-millionth person had interesting ideological
overtones, and so I chose to pursue the matter.

On November 14, 1958, the millionth viewer saw the film. The *Colonial
Williamsburg News* recorded the ceremony in these terms: "The excitement of the millionth viewer of *The Story of a Patriot* caused a rustle of
anticipation among CWers at the Information Center on Nov. 14. At
10:43 a.m. on that morning, attractive Mrs. John Trapnell, wife of a

Philadelphia physician, walked through the doorway into the theatre to become that millionth person . . . Mrs. Trapnell was quite overwhelmed at being a milestone in the history of the film. 'Imagine being the millionth anything,' she laughed when informed that she was the lucky lady" (vol. 16, no. 2, p. 1). According to the *News*, the entire audience was told that "the millionth viewer was somewhere among them," and all were treated to a VIP "backstage" tour of the theater. Mrs. Trapnell herself was given more extended VIP treatment, including gifts (presented by the foundation president) and a complimentary meal.

Knowing nothing more about such rituals, it is still possible to interpret them by reference to the egalitarian dilemmas I mentioned above. Institutions such as Colonial Williamsburg cater to a mass public of anonymous individuals who, it is thought, must be made to feel they are receiving "personalized" treatment. At the same time, Colonial Williamsburg receives VIP visitors (government officials, movie celebrities, wealthy donors) who receive special treatment and whose presence is thought by insiders to enhance the prestige of the museum. Yet the anonymous crowds must not be made to feel slighted in comparison to VIPs, so that, for example, special tours which bypass long waiting lines are often hidden from the mass public who might resent such privileges were they to catch on to them.

Such tensions of egalitarian ideology are never far from the surface at Colonial Williamsburg. The ritual of the millionth viewer enacts and resolves such tensions (on a small stage, it must be admitted, since these are rather insignificant events in the daily life of the museum). The ritual displays the egalitarian value of impartiality and the refusal of social privilege. Our base-ten number system bestows, at random and with no possibility for favoritism, celebrity status on a face in the crowd. The randomness of this creation of a celebrity is emphasized in the structure of the ritual, which singles out first an audience and then an individual from among the chosen audience. The audience is granted VIP status en masse in the backstage tour but is quickly returned to its status of anonymous mass, at which point one individual is selected as a celebrity. She is feted more elaborately than was the audience, but in the end, she, too, is sent on her way. Thus the ritual creates and celebrates the millionth anything as at once a distinctive and an anonymous individual.[35] It enacts Tocqueville's "imaginary equality."

But of course there are backstages at institutions that are more backstage than the back of the theater the audience was allowed to tour during the ritual. As luck would have it, I was able to interview a retired executive who had been in charge of the ritual during the 1950s and 1960s. He explained that his office was informed, a few hours in advance, when the n-millionth person would be in the audience for a particular showing of the film. He and his staff would then attend that showing and *choose* who in the audience was to be considered the n-millionth person. His account made it clear that there were two criteria guiding the choice. First, the person could not be a "local" visitor, because (in his words) "we wanted to get some out-of-state publicity." Second, the person had to be "attractive," which seems to mean the person had to be female, either a woman like Mrs. Trapnell or a child (for another of his choices, he explained, "I picked this cute little freckle-faced gal . . . just because she looked like she'd take a good picture").[36]

To control the apparently random selection of one person among many in a crowd, and to do so by making unacknowledged use of criteria for differentially evaluating various aspects of personhood, might be deemed manipulative or even "unfair" by people in an egalitarian society. From a principled egalitarian perspective, counting by itself should select the n-millionth person, and furthermore, all persons should be counted as "just persons," as we say, with no distinctions separating them that can be considered more meaningful than the abstract personhood that makes them all alike. And comparative analyses of personhood and individuality can help us to see this, for in the anthropologist's cross-cultural perspective, the modern notion of "just a person" (or abstract personhood) stands out as unusual, if not unique. Indeed, it is conceptually difficult to imagine an abstract person, devoid of particularities. Any form of individualism requires a basic definition of the qualities a person must possess to *be* a person, or, what amounts to the same thing, to *be recognized* as a person by other persons. Thus, despite the abstract notion of the individual that seems to underlie American egalitarianism, one can say that our history has been a succession of struggles over the definition of full personhood. At any particular place and moment, such as mid-century Colonial Williamsburg, to select an n-millionth person would bring into play a set of assumptions (partially contested, no doubt) about the particular features generic persons ought to possess.

Comparative Incommensurabilities

Scholars from other disciplines and other theoretical perspectives who happened across the ritual of the n-millionth viewer could no doubt recognize and critically interpret egalitarian dilemmas at places like Colonial Williamsburg. That such scholars do not carry around in their heads a canonical set of cross-cultural comparative examples, as many anthropologists do, does not mean they would not have access to other, equally useful comparative perspectives. In the cultural studies tradition of the past thirty years, for example, researchers trained in critical race theory or in the analysis of class and gender in capitalist societies or in disability studies would have all sorts of insights about the museum's treatment of apparently equal individuals. Such insights have been gained from paying attention to persons whose experience of and ideas about modern American society had been ignored, caricatured, or scorned by earlier generations of literati and scholars. One does not need to go halfway around the world, as anthropologists do, to find incommensurable difference that can be turned to comparative account. One does, however, have to be alert to the interpretive possibility that difference affords and willing to engage in the always imperfect work of translation that can render difference not only meaningful, but critically indispensable.

I have long thought that comparative studies of different kinds of incommensurability would be useful. We could start by comparing what I shall call deep grammatical difference (including cognitive differences linked, apparently, to linguistic difference) and those based on difference of social placement and consequently difference of social experience. Both kinds of incommensurability have the potential to bring to light hidden assumptions of the analyst, which is what makes the comparison of incommensurables interpretively productive. But the anthropologist's explication of deep grammatical difference entails a translation process that is largely absent from the study of incommensurable social experiences enacted in a common language and in the "same" nation or society. On the other hand, the second kind of incommensurability can provide an imaginative recognition that can be more easily "owned" and even "tried out" by an analyst who can readily understand the linguistic terms of the comparison but had never grasped their implications in familiar daily life.[37]

With respect to deep cross-cultural difference, we might ask what *different* insights we can gain from different comparative studies of the same culture. From the classic tradition of comparing egalitarian modern societies to traditional hierarchical ones, what do different traditional societies reveal about modernity? What does Dumont's India reveal that Benedict's Japan does not? What might Tocqueville's understanding of late European feudalism teach us about Japanese modernity, or Japanese feudalism, for that matter? And what could a study of Japanese principles of social obligation reveal about classical Indian ideas of "circular" hierarchy?[38] With respect to different kinds of intrasocietal, social marginalization, there is already a well-developed literature comparing the intersection of "race, class, and gender," and, more particularly, the different kinds of analytic or critical leverage to be gained from work in each of these areas.

In the end, a distinction between deep (or perhaps "far-apart") cross-

cultural difference and difference based on extreme social marginalization will break down, for, after all, at what point does social marginalization give rise to cultural difference? And when are contacts between
cultures *not* fraught with power imbalances, or at least the potential for
the institutionalization of social inequalities? We can imagine utterly
separate, distinct cultures that can deliver "pristine" comparative insights,
and in addition, it makes a certain sense to speak of two cultures that are
relatively far apart, or more different (at least in some ways) than two
other cultures are different. But in the last three decades it has become
impossible for anthropologists to maintain the fiction that we were (in
the "Golden Age" of our discipline[39]) studying "unspoiled," "precontact"
others. We have had to learn the hard way that the comparative study of
"non-Western" peoples in the modern world system must draw its insights
from both deep cultural differences and extreme social marginalization.

NOTES

1   Émile Durkheim, *The Rules of Sociological Method*, trans. Sarah Solovay and John Mueller
(1895; New York: Free Press, 1966), 14. For Durkheim on social facts, see Robert Murphy,
The Dialectics of Social Life: Alarms and Excursions in Anthropological Theory (New York: Basic
Books, 1971), 37–45.
2   On epistemological dualism in anthropology, see George Stocking, "The Ethnographic
Sensibility of the 1920s and the Dualism of the Anthropological Tradition," in *The Ethnographer's Magic and Other Essays in the History of Anthropology* (Madison: Univ. of Wisconsin
Press, 1992), 276–341.
3   "Theoretical Setting—1954," in *Childhood in Contemporary Cultures*, ed. Margaret Mead
and Martha Wolfenstein (Chicago: Univ. of Chicago Press, 1955), 9.
4   Stocking, "Delimiting Anthropology: Historical Reflections on the Boundaries of a
Boundless Discipline," in *Delimiting Anthropology: Occasional Inquiries and Reflections* (Madison: Univ. of Wisconsin Press, 2001), 311; Eric Wolf, *Europe and the People without History*
(Berkeley: Univ. of California Press, 1982).
5   Carol Ember, "Cross-Cultural Research," in *Encyclopedia of Cultural Anthropology*, ed.
David Levinson and Melvin Ember (New York: Henry Holt, 1996), I:261.
6   Edward Burnett Tylor, "On a Method of Investigating the Development of Institutions;
Applied to Laws of Marriage and Descent," *Journal of the Royal Anthropological Institute* 18
(1888): 245.
7   Tylor, "Method," 245–46, 267.
8   Galton in Tylor, "Method," 270; see Ember, "Cross-Cultural Research," 262, and George
Stocking, *After Tylor: British Social Anthropology 1888–1951* (Madison: Univ. of Wisconsin
Press), 10–11.
9   Edward Sapir, "Cultural Anthropology and Psychiatry" and "Psychiatric and Cultural
Pitfalls in the Business of Getting a Living," in *Selected Writings of Edward Sapir in Language,
Culture, and Personality* (Berkeley: Univ. of California Press, 1949), 509–21, 578–89; Mar-
garet Mead, "National Character," in *Anthropology Today*, ed. Alfred L. Kroeber (Chicago:
Univ. of Chicago Press, 1953), 642–67; Alfred L. Kroeber, *Configurations of Culture Growth*
(Berkeley: Univ. of California Press, 1944).
10   Ruth Benedict, *Patterns of Culture* (Boston: Houghton Mifflin, 1934), 17.
11   Benedict, *Patterns*, 19.

12 Benedict, *The Chrysanthemum and the Sword: Patterns of Japanese Culture* (Boston: Houghton Mifflin, 1946), 117–19, 133.

13 George Stocking, "The Basic Assumptions of Boasian Anthropology," in *The Shaping of American Anthropology 1883–1911: A Franz Boas Reader* (New York: Basic Books, 1974), 5–9.

14 Benedict, "Psychological Types in the Cultures of the Southwest," in *An Anthropologist at Work: Writings of Ruth Benedict*, ed. M. Mead (Boston: Houghton Mifflin, 1959 [1930]), 248–61 and "Configurations of Culture in North America," *American Anthropologist* 34, no. 1 (1932): 1–27.

15 Mead, *Ruth Benedict* (New York: Columbia Univ. Press, 1974), 38–41.

16 Benedict, *Patterns*, 46, 223.

17 Benedict, *Chrysanthemum*, 1 (hereafter cited in text).

18 Mead, *And Keep Your Powder Dry: An Anthropologist Looks at America* (New York: William Morrow, 1942), 6–7.

19 This movement is documented by the steady production of notable edited volumes: *The Science of Man in the World Crisis*, ed. Ralph Linton (New York: Columbia Univ. Press, 1945); *Anthropology Today: An Encyclopedic Inventory*, ed. Alfred Kroeber (Chicago: Univ. of Chicago Press, 1953); *Reinventing Anthropology*, ed. Dell Hymes (New York: Pantheon, 1972); *Recapturing Anthropology: Working in the Present*, ed. Richard Fox (Santa Fe, NM: School of American Research Press, 1991); *Exotic No More: Anthropology on the Front Lines*, ed. Jeremy MacClancy (Chicago: Univ. of Chicago Press, 2002). The phrase "the savage slot" comes from Michel-Rolph Trouillot, "Anthropology and the Savage Slot: The Poetics and Politics of Otherness," in *Recapturing Anthropology*, 17–44.

20 The work of the Committee for the Comparative Study of New Nations at the University of Chicago is paradigmatic; see, for example, *Old Societies and New States: The Quest for Modernity in Asia and Africa*, ed. Clifford Geertz (New York: Free Press, 1963).

21 Benedict Anderson, *Imagined Communities: Reflections on the Origin and Spread of Nationalism* (London: Verso, 1983); Louis Dumont, *Homo Hierarchicus: An Essay on the Caste System*, trans. Mark Sainsbury (Chicago: Univ. of Chicago Press, 1970) and "Religion, Politics, and Society in the Individualistic Universe," *Proceedings of the Royal Anthropological Institute of Great Britain and Ireland* (1970): 31–45.

22 Dumont, "Religion, Politics, and Society," 33.

23 On Uncle Sam and prior personifications of American nationhood, see John Higham, "America in Person: The Evolution of National Symbols," in Higham, *Hanging Together: Unity and Diversity in American Culture* (New Haven, CT: Yale Univ. Press, 2001), 23–55.

24 Anderson, *Imagined Communities*, 7.

25 Dumont, *Homo Hierarchicus*, 9.

26 I have explicated the ideological structure of nationalism in relationship to individualism more fully in *Nationalism and the Politics of Culture in Quebec* (Madison: Univ. of Wisconsin Press, 1988), 30–51. The term "possessive individualism" comes from Crawford Brough Macpherson, *The Political Theory of Possessive Individualism: Hobbes to Locke* (Oxford: Oxford Univ. Press, 1962); see also Dumont, "Religion, Politics, and Society."

27 "The Conception of the Self among the Wintu Indians," in Lee, *Freedom and Culture* (Englewood Cliffs, NJ: Prentice-Hall, 1959), 134, 136.

28 Lee's essays are collected in *Freedom and Culture* and in *Valuing the Self: What We Can Learn from Other Cultures* (Englewood Cliffs, NJ: Prentice-Hall, 1976).

29 See Sheldon Wolin, *Tocqueville between Two Worlds: The Making of a Political and Theoretical Life* (Princeton, NJ: Princeton Univ. Press, 2001). My brief remarks on Tocqueville are based on a more extended analysis, "Individualism Inside Out: Tocqueville's *Democracy in America*," in *Critics against Culture: Anthropological Observers of Mass Society* (Madison: Univ. of Wisconsin Press), 22–48.

30 Clifford Geertz, "Common Sense as a Cultural System," in *Local Knowledge: Further Essays in Interpretive Anthropology* (New York: Basic Books, 2000), 73–93.

31 The passage is from Tocqueville's magnificent chapter, "How Democracy Affects the Relations of Masters and Servants," in *Democracy in America*, trans. Henry Reeve (New York: Vintage Books, 1955), 2:187–95.

32 Eric Gable, Richard Handler, and Anna Lawson, "On the Uses of Relativism: Fact, Conjecture, and Black and White Histories at Colonial Williamsburg," *American Ethnologist* 19, no. 4 (1992): 124–32; Richard Handler and Eric Gable, *The New History in an Old Museum: Creating the Past at Colonial Williamsburg* (Durham, NC: Duke Univ. Press, 1997).

33 Anna Lawson, *"The Other Half": Making African-American History at Colonial Williamsburg* (PhD diss., Univ. of Virginia, 1995); Eric Gable and Richard Handler, "Persons of Stature and the Passing Parade: Egalitarian Dilemmas at Monticello and Colonial Williamsburg," *Museum Anthropology* 29, no. 1 (2006): 5–19.

34 The *Colonial Williamsburg News* recorded the one-, three-, and four-millionth viewer (12[6]:1, 3 [1958], 16[2]:1 [1961], 17[8]:3 [1963]). I learned of other milestones from an interviewee. As of the summer of 2009, the foundation Web site reports that the film continues to be shown after having been digitally restored; the thirty-millionth viewer was celebrated in a 2002 ceremony that seems identical to those discussed here.

35 This ritual is more elaborately contextualized in Gable and Handler, "Persons of Stature."

36 Anonymous consultant at Colonial Williamsburg, interviewed by the author June 21, 1990; interview transcript in the files of the author.

37 Predictably, the second kind of incommensurability provides modern readers with a standard fictional structure, that of "trading places," as the title of the 1983 Eddie Murphy / Dan Aykroyd movie has it; it would seem to be less easy to interest a broad audience in a sustained presentation of deep cultural difference, although of course Jonathan Swift and Montesquieu (and even Herman Melville) provide classic examples. Clifford Geertz interprets Ruth Benedict as a Swiftian moralist, one whose plot structure is, simply, us / not us: "Us / Not-Us: Benedict's Travels," in *Works and Lives: The Anthropologist as Author* (Stanford, CA: Stanford Univ. Press, 1988), 102–28. On incommensurability and cultural criticism see Elizabeth Povinelli, "Radical Worlds: The Anthropology of Incommensurability and Inconceivability," *Annual Review of Anthropology* 30 (2001): 319–37.

38 Indian circular hierarchy is explicated by Frédérique Apffel-Marglin in "Smallpox in Two Systems of Knowledge," in *Dominating Knowledge: Development, Culture, and Resistance*, ed. Frédérique Apffel-Marglin and Stephen A. Marglin (Oxford: Clarendon Press, 1990), 102–44. See also Arjun Appadurai, *Worship and Conflict under Colonial Rule: A South Indian Case* (Cambridge: Cambridge Univ. Press, 1981).

39 I don't know whether anyone other than Margaret Mead could use such a phrase in an apparently nonironic way, as in the title of a volume she and Ruth Bunzel edited, *The Golden Age of American Anthropology* (New York: G. Braziller, 1960). Nonetheless, Mead's introduction to the volume takes account both of white Americans' romance of the American Indian and of their genocidal campaigns against them, while asking the astute question: what difference have the cultural particularities of American Indian societies made to the development of American anthropology, considered as a national tradition built on a colonialism that differs from those associated with British, French, and German anthropology?

CHAPTER FIFTEEN

Anthropology, Migration, and Comparative Consciousness

Caroline B. Brettell

FOR SOME TIME, SCHOLARS HAVE WRITTEN about the two opposing poles that characterize anthropological thought—the particularizing and the generalizing.[1] James Peacock, a past president of the American Anthropological Association, has portrayed the particularizers exceedingly well. They are the ones who see the world through the lens of the population with whom they worked in their ethnographic field site, consistently taking exception by asserting that "my people don't do it that way." Particularizers reject comparison and place their emphasis on infinite cultural diversity and on differences. Their methods are those of description and interpretation. Generalizers, by contrast, recognize differences but also emphasize the similarities that can be found across both the breadth and depth of cultures around the world. Their goal reaches beyond description and interpretation to scientific explanation. This opposition between the particular and the general is central to a long-standing debate about the role of the comparative method in anthropological research.[2]

Of course, for some of us, there is no debate about the centrality of comparison to the discipline of anthropology since the endeavor itself—one of cross-cultural translation—is by its very nature comparative.[3] As Carol and Melvin Ember have observed, "ethnography employs words, and words are always applicable to more than one instance. It is impossible to describe a particular culture (or anything else for that matter) without using words that have meanings for others."[4] Harold Scheffler, in an essay that otherwise addresses sexism and naturalism in the study of kinship, has written that "ethnographic inquiry begins and ends as a theory-laden act of comparison. In the course of it we try to detect in the speech and actions of another people concepts and practices that are analogous to those we know from our own social experience or from other ethnographic studies."[5] In a provocative book that tackles the uncanny similarities between the societies of the Amazon and those of Melanesia, Thomas Gregor and Donald Tuzin present an excellent example of the "inherentness" of comparison and its relationship to words by observing that "when we speak of a society as having men's cults . . . we have in mind similar organizations in other societies."[6] Allen Johnson offers a slightly different perspective, although again one shared by many anthropologists, when he observes that it is "impossible to undertake anthropological fieldwork in an unfamiliar culture and not draw comparison between one's own culture and the one being studied." He goes on to argue that any recognition of difference is a comparative process. Thus, he asserts: "For all the emphasis on cultural relativism and the uniqueness of particular cultures in anthropology, ours is a pervasively comparative science."[7] Finally, Rena Lederman, in an essay on the future of culture areas in anthropological research, writes that rarely has anthropological area expertise "not been motivated by comparativist projects of one sort or another: whether positivist projects of typologizing for functional and developmental analysis (emphasizing cross-cultural similarities) or interpretive projects, reflexive or otherwise (emphasizing differences)."[8]

Despite all these assertions about the centrality of comparison to the anthropological project, each of these authors is cognizant of the "troubled history" of the comparative method in anthropology. This essay begins with a brief and broad-brushstroke review of this troubled history in order to outline the various ways, from informal to formal, that the comparative method has been engaged within one discipline.[9] I then turn to a discussion of the importance of a comparative consciousness, to borrow a term from anthropologist Laura Nader, to the study of migration, a topic I have engaged throughout my professional career. I argue that comparisons are essential if we are to avoid both national and temporal exceptionalism in our understanding of the causes and consequences of migration. I move therefore from a theoretical and methodological approach formulated within a single discipline to its application in addressing an important problem in human experience that concerns scholars across a range of disciplines.

Debating the Comparative Method in Anthropology: A Brief Dip in Troubled Waters

In anthropology, the comparative method has its roots in nineteenth-century evolutionary anthropology and particularly the work of Sir Edward Tylor. The explanatory models of Tylor and others were built on an assumption of survivals—that is, the customs and habits of so-called primitive peoples living in the present represented earlier stages of human society and cultural development through which all people had passed on the progressive march from "savagery" to "civilization."[10]

This paradigm, equally present in the work of contemporaries of Tylor such as James Frazer and A. Lane-Fox Pitt Rivers in Europe and Lewis Henry Morgan in the United States, prevailed in the field until it was challenged and disrupted by Franz Boas, founder of the Department of Anthropology at Columbia University.

Under Boas, anthropology, and especially U.S. anthropology, took a dramatic theoretical turn toward what is now labeled historical particularism. Boas was suspicious of evolutionary frameworks and, by extension, generalization, which he argued should only proceed after exhaustive historical and ethnographic research of individual cases. In what is repeatedly cited as one of his most important and "classic" essays, "The Limitations of the Comparative Method of Anthropology," Boas argued that the comparative method had been misleading in its assumptions of "connections wherever similarities of culture were found. The comparative method," he asserted, "has been remarkably barren of definite results, and I believe it will not become fruitful until we renounce the vain endeavor to construct a uniform systematic history of the evolution of culture, and until we begin to make our comparisons on the broader and sounder basis . . . [emerging from] historical researches which are devoted to laying clear the complex relations of each individual culture."[11]

Although Boas acknowledged in this essay that following extensive historical and ethnographic research it might be possible to discover "certain laws [that] exist which govern growth of human culture" and that "it is our endeavor to discover those laws," it is commonly agreed that his approach dealt a severe blow to comparison within anthropology.[12] Anthropologist Marvin Harris has suggested that "ludicrous errors were committed by the Boasians in their attempt to discredit the comparative method," citing several examples of what he labeled as "imaginative and ridiculous associations of cultural traits."[13] However, in relation to this paradigmatic shift from cultural evolution to historical particularism, two different approaches to comparison emerged, one rooted in the statistical comparison of a large number of cases and the other in careful, contextualized, and controlled comparisons of a limited number of cases.

The first approach was best represented by the work of George Peter Murdock in the 1940s and the development of the Cross Cultural Survey at Yale University's Institute of Human Relations, which eventually became the Human Relations Area Files (HRAF). Murdock compiled data from ethnographic reports for more than three hundred societies and organized them according to more than seven hundred categories. The goal was to draw on this sample to discover statistical correlations among different cultural features.[14] The research that HRAF has generated is, as Ember and Ember point out, systematic, and focused on testing hypotheses about the "incidence, distribution and causes of cultural variation."[15] A good example of this work is Jack Goody's comparison of patterns of inheritance in Africa and Eurasia. Goody linked what he called diverging devolution in Eurasia (basically, bilateral inheritance) to the prevalence of dowry rather than bridewealth, and monogamy rather than polygamy, as well as to a range of other cultural practices such as adoption, late marriage, and high rates of permanent celibacy.[16]

While some still find merit in this particular body of research by Goody, as well as that of other scholars who have drawn on the wealth of ethnographic data contained in the Human Relations Area Files, many anthropologists consider the HRAF approach sterile and fault it for taking elements of culture out of context and hence overgeneralizing. As Susan Gillespie has observed, in a broader critical analysis of categories and typologies in the study of social organization, "too much detail was being lost in reducing cross-cultural comparisons to their lowest common sociological denominator."[17] Joseph Tobin rightly points out that by 1970 the HRAF had become "the embodiment of anthropology as science, in contradistinction to the thickly descriptive, anthropology-as-interpretive-art approach exemplified by Clifford Geertz." For many, he suggests, it was "taxonomic imperialism."[18] Criticism of HRAF became criticism of the comparative method, although it represented only one way in which anthropologists engaged this method.

The second approach to comparison that prevailed between 1940 and 1960 was associated with British structural functionalism. With concerns about the equivalence of units of comparison being primary, those who pursued this approach emphasized a limited number of cases within a tightly defined region such that variation could be controlled. Max Gluckman, and others who were affiliated with what came to be known as the Rhodes-Livingstone / Manchester Research Program, were strong proponents of this method. Bruce Kapferer has observed that in Gluckman's view

comparison should not involve the consideration of examples taken at random or out of context and engaged merely to illustrate preformulated ideas . . . that were not thoroughly questioned through the ethnography itself. Rather, comparison should initially develop systematically, attending to variations in practice across a region in which there are broad similarities in historical circumstance, institutions, language, and customs between people. Only after this has been done (and a relatively secure basis for ideas established) should the method be extended farther afield, and here the comparative method should be thoroughly alive in contextual and value divergences, testing the extent to which such differences permit the confirmation (or not) of larger generalizations that are built through comparison.[19]

A good example of this controlled comparison approach is Siegfried Frederick Nadel's analysis of witchcraft in four African societies. Nadel's richly layered discussion, which can only be briefly summarized here, is built on a comparison of two pairs of ethnic groups, the neighboring Nupe and the Gwari of Nigeria and the neighboring Korongo and Mesakin of central Sudan. Each pair showed linguistic and cultural similarities but diverged in their witchcraft beliefs. Among the Nupe, women are generally accused of being witches, women who often hold a good deal of economic power that contradicted the ideology of male dominance. This results in sexual tensions that are manifested in witchcraft accusations. By contrast, among the Gwari there is very little sexual antagonism or tension in daily life, and men and women are equally accused of witchcraft. In his analysis of the Korongo / Mesakin pair, Nadel identified a different source of tension. Mesakin men pass through three age grades while aging, while Korongo men pass through six—that is, a more gradual process. Witchcraft beliefs are absent among the Korongo while the Mesakin were obsessed by fears of witchcraft. To pass from one age grade to the next, Mesakin men had to give up the privileges of the group they were leaving. Suspicions and accusations were extensive between the young men and those in the middle grade who were reluctant to move into old age and relinquish sexual activities and other privileges they had enjoyed. It was between these two groups that witchcraft accusations were strongest. Nadel drew upon the frustration-aggression hypothesis—when one's interests are frustrated, aggressive behaviors may erupt—to explain these differences in witchcraft beliefs and accusations. The emphasis in Nadel's work, and that of others in both Europe and America, for example Fred Eggan, was on identifying functionally significant relationships among traits within different societies.[20]

By the 1960s, and particularly after 1970, both generalizing and comparison began to lose their footing within anthropology as more idiographic (as opposed to nomothetic) approaches entered the field.[21] Richard Fox and André Gingrich suggest that the distancing from the comparative method was a result of a field that had matured enough to be concerned about its complicity with European imperialism and more aware of the shortcomings of assumptions about self-contained, stable, and integrated cultures in the face of a capitalist world system of great historical depth.[22] One should add to this a growing concern with the application of Euro-American models to the rest of the world.

One of the strongest voices for this last concern was that of David Schneider, who redirected the study of kinship, a key subject of research in anthropology since the nineteenth century, from functional and structural analysis toward meaning-centered symbolic analysis.[23] While Schneider was not against comparison, he was leery of the bases on which anthropologists were making them. He argued that comparative studies of kinship either had to find a more solid foundation or be abandoned.

He wrote: "The first step, prerequisite to all others in comparative work, is to establish the particular categories or units which each particular culture itself marks off; that is to say, the symbols and meanings of a particular culture. Once this is done, without being prejudiced by theories about functional prerequisites to social life or assumptions about universal activities, then comparison can begin and analytic procedures and tools can perhaps be developed."[24]

There are those who argue that Schneider's culturalist critique of kinship and his emphasis on local meanings impeded "the classic anthropological project of comparison and contrast."[25] To some extent the debate was recast at this time as one between comparativists and relativists. Anthropologists David Kaplan and Robert Manners wrote: "The relativist tells us that a culture must be examined as a totality and only in terms of itself; while the comparativist says that an institution, process, complex, or item must be removed from its larger cultural matrix so that it can be compared with institutions, processes, complexes or items in other sociocultural contexts."[26] While I would challenge their emphasis on removing something from its cultural context (many of those who continued to adhere to the value of generalizing and comparison understood full well how important context was / is), it is safe to say that Kaplan and Manners recognized the shortcomings of what they thought were the excesses of relativism which made scientific inquiry difficult and theory-building virtually impossible. Theirs was a heroic defense of the value of comparison to the development of culture theory, but by the mid-1980s postmodernism—with its challenges to concepts of ethnographic authority and its promotion of ethnographies as texts—assumed supremacy.[27] Postmodernists, together with poststructuralists, became just the latest to weigh in on critiques of the role of comparison in the anthropological enterprise. Comparison, in the words of Victor de Munck, assumed a "refugee status."[28]

While postmodern thought has many roots, within anthropology its beginnings can be found not only in the symbolic approach of David Schneider but also in the interpretivist approach of Clifford Geertz. Geertz argued that the analysis of culture is "not an experimental science in search of law but an interpretive one in search of meaning."[29] He steered anthropology away from generalizing across ethnographic cases (that is, comparison) toward the in-depth analysis of a single case. The rejection of generalization is certainly key to the postmodern approach, which Nigel Rapport and Joanna Overing describe as reactive to "things and thingness . . . to conceptions of reason and rationality, objectivity and truth, scientific method and the progress of history and knowledge."[30] As developed by scholars such as George Marcus, Michael Fischer, and James Clifford, postmodernism became concerned about

the presumptuousness of ethnographic authority, critical of anthropological imperialism, and doubtful about the goal of a science of culture.
John Borneman and Abdellah Hammoudi have recently encapsulated
the postmodern assessment of anthropological practice as follows: "Ethnographers, primarily members of Euro-American societies engaged in
the pursuit of science, were accused of fixing other people in totalizing
cultures and representing them as radically distinct from their Western
selves in time and space."[31]

Anthropological postmodernists not only echoed Geertz's call for a
focus on meaning rather than causality, but also emphasized multivocality,
relativism, and the analysis of ethnographies as texts. They asserted the
need for anthropology to abandon positivism and, as Patricia Greenfield
has bluntly stated, considered generalization "oppressive."[32] Perhaps
one of the best and most successful examples can be found in Lila
Abu-Lughod's *Writing Women's Worlds*, a book that adopts "many of the
techniques of humanistic writing" in order to give the Bedouin women
she has worked with their own voice. Abu-Lughod explicitly writes against
culture and generalization. "Anthropologists . . . have two reasons to be
especially wary of generalization. The first is that as part of a professional
discourse of objectivity and expertise, it is inevitably a language of power
. . . the second and more serious problem with generalization is that by
producing the effects of homogeneity, coherence, and timelessness, it
contributes to the creation of 'cultures' . . . The effort to produce general
ethnographic descriptions of people's beliefs or actions risks smoothing
over contradictions, conflicts of interest, doubts, and arguments, not to
mention changing motivations and historical circumstances."[33]

The debate over scientific versus humanistic approaches in anthropology, as well as between objectivity and subjectivity and generalizing and
particularizing, became pervasive (if not sometimes bitter), ultimately
resulting by the late 1990s in books that attempted to reclaim a scientific
anthropology.[34] Doyens of anthropology, such as Roy D'Andrade, argued
that objective approaches in anthropology were not necessarily dehuman-
izing and that science "works not because it produces unbiased accounts
but because its accounts are objective enough to be proved or disproved
no matter what anyone wants to be true."[35] After 2000, the criticisms
of postmodernism became even more vocal and were often strongest
among those writing about the place of comparison in anthropology.[36]
Taking a somewhat ironic swipe, Gregor and Tuzin wrote: "If cultures
are islands unto themselves or texts composed in the imaginations of
pseudo-observers, if all classification and generalization are nothing but
the exercise of Western hegemony and arrogance, if, in short, all is vanity,
then comparison would be at best impossible and at worst immoral."[37]

In an early effort to thoughtfully and perhaps less antagonistically resurrect comparison within anthropology, Laura Nader observed that postmodernism had contributed to our understanding of the "rhetoric of science and the limitations of positivist science in anthropology," as well as to our understanding of the limitations of nonscientist humanists "who also arrogantly conceive of understanding as possible from unidimensional frames."[38] But Nader also argued that debunking comparison eliminates any possibility to explore aspects of the human experience that are shared. Nader concluded by challenging the field to develop a comparative approach that could address questions of process and hegemony, an "area in between, a place which holds the possibility of a comparative consciousness that illuminates connections—between local and global, between past and present, between anthropologists and those they study, between uses of comparison and implications of its uses." She called for a comparative consciousness, broad in its "methodological scope and intellectual style."[39]

This opened the door for further measured and collective considerations—for example, a special issue of the journal *Ethnology* published in 2000 and a volume edited by André Gingrich and Richard G. Fox (*Anthropology, By Comparison*), where several authors argue for the future of comparison in anthropology, not only for purposes of cross-cultural analysis and understanding, but also as a public responsibility. In trying to unify the voices in their edited collection, Fox and Gingrich call for a "rich plurality of qualitative comparative methodologies" that are sensitive to context, and able to encompass scalar (local, regional, transnational) differences and temporal transformations.[40] It is precisely this kind of approach that has proved fruitful in the study of migration. An anthropology of migration addresses the way in which a global process manifests itself locally, whether in sending or receiving societies. A comparative consciousness can help to illuminate the links between the global and the local, as well as illustrate how these are mediated by difference at the national scale.

Comparative Approaches to the Study of International Migration

Ernest George Ravenstein (1834–1913), a contemporary of Sir Edward Tylor (1832–1917), delivered a famous paper about migration to the Royal Statistical Society of London in 1885. In this paper, Ravenstein formulated a series of laws of migration to describe patterns of both internal and cross-border population movement. Ravenstein not only compared data from one decade to the next, but also compared counties of "dispersal" with those of "absorption" as well as male migration with female migration. His findings that "females are more migratory than males" and that their movements are generally shorter distance (internal) when compared with those of men are often cited in the more recent and by now extensive literature on gender and migration, a topic left underresearched until the last three decades of the twentieth century.[41] Ravenstein's work reminds us of the fundamental contribution of the comparative method to an understanding of migration as a social process as well as to how similarly or differently it is experienced in different locations and by different populations by gender, national origin, age, and the like.

Theory-building in migration studies often begins with the particularities of an individual case—one group, one receiving society, one urban context, one historical period. But it must not end there, because the ultimate goal is to understand patterns in the causes and consequences of migration, how these might occur repeatedly or distinctively across the range of sending and receiving societies or ethnic groups, and how they might change over time. To delineate these patterns and processes, comparisons are essential. In the study of migration, comparison can proceed at several levels or scales of analysis. It can be global in scope, cross-national, intranational, or regional. It can draw upon large secondary data sets or primary and generally more qualitative data generated from field research in one or more sites (either by the same researcher or more than one researcher) that are often presented as case studies. It can be diachronic or synchronic—that is, tracing change over time in a single or a few places or differences across space at similar points in time. Here I focus on a few examples of comparative approaches in migration studies, drawing on my own work and that of others who engage the qualitative and more informal comparative methods identified by Fox and Gingrich. While a good deal of theorizing about migration focuses on the causes of migration,[42] my emphasis is on how comparative projects that are rooted in a case study method, and that are sensitive not only to local context but also to national and transnational scalar influences, can illuminate some of the consequences of migration and assist in the development of more systematic models of immigrant incorporation. Like Harlan Koff (who refers to integration, a term used more commonly by European scholars), I consider incorporation to involve a set of simultaneous processes—economic, political, social, and cultural.[43]

Thirty years ago, I moved from conducting research on Portuguese immigrants in U.S. and Canadian contexts to a study of Portuguese immigrants in France. As a result of this transition, I was confronted head on by the limitations of our theories about the settlement patterns of first-generation immigrants in cities, and was forced to search for meaningful explanations of the differences that I saw on the ground.[44] At the time, the prevailing theoretical model explaining how immigrants settled in cities derived from the Chicago School of Sociology and described first-generation immigrant enclaves that were located in city centers where cheap housing and jobs were plentiful. As the second generation grew to maturity, they moved out of these inner city "ghettoes" into the suburbs. By the third generation, their assimilation and their transformation into "white ethnics" was complete. This was a model based on the analysis of American cities and the American immigrant experience. The comparison with a European city and a European national context revealed something quite different, thereby necessitating the identification of a range of factors that should be considered in order to understand and theorize more broadly processes of immigration incorporation.

What I found in the Parisian urban landscape of the mid-1970s was a foreign-born population that was fairly evenly scattered throughout the urban fabric with a slightly higher concentration in the second and third *arrondissements*. There was certainly no Portuguese enclave like the one I had found in central Toronto. To some extent, this was associated with the housing to which Portuguese immigrants had access, which itself was in many instances related to the jobs that Portuguese women held as building caretakers (*concierges*) and private domestics. In a vertically stratified Paris, in contrast to a horizontally stratified Toronto, Portuguese families were found either in first-floor apartments or in sixth-floor maids' rooms. The other locus for the settlement of Portuguese and other early postwar immigrants to Paris was in the Parisian suburbs, generally in the public apartment housing, *habitation à loyer moderé* (HLMs), which was being constructed around the city in all directions and connected to the city by new networks of urban transportation. At the time, the policy was that the dispersal of immigrants of various nationalities in these housing projects would avoid the *ghettoes à l'americaine*, supposedly, at least from a French perspective, the source of all of America's urban problems, and particularly its problems with race.

But we can take this comparison of different settlement patterns and their relation to urban and national context further by fast forwarding to the present. Today, in many metropolitan areas in the United States, and in the *région parisienne*, we have suburbs in which first-generation immigrants have been settling soon after arrival.[45] But if in American metropolitan areas suburbs have been diversified, spawning such analytical concepts as "ethnoburbs" or "melting pot suburbs,"[46] the Parisian suburbs (which have also changed in the last thirty years) have been "burning" and the ghettoes that policy makers of the 1970s wished to avoid have in fact emerged. The metaphors of melting pot and burning suburbs describe the different ways that immigrants of the late twentieth and early twenty-first centuries have been claiming space and making place in the global cities of immigration. By comparison with the ethnically diverse suburbs of many North American cities, which are represented as nodes of new development and employment where immigrant institutions can locate themselves and where ethnic festivals, soccer leagues, and cricket matches are promoted, many of the Parisian suburbs are described as areas of marginalization and unemployment where immigrants are segregated in concrete high-rise ghettoes. These are places that Nicholas Sarkozy, the Minister of the Interior at the time of the fall 2005 riots in Parisian suburbs and later the president of France, wanted to sweep clean.[47] Riva Kastoryano has emphasized that living in the suburbs in France is no longer a move of choice and that the spatial immobility of immigrants in these suburbs reflects their social immobility. In these suburbs, as Stephane Dufoix has noted, immigrant youth have claimed the night, and their discourse of claims making was violence. "Rage," writes Kastoryano, "has settled in those spaces."[48]

To cut to the chase, the relationship between suburbs and immigrants in France (spaces of immobility) and the United States (spaces of mobility) is distinctly different and well worth more serious comparative ethnographic treatment. What kinds of activities take place in the public sphere in these suburbs? Can they be read as texts for what they tell us about immigrants in cities, comparative processes of claims making and incorporation, the process of national identity construction, and the fundamental matter of how nations relate to immigrants? If we limit our consideration of this question to one national context, as I, with colleagues Audrey Singer and Susan Hardwick, have recently done in a book that compares suburban incorporation in nine twenty-first century U.S. gateway cities, we paint only a partial portrait of important processes of immigrant settlement because we narrate only one national history of suburbanization. As a result, our theories about immigrant incorporation are also limited.[49]

There are other comparative considerations beyond the question of different urban and suburban settlement patterns that struck me years ago and that still resonate in the present. For the Portuguese in the Paris of the 1970s, the church provided one locale for claiming urban space, but not in the same way that immigrants in America have claimed space through their religious institutions, including ethnic-based Catholic parishes. Because they were Roman Catholic, the Portuguese were quickly accommodated into the French Catholic churches of Paris, sometimes with a special mass in their own language. There were no strictly Portuguese parishes like the Irish or Italian parishes that emerged in nineteenth- and early twentieth-century America, or the Polish and Mexican parishes that exist in twenty-first-century American cities. The broader national differences regarding religion—whether it is religious hegemony as opposed to religious diversity, or where a nation through its national policies situates itself on a continuum between the sacred and the secular in public life—are extremely important to deconstruct. Studying one national context does not give us the full range of experience upon which to build a theory about the role of religious institutions in the process of immigrant incorporation. Further, France's / Paris's immigration issues today are quite different from what they were several decades ago (hence, demonstrating the importance of a temporal as well as a spatial comparative consciousness). A large Muslim population raises new issues that were not there in relation to a similarly European and similarly Catholic Portuguese immigrant population. Who is asking to be included and incorporated matters!

Nancy Foner and Richard Alba have recently argued that religion in the United States has often been theorized as a bridge to inclusion, while in Europe it has become a barrier, "a marker of a fundamental social divide." Using a case-study approach that draws on a broad range of evidence from four European countries (France, Germany, Britain, the Netherlands), these authors identify three important differences to explain the contrast with the United States: the religiosity of the native populations (Western Europeans are more secular than Americans); the religious backgrounds of immigrants in the United States and Western Europe (largely Christian in the United States and largely Muslim in Western Europe); and the historical relationship between the state and various religious groups. In many European countries religion is excluded from affairs of state, but at the same time European states often own and maintain Christian churches and often support religious schools "as long as they teach the national secular curriculum."[50] Foner and Alba describe a Europe marked by "cultural racism" and a United States "plagued by deeply rooted biological racism, which stigmatizes and disadvantages recent immigrants, who are overwhelmingly Asian, Latino, and Black and thus outside the pale of whiteness."[51] The comparison these authors draw between different national contexts clearly lays the ground for more subtle theory-building regarding the ways in which immigrants are either included or excluded.

My own more limited comparative analysis of the settlement of Portuguese immigrants in one North American city and one European city revealed another important difference. At the time that I worked in France, the Portuguese had no associations that they had built for themselves—again startling to a North American trained scholar of immigration brought up on the idea of "institutional completeness" or an urban anthropologist well versed in the theoretical literature on the integrative role of voluntary associations that had emerged among

African "tribesmen" who had become "townsmen."[52] In 1970s France, foreign associations were severely controlled. Their creation required the authorization of the minister of the interior, and only a French citizen could be at their head. Further, there is an important difference between organizations that are grass roots, emerging from the immigrant community, and those that are formed by a paternalistic state to serve immigrants. The primary point here is that the comparative consciousness that I brought with me to France, one forged from training in my discipline, helped me to see things that were absent as well as those that were present, and to begin to ask questions about this absence as well as attempt to explain it. I was led into the realm of law and policy as I searched for answers.

Canadian immigration policy, rooted in a model of multiculturalism, can be contrasted with French immigration policy, which adheres to an assimilation model. As one reporter recently observed, in a reflection on the Muslim head scarves issue in France, France has been the European country most open to immigration but the most insistent on assimilation.[53] Anthropologists Carolyn Sargent and Stephanie Larchanché-Kim have noted that since 1993, when the Pasqua laws of restrictive immigration were put in place and a goal of zero immigration was established (*la France ne veut plus être un pays d'immigration* ["France no longer wants to be a country of immigration"]), anti-immigrant discourse has been strident, persistent, directed toward specific populations, and fundamental to French politics and policies.[54] Robert Levine, offering further support to Foner and Alba's formulation of cultural racism, bluntly observes that French culture has not changed "to allow any significant entry of Muslim elements."[55] What I identified as important differences in policy more than a quarter-century ago have only become more stark in the face of an immigrant population that is more different, and hence essential to explanatory models of immigrant incorporation.

My thoughts returned to the comparisons I had drawn between the Portuguese immigrants in Paris and those in Toronto a few years ago as I began to think in more theoretical terms about how the structure and nature of cities affect the immigrant experience. In my view, there are four important comparative dimensions to be considered.[56] First, how do cities differ in their temporal and spatial dimensions: that is, what is the historical depth of immigration, has the city defined itself for some time as a city of immigrants, how is the city laid out geographically, and where is the oldest housing stock located? Second, what is the social context of the city: that is, how heterogenous is the urban population, how divided is it—does one ethnic group hold the reins of power and how are different ethnic groups interrelated—and when, where, and how do identity politics emerge? Here the comparative efforts of political scientist John Mollenkopf are particularly illustrative of both these dimensions.

Mollenkopf observes that New York and Los Angeles differ in the extent to which they have been able to contain native backlash toward immigrants. He explains this difference in relation to distinct ways in which the respective political systems in the two cities "create (or lack) incentives for dominant white elites to recognize, incorporate, or co-opt claims from subordinate groups (including new immigrant groups) and for leaders of subordinate groups to accommodate one another."[57] Mollenkopf suggests that while in New York all groups, including whites, have immigrant roots, and access to the political system, in Los Angeles "nativity pits groups against each other" and access to the political system has been more limited. He writes: "All groups must fight it out in one, highly partisan system in New York, while Los Angeles County has eighty-eight separate, nonpartisan jurisdictions."[58] Local political structures as well as local histories of immigration generate different outcomes of exclusion and inclusion and, ultimately, political participation. Without the systematic comparison that Mollenkopf draws between two metro-politan areas, we would not learn about the significant impact of these subtle differences in how local politics operate on the lives of immigrants.

A third dimension of cities that is important to consider in an effort to build a model for comparative processes of immigrant incorporation is the nature of the urban labor market: that is, how do differences in local economic structures result in diverging opportunity structures for both native and foreign born populations? Fourthly, it is important to address what I call the cultural ethos of a city: that is, how does a city look at and represent itself and the other? Here, Kevin Keogen's delineation, based on a content analysis of *The Los Angeles Times* and *The New York Times*, of important differences in the symbolic construction of immigrants that affect their adaptation in these two metropolitan areas is illustrative. His analysis shows an exclusive "threat narrative" in Southern California and a more inclusive "immigrant as victim narrative" in New York. He explains these differences in relation to distinct material and symbolic contexts. "In the New York area, immigrants are understood in terms of an immigrant origin mythology, represented through salient landmarks and immigrant-ethnic celebrations that embody a specific positive narrative of immigrants and their historic place in the community. The Los Angeles metropolitan area is relatively void of popular, positive symbols of immigrants."[59] Keogan goes on to suggest that, as a result, immigrants in Southern California are more susceptible to exclusionary politics, especially during times of economic insecurity. Proposition 187 is one example. In Keogan's view, there is an "immigrants as us" identity in New

York City that can be contrasted with an "immigrant as other" emphasis
in Los Angeles, a city with a long historical tradition of nativism.[60] Keogan
concludes by suggesting that "the social status accorded foreign-born
persons at the federal level may be either reinforced or renegotiated at
the more local level through a process of symbolic association and narrative identity-politics. In turn, these more local interpretations influence
federal immigration policy."[61] He calls for more studies of the material
and cultural factors influencing the politics of immigration, as well as
more studies of local immigration politics in other urban spaces.

Political sociologist Irene Bloemraad has recently responded to this
call in her comparative case study of processes of political incorporation as structured mobilization among Vietnamese and Portuguese
immigrants in Boston and Toronto. As I did years ago, Bloemraad pays
particular attention to the multicultural and hands-on approach to the
integration of immigrants in Canada. But she compares it with the more
laissez-faire approach in the United States. She argues that in Canada,
as a direct result of the differences in policy and approach, immigrants
pursue citizenship and develop political skills with much greater alacrity
and more extensively than in the United States.[62] Although Bloemraad
includes two different nationality groups in her research, her emphasis
is primarily on different urban and particularly different national contexts in order to answer the question of whether it is worth embracing
multiculturalism, a policy that several countries, including the United
States and Australia, are backing away from because they view it as a path
to fragmentation and the loss of national unity. Her extensive analysis
of the role of government and community organizations as well as of
the rates of naturalization and the meaning of citizenship lead her to
the conclusion that,

in cases of citizenship acquisition, political participation, and electoral representation . . . on average Canada has been doing better than the United States,
in part because multiculturalism provides the symbolic and material resources
needed to take out and exercise political membership. Some of the dynamics that
facilitate political incorporation in Canada—support of ethnic organizations and
promotion of community leadership—find parallels in U.S. refugee resettlement
policy. It is no coincidence that Cuban Americans are one of the most politically
successful and vocal migrant groups in the United States.[63]

Bloemraad puts her nuanced comparative analysis to good use (pace
Laura Nader) by responding forthrightly to alarmists like Samuel Huntington, who pin what they identify as a crisis of political incorporation
among immigrants on the recognition of difference rather than on the
absence of public resources extended to immigrant communities.[64]

I have been emphasizing the comparative analysis of cities as contexts as a useful approach for theory-building regarding processes of immigrant settlement and incorporation, but the work of Bloemraad also directs our attention to intergroup differences. Such comparisons across groups are in fact quite common among scholars of immigration who are interested in teasing out the relative impacts of structural as opposed to cultural factors as these influence the process by which immigrants are incorporated in receiving societies.

For example, Pyong Gap Min and Mehdi Bozorgmehr focus their attention on Korean and Iranian entrepreneurs in Los Angeles. They take on theoretical debates about both the causes and consequences of immigrant entrepreneurship. Their comparison reveals that while Korean immigrants draw more on ethnic resources to help them establish their businesses, Iranians draw on class resources. The result of this difference is that while Korean businesses are smaller, more spatially concentrated, and serve more low-income, minority, and coethnic customers, Iranian entrepreneurs are larger, more spatially dispersed, and serve more white customers. The result is that Iranians have escaped the conflicts to which Korean entrepreneurs have been subjected, most notably during the 1992 Los Angeles riots following the Rodney King trial.[65] These authors conclude by arguing that this comparison refines current theory by suggesting that while all forms of immigrant/ethnic businesses can contribute to ethnic attachment, only middleman businesses lead to a strengthening of ethnic solidarity.

In an essay exploring similarities and differences in ideas about political and cultural belonging, and citizenship, I compare four different populations—Salvadorans, Indians, Vietnamese, and Nigerians—who have settled in the Dallas-Fort Worth metropolitan area. The data for this essay emerged from participant observation as well as interviews with one hundred individuals, both male and female, in each population. All respondents were first-generation immigrants.[66] Salvadorans, Indians, Vietnamese, and Nigerians differ in their auspices of immigration, their level of education, their occupational profiles, and their rates of naturalization. The Vietnamese have come as refugees, while Salvadorans, Indians, and Nigerians are economic migrants. However, many Indians and Nigerians first enter the United States on student visas, and some Nigerians are in the United States as a result of winning the diversity lottery. Salvadorans have often entered without authorization although many are now on temporary protective-status visas. When individuals from each of these populations naturalize, it is often for different reasons. Indians emphasize family sponsorship and civic mindedness more than other groups. The Vietnamese, the group with the highest rate of naturalization, emphasize that they really have no alternative. While Indians mentioned the desire to vote, Nigerians emphasized this even

COMPARISON IN THE DISCIPLINES

more. Salvadorans, with the lowest rate of naturalization, indicated their ineligibility, lack of time, and, occasionally, the fear of an investigation into their past. Yet, despite these variations, a very pragmatic attitude toward citizenship, particularly that it facilitates travel in this flat and global twenty-first-century world, is characteristic of individuals across all groups. Further, across all groups, individuals emphasized a distinction between political belonging and cultural belonging—that they could be both American and of their own national origin at the same time. In other words, while there are subtle differences across the four immigrant populations in reasons for naturalization and their understandings of what it means to be a citizen, they share the idea of operating with two or more identities and, by extension, of operating in transnational social fields. This transnationalism does not obviate the process of incorporation.

Conclusion

In a provocative and thoughtful essay, sociologist Adrian Favell recognizes the often empty call for cross-national comparativism in migration studies. He describes American international conferences that are not well attended by European scholars "who are too busy in their local struggles and commitments to take time out for a sabbatical year in the United States, and often do not publish much in English" as well as American scholars who "pop over to Europe during the summer recess or an occasional international conference who might try to build in a comparative agenda, but rarely stick around long enough to develop a plausible local knowledge." Favell also points to the realization among U.S. immigration scholars that transatlantic comparative work "is going to necessitate thoroughly rethinking the theoretical assumptions and data reflexes on which the American canon is based."[67] Favell suggests that this realization has often deterred real and meaningful comparisons.

While Favell may be correct in broad disciplinary terms, it is safe to say that anthropologists who have been studying migration for some time have consistently operated within a comparative framework, particularly when their work has straddled more than one field site or when it has followed migrants from their home communities to their destination.[68] The comparative approach of these anthropologists, particularly those interested in theorizing the process of migration, is not like that developed by those working with the Human Relations Area Files. Nor is it like the controlled comparison method of British structural functionalists who made assumptions about bounded social communities, assumptions that no longer hold in a globalized world and that are impractical in the study of a process, migration, that is by its very nature unbounded.

Rather, it is a case study approach that can draw on both qualitative and quantitative methodologies and that is attentive to both scale and context.

In his book on the comparative imagination, historian George Frederickson suggests that comparison calls into question two risky assumptions, that of absolute uniqueness and that of uniform regularity.[69] These two assumptions have characterized the poles of anthropological thought over the course of its first century, from the evolutionary paradigm to the postmodern paradigm. The comparative consciousness that Nader proposed a little more than a decade ago is precisely what the anthropological discipline requires and it is precisely what migration scholars, who must be both interdisciplinary and comparative in their approach, need to implement in order to avoid making any single migration context or migration stream exceptional. Without this consciousness, differences are made more unique than they should be and similarities can be overstated. Further, without it we are condemned to reinvention and to claims of newness about characteristics that in fact often have appeared elsewhere or at another time. In my early research on postwar Portuguese immigration to France, I identified an ideology of return that has many parallels to the transnational practices and transnational social fields that have been described in scholarship beginning in the 1990s; and more recently anthropologist Nancy Foner has rightly and pointedly asked "what is new about transnationalism?"[70] Today there is a good deal of discussion about emigrant remittances that bolster the economy of Mexico, but similar remittances were bolstering the economy of Portugal in the 1960s and 1970s. Such behaviors are part of migration as a process no matter when or where it occurs. Finally, and as Nancy Foner has emphasized, "a comparative analysis can deepen our understanding of migration by raising new questions and research problems and help to evaluate, and in some cases modify, theoretical perspectives and formulate explanations that could not be made on the basis of one case—or one time period—alone."[71] By framing one case against another, we learn more about each and we refine our theories in the process—this is the ultimate importance of the comparative consciousness in the study of migration, in anthropology, and undoubtedly in scholarship in general. If there is something exceptional, we find it rather than assume it.

NOTES

1   See for example Marvin Harris, *The Rise of Anthropological Theory* (New York: Thomas Y. Crowell Company, 1968). It is worth noting that in the May 2009 issue of *Anthropology News*, National Science Foundation Program Officer for Anthropology Deborah Winslow reported the following after two proposal review panels that had just occurred: "We have yet to bridge the gap between those who do 'cases-and-interpretations' anthropology (as

Renato Rosaldo once described the work of Clifford Geertz) and those who stay resolutely focused on grander theory designed to reveal the political and economic realities of contemporary human life or contribute to Science-writ-large." "Doing Anthropology Well?" *Anthropology News* 50, no. 5 (2009): 36.

2   James Peacock, *The Anthropological Lens: Harsh Light, Soft Focus* (Cambridge: Cambridge Univ. Press, 1986), 75. Anthropology is not the only discipline characterized by this debate. Robert Segal ("In Defense of the Comparative Method," *Numen* 48, no. 3 [2001]: 339–73) identifies a similar debate in the field of religious studies.

3   Further, many ethnographers have noted that the people they study themselves engage in comparisons. Mark Busse ("Wandering Hero Stories in the Southern Lowlands of New Guinea: Culture Areas, Comparison, and History," *Cultural Anthropology* 20, no. 4 [2005]: 443–73) in fact argues for an approach in anthropology that acknowledges peoples' own understandings of similarities and differences.

4   Carol R. Ember and Melvin Ember, *Cross-cultural Research Methods* (Lanham, MD: Altamira Press, 2001), 2.

5   Harold W. Scheffler, "Sexism and Naturalism in the Study of Kinship," in *Kinship and Family: An Anthropological Reader*, ed. Robert Parkin and Linda Stone (Oxford: Blackwell, 2004), 298.

6   Thomas A. Gregor and Donald Tuzin, "Comparing Gender in Amazonia and Melanesia: A Theoretical Orientation," in *Gender in Amazonia and Melanesia: An Exploration of the Comparative Method*, ed. Thomas A. Gregor and Donald Tuzin (Berkeley: Univ. of California Press, 2001), 2. Of course there are those who object to such terms as "men's cults" suggesting instead that we use the emic terms—that is, those of the people themselves in their language.

7   Allen Johnson, "Regional Comparative Field Research," *Behavioral Science Research* 25, no. 1–4 (1991): 3.

8   Rena Lederman, "Globalization and the Future of Culture Areas: Melanesianist Anthropology in Transition," *Annual Review of Anthropology* 27 (1998): 433. See also Aram A. Yengoyam, ed., *Modes of Comparison: Theory and Practice* (Ann Arbor: Univ. of Michigan Press, 2006).

9   For a much more complete discussion see various essays in André Gingrich and Richard G. Fox, eds., *Anthropology, by Comparison* (New York: Routledge, 2002) and particularly the essay by Fox, "The Study of Historical Transformation in American Anthropology," 167–84. See also Allen Johnson, "Regional Comparative Field Research," *Behavioral Science Research* 25, no. 1–4 (1991): 3–22.

10   Marvin Harris (*The Rise of Anthropological Theory*, 153), who locates the origins of the comparative method in the Enlightenment, points out that it "is closely related to the rise of scientific theory in many different disciplines." He goes on to discuss its applications in the natural and linguistic sciences.

11   Franz Boas, "The Limitations of the Comparative Method of Anthropology," in *Race, Language and Culture* (1896; New York: Macmillan, 1940), 280.

12   Boas, "Limitations of the Comparative Method of Anthropology," 276, 279.

13   Marvin Harris, *Rise of Anthropological Theory*, 155.

14   For further discussion of the Human Relations Area Files and the kind of comparative research it supports, see Ember and Ember, *Cross-cultural Research Methods*. The discussion in Marvin Harris (*The Rise of Anthropological Theory*) is also useful as is Aram Yengoyan, "Comparison and Its Discontents," in *Modes of Comparison: Theory and Practice*, 139–40. For a more complete discussion of the critique of Murdock's approach within anthropology, see Joseph Tobin, "The HRAF as Radical Text?," *Cultural Anthropology* 5, no. 4 (1990): 473–87.

15   Ember and Ember, *Cross-cultural Research Methods*, 2. See also Ruth Mace et al., "The Comparative Method in Anthropology," *Current Anthropology* 35, no. 5 (1994): 549–54.

16   Jack Goody, "Inheritance, Property, and Marriage in Africa and Eurasia," *Sociology* 3, no. 1 (1969): 557–66.

17   Susan D. Gillespie, "Lévi-Strauss: Maison and Société à Maisons," in *Beyond Kinship: Social and Material Reproduction in House Societies*, ed. Rosemary A. Joyce and Susan D. Gillespie (Philadelphia: Univ. of Pennsylvania Press, 2000), 42.

18   Tobin, "The HRAF as Radical Text," 478, 476.

19   Bruce Kapferer, "Situations, Crisis, and the Anthropology of the Concrete: The Contributions of Max Gluckman," in *The Manchester School: Practice and Ethnographic Praxis in Anthropology*, ed. T. M. S. Evens and Don Handelman (New York: Berghahn Books, 2006), 124. Other essays in this volume offer extensive analysis of the extended case-study approach developed by Gluckman and other anthropologists of the Manchester School.

20   Siegfried F. Nadel, "Witchcraft in Four African Societies: An Essay in Comparison," *American Anthropologist* 57 (1952): 661–79; Fred Eggan, "Social Anthropology and the Method of Controlled Comparison," *American Anthropologist* 56 (1954): 743–63.

21   Idiographic approaches are focused on in-depth description of single cases and rely heavily on qualitative methods. Nomothetic approaches are generalizing and generally use more quantitative methods.

22   Fox and Gingrich, introduction to *Anthropology, by Comparison*, 2.

23   David M. Schneider, "What Is Kinship All About?" in *Kinship Studies in the Morgan Centennial Year*, ed. Priscilla Reining (Washington, DC: The Anthropological Society of Washington, 1972), 32–63. Schneider laid out his arguments more fully in his book *A Critique of the Study of Kinship* (Ann Arbor: Univ. of Michigan Press, 1984). For a discussion of the work of Schneider see *The Cultural Analysis of Kinship: The Legacy of David M. Schneider*, ed. Richard Feinberg and Martin Ottenheimer (Urbana: Univ. of Illinois Press, 2001).

24   Schneider, *Critique of the Study of Kinship*, 184.

25   Janet Carsten, *After Kinship* (Cambridge: Cambridge Univ. Press, 2004), 22.

26   David Kaplan and Robert A. Manners, *Culture Theory* (Englewood Cliffs, NJ: Prentice Hall, 1972), 5.

27   See George Marcus and Dick Cushman, "Ethnographies as Texts," *Annual Review of Anthropology* 11 (1982): 25–69; George Marcus and James Clifford, *Writing Culture: The Poetics and Politics of Ethnography* (Berkeley: Univ. of California Press, 1986); George Marcus and Michael Fischer, *Anthropology as Cultural Critique: An Experimental Moment in the Human Sciences* (Chicago: Univ. of Chicago Press, 1986).

28   Victor de Munck, "Introduction: Units for Describing and Analyzing Culture and Society," *Ethnology* 39, no. 4 (2000): 279–91.

29   Clifford Geertz, *The Interpretation of Cultures* (New York, Basic Books, 1973), 5.

30   Nigel Rapport and Joanna Overing, *Social and Cultural Anthropology: The Key Concepts* (New York: Routledge, 2000), 295.

31   John Borneman and Abdellah Hammoudi, "The Fieldwork Encounter, Experience, and the Making of Truth: An Introduction," in *Being There: The Fieldwork Encounter and the Making of Truth*, ed. John Borneman and Abdellah Hammoudi (Berkeley: Univ. of California Press, 2009), 2.

32   Patricia M. Greenfield, "What Psychology Can Do for Anthropology, or Why Anthropology Took Postmodernism on the Chin," *American Anthropologist* 102, no. 3 (2000): 573.

33   Lila Abu-Lughod, *Writing Women's Worlds: Bedouin Stories* (Berkeley: Univ. of California Press, 1993), 8–9.

34   See for example Lawrence A. Kuznar, *Reclaiming a Scientifc Anthropology* (Walnut Creek, CA: Altamira Press, 1997); James Lett, *Science, Reason and Anthropology: The Principles of Rational Inquiry* (Lanham, MD: Rowman and Littlefield, 1997).

35   Roy D'Andrade, "Moral Models in Anthropology," *Current Anthropology* 36, no. 3 (1995): 404.

36   See for example Homayun Sidky, *A Critique of Postmodern Anthropology: In Defense of Disciplinary Origins and Traditions* (Lewiston, NY: Edward Mellen Press, 2003).
37   Gregor and Tuzin, "Comparing Gender in Amazonia and Melanesia," 5.
38   Laura Nader, "Comparative Consciousness," in *Assessing Cultural Anthropology*, ed. Robert Borofsky (New York: McGraw-Hill, 1994), 85.
39   Nader, "Comparative Consciousness," 88.
40   Fox and Gingrich, introduction to *Anthropology, by Comparison*, 12.
41   Ernest G. Ravenstein, "The Laws of Migration," *Journal of the Royal Statistical Society* 48, no. 2 (1885): 167–235. See also Ernest G. Ravenstein, "The Laws of Migration," *Journal of the Royal Statistical Society* 52, no. 2. (1889): 241–305. For a collection of recent essays on gender and migration, see volume 40, no. 1 (2006), of the *International Migration Review*.
42   See, for example, Douglas S. Massey et al., "Theories of International Migration," *Population and Development Review* 19, no. 3 (1993): 431–66. For a discussion of theories of migration that have emerged from various disciplines, see Caroline B. Brettell and James F. Hollifield, eds., *Migration Theory: Talking across Disciplines*, 2nd ed. (New York: Routledge, 2008).
43   Harlan Koff, *Fortress Europe or a Europe of Fortresses? The Integration of Migrants in Western Europe* (Brussels: P. I. E. Lang, 2008).
44   Caroline B. Brettell, "Is the Ethnic Community Inevitable? A Comparison of the Settlement Patterns of Portuguese Immigrants in Toronto and Paris," *Journal of Ethnic Studies* 9 (1981): 1–17. Republished in Caroline B. Brettell, *Anthropology and Migration: Essays on Transnationalism, Ethnicity, and Identity* (Walnut Creek, CA: Altamira Press, 2003).
45   For studies of the suburban settlement of immigrants in U.S. cities, see Sarah Mahler, *American Dreaming: Immigrant Life on the Margins* (Princeton, NJ: Princeton Univ. Press, 1995); Richard Alba, John Logan, Brian Stults et al., "Immigrant Groups and Suburbs: A Reexamination of Suburbanization and Spatial Assimilation," *American Sociological Review* 64 (1999): 446–60; and Audrey Singer, Susan W. Hardwick, and Caroline B. Brettell, eds., *Twenty-First Century Gateways: Immigrant Incorporation in Suburban American* (Washington, DC: The Brookings Institution, 2008).
46   Wei Li, "Anatomy of a New Ethnic Settlement: Chinese Ethnoburbs in Los Angeles," *Urban Studies* 35 (1998): 479–501; William H. Frey, *Melting Pot Suburbs: A Census 2000 Study of Suburban Diversity* (Washington, DC: The Brookings Institution, Center on Urban and Metropolitan Policy, 2001).
47   Catherine Wihtol de Wenden, "Reflections 'à Chaud' on the French Suburban Crisis," in *Civil Unrest in the French Suburbs* (New York: Social Science Research Council, 2005), http://riotsfrance.ssrc.org.
48   Riva Kastoryano, "Territories of Identities in France," in *Civil Unrest in the French Suburbs* (New York: Social Science Research Council, 2006), http://riotsfrance.ssrc.org; Stephane Dufoix, "More Than Riots: A Question of Spheres," in *Civil Unrest in the French Suburbs*.
49   Audrey Singer, Susan W. Hardwick, and Caroline B. Brettell, *Twenty-First Century Gateways*. A book with a more global comparative perspective is *Migrants to the Metropolis: The Rise of Immigrant Gateways*, ed. Marie Price and Lisa Benton-Sort (Syracuse, NY: Univ. of Syracuse Press, 2008).
50   Nancy Foner and Richard Alba, "Immigrant Religion in the U.S. and Western Europe: Bridge or Barrier to Inclusion?," *International Migration Review* 42, no. 2 (2008): 382. In many European countries, state policies and institutional structures have explicit and direct involvement in what is and is not permissible—including whether it is permissible to wear Muslim dress. During the summer of 2008, a Moroccan woman applied for citizenship in France and was turned down because she chose to wear the niqab, a robe that covers her entire body and from which she looks out through a narrow slit in her facial veil.
51   Foner and Alba, "Immigrant Religion," 384.

ANTHROPOLOGY, MIGRATION, AND COMPARATIVE CONSCIOUSNESS 313

ANTHROPOLOGY, MIGRATION, AND COMPARATIVE CONSCIOUSNESS 313

52 Raymond Breton, "Institutional Completeness of Ethnic Communities and the Personal Relations of Immigrants," *American Journal of Sociology* 70, no. 2 (1964): 193–205; Kenneth Little, "The Role of Voluntary Associations in West African Urbanization," *American Anthropologist* 59 (1957): 579–96; Philip Mayer, *Townsmen or Tribesmen* (Capetown: Oxford Univ. Press, 1961).

53 William Pfaff, "Why France Still Insists on Cultural Assimilation: Head Scarves," *International Herald Tribune,* January 17, 2004.

54 Carolyn F. Sargent and Stephanie Larchanché-Kim, "Liminal Lives: Immigration Status, Gender, and the Construction of Identities among Malian Migrants in Paris," *American Behavioral Scientist* 50, no. 1 (2006): 10–11.

55 Robert Levine, *Assimilating Immigrants: Why America Can and France Cannot* (Santa Monica, CA: Rand Corporation, Occasional Papers, 2004), 16.

56 See Caroline B. Brettell, "Bringing the City Back In: Cities as Contexts for Immigrant Incorporation," in *American Arrivals: Anthropology Confronts the New Immigration*, ed. Nancy Foner (Santa Fe, NM: School of American Research Press, 2003), 163–95. Earlier considerations of "the city as context" can be found in Jack Rollwagen, "Introduction: The City as Context. A Symposium," *Urban Anthropology* 4 (1975): 1–4; and Nancy Foner, "Introduction: New Immigrants and Changing Patterns in New York City," in *New Immigrants in New York*, ed. Nancy Foner (New York: Columbia Univ. Press, 1987), 1–33.

57 John Mollenkopf, "Urban Political Conflicts and Alliances; New York and Los Angeles Compared," in *The Handbook of International Migration*, ed. Charles Hirschman (New York: Russell Sage Foundation, 1999), 413.

58 Mollenkopf, "Urban Political Conflicts and Alliances," 413.

59 Kevin Keogan, "A Sense of Place: The Politics of Immigration and the Symbolic Construction of Identity in Southern California and the New York Metropolitan Area," *Sociological Forum* 17, no. 2 (2002): 230.

60 Anthropologist Leo Chavez (*The Latino Threat: Constructing Immigrants, Citizens and the Nation* [Palo Alto, CA: Stanford Univ. Press, 2008]) writes about a more pervasive nationwide Latino threat image in the United States but this does not obviate local differences such as those that Koegan describes.

61 Koegan, "Sense of Place," 249.

62 Irene Bloemraad, *Becoming a Citizen: Incorporating Immigrants and Refugees in the United States and Canada* (Berkeley: Univ. of California Press, 2006).

63 Bloemraad, *Becoming a Citizen*, 236–37.

64 Samuel P. Huntington, "The Hispanic Challenge," *Foreign Policy* (March April, 2004): 30–45, and *Who Are We? The Challenges to America's National Identity* (New York: Simon and Schuster, 2004).

65 Pyong Gap Min and Mehdi Bozorgmehr, "Immigrant Entrepreneurs and Business Patterns: A Comparison of Koreans and Iranians in Los Angeles," *International Migration Review* 34, no. 1 (2000): 707–38. For further analysis of the impact of the LA riots on Korean immigrants, see Pyong Gap Min, *Caught in the Middle: Korean Communities in New York and Los Angeles* (Berkeley: Univ. of California Press, 1996).

66 Caroline B. Brettell, "Political Belonging and Cultural Belonging: Immigration Status, Citizenship, and Identity among Four Immigrant Populations in a Southwestern City," *American Behavioral Scientist* 50, no. 1 (2006): 70–99. The research was supported by the National Science Foundation.

67 Adrian Favell, "Rebooting Migration Theory: Interdisciplinarity, Globality, and Post-disciplinarity in Migration Studies," in *Migration Theory*, 264.

68 See, for example, Nancy Foner's reflection on her thirty-year career studying Jamaicans in London and New York as well as immigration in New York then and now in Nancy Foner, *In a New Land: A Comparative View of Immigration* (New York: New York Univ. Press, 2005).

See also, Nancy Foner, *From Ellis Island to JFK: New York's Two Great Waves of Immigration* (New Haven, CT: Yale Univ. Press, 2000).

69   George Fredrickson, *The Comparative Imagination: On the History of Racism, Nationalism, and Social Movements* (Berkeley: Univ. of California Press, 1997), 65.

70   For further discussion, see Brettell, *Anthropology and Migration,* and Foner, "What's New About Transnationalism? New York Immigrants Today and at the Turn of the Century," *Diaspora* 6 (1997): 355–76.

71   Foner, *In a New Land,* 3.

CHAPTER SIXTEEN

A Meditation on Comparison in Historical Scholarship

Linda Gordon

I.

Like many well-trained and experienced historians, I've been afraid to try comparative scholarship. This fear kept me minding the boundaries of my field—the United States—despite having already crossed them once, with a PhD in Russian history. From exploring the sixteenth- and seventeenth-century borderlands at the intersection of the Polish Empire, the Ottoman Empire, and the nascent Muscovite state, I transformed myself into an obedient Americanist of the late nineteenth and twentieth centuries. Always a good student, I did not color outside the lines.

The anxiety about coloring outside the lines came not only from external expectations but also from my own research experience. It required a tremendous amount of work to begin to understand the complications of nation-building in the southeastern European borderlands. My dissertation and the book it became rested, I knew, on a very thin grasp of Ottoman and Polish-Lithuanian political cultures.[1] On this frontier just north of the Black Sea, adventurers, pirates, and runaway serfs mingled in an essentially stateless territory. Despite religious differences, they lived jointly in a borderland dominated by private armies, often mere gangs, united by a masculinist warrior consciousness. Oddly enough, their very detachment from established state powers allowed me to write a decent book despite areas of ignorance, but it left me well aware of the limits of my knowledge.

You might think that becoming a "women's historian" could have encouraged defiance of national boundaries. In contrast to a common misconception, the pioneers of this second wave of women's history[2] were from their start exploring the diversity of women's experiences. Far from generalizing about "woman," far from postulating a universal sisterhood, already in the 1970s Gerda Lerner was writing about black women, Mari Jo Buhle about socialist women, Tom Dublin about factory women, Alice Kessler-Harris about women in the labor movement, and I was denouncing Margaret Sanger for the whiteness and professionalism of her later campaigns. Others like Nell Painter, William Chafe, and Jane DeHart came to women's history from the study of "difference" in America. The difference slogan masked constant implicit comparison—black with white, middle class with working class, employed with stay-at-home women.

The diversity they documented does not usually count as comparative in the history profession, however. Despite Marc Bloch's insistence of sixty years ago that all sorts of units could be compared,[3] if you say "comparative" to historians today, most of us think of two or more nations. It was in the nineteenth century, the acme of nation-states, that professional historians dislodged amateurs. The older empires were falling behind (the Russian, the Ottoman ["the sick man of Europe"], the Spanish, the Chinese), while the thriving newer empires of Britain, Germany, Belgium, the Netherlands, and so on were understood not as imperial entities but as emanations of nations—that is, nations with colonies—the different syntax implying importantly different conceptualizations. In fact, not only did almost all historians focus within national boundaries, but most of them gave little attention to the colonies. The classic modern European history textbook from which I was taught in college barely mentioned colonies;[4] only the Marxist historians did. At the University of Wisconsin when I taught there (1984–99), as at most large universities, there were, for example, several historians of France, of Germany, and of Britain, two of Russia, one covering Spain, another Italy, another Turkey. The number per country expressed the scholarly estimation of the power and status of that country. Where more than one historian shared a single country, they covered different centuries. There were exceptions, but this was the dominant pattern. And the European historians' model was normative among the rare birds who thought and wrote comparatively.

Comparative work has not only reflected but also continually confirmed the inevitability of nations and their teleological placement as characteristics of advanced states and political development in general. As Robert Gregg put it, comparative work often adds "extra layers of cement" to the nation-state assumptions, "fixing people in columns of transhistorical meaning."[5] Using nations as the comparative unit also discourages comparative studies because nations are usually large. They "prove too grand, too comprehensive for the kind of fruitful comparison that uses discriminating logic to make a discovery or establish a point not visible before," Raymond Grew writes.[6] To be saturated with the facts of a national history carries the risk of getting so lost in the details that comparison of anything but minutiae becomes impossible.

Certain historical subfields have been by necessity comparative, such as military and intellectual history. The former has always been cross-national, as the weapons and strategies of warfare are usually directed against aliens. Until recently, the field of intellectual history, engendered by the European disciplines of *Kulturgeschichte* and *Geistesgeschichte*, concerned itself with a small intelligentsia that traveled across Europe, so these historians studied ideas across national lines. Intellectual history thus defined lost status as the discipline of history became democratized, especially with the reinvention of social history, starting after World War II under the influence of Marc Bloch, Fernand Braudel, Emmanuel Le Roy Ladurie, and E. P. Thompson in England. In the 1970s, intellectual history was startled into new life by the "linguistic turn" and became somewhat absorbed into cultural studies and cultural history.[7] Despite this broadening, most of the work continues to focus on single countries and even single individuals.[8]

Two other aspects of the dominance of European history as a model furthered fear of attempting cross-national comparison: that European historians had to master an extensive national historiography, and that they had to do so in a foreign language. The long tradition of literacy in these old, rich nations had produced voluminous scholarship so vast that one could hardly assimilate all the material on one country, let alone two. Yet the standards of historical scholarship require being able to place one's work in conversation with earlier work, and this is a good standard. Meanwhile, American high schools and colleges teach foreign languages so poorly that most graduate students struggle to be able to read widely outside of English.

Historians of the United States have yet another tradition that weighs against comparative work: the idea of American exceptionalism. This has recently been repoliticized in a conservative direction, with the charge that denying American uniqueness denotes a lack of patriotism. Anyone deeply knowledgeable about a nation or even a region within a nation will find their area exceptional in some ways, but nowhere was the claim as strong as in U.S. history. That exceptionalist claim has been well demolished by historians of the past few decades, but its hold on history teaching continues.

Is not American exceptionalism itself an implicitly comparative claim? And is it not simultaneously a defense against comparison, against finding uncomfortable similarities and differences?

II.

Of course, numerous scholars have done comparative historical work. Historical sociologists and social-scientifically inclined historians use comparative studies widely. Among the greatest of these was Barrington Moore, who, starting in the 1960s, pioneered a new form of comparative historical analysis, one grounded in political economy with a powerful moral purpose. (I think particularly of his *Social Origins of Dictatorship and Democracy: Lord and Peasant in the Making of the Modern World*, 1966.) Before his death in 2005, Moore's writings encompassed not only England and France but also the United States, China, and Japan. Influenced by Herbert Marcuse and, through him, the Frankfurt School, Moore examined how the intersection of traditional agrarian regimes of power with capitalism and industrialism conditioned further political development. Like his political-intellectual precursors, he combined empirical with theoretical and political-philosophical work, notably in *Injustice: The Social Bases of Obedience and Revolt*, 1978; *Privacy*, 1983; and his essay in *A Critique of Pure Tolerance*, 1965.[9] Thus Moore was as much a humanist as a social scientist.

The school of comparative historical sociology that followed Moore, influenced by his student Theda Skocpol, turned to a more "scientific" sociology. Members of this school do rigorous comparative studies using social-science methods, notably hypothesis testing and taxonomizing, both based on precisely defined variables. They determine patterns, typicalities, as well as outliers. In the field of gender, the field I know best, one scholar measured the woman-friendliness of American states by counting membership in the National Organization of Women. Many have categorized the woman-friendliness of welfare states on the basis of the existence of programs such as child allowance and affirmative action, as well as the proportion of women in governmental positions. Or they trace patterns of longitudinal development by looking at the dates and the order in which such programs were instituted, or by identifying functional similarities despite structural differences; that is, how different social systems meet similar human "needs."[10] These scholars usually identify history as a social science, or social science as an appropriate aspiration of historians, who should attempt to make their studies maximally scientific. And science requires intersubjective repeatability, as a means of determining objectivity. Social-science historians are perfectly aware that controlled experimental testing of hypotheses is never possible in studying human beings, but nevertheless they try to move as close to scientific validity as possible.

Many historians, however, including myself, have pointed out the limits of that approach.[11] We don't deny the usefulness of comparative conclusions based on rigorous definitions of variables, so as to achieve comparisons between like and like, or comparisons that reveal unlikeness or difference. But most historians consider themselves practitioners of the humanities. We see historical scholarship as inevitably an interpretive discipline. A few critical questions regarding the development of welfare states, to continue that example, may illustrate the historical critique of social-scientific comparison. For example, the "variables" that influence any historical development can be infinite—by reducing them to a practicable number, are not many influences eliminated? And is it not extremely difficult to define the variables precisely? How is one to measure and define American "individualism" precisely enough to compute its strength vis-à-vis, say, that of France? How would we measure the impact of the American Horatio Alger myth? To make comparisons rigorous in the social scientific sense, one must either define variables narrowly or define questions narrowly.

Another problem: historical studies of welfare states have typically compared programs established in, say, 1870, to those of 1890 to those of 1920, and so on. But these individual snapshots, frozen moments in time, tend to ignore the *processes between* particular dates, while process may be of the essence of historical understanding. Comparisons of welfare outcomes—for example, who receives old-age pensions, from which sources, with what eligibility criteria—may ignore the vital cultural aspects of welfare, that is, how people understand who has economic responsibility for whom and on what moral bases. Humanistic historians will want to include evidence that is not quantifiable, not reducible to discrete variables that could then be compared to another set of similarly derived variables. Furthermore, historians are of necessity conscious of the fragmentary nature of our evidence. If we use diaries, we are aware of how indeterminate is the number of diaries that have not survived, not to mention the people that did not keep diaries. If we use oral history, we understand the fluidity of memory. If we use court documents, we can only imagine how many similar cases never got to court. To humanistic historians, this social-science type of comparison may appear to create a false precision.

Perhaps the most fundamental problem with the variables used in social-scientific comparative work is the assumption that words and concepts mean the same things across cultures and languages. Concepts such as nation, government, the people, security, freedom, family, rights, the church, and the like cannot be neatly translated word for word. A social-scientific comparison requires matching descriptions or definitions of what is being compared. But historians must work with concepts that don't match: what Europeans called a colony did not match American definitions of colony—yet comparing U.S. and European colonialism has been most productive. Forcing identical definitions on multivalent and historically changing political, social, cultural, legal concepts in order to create scientific findings may factor out important parts of the meanings of historical relationships. As German historian Erich Angermann put it: "Can we at all apprehend other people's patterns of thought and feeling without having shared their educational experiences, including nursery rhymes, fairy tales, tall tales, myths, superstitions, plays, entertainments, outdoor life, and God know what? Does it make a difference, for instance, whether one grew up with *Alice in Wonderland* or *Struwwelpeter*?"[12] One can multiply these questions infinitely. What assumptions do residents draw from the distribution of powers among local and statewide authorities? From the laws governing markets? From the degree of religious homogeneity? Ethnic homogeneity? If assumptions regarding the dissolubility of national unity changed over time, as they did in the United States between the Declaration of Independence and the 1880s, what were the crises, events, and processes that changed them, and what marks did they leave?

III.

Is it possible to conceive of an analytic project that is *not* implicitly comparative? Comparing, taxonomizing, distinguishing—these intellectual operations are, after all, the fundamentals of thought. Children learn language through such mental operations: they recognize that a table is different from a chair, that tables may have different features but nevertheless bear enough similarity that they are called tables. A historian understands a republic because she also knows the characteristics of a monarchy. Scholarly attitude toward comparison, therefore, depends on the size and degree of differentness. The more different, the more the comparative operation appears to have the "apples and oranges" problem and to be therefore illegitimate. But all comparison takes on some part of the apples and oranges problem, because if there were no differences, we would soon declare the several objects identical.

So all comparison is partial. It is from this perspective that I would like to respond to historians' hesitance about comparative study. I want to defend the validity of a humanistic as well as a social-scientific method of comparison. To do so means defending *inexact* comparison, admitting the fuzziness and variability in the key concepts employed. Comparisons do not have to be equations to be of value; they do not require comparing commensurate objects. It could be fruitful, for example, to compare slave revolts in the United States and South Africa, although South African blacks were not slaves in our understanding of the word. Logicians speak of cluster concepts, in which similar but not identical phenomena each share some but not all of the attributes of an ideal type. We can acknowledge that "welfare state" and "colonialism" are such ideal types, while no actual welfare or colonial state exhibits all the attributes. In this type of comparison, the concept may even be metaphorical, a figure of speech intended to call to mind a similar feel and culture.

I also want to defend *unequal* comparison, a kind that does not require equal knowledge of both sides of the comparison. To compare American racial segregation to South African apartheid does not require equal knowledge of both countries, although it does require some knowledge of both, enough to delineate the boundaries of similarity and the general nature of the distinctiveness on the other side of that boundary. Teaching about apartheid, however superficially, illuminates for students new aspects of race segregation and domination in the United States. If the comparison illuminates one side more than the other, that is still a net gain.[13]

Neither does a comparison need to be *sustained*. Sociologist Robert Merton coined the term "strategic research site" to identify case studies that can be made to carry larger implications and reveal broader patterns. Historians sometimes use strategic research moments, events that are both places and times. But a useful comparison can also be momentary, a simile or metaphor subsidiary to a main argument. I frequently mention to students something that gay rights and birth control issues share, a commitment to separating sex from reproduction; that point is usually quite ancillary to my main theme, but it still seems worth pointing out.

Often the major value of comparison is to raise questions, questions that might never be thought of without the analogy. I should like therefore to praise small comparisons: thin comparisons, limited comparisons, even comparisons as minor "asides" within a sustained argument.

IV.

Let me illustrate the usefulness of comparison with two examples from my research. Their relations to comparison are quite different, forming a comparison of two uses of comparison in history writing. The first is an American story, the interpretation of which was influenced by questions resulting from my reading about Asia and Africa. The second is comparative on its face, an essay in which comparison is the topic.

My analysis in *The Great Arizona Orphan Abduction* derived in part from European historiography. That influence entered through a photograph taken in the early twentieth century that I found in a Clifton, Arizona, attic.[14] It showed a group of Anglo men seated on the balcony of the Morenci Club—a club that I knew permitted only Anglos to enter as members or guests—looking down on Mexican workers on an unpaved plaza below, in the Arizona mining town of Morenci.[15] The managers were relaxed, in shirtsleeves, drinking and smoking; the workers were scurrying, tiny because the photo was taken from the balcony. It looked somehow familiar when I found it, though I had never seen it before.

Somehow it reminded me of India, of images I had seen in films or imagined from novels of British managers or company men drinking gin and tonic. (Now I would call it a Dorothea Lange–like image, where the spatial relations in the photo replicate the power relations being produced.[16]) It smelled of colonialism.[17] It led me to consider the relation between Anglos and Mexicans in Arizona at the time as a kind of colonialism, an internal colonialism, not in the sense that it replicated British India, but merely in the sense that the Arizona place and time had colonial aspects. The comparison began as a sensory metaphor—an echo, an image, a glance. My sense of the comparative, to repeat, is often not fully analogical but metaphorical, meant only to suggest.

The reader may notice that the "Mexicans" I refer to consist of both Mexican Americans and citizens of Mexico. I conflate them for two reasons: because this is the way Arizonans of the time spoke and thought, and because at the time these people were a transnational group. The border was not marked at this time; men and women crossed freely, as did individual identities. So, too, in examining European colonialism and its subjects, my reference points were not nations but governmentalities, strategies of domination and accommodation, methods of economic exploitation, shifts in racial and ethnic categories, structures of enforcement. Thus I was not comparing nation to nation here, contrary to the complaint that comparative history reifies nation-states.

Studying the methods of European imperialism elsewhere allowed new features of the Clifton/Morenci situation to appear. As in South Africa and Zimbabwe, the Arizona miners were "natives" of Mexican territory, whether from regions that had been seized by the United States in the 1848–54 period or regions that remained in the Mexican nation. Since most of them came to the Clifton/Morenci mine as single men and as sojourners, workers doing targeted labor—intending to stay long enough to earn funds for specific projects back home—usually left families behind. The African cases reminded me to look for gendered consequences of this separation, such as prostitution and other money-earning opportunities for women who provided cooking, sewing, laundry, nursing, and the like. Luise White's work on Kenya in particular showed that these domestic services were not always understood as separate from the sexual services: both were "wifely."[18] Moreover, among African and Mexican migrant workers, separation from family did not mean alienation from family, as amazingly large proportions of U.S. earnings were sent or taken back home to support family members and to improve home property: to put a tin roof on an adobe house, to buy a sewing machine for a wife (which enabled her to earn), to invest in more land or a small store.

The African comparison led me to ask how the male laborers were received when they returned home: they became returning heroes, bearing gifts and money and thereby supporting a masculine pride that had been undercut by subordination to mine bosses. But they also encountered family members resentful of the men's absence and the added burdens carried by those left behind. To wives, they were sometimes outsiders disrupting the rhythms of woman-headed households, while the husbands encountered women accustomed to greater independence. The miners came needing rest and pleasure; the women and children received them with demands.[19] The separation of men from children weakened those ties, while women's ties with other women and with children strengthened.

In early European settler colonies, where white men came as managerial, policing, and commercial operators, many of them took native women in concubinage, positions often advantageous for the women.[20] Similarly in Arizona. These practices were accompanied by an American version of Orientalism, exoticizing and sexualizing *mexicanas* in contrast to white women. In the late nineteenth century, many of these relationships had resulted in marriages, and in many locations these "intermarriages" were socially as well as legally legitimate. White men in other parts of the southwestern United States often used these marriages to accumulate property from their wives' inheritance or dowry, and the wives were typically accepted in elite society.[21] In Arizona as in African and Indian settler colonies, when white women started to arrive in critical numbers, they conducted sometimes vehement and usually successful campaigns against "intermarriage." As missionaries, teachers, and wives, they built a new standard of morality that made love between "races" ipso facto immoral. Their campaign against concubinage was less successful, but it often had negative consequences for the women involved, eroding their respectability, debasing their reputations, forcing them into hiding, and degrading their living conditions—which constituted, of course, their wages, as they were often "paid" by being "kept."[22]

The Anglo women's hostility to intermarriage stigmatized, of course, mixed-race children. It also required (re)defining and sharpening racial formations. Anglo women in the southwestern United States contributed considerably to new racial categories and boundaries, an influence parallel to that of European colonial women. Out of a complex mixture of peoples and labels—Indians, *mestizos*, Spaniards, Cornishmen, Italians, Chinese—Anglos created a binary: white and nonwhite. The result was a segregation and a disempowerment as thorough as that in Mississippi: Mexican were disfranchised, clubs and restaurants put up "No Mexicans" signs, schools and neighborhoods were segregated. In this respect, conditions were markedly different from those in European colonies, and the difference reveals the variation in racial structures within the United States. In European colonies, voting rights had rarely been granted to natives, so disfranchisement was unnecessary. More importantly, Anglos regarded Mexicans as aliens, even if they had lived in the Southwest when it was a part of Mexico and had been legal U.S. citizens since the mid-nineteenth century. Soon, in the dominant usage, "American" came to mean "white." This process was less common in European colonies, although it resembled some aspects of British- and then Boer-controlled South Africa.

Wherever men were drawn into labor in places remote from families, prostitution was particularly extensive, and as intermarriage and concubinage declined, prostitution expanded. This intensified the discourse that distinguished respectable Mexican women from immoral ones. In Clifton/Morenci as in colonial Africa, women performed many services for wifeless men, providing not only sex but also cleaning, cooking, sewing, washing, shopping, and so forth. The comparison thus requires interrogating the very definition of prostitution.

White wives in Arizona hired subject women as servants, just as they did in European colonies, but the differences called to my attention unique aspects of servitude in Arizona. Whether because of the rougher conditions of the southwestern U.S. frontier, or the more democratic culture of Americans, or that Anglo women in Arizona had migrated from places where they did some of their own housework, there was less hierarchy and fewer markers of rank between mistress and maid in Arizona: no uniforms, no coming in the back door. Live-in domestics were rare. Still, the availability of inexpensive household servants gave white wives a vested interest in maintaining these colonial subjects as a low-wage labor force. Dependence on servants stood in contradiction to white women's claims that they aimed to uplift native women. Educational institutions for natives showed the self-interest of their sponsors, training native women almost exclusively for domestic service—in Arizona as in Puerto Rico or the Philippines.

Colonialism everywhere produced among its subjects a romanticized view of precolonial societies. An invented/remembered history of an allegedly precolonial society colored it sunny and harmonious, ignoring or de-emphasizing its inequalities, tyrannies, and brutalities. This additional axis of comparison, between past and present, is commonly repeated in political discourse, even in postcolonialism, and usually operates by comparing unlike phenomena: the ideal to the real, the imagined to the actual. It operates particularly seductively when the preferred past can be imaged as authentic—that is, of one's own making—in contrast to a present of subordination to dominators who are nonindigenous. The precolonial hierarchy of domination is forgotten, as the present effects a continuing reconstruction of memory. That rosy memory was embedded in the homesickness, nostalgia, and depression of migrants far from home. Mexican American and Mexican workers alike romanticized the human-scale, communitarian village life, just as African workers did. This tendency also engaged both national liberation movements and first world, anti-imperialist scholars.[23]

This view was particularly strong with respect to gender systems and women's status, often proposing a precolonial era in which women were respected and even powerful.[24] Ironic as this appears to historians and anthropologists familiar with traditional—that is, premodern—forms of domination, the dream of an age of "matriarchy," an often-used misnomer, is not entirely without evidence. For some scholars, the prominence of women as goddesses and saints signals a culture of respect for women. Among Mexican Americans, one might see it in the *Marianismo* of Hispanic and Latino Catholicism and in the Mexican adoration of the Virgin of Guadalupe. More convincing evidence is the traditional division of resources and labor that guaranteed women monopolized control over many social necessities, including water, land, agricultural products, livestock, dwellings, children; essential skills such as weaving, sewing, and pottery; and cultural and ritual practices necessary for social cohesion and survival. Assaulted by colonial control and the commoditization of labor in tandem, women often lost these sources of power. But those same historic changes—colonialism and wage labor—also reduced the power of subjected men and created opportunities for women to find autonomy and voice in new ways. It is not surprising that, in the primary sources, men express vociferously a preference for the precolonial, while women express themselves with far more equivocation, ambivalence, and complexity.[25] My point here is far simpler: that understanding what was happening to Mexican women in the Arizona territory is illuminated by reference to colonial situations in other parts of the world.

V.

In the above comparison, observations from one situation raised questions of another, questions one might not have thought to ask otherwise. This method carries the risk that searching for similarity may bias a researcher toward finding it, or exaggerating it. But there are all sorts of interpretive errors to avoid. In a new project based explicitly on comparison, I begin from fairly obvious similarity and move toward difference, a method that carries yet other risks.

At least one art critic has noted a resemblance between American Depression-era social-realist visual art and Soviet socialist-realist art.[26] Other critics have noted how the visual art of the German Third Reich resembled that of the Soviet Union, as did, to a lesser extent, some of the art of fascist Italy. Several of the latter, notably refugees from the totalitarian regimes, have argued or suggested that there was a uniquely totalitarian art.[27] The addition of American official art obviously challenges this interpretation, because no one could seriously call Franklin Roosevelt's America totalitarian. No scholar has offered an explanation that includes the United States, and this of course illustrates the reluctance of art critics and historians to venture into an area that they believe requires extensive expertise about art and politics in each nation. My basis of knowledge is uneven: I know a great deal about American 1930s art, a good bit about Soviet art, and very little about art in Germany or Italy. But I grew un-repressibly interested in studying and trying to explain this convergence. It is perhaps the fool in me that rushes in, that I lack the knowledge to have the proper humility. Folly or not, my procedure is a standard historical one, first looking at the evidence to evaluate these hunches about similarity.

Before turning to the common visual themes, however, certain differences must be stipulated. The media were different and in turn reflect unique conditions, purposes, and meanings. The poorest country, the Soviet Union, primarily used posters: they were mass produced and mass distributed; they could be posted where many would see them; they provided visual messages to the many millions still illiterate; and there wasn't enough money for the thousands of muralists, sculptors, and painters hired in the United States. Posters were used for specific campaigns in the other countries, but fine artists were also hired to create public art of the highest caliber. Wealthier Germany supported sculptors more than other nations, and produced many massive bronze monuments to the might of the Third Reich. Everywhere new advances in photography and photographic reproduction made it possible to print photographs cheaply in newspapers and magazines; *Life* and *Look* were born in the United States, and there were similar publications elsewhere, but their distribution was limited in the Soviet Union.

Another major area of difference correlates with the political structures of the four regimes: German, Italian, and Soviet leaders had their images plastered everywhere—in posters, paintings, photographs, statues, and billboards. Not so FDR. It is true that many people, particularly the poor, put up Roosevelt's image in their homes, but these were private decisions. Although the U.S. president is always shown in post offices and other federal buildings, he did not commonly appear in public, outdoor display. Moreover, the visage of the leaders also correlates with political cultures. Lenin, for example, appears in action—an arm raised forcefully in a public lecture or leaning in to a conversation with workers—he is connected to his people. Stalin, by contrast, is mostly still, posing, his unmoving solidity at once stolid and comforting, the unmovable father protector. That shift might be said to represent the move toward totalitarianism. Hitler's preferred image—and he carefully monitored every one—was fierce; he almost never appeared smiling. There is nothing lighthearted in the German quest for revenge and domain. With his bald head, thick jaw, and stubbornly upturned chin, Mussolini seems (admittedly with a bit of hindsight) a junior partner, conveying an adolescently provocative defiance. It is FDR who stands apart from the others: he is usually seated (due to his disability), the only leader who is almost always smiling, and his cigarette in holder points upward at a cocky angle; he connotes nationalist confidence, but without fearsomeness.

A third immediate difference: the militarism of German and Italian art. Both countries were *revanchist*: resenting WWI defeats, blaming them on disloyalty and unmanliness, determined to build up to military glory. Recently unified, both were eager for more land. Both were imperial colonizers of Africa, Italy already embroiled in war over Abyssinia. Soviet leaders, trying merely to defend their new union, had already exhausted their military capability fighting off intervention after the revolution and may have willed themselves into believing, until well into the 1930s, that they could forestall a German invasion. And in the United States, reeling from economic depression, isolationists held strong.

Bracketing these major national differences, the similarities are striking. Since I am considering only "official" art—that is, art that is publicly funded and promoted—it is by definition politicized and statist.[28] Beyond that, I identified seven visual themes that appear in all four places: honoring the "common people"; heroizing them through enlarging, monumentalizing them as paragons of physical strength; creating architecture featuring block- or phallic-like masses; promoting mass pageantry; racialized nationalism; paradoxically, making peasants the ideal type that stands for the nation; and reverting to conventional, even Victorian, images of women. (The reader will have to take my word for these at this time, because the evidence—scores of images—does not appear with this essay.)

The honored "common people" are mainly male. Their maleness is in fact much magnified; an immense masculinism prevailed in all the official art. The male workers are all Paul Bunyans or Stakhanovites, heavily muscled with strong facial features; the Soviet workers are frequently shown with the dust and sweat of heavy labor on their faces—they were often represented through photographs, and in this sense could perhaps be said to be more "realistic." They are larger than life and command respect, even awe. Photographers frequently shot from below in order to maximize that awesomeness.

The men wield heavy tools—axes, hammers, sledgehammers, drills— or guide heavy equipment. There are no men shown on assembly lines, even though this form of production was widespread in Germany and the United States. Assembly lines are too feminine inasmuch as they reduce men to minuscule, dehumanized pieces of a vast machine, and in fact one does see Soviet women minding looms. Moreover, they must have physical strength, must in fact monopolize physical strength—none is left over for women, as we will see below. Heroic workers were by definition creating heroic structures: the large buildings, bridges, and metallurgy, the *magnitogorsks* and Boulder dams of an industrial society. Or they work in foundries, pictured with huge vats of molten metal or in front of red-hot furnaces. The heroic builder of massive constructions is merged with those constructions.

This monumentality was particularly visible in architecture. At the International Exhibition of Arts, Crafts, and Sciences in Paris in 1937, the organizers placed the German and Soviet pavilions opposite each other, perhaps in recognition of their impending conflict, but also perhaps in recognition of their similarities. Both are massive vertical rectangles, articulated only by the high, square columns, sharp edged, lacking a single curve. Many New Deal American buildings look like this. The architectural, stone, and concrete monumentality evokes national pride, of course, even as it serves to diminish actual people.

The monumentalism appeared also in another common visual trope: mass pageantry.[29] The synchronized movement of masses of people creating large-scale shifting patterns became a beloved art form, and until the Chinese choreography at the 2008 Olympics opening ceremony, no one did it better than the Nazis. They had been fans of rigorous, in-unison marches well before taking power; the *Sturmabteilung* (SA) conducted in-step marches, in matching uniforms, through the streets in the 1920s. Nazi and fascist salutes were ideal for creating vast displays of unison, and instruction books taught the precise angle at which to hold the arm.[30] Pageantry drew observers as well as paraders into feeling a part of a mighty military force.[31] The perfect synchronicity of movement and the use of thousands of bodies to create stunning shapes in space and time symbolized national unity. All three European regimes established government/party organizations for children that featured uniforms (although the poorer Soviet Union sometimes had to be content with supplying only red neck scarves) and parades and calisthenics. Italian fascist youth clubs paraded with rifles. The children and youth, always robust and rosy cheeked, signaled to parents that these activities were good for the children. The displays both represented and constructed the willingness of the masses to cooperate, to follow, to allow themselves to be deployed in the service of the motherland, the fatherland, the construction of socialism. In Gramscian terms, one could call them spectacles of consent.

The United States, by contrast, was far less militaristic and less interested in mass conformity. Except for occasional military parades, most parades were local and never in unison. Participants wore varieties of costumes or none at all and created "floats" representing all sorts of groups; here civil society continued to flourish. Choreographed and architected pageantry appeared, of course, in dozens of Busby Berkeley movies, and their message was quite different, frequently called "escapism" by the critics. Escape from economic worry, true, but other critics have pointed out that the synchronized performances also symbolized and promoted acceptance of Taylorist, mass-production organizational forms.

The monumentality and unison movement represented national unity. The unity becomes identity in representations of people, through their lack of individuation: faces and bodies all look alike (except, of course, in photography). The alikeness is, moreover, a racial identity. These heroic common people were mostly blond and almost always tall, broad shouldered, pink cheeked, and blue eyed. This "white" race *is* the national identity. It is not the Nazis alone who believed in an Aryan purity; in New Deal America, murals depicting people of color are rare.[32] There are no black or Japanese farmers; the millions of black sharecroppers and Mexican migrant farmworkers—who were producing most of America's fruit and vegetables by this time—are erased. The Soviet Union is a bit of an exception. Trying to win the loyalty of its many non-Russian national groups, from Siberian trappers to Kazakh and Tatar herders to Ukrainian peasants, Soviet official art featured these faces in some posters. People of color, notably Jews and gypsies, appeared only as vile in Nazi imagery, of course, as did Ethiopians in fascist imagery.

Despite the emphasis on industrial construction, in all four countries the quintessential national figure in art for mass distribution was paradoxically rural, not proletarian; a man of the earth, not of concrete. In the United States, agrarian images overwhelmingly dominated (in contrast to the work of non-official Left artists, who often depicted class struggle and racist terror in the South). This is a case of overdetermination, arising from intersecting factors at several levels of analysis. The U.S. electoral system overrepresents rural and small-town dwellers, so that the Roosevelt administration mustered political support for its arts programs by catering to those nonurban tastes and locations. For example, mural painting filled the walls of small-town post offices—the only organs of the federal government encountered by most of its citizens. American cultural nationalism rested on nostalgia for rural life, with its alleged nuclear family self-reliance. And there was the influence of the Farm Security Administration (FSA) photography project and its assignment to document rural life, as well as the fact that it was ultimately situated

in the Department of Agriculture, the largest federal agency, thus tying
the conjunctural, contingent origin of that project to the overall political structure of the nation. The artists, meanwhile, were influenced by
the earlier "regionalist" painters and the even greater influence of the
Mexican muralists, especially Rivera, whose subjects were mainly rural.

In Germany, Italy, and the United States, rural people always represented a beloved past. They are above all family farmers, expressing
a nostalgia for a dying form and/or providing a compensation to the
population for their actual lives. But not in the Soviet Union, where
the future was always the underlying motivator. There, modern farmers,
pictured surrounded by bountiful produce, appeal to other peasants to
join the collective farms. Collectivization means bigger harvests through
mechanization, and in Soviet posters the lovable cow—its bovine equa-
nimity both reassuring and symbolizing the dull, unchanging, stupid old
peasant life—appears next to a tractor. Tractors are in fact the single
most common element in all Soviet rural imagery of the 1930s. But unlike the tractors that appear from time to time in the FSA photography
of Dorothea Lange and others, Soviet tractors are nearly always driven
by women. These women are not the old peasant *babas* in the early
campaigns against superstition and ignorance, but new women: young,
assertive, confident, and strong.

Strong, even leader-like, peasant women were part of a profoundly
gendered imagery that symbolized the Bolshevik party and the essence
of the Soviet Union: the hammer and sickle. That image represents
industry and agriculture, workers and peasants united, the alliance (or
rhetorical alliance) crafted by Lenin. Millions of Soviet citizens saw a
logo in its explicitly gendered form of one of the country's most famous
works of art and its most famous sculpture, Vera Mukhina's image of a
man holding aloft a hammer and a woman holding a sickle. The male
worker partners with the female peasant. Originally made to rest on
the Soviet pavilion in the Paris exhibition of 1937, the sculpture was
recast repeatedly and its photograph published widely. The emblematic
nature of this sculpture is underscored by the fact that she pronounced
it analogous to the American Statue of Liberty.[33] There may have been
some political basis for this gendered representation: among the proletariat, men certainly commanded the best jobs with the fewest domestic
responsibilities; among the peasantry, women may have looked more
favorably upon the cooperative possibilities inherent in collectivization.

The greater strength of women in the Soviet Union is another case of
overdetermination: first, stuck with a backward, barely industrialized
economy, the Soviet communists needed all possible hands to create the
material basis for socialism; second, following Marx, they saw women's

confinement to the home as one of the conservative values they had to overcome and as feeding the conservative opposition; and third, they began to see a German invasion as inevitable and therefore needed to create industries capable of supplying a massive defensive armed force. Although the Stalinist regime conducted a radical repression of previous gains in women's and sexual rights, the posters underline another aspect of the Soviet gender system: the need for female labor created a considerable revision of the Victorian system by normalizing and even naturalizing women's participation in wage labor. The physical robustness and strength of women in Soviet imagery broke from Victorian images of delicacy, and indeed this very thickness of Soviet women was much parodied and disdained in the American anticommunist press.

One of the biggest surprises in this comparison: all except the Americans honored women's physical strength in athletics. Soviet, German, and Italian art honored women track and field competitors in posters, stamps, and photographs. The relative scarcity of images of female athletes in the United States has been unnoticed in the historical scholarship both on images of women and on women's athletics. A question that merits further—comparative—study.

The 1930s robust women were a throwback in some ways to pre-Victorian imagery. They were not, however, allowed to break with Victorian gender rules in other ways. True, they were neither sylphlike nor fragile; like men, they had a solidity that connoted and symbolized strength. But for Nazis, fascists, and Americans, women were usually pictured with babies or children, and frequently in Christian imagery of self-sacrifice and purity. They are maternal even when they are not shown with children. Sexualized women were, it seems, degenerate. Women's primary duty and fundamental purpose in life was domestic. In the United States the rural ideal remained the family farm—no matter that these were virtually outmoded economic structures, failing by the hundreds of thousands, forced out by the huge corporate plantations of the West that were powered not by "farmers" but by wage workers. Ironically, however, the family farm model in the depression both reflected and helped reproduce a family wage model in which men produced and women reproduced, a model substantially inaccurate about the typical division of labor on family farms. In much imagery, particularly the growing number of murals in public buildings, farm women remained passive—the givers of food, not the growers of food. American representations of women are inactive, stolid, even passive.

In the more war-ready European countries, however, the characteristic maternal image is stubborn, even fierce. She is Mother Courage. In the Soviet Union, she occasionally possessed startling levels of strength, imagery that might be considered unfeminine. The sturdiness is a class marker, reminding the viewer that these are not aristocrats, not pampered women. The Russian women work the hardest, the Bolsheviks having denounced the notion that women should stay home. But even in the Soviet Union, hardworking women were most commonly figured on farms, where women's labor did not threaten the gender system, because their rural labor is naturalized as an organic aspect of a nurturing conceived as biological. They are typically assigned by the system to caring for animals and growing subsistence crops, thereby understood as reproducing rather than producing.

In all representations of women, the United States is the most conservative. Outside of the photography of Dorothea Lange, the American women represented are placid, immobile, and engaged in reproduction, rarely production. These restrictions shifted radically during wartime, and no one familiar with gender analysis would be surprised that wartime imagery, intended to mobilize a new labor force, would bear cross-national, cross-ideological similarities. Heroic images of women multiplied once the war started and women's services were needed. These were strongest in the United States and the Soviet Union. Rosie the Riveter photographs have become an American cliché. The Soviet Union and the United States occasionally honored female paratroopers and pilots. But everywhere, mobilizing women for defense industry work made it necessary to reassure the public of their continuing femininity—again a trope strongest in the United States, where the female defense plant workers are always perfected coifed and made up, with flowered scarves tying back their hair.

One aspect of Nazi gendered imagery stands out as unique: its devotion to heavily muscled male nudes. Much has been said about homoerotic themes among the Nazis, but here I am concerned with the superficial lack of prudery, quite possibly an influence remaining from Weimar. Italian fascists indulged, as well, always in the guise of the classical tradition; they used classical male nudes in paintings and posters and literally copied classical sculpture. Any such exposure of the body was entirely forbidden in official art in the Soviet Union and the United States.

This comparison yields myriad questions. Even in the case of those questions for which I have hypothesized an answer—for example, why women are stronger in Soviet propaganda, why American mass pageantry was confined to the movies—more research could prove me wrong. To other questions I can't even begin to suggest an answer—why the Europeans honored female athletes most, why Hitler never smiles, why women don't drive tractors in Germany or the United States. But my point has been much less ambitious: I spent ten years with American 1930s official visual art, but I hadn't thought to ask these questions until I compared it to that of other places.

VI.

I have argued here for the encouragement of what we might call "light" comparison: comparison unbalanced, unequal, partial, even reduced to "asides" or parenthetical comments. Some might call this a move away from scholarly rigor, but I don't agree. Once it would have been possible for Americans or Europeans to "master" the history of India by reading, say, twenty-five books. Now it might require a lifetime to know the history of one Indian state. If we are to adapt to those new circumstances without losing our openness to questions that we may not see without "outside" input, we have to do comparative work.

All comparison has a politics.[34] Although comparison may reveal new questions, you cannot begin, let alone structure, a comparison without questions already guiding the way. The scholar's choice of working definition, anecdote, or fact deployed as evidence always has a purpose. Like all history writing, comparison can be misleading and prejudiced. The remedy is not to avoid comparison but to remember a useful scholarly rule: just as in criticizing, one is obligated to make the strongest possible case for that which is criticized, and in praising, one must never minimize the defects of that which is praised, so in comparing, one must never minimize difference, or fail to point it out. In other words, comparison operates with standard scholarly rules; it need not be reserved for polymaths.

NOTES

1 Linda Gordon, *Cossack Rebellions: Social Turmoil in the 16th Century Ukraine* (Albany: State Univ. of New York Press, 1983).

2 There had been a smaller first wave of women's history growing out of the women's rights movement and peaking in the 1920s.

3 William H. Sewell, Jr., "Marc Bloch and the Logic of Comparative History," *History and Theory* 6, no. 2 (1967): 208–18.

4 R. R. Palmer, *A History of the Modern World* (New York: Knopf, 1966).

5 Robert Gregg, *Inside Out, Outside In: Essays in Comparative History* (Basingstoke: Macmillan, 2000), quoted in Philippa Levine, *Prostitution, Race and Politics: Policing Venereal Disease in the British Empire* (New York: Routledge, 2003), 16.

6 Raymond Grew, "The Comparative Weakness of American History," *Journal of Interdisciplinary History* 16 (Summer 1985): 93.

7 "The Current State of Intellectual History: A Forum," *Historically Speaking* (September 2009): 14–24.

8 Examples in U.S. history include Louis Menand, *The Metaphysical Club* (New York: Farrar, Strauss and Giroux, 2001); Jeffrey P. Sklansky, *The Soul's Economy* (Chapel Hill: Univ. of North Carolina Press, 2002); Louis Mitchell, *Jonathan Edwards on the Experience of Beauty* (Princeton, NJ: Princeton Theological Seminar, 2003); Michael O'Brien, *Conjectures of Order* (Chapel Hill: Univ. of North Carolina Press, 2004); Richard D. Richardson, *William James: In the Maelstrom of American Modernism* (Boston: Houghton Mifflin, 2006); Sarah Elizabeth Igo, *The Averaged American* (Cambridge, MA: Harvard Univ. Press, 2007).

9   Notably, Barrington Moore, *The Social Origins of Dictatorship and Democracy* (Boston: Beacon Press, 1966); *Reflections on the Causes of Human Misery and upon Certain Proposals to Eliminate Them* (Boston: Beacon Press, 1969).

10   See the journal *Social Politics.*

11   "Debate with Theda Skocpol," *Contention* 2, no. 3 (spring 1993): 138–56.

12   Erich Angermann, "Challenges of Ambiguity: Doing Comparative History," German Historical Institute Annual Lecture Series, no. 4, Washington, DC. Accessed August 19, 2012, www.ghi-dc.org/publications/ghipubs/annual/al04.pdf.

13   Historian George M. Fredrickson, the pioneering comparativist who first placed American and South African racism next to each other, might disagree; in 1995 he wrote that to do comparative history without claiming exceptionalism, one must deal "with several countries even-handedly, without privileging one case." Thus he might deny that my description of the comparative is actually comparative, and I have no wish to argue about what we call it. George M. Fredrickson, "From Exceptionalism to Variability: Recent Developments in Cross-National Comparative History," *Journal of American History* 82, no. 2 (September 1995): 595. Fredrickson's powerful comparative work includes, notably, *The Comparative Imagination: On the History of Racism, Nationalism and Social Movements* (Berkeley: Univ. of California Press, 1997).

14   Linda Gordon, *The Great Arizona Orphan Abduction* (Cambridge, MA: Harvard Univ. Press, 1999), p. 14 of photographs.

15   Arizona was not yet a state. The events in my book took place in 1903–4.

16   Linda Gordon, *Dorothea Lange: A Life beyond Limits* (New York: Norton, 2009).

17   Internal colonialism was a concept widely discussed by Left scholars in the 1960s and early 1970s, and neglected thereafter. My own discussion of the concept appears in "The Imperial Within: Internal Colonialism and Gender," in *Haunted by Empire*, ed. Ann Laura Stoler (Durham, NC: Duke Univ. Press, 2006), 427–51, and in *Labrys: Estudos Feministas* 8 (agosto/dezembro 2005).

18   Luise White, *The Comforts of Home: Prostitution in Colonial Nairobi* (Chicago: Univ. of Chicago Press, 1990); George Chauncey, Jr., "The Locus of Reproduction: Women's Labour in the Zambian Copperbelt, 1927–1953," *Journal of Southern African Studies* 7, no. 2 (April 1981): 135–64.

19   Chauncey, "The Locus of Reproduction"; Cheryl Walker, "Gender and the Development of the Migrant Labour System 1850–1930," in *Women and Gender in Southern Africa to 1945*, ed. Cheryl Walker (Cape Town: David Philip, 1990), 168–96.

20   Ann Laura Stoler, *Carnal Knowledge and Imperial Power: Race and the Intimate in Colonial Rule* (Berkeley: Univ. of California Press, 2002), and "Carnal Knowledge and Imperial Power," in *Gender at the Crossroads of Knowledge: Feminist Anthropology in a Postmodern Era*, ed. Micaela di Leonardo (Berkeley: Univ. of California Press, 1991), 55–101.

21   Maria E. Montoya, *Translating Property: The Maxwell Land Grant and the Conflict over Land in the American West, 1840–1900* (Lawrence: Univ. of Kansas Press, 2002).

22   Lora Wildenthal, *German Women for Empire, 1884–1945* (Durham, NC: Duke Univ. Press, 2001).

23   Judith Whitehead, Himani Bannerji, and Shahrzad Mojab, eds. "Introduction," in *Of Property and Propriety: The Role of Gender and Class in Imperialism and Nationalism* (Toronto: Univ. of Toronto Press, 2001), 10.

24   In pointing out this widespread tendency, I do not mean to deny that colonialism often brought new indignities and sufferings to women (and men), or that women had traditional sources of power that they frequently lost.

25   Manuel Gamio, *The Mexican Immigrant* (Chicago: Univ. of Chicago Press, 1931).

26   Leah Bendavid-Val, *Propaganda & Dreams: Photographing the 1930s in the USSR and the US* (Zurich: Edition Stemmle, 1999).

27 Boris Groys, *The Total Art of Stalinism: Avant-Garde, Aesthetic Dictatorship, and Beyond*, trans. Charles Roughe (Princeton, NJ: Princeton Univ. Press, 1992); Igor Golomstock, *Totalitarian Art in the Soviet Union, the Third Reich, Fascist Italy and the People's Republic of China* (New York: Icon, 1990); Hellmut Lehmann-Haupt, *Art under a Dictatorship* (New York: Farrar, Straus and Giroux, 1973; orig. Oxford Univ. Press, 1954).

28 In further work I will attempt to explain to explain these similarities. My hypothesis is threefold. First, and most obvious, the art is all nationalist in varying degrees and at a time when economic and geopolitical crises were escalating nationalism. Second, visual art was responding to the impact and contradictions of imposing Taylorized, mass-production labor in a push to increase production and productivity. That response was largely compensatory or ideological; it expressed a longing for, a constructed nostalgia for, a life with less alienation and produced those nostalgic images as a false reassurance to the "masses" about where their societies were headed. Third, and closely connected to my other claims, all four governments were engaged in expanding the role of the state in managing production. Still, the ideologies propounded by the four governments must have meant that images contained different meanings, and although it is impossible for the historian to get evidence of how the images were actually read, I had to surmise that the propagandists knew what they were doing. Certainly the evidence shows that all four regimes succeeded into interpolating widespread consent and even enthusiasm.

29 Robert Edelman, "A Small Way of Saying 'No': Moscow Working Men, Spartak Soccer, and the Communist Party, 1900–1945," *American History Review* 107, no. 5 (December 2002): 1441–74.

30 Steven Heller, *Iron Fists: Branding the 20th-Century Totalitarian State* (London: Phaidon, 2008).

31 Jeanine P. Castello-Lin, *Identity and Difference: The Construction of das Volk in Nazi Photojournalism, 1930–33* (PhD diss., Rhetoric, Univ. of California, 1994), 238.

32 The exceptions were Left artists such as Jack Levine, William Gropper, and Ben Shahn.

33 Alison Hilton, "Feminism and Gender Values in Soviet Art," in *Slavica Tamperensia*, ed. Marianne Liljectrome, Eila Mantysaari, and Arja Rosenholm, vol. II (Tampere, Finland: Univ. of Tempere, 1993), 102.

34 This is a point perhaps more obvious to cultural studies scholars than to historians, and so this is not the place to belabor the argument among historians about what "objectivity" is possible.

NOTES ON CONTRIBUTORS

Caroline B. Brettell is the University Distinguished Professor of Anthropology at Southern Methodist University. In addition to numerous journal articles and book chapters, she is the author, coauthor, editor, or coeditor of fourteen books. Her most recent books are *Civic Engagements: The Citizenship Practices of Indian and Vietnamese Immigrants* (coauthored with Deborah Reed-Danahay) and *Citizenship, Immigration and Belonging: Immigrants in Europe and the United States* (coedited with Deborah Reed-Danahay).

Pheng Cheah is Professor of Rhetoric at the University of California, Berkeley. He is author of *Inhuman Conditions: On Cosmopolitanism and Human Rights* and *Spectral Nationality: Passages of Freedom from Kant to Postcolonial Literatures of Liberation,* and coeditor of *Derrida and the Time of the Political; Grounds of Comparison: Around the Work of Benedict Anderson;* and *Cosmopolitics: Thinking and Feeling Beyond the Nation.* He is completing a book on theories of the world and world literature from the postcolonial South in an era of global financialization.

Rita Felski is the William R. Kenan, Jr., Professor of English at the University of Virginia and the editor of *New Literary History.* She is the author of *Beyond Feminist Aesthetics; The Gender of Modernity; Doing Time: Feminist Theory and Postmodern Culture; Literature after Feminism;* and the Blackwell manifesto *Uses of Literature,* and the editor of *Rethinking Tragedy.* She is currently completing a book on the hermeneutics of suspicion called *Schools of Suspicion: Literary Studies and the Limits of Critique.*

Susan Stanford Friedman is the Virginia Woolf Professor of English and Women's Studies and Director of the Institute for Research in the Humanities at the University of Wisconsin–Madison. She is the author or editor of books on H. D. and James Joyce, as well as *Mappings: Feminism and the Cultural Geographies of Encounter.* She is completing a book on transnational modernisms and is at work on a book on women's diasporic writing.

Linda Gordon is Professor of History at New York University. Her most recent books are *The Great Arizona Orphan Abduction* and *Dorothea Lange: A Life beyond Limits,* both of which won the Bancroft Prize for best book in U.S. history, among other prizes. Earlier books include *Pitied but Not Entitled: The Politics and History of Family Violence—Boston, 1880–1960* and *The Moral Property of Women: A History of Birth Control Politics in America.*

Richard Handler is Professor of Anthropology and Director of the Program in Global Development Studies, University of Virginia. His most recent

book is *Critics against Culture: Anthropological Observers of Mass Society.*
He is currently writing a series of essays on the American sociologist
Erving Goffman.

Mary N. Layoun is Professor of Comparative Literature, University of
Wisconsin, Madison. Her research, teaching, and community work
focus on intersections of politics, culture, and literature; transnational
regimes and constructions of citizenship and community; "terror" and
human security; visual culture, comic books, and history. Current book
projects include *Worlds of Difference: Graphic Narratives and History* and
*Occupying the National Family: Sexuality, the Family, and Citizenship in Oc-
cupation Japan and in the U.S. (1945–47).*

Ania Loomba is the Catherine Bryson Professor of English at the University
of Pennsylvania. Her writings include *Gender, Race, Renaissance Drama*;
Colonialism / Postcolonialism; and *Shakespeare, Race, and Colonialism.* She
has edited a critical edition of Shakespeare's *Antony and Cleopatra* and
coedited *Post-colonial Shakespeares*; *Postcolonial Studies and Beyond*; *Race
in Early Modern England: A Documentary Companion*; and *South Asian
Feminisms.*

Walter D. Mignolo is the William H. Wannamaker Distinguished Professor
and Director of the Center for Global Studies and the Humanities at
Duke University. Among his major works are *The Darker Side of The
Renaissance: Literacy, Territoriality, and Colonization*; *Local Histories / Global
Designs: Coloniality, Subaltern Knowledges, and Border Thinking*; and *The
Idea of Latin America. The Darker Side of Western Modernity: Global Futures,
Decolonial Options* was published in December 2011.

R. Radhakrishnan is the Chancellor's Professor of English and Comparative Literature at the University of California, Irvine. He is the author
of *A Said Dictionary*; *History, the Human, and the World Between*; *Theory in
an Uneven World*; and *Diasporic Mediations: Between Home and Location*,
editor of *Theory as Variation*, coeditor with Susan Koshy of *Transnational
South Asians: The Making of a Neo-Diaspora*, and coeditor, with Kailash
Baral, of *Theory after Derrida.*

Bruce Robbins is the Old Dominion Foundation Professor in the Humanities in the department of English and Comparative Literature at
Columbia University. He is the author of *Perpetual War: Cosmopolitanism from the Viewpoint of Violence* and a companion volume entitled *The
Beneficiary: Cosmopolitanism from the Viewpoint of Inequality.* He is at work
on a documentary about American Jews who are critical of Israel.

Haun Saussy is University Professor of Comparative Literature at the
University of Chicago. A former president of the American Compara-
tive Literature Association, he edited its volume *Comparative Literature
in an Age of Globalization.* He is the author of *The Problem of a Chinese
Aesthetic* and *Great Walls of Discourse and Other Adventures in Cultural
China* and coeditor of *Women Writers of Traditional China: An Anthology*

of Poetry and Criticism; Sinographies: Writing China; and *Partner to the Poor: A Paul Farmer Reader.*

Shu-mei Shih is Professor of Comparative Literature, Asian Languages and Cultures, and Asian American Studies at the University of California, Los Angeles. She is the author of *The Lure of the Modern: Writing Modernism in Semicolonial China, 1917–1937* and *Visuality and Identity: Sinophone Articulations across the Pacific.* She is the guest editor of *PMLA*'s special issue "Comparative Racialization" and coeditor of *Minor Transnationalism; The Creolization of Theory;* and *Sinophone Studies: A Critical Reader.*

Ella Shohat is Professor of Cultural Studies at New York University. Her books include: *Taboo Memories, Diasporic Voices; Talking Visions: Multicultural Feminism in a Transnational Age; Israeli Cinema: East/West and the Politics of Representation; Le sionisme du point de vue de ses victimes juives: Les juifs orientaux en Israel;* and, with Robert Stam, *Unthinking Eurocentrism, Flagging Patriotism: Crises of Narcissism and Anti-Americanism* and *Race in Translation: Culture Wars around the Postcolonial Atlantic.*

Gayatri Chakravorty Spivak is University Professor in the Humanities at Columbia University. Among her books are a translation with critical introduction of Jacques Derrida's *Of Grammatology; A Critique of Postcolonial Reason; Death of a Discipline; Nationalism and the Imagination;* and *An Aesthetic Education in the Era of Globalization.*

Robert Stam is University Professor at New York University. Some of his books include *François Truffaut and Friends; Literature through Film; Film Theory: An Introduction; Tropical Multiculturalism;* and, with Ella Shohat, *Unthinking Eurocentrism, Flagging Patriotism* and *Race in Translation: Culture Wars around the Postcolonial Atlantic,* from which the present essay is partly taken. He has taught in France, Tunisia, and Brazil, and his work has been translated into fifteen languages.

Rebecca L. Walkowitz is Associate Professor of English at Rutgers University. She is the author of *Cosmopolitan Style: Modernism beyond the Nation* and the editor or coeditor of several other books, including *Bad Modernisms* (with Douglas Mao) and *Immigrant Fictions.* Her current book project is *Born Translated: The Contemporary Novel in an Age of World Literature.* She coedits the book series "Literature Now," published by Columbia University Press.

Zhang Longxi is Chair Professor of Comparative Literature and Translation at the City University of Hong Kong. Among his many books are *The Tao and the Logos; Literary Hermeneutics, East and West; Mighty Opposites: From Dichotomies to Differences in the Comparative Study of China; Allegoresis: Reading Canonical Literature East and West; Unexpected Affinities: Reading across Cultures;* and the edited volume *The Concept of Humanity in an Age of Globalization.*

INDEX

Abbot, George, 150
Abel, Karl, 47
Abu-Lughod, Janet L., 79, 81, 82
Abu-Lughod, Lila, 298
Achebe, Chinua, 20
Adam, Paul, 126
Addison, Joseph, 212, 215
Aesop, 165n15
Alba, Richard, 303
Allan, Lewis, 132
Allen, Roger, 233n41
Ambai. *See* Lakshmi, C. S.
Ambedkar, Bhimrao Ramji, 156, 160–61
Anderson, Benedict: Chatterjee's critique of, 20; hierarchical societies as comparative reference used by, 284; *Imagined Communities* by, 64, 241–45, 249, 282; on non-Eurocentric method of comparison, 189n20; on "spectre of comparisons," 74n1, 189n20, 215, 230n9; on translation, 244; and transnationalism, 243
Anderson, Perry, 208n27
Angermann, Erich, 319–20
Appiah, Kwame Anthony, 51–53
Apter, Emily, 3–4, 45n27, 56, 58–59, 213, 215, 228
Arendt, Hannah, 254
Aristotle, 107
Asad, Talal, 201, 203–6
Auden, W. H., 217
Auerbach, Erich, 253
Augustine, St., 150, 165n13
Aykroyd, Dan, 291n37

Bachelard, Gaston, 255
Badiou, Alain, 58–59
Bakhtin, Mikhail, 60, 63n55, 133, 134
Bakunin, Mikhail, 202
Balibar, Etienne, 154, 155
Balzac, Honoré de, 52, 53, 55, 103
Bardolph, Jacqueline, 127
Barroso, Ary, 132
Bartlett, Robert, 155
Bassnett, Susan, 237
Bastide, Roger, 140–42, 146n29
Bateson, Gregory, 268, 269n10

Baudelaire, Charles, 74n2
Bayly, Susan, 160
Beckett, Samuel, 238
Bellow, Saul, 21
Benedict, Ruth, 9, 275–82, 284, 288, 291n37
Benjamin, Walter, 29–30, 57, 59, 60, 213
Ben Jar, Jorge, 132
Berberian, Viken, 259
Berkeley, Busby, 329
Berman, Antoine, 57
Bermann, Sandra, 56–57
Bernards, Brian, 97n40
Bernheimer, Charles, 254
Bérubé, Michael, 196
Béteille, Andre, 157
Bilgrami, Akeel, 157
Bin Laden, Osama, 193
Bloch, Ernst, 213–14
Bloch, Marc, 316, 317
Bloemraad, Irene, 306–7
Boas, Franz, 268, 275–77, 279, 282, 294
Bodin, Jean, 151
Boellstorff, Tom, 97n16
Bonnard, Abel, 128
Borges, Jorge Luis, 110, 129
Borneman, John, 298
Bourdieu, Pierre, 69, 75n15, 121
Bowker, Geoffrey C., 148
Boyle, Robert, 165n25
Bozorgmehr, Mehdi, 307
Brackenridge, Henry M., 129–30
Brathwaite, Edward Kamau, 85, 143
Braudel, Fernand, 317
Brecht, Bertolt, 217
Brennan, Timothy, 215
Brettell, Caroline B., 10, 292–314, 337
Brodsky, Joseph, 217
Brown, Thomas O., 255
Buarque de Holanda, Sérgio, 131–32
Buhle, Mari Jo, 315
Bunzel, Ruth, 291n39
Burgess, Anthony, 238
Burnichon, Joseph, 128
Bush, George W., 194
Busse, Mark, 310n3
Butler, Judith, 25, 204–6, 236–37

Friedman, Susan Stanford, 1–12, 34–45, 337
Friedman, Thomas, 193, 194
Frost, Robert, 48, 61n6
Frye, Northrop, 255

Gable, Eric, 285
Galdós, Benito Pérez, 103
Galton, Francis, 274–75
Galtung, Johan, 6, 71–72, 73, 74, 75–76n26
Gandhi, Mahatma, 114, 155, 160
Garibay, Angel María, 110
Geertz, Clifford, 3, 36, 284, 291n37, 295, 297–98, 309–10n1
Ghosh, Amitav, 25, 162, 167n69
Gilroy, Paul, 143
Gingrich, André, 296, 299, 300
Ginzburg, Carlo, 53
Glissant, Édouard: on Faulkner, 80, 87–88, 91, 92, 95; Melas on, 231n14; on plantation system, 86; relational poetics of, 4, 6, 79–80, 84–88, 95, 231n14; Shih on, 4, 6, 79–80, 84–88, 95; on "transversalities," 144
Glover, Danny, 265
Glück, Louise, 217
Gluckman, Max, 295, 311n19
Godard, Jean-Luc, 129
Godwyn, Morgan, 153
Goethe, Johann Wolfgang von, 102, 103, 104, 215, 253, 268
Goldberg, David Theo, 166n31
Goldschmidt, Victor, 75n22
Goody, Jack, 295
Gordon, Linda, 4, 10, 315–35, 337
Gramsci, Antonio, 328
Greenfield, Patricia, 298
Gregg, Robert, 316
Gregor, Thomas, 292–93, 298
Grew, Raymond, 316
Guattari, Félix, 269–70n15

Hadas, Rachel, 217
Hafez, Sabry, 221, 223, 232n38
Hall, Stuart, 155
Hamid, Mohsin, 239
Hamilton, W., 167n53
Hammoudi, Abdellah, 298
Handler, Richard, 9–10, 241, 271–91, 337–38

Hardwick, Susan, 302
Harootunian, Harry, 212–15, 227, 228, 230n4, 230n9
Harris, Marvin, 310n10
Hass, Robert, 217
Hayot, Eric, 54
H. D., 35
Hegel, G. W. F.: Cheah on, 8, 174–76; Eurocentric view of world history by, 102, 105, 114, 125, 126, 133, 142, 174–76, 180; Marx's inversion of, 160, 187; North/South schema of, 124–25; pseudo-Hegelian pronouncements, 184–85; on Spirit and progress of history, 114
Heidegger, Martin, 23
Heraclitus, 63n55
Herman, Edward, 205
Hitler, Adolf, 278, 327
Hobbes, Thomas, 69
Hobson, John M., 79, 82–83
Ho Davies, Peter, 239
Hofmeyr, Isabel, 238
Holquist, Michael, 63n55
Hom, Marlon, 97nn35–37
Homer, 175–76
Horkheimer, Max, 112–14
Huntington, Samuel P., 28, 133, 197–98, 306

Ikuo, Shinjou, 270n18
Ishiguro, Kazuo, 239, 244

Jakobson, Roman, 49–50
Johnson, Allen, 293
Jones, William, 159
Joyce, James, 238, 239
Jung, C. G., 255

Kadir, Djelal, 41, 249n4
Kafka, Franz, 22
Kant, Immanuel: Cheah on, 8, 69, 173–74, 176; on comparison as pluralism, 173–74, 176; on comparison as unsocial sociability, 174; on discipline, 118n7; on Europe and colonial and imperial differences, 105; and Osborne on comparability, 213; on thinking as speaking to oneself, 56
Kao, Yu-kung, 50
Kapferer, Bruce, 295

344